REMEMBER ELVIS

PRODUCED BY JOE ESPOSITO

A TCB JOE PUBLISHING HARDCOVER

A TCB JOE PUBLISHING HARDCOVER

Published by
TCB JOE Publishing
A division of
TCB JOE Enterprises, LLC

Narration by Darwin Lamm, Founder of Elvis the Magazine,
an official EPE recognized and licensed publication.
www.ElvisTheMagazine.com

Art Direction by Lauren McMullen, Founder of The Dream Factory
Book & Cover Design by The Dream Factory

Poems composed by Marion Lindsay

TCB JOE books may be purchased for business or promotional use or for special sales.
For more information please write to: info@tcbjoepublishing.com

ISBN: 0-9778945-0-9

THIS BOOK IS DEDICATED IN LOVING MEMORY, TO MY BEST FRIEND, ELVIS PRESLEY....

Elvis, you wondered if you would be remembered after you were gone....
My friend, I wish you could see how much you are still loved today
How the whole world knows you by your first name alone,
That the legacy you left behind is here to stay.

Remembered for the gift you gave us in song
As you rocked the world with body and soul
With a voice that remains "Second to None"
The one who created Rock 'n' Roll.

A nonconformist, not afraid to step out
With a new kind of music with a different feel.
You made it happen, showed what you were about
You dreamed the dream, and you made it real.

Referred to still as the "handsomest man ever known"
Whose presence in the room was electrifying
Causing all heads to turn towards you alone.
Elvis, the world remembers, of that there is no denying.

Elvis, you are a legend and the world will not forget
Not just your music, but the joy you found in giving....
Houses, cars, money, you gave all with no regret,
For to you, it was a necessary part of living.

You believed that God destined you from your birth
To make others happy, lifting their spirits for a while.
Having fulfilled your destiny, you then left this earth,
But your voice lives on, still making the world smile.

Thank you, Elvis, for making the world brighter,
For being a friend that I was privileged to know.
My hope in sharing this book as its producer,
Is to record for the world why we still love you so.

Your friend, Joe Esposito

Our deepest gratitude goes out to:

Fred Cole
Daniel Lombardy
Lauren McMullen & The Dream Factory
Veronica Heeres
Holly McMullen
Darwin Lamm
George Di Domizio
Marion Lindsay
Sam Thompson

We would also like to show our appreciation to all of the fans around the world that have shown their loyalty and support to Elvis Presley over the years. We would also like to thank our families and friends for their continued love, support and friendship. *Joe Esposito and the TCB JOE Team*

THE STORY BEHIND THE COVER ART AND TITLE

The front and back book colors were inspired by the American flag reflecting Elvis's deep pride and patriotism he had as an American.

The image of Elvis seen on the cover was intended to serve a dual purpose. The first, captures Elvis on stage, sharing his unforgettable charisma, talent, energy and showmanship. The second, a bit more subtle, conveys the undying love and loyalty his fans and friends will always feel towards Elvis Presley. This was accomplished by creating the image silhouette in white making it possible for the form to look like a white rose when seen out of focus or at a distance.

The book title was carefully chosen to reflect our shared mission as Elvis fans to always **REMEMBER ELVIS**

Lauren McMullen & The Dream Factory '06

FEATURING

REMEMBER ELVIS. WHAT A GREAT BOOK TITLE. AND, WHAT A THRILL IT IS TO BE ASKED TO WRITE THE FOREWORD FOR WHAT I THINK WILL BE A TREASURY OF MEMORIES FOR ELVIS FANS AROUND THE WORLD.

I'm one of the lucky people who had a chance to meet Elvis and get to know him as the down-to-earth guy he was. For me, the Elvis adventure started in 1959 when Joe Esposito, my Army buddy and roommate at Ray Barracks in Friedberg, Germany, introduced me to Elvis and opened the door to the private side of Elvis. At our first meeting at his rental home in Bad Nauheim, I was struck by his personal style of greeting people – "Hi, I'm Elvis Presley." He has the most recognizable face in the world, and he opened every first contact with the same line – "Hi, I'm Elvis Presley -- what's your name?"

When I said George Di Domizio, he stepped back, flashed his famous grin and said: "I'll call you D." I said, "OK. And I'll call you E." That produced one of the Elvis laughs that seem to start in his toes. At some point in the conversation that night, I mentioned that I played quarterback for Lansdale Catholic and that got me an invitation to play football the coming Sunday. All the guys in the touch football games wore Elvis-supplied sweatshirts, either black or white. The Elvis team always wore black. As we were leaving the house for the football field and my first game, he asked me to grab a black shirt.

After that first football game, Joe and I became regular guests at his Bad Nauheim home and would marvel at the crowds gathered every day to get a glimpse of Elvis and perhaps an autograph. Before we left Germany for the states, Elvis invited me to come to Hollywood for a visit. I took him up on his offer and in September of 1960, showed up at the Beverly Wilshire Hotel in Beverly Hills. Not only did he give me a VIP welcome, he asked me to bunk down at the hotel for the night so I could ride with

the Memphis Mafia for a 5 a.m. trip to the location shooting for Flaming Star. He gave me Gene Smith's room for the night. Poor Gene had to sack out on the floor in Elvis's room.

As luck would have it, during my two-week stay with Elvis and company, we moved from the hotel to the rental house on Perugia Way in Bel Air. What great fun that was. Hanging out with Elvis at the pool, being part of his karate practice sessions, joining the entourage each day on location or at the 20th Century Fox studios, and meeting famous stars who would drop by the set.

Over the years, I was busy with my job at Merck, but was able to keep up with the Elvis adventures through periodic contact with Joe. I had a chance to visit with Elvis on location in Crystal River, Florida, for the shooting of Follow That Dream, and dropped by Graceland several times where in 1967 I got a personal tour of the renovated second floor living quarters.

One of the major highlights came in 1968, the year I married June. We had decided to honeymoon in Scottsdale, Arizona, then head west to Vegas by car. As I often did while traveling for Merck, I would touch base with Joe's wife to learn where Elvis and Joe were working. To my delight, Joan told me they were on location in Apache Junction, an Arizona hop and skip from Scottsdale, staying at the Superstition Inn. When I called the motel and asked for Joe, Elvis answered the phone. The famous Elvis laugh shook the phone line when I asked him if he was now work-ing for Joe. He invited June and me to the set where they were shooting Charro.

One of the most memorable Elvis moments came when Elvis delayed shooting a scene by coming over to meet June while the director and about 50 cast and crew waited and wondered who we were.

Not a day goes by without some contact with an Elvis memory. It could be a phone call from Bill Greene, a Philadelphia Army buddy, who was part of the football games in Germany. It could be an e-mail from Rockin Ron Cade, who has a Sunday radio show: "Elvis and Friends," or something on TV or in the papers about Joe and Elvis. Speaking of TV and Joe, one of the adventures was a trip to Hollywood in 1989. Joe invited me to be his partner in a quiz show, the "Third Degree," where we won $1,000 each by stumping the panel about our special relationship – Army buddies of Elvis.

My job these days is coming up with names for phar-maceutical products. One of the creative techniques I use is Brain Writing with a small group of people from the client company. During the exercise, I play Elvis music to stimulate creativity and it always works. Elvis is magic.

It's easy for me to REMEMBER ELVIS. Now, I think it will be easy for readers to REMEMBER ELVIS with a little help from all that follows in this wonderful book by Joe and his TCB Joe team.

By George Di Domizio

THE CRADLE THAT ROCKED THE WORLD

"GROWING UP, EVEN FOR A FUTURE KING, IS ALWAYS DIFFICULT."

— DARWIN LAMM

In 1935 Tupelo, Mississippi, was little more than a poor southern town struggling to make itself into a city.

Its only claim to fame up to that point was that novelist William Faulkner had been born only 35 miles away. With the Great Depression raging across the nation and Jim Crow the law of the land down South, little had changed in Tupelo since it had been founded in 1870.

There was no fanfare on January 8th, 1935, when a baby boy was born to Vernon and Gladys Presley in a two-room shotgun shack on the outskirts of town. The boy was the second of a set of twins that had been delivered with some difficulty. The first twin was stillborn. The Presleys decided to name the child nonetheless and chose Jesse Garon Presley as the name of their first son who would soon be buried at Priceville cemetery. They christened their surviving son Elvis Aron Presley in honor of his father's middle name and as a rhyming tribute to his brother.

A poor boy born into the last dying breath of the Old South, there was no indication that the baby now resting in a blanket next to his mother by the light of oil lamps in their modest home would spark a cultural revolution the likes of which mankind had never seen.

Elvis Presley was going to change the world… But growing up, even for a future king, is always difficult. Tupelo, Mississippi, with its dirty streets and its moonshine whiskey had served its purpose as the beginning of a story that would one day enthrall people all over the world.

But the real story would always lead to a city on the Mississippi River, one whose name went all the way back to ancient Egypt as a mythical and powerful city where Gods were born, one whose name is still spoken with awe… Memphis.

Vernon, Gladys, and Elvis Presley arrived in Memphis, Tennessee, in 1948 with their worldly possessions strapped to the top of their car. The young family hoped that by moving to a new city they could escape the poverty that had dogged them in Tupelo. But it will be a hard climb from the underbelly of society.

The Presleys would have some assistance however. They managed to get an apartment at a public housing project called Lauderdale Courts, which as luck would have it, was within walking distance of Vernon's job and would only cost them $35 a month in rent. The complex also served as Elvis's home, playground and hideaway during the formative years of his later childhood.

America was also undergoing a transformation during those years... World War II had left the nation with more prosperity than it had seen in a generation... People were working hard now not just to survive but to afford some of the new comforts life had to offer, like automated kitchens, big cars, and a new device that was making entertainment not only a part of life but almost a necessity... the television set.

For his part, young Elvis was traumatized by the move... Though he had always been somewhat separate from his classmates in Tupelo, he had at least known them all. Now, he was faced with having to go to a new school where he would feel even more like an outsider. With his outlandish hair and shy demeanor, young Elvis cut quite a striking figure in early 1950's Memphis, but Memphis had always been a city that embraced its differences while managing to exploit them at the same time. It was the home of WDIA, the first all-black radio station in the nation which featured DJ's like schoolteacher by day Nat D. Williams and future Blues legend B.B. King.

It was also the birthplace of something that would change the world, although it didn't have a champion or even a name. On March 5th, 1951, a small group of musicians, including a young piano player named Ike Turner, gathered at the Memphis Recording Service at 706 Union Avenue. That night they recorded a single called Rocket 88. Though they considered it a strictly rhythm and blues record, the press and the public started calling it by a new name... Rock 'n' Roll. Soon afterwards, the Memphis Recording Service also had a new name... Sun Records.

George Klein: Elvis moved up from Tupelo, Mississippi, in 1948 and enrolled in Humes High School. Coincidentally and ironically, we were in the exact same classes from the eighth grade until the 12th grade.

Bob Morrison: You know, everybody tried to dress like everybody else, but Elvis didn't. The thing that I remember about him more than anything else was it could be the coldest day, and he would have a suit coat on with the flap up on his collar. I always thought that maybe he couldn't afford a jacket.

Buzzy Forbes: I met Elvis about 1949 when I moved to Lauderdale Courts. We lived in an apartment building. It was probably 54 apartments in the building. And some time within the first two or three months I met Elvis.

Joe Esposito: Elvis, when he was young, didn't have too many friends. He was always the strange kid in high school and in his neighborhood. He was the one with long hair and the weird clothes. Everybody else wore T-shirts and crew cuts. So he didn't have too many friends.

Dixie Locke-Emmons: Elvis and I first met in January '54. He of course had already graduated from school, and I was in school, a sophomore at South Side. And I think Elvis pretty – always dressed flashy. The first time I saw him at church, he had on a dark sport coat and light pants. He was very striking and handsome. His long hair and that beautiful face that a lot of his persona that he wanted people to see was really an effort for him to do because he was not that confident in himself and basically very shy.

Bernard Lansky: Well Elvis came there one day and looking at the window. He always come by here, but I never knew who he was. So one day I invite him in. I said, "Come on in young man. Could I show you around?" He said, "Okay." So he walked in and I showed him everything. And he said, "One of these days I'm going to buy you out." I said, "Do me a favor, don't buy me out. Just buy from me", which he never forgot.

Bob Morrison: The class was large, 350 something like that. But everybody knew Elvis. He stood out in a way that you couldn't help from knowing him.

Buzzy Forbes: We did everything that you could do without money. Played an awful lot of football, dated, had our own parties. We lived close to swimming pools. We went to a lot of movies, a lot of times just sitting around talking, Elvis playing his guitar singing.

Around this time, Elvis began to seriously ponder life after Humes High. Although he had never shied away from hard work and had always been humble and unassuming, his fondest desire was to be an entertainer.

Presley spent hour after hour listening to Dewey Phillips' Red, Hot and Blue on the radio and watching movies starring a new breed of actor personified by James Dean and Marlon Brando, who were known for their smoldering sex appeal and brooding melancholy performances. He also admired Tony Curtis's hair.

Although Elvis had always sung to friends and family, he hadn't performed in front of a live audience since a contest at the Tupelo fairgrounds when he was 11 years old. That day, he had placed second with his rendition of the tearjerker "Ol' Shep," winning five dollars and free admission to the rides. In his senior year of high school, Elvis decided to enter the talent show competition in the hopes of furthering his private ambitions. This time he came in first.

Buzzy Forbes: He won the talent contest. And that really helped his self-esteem. From that time on, you could really see the difference.

Elvis, I'm sure at that time it had a lot to do with him deciding he really liked being in front of people performing.

Bob Morrison: Near the end of the year around May, we were talking about what we were going to do, and I said, "Well my mom and dad want me to go to Business College," and he put out a big laugh. Man he laughed real hard; he wasn't laughing at me.

He just was laughing of the idea of going to school after getting out. And I said, "Well, what do you want to do?" And he said, "Well, one of these days, I want a hillbilly band."

For his part, Elvis was busy with the same things most teenage boys are concerned with… school, cars and most of all… girls. After he graduated high school, Elvis faced an uncertain future. Although he had always been a decent student, there was no question of his proceeding to college. His parents simply couldn't afford it, and besides, he had no desire to remain in a school environment.

The Presleys had been evicted from their home in Lauderdale Courts because their income exceeded the allowable limit for assisted housing, but it wasn't enough to support a family of three. So Elvis's future was clear. In order to help his family survive, he would have to go to work. Although Elvis had taken part-time jobs in the past, most significantly at the Loew's State Theater in town, he began looking for something that could actually lead to a career.

On the day of his graduation, Elvis Aron Presley walked into the Tennessee Employment Security Offices on Union Avenue and asked to be tested and placed into a job, any job. Although he did say his preference would be to drive a truck.

His first assignment was a short-term job at the M.B. Parker Company, where one day his employer found him close to tears.

Elvis told him that he needed an advance on his salary to make his car payment. His boss told him that was against company policy, but he would personally loan Elvis the $33. True to his word, Elvis paid him back two days later after receiving his paycheck.

The strange part about this incident is that Elvis's car was already paid for. That same week, he showed up at the Memphis Recording Service to pay for and cut a record called "My Happiness."

The receptionist, Marion Kesker, was impressed enough by the young man with the deep set eyes and shy demeanor that she made a note to herself to mention the boy to her boss...Sam Phillips.

Elvis next went to work for Precision Tool making artillery shells for the government. But after only a few months, fate intervened answering one of his dreams. Elvis Presley was going to be a...truck driver.

Sam Phillips: That truck kept going by here, I noticed, quite frequently, and I thought hell these people got a lot of business in this area, you know. But anyway, he finally got up the courage to come in and tell Marion that he wanted to make a record for his mother, a birthday record. Elvis came back, and I just saw the guy, and I couldn't refuse him. And I thought, "Hey yeah...I'll make you a record, Elvis. You got four bucks?" Some jazz like that, you know. The thing was I listened to him and he sang "My Happiness." And this dang guy was just unusually distinct, and I just simply knew that this guy was as potentially good as any person I had auditioned.

SAM PHILLIPS
FOUNDER OF SUN RECORDS

Vernon Presley: He just went down to-to make a record to see, you know, just how he would sound. So Mr. Sam Phillips was the owner of the recording studio at the time. So he told him, and he said I want to get your name and address before you leave because I might use you, you know. Something might come up. So about eight months later, they called him one night to come down. I think we have something you can use.

Dixie Locke-Emmons: When Elvis and I first met Sam, we were both a little intimidated. And I was almost frightful of him because we would go to recording sessions with him and that kind of thing. And he was very aggressive, and I see now that I'm older it was the professionalism in him that he knew exactly what he wanted, and he was going to get it. But I think he knew from the beginning that he had Elvis's best interest at heart.

George Klein: Elvis had met Sam Phillips and he said, "Well, let's see if we can work with you, and I'll put you together with two great musicians here: Scotty Moore and Bill Black." Bill Black was working over at Firestone at the time. Scotty was an accomplished guitar player right there in Memphis. And so Elvis came over there, and he was in his Lincoln, and he was wearing a pink shirt and black pants with a pink stripe down the side I think. And he came in with that Lincoln smoking, and that's when they met him.

Sam Phillips: I knew Scotty Moore had a lot of patience and Bill Black was the best upright, slap-base player, and so Scotty and Bill, they worked back and forth and they wouldn't have it and so. I don't know. After the fifth, sixth, seventh, eighth time we were about ready to sack everything up that night and come back again later on.

George Klein: Elvis wanted to do all these Dean Martin songs, and it just wasn't cutting it. And then I can just see Sam in the studio, you know, just getting ready to say, "Oh that's it. That's it." And then Elvis just start strumming on this Arthur "Big Boy" Crudup tune, "That's All Right Momma." And then Scotty and Bill just come to it. And then Sam comes out and says, "Hey. Hey guys, what are you doing?" And Elvis says, "You like that?" And he says, "Hell, yeah. I like that. Let's do it again."

Sam Phillips: When I heard it, it just broke me up. I mean, I said, "Golly. A rhythm and blues thing." Almost a gut bucket thing but with the tempo up, it became a quote on quote "Rhythm and blues thing." And so that's how really we got started. And when I heard that, I knew that's what I was looking for, and I hoped and prayed that it was the thing that would help us to get Elvis get started.

SAM PHILLIPS
FOUNDER OF SUN RECORDS

Dewey Phillips: Knock. Knock. It's Dewey Phillips' Red, Hot and Blue coming through WHPQ in Hotel Teska on the Maybelline floor right here in good old Memphis, Tennessee.

George Klein: Daddy old Dewey. What do you want to know? Oh, yes. I get people so Daddy o' Dewey, WPHQ. Come get your Red, Hot and Blue. Nine to midnight. We're going to rock. We're going to roll. And I'm going to take all this payola and have a whole lot of fun.

GEORGE KLEIN
MEMPHIS MAJOR FRIEND

Dewey Phillips was an unorthodox disc jockey. He had his own style, not sounding like anybody else. His main popularity was from nine to midnight at night at WHPQ playing black music, rhythm and blues songs. We called it race music at that time. So the black audience was zeroing in on Dewey at night. And then the white kids were starting to pick up on that music at that time. It was the thing to listen to Dewey Phillips at night. Everybody wanted to listen to Dewey Phillips.

Dewey Phillips thought the moon rose and set on Sam Phillips. So Sam would bring up new artist records to Dewey and let Dewey be the first disk jokey in Memphis to play them. Well, Sam brought Elvis up, "That's All Right Momma." And he said, "Dewey." He said, "I got an act here that is very unique and very unusual. You got to listen to this guy. It's a white guy sounding black. And so Dewey put it on and listened to it. And he had a phrase, "Hey mother. That's a hit. That's a smash, you know."

Vernon Presley: Yeah. Disc jockey by the name of Dewey Phillips. Well, he called the house and wondered where Elvis was. I said, "Well, he's gone to the show." He said, "Well, see if you can get him down here." He said, "The phone is ringing off the wall, and a telegram is coming in. I can't answer the phone. I got to do my job, you know." So we walked up to the theater and got him, and he went down to the station.

Dixie Locke-Emmons: Dewey Phillips was a character. I went with Elvis a few times to the studio when he was broadcasting and, you know, he was fascinating to watch. But he would put on a record, and then while that was playing he would turn around and say things to Elvis, you know, talking to him and trying to get interviews going, and he was a crazy man.

George Klein: An advertising agent, he'd hired me to play records like a mobile DJ thing, and they had a flatbed truck, and it was just Elvis, Scotty and Bill. And I introduced Elvis on stage. Well, that was the first time I'd seen him in person having turned professional and had a record out. Of course, I'd seen him a lot in high school and around the neighborhood and all. But I think that really was his very first official public appearance in Memphis.

With the success of "That's All Right", Elvis, Scotty, and Bill began playing local shows as the Blue Moon Boys, a name that capitalized on the song "Blue Moon of Kentucky" which was the B-side of their hit single and one that helped maintain a sense of fairness in the billing. That would change as it became increasingly evident that even though Elvis couldn't have done the record without them, no one was coming to see Scotty Moore and Bill Black. Their first performance was at the Overton Park band shell in Memphis.

Sam Phillips: That little show at Overton Park shell right here in midtown Memphis, Tennessee, was a turning point in that man's career so far as is in a feeling toward whether or not people were going to love him, like him, and appreciate what he was giving em, and doing his best to do it. My God, when he got on that stage, unless you were there, you're not going to believe the response.

But playing small gigs in their hometown, however thrilling local celebrity status might be, was never going to further their careers. The trio decided to expand their horizons. Sam Phillips and Bob Neal, who functioned as Elvis's manager, arranged to get the Blue Moon Boys booked on a couple of country music radio programs...the Louisiana Hayride and the legendary Grand Ol' Opry. The Opry was the peak of success for a country music star, and it was rare that an unknown like Elvis Presley would be afforded the opportunity of playing on its valuable airwaves.

Elvis Presley: I was working for about a year and a half in nightclubs and football fields, barns, Louisiana Hayride, yes, sir. They threw me off the Grand Ol' Opry. I went to the Grand Ol' Opry, man. They gave me six dollars and said, "Look, go home, man."

Sam Phillips: I knew Jim Denney, who was the program director for Grand Ol' Opry. But they weren't interested in what we were doing on Elvis. After the fourth or fifth time, we had discussed this. He said, "If the boys in the neighborhood some time wants to drop by, we'll – we'll see if we could maybe get him on there." Finally got him to commit to put him on the old Hank Snows portion at 10:15 at night. When we finally got him on, Elvis went on stage, and he didn't get the greatest introduction.

SAM PHILLIPS
FOUNDER OF SUN RECORDS

Eddy Arnold: Some of them thought he was a little wild, you know. You know, he'd just wiggle his knees. I – I thought he was pretty good.

EDDY ARNOLD
COUNTRY SINGER

Buddy Killen: I met Elvis the first time when I was working on the Grand Ol' Opry as the bass player, and I was walking across the stage, and I see this guy standing over in the corner. He's got a guitar strapped over his back. And he's standing there all alone. He's pacing around, and I walked over to him. And I said, "My name is Buddy Killen. I work on the Opry." I said, "What's the matter with you?" He said, "I'm Elvis Presley and I'm scared to death." And I said, "Of what?" He said, "These people are going to hate me." I said, "No. They're not going to hate you." He said, "Yes, they are. They're going to hate me." But he went on stage and he did "Blue Moon of Kentucky". You wouldn't know he was nervous once he got on the stage.

BUDDY KILLEN

D.J. Fontana: He went to audition for them, and somehow they didn't really care for him, I mean the management. They said, "You better keep your job, you know. And go back to driving a truck or something." So that kind of hurt his feelings, and I don't think he ever got over that one.

Buddy Killen: Jim Deney is quoted as saying, "Don't give up your day job." I have trouble believing that he said that. But Scotty Moore says he heard him say it. So if Scotty heard him say it...

Dixie Locke-Emmons: That was kind of a shock for him, I think, because he was excited to do it and, you know, ready to perform on stage, but he wasn't received well. He was hurt over that I think and not so much hurt that they didn't like his music, but hurt that another person would be so blunt and so hurtful to say something to him like, "Don't give up your day job."

George Klein: Scotty Moore told me that Elvis cried all the way back from Nashville to Memphis. And the truth be known, Elvis was not a fan of Nashville, Tennessee, and it was mainly because of that. He liked the fact that the musicians were great in Nashville. He liked the fact that the studio was great. At the same token, mister, he never bought a house there. Never partied there. Never hung out in Nashville. What does that tell you?

The Blue Moon Boys were crushed by the response to their performance. That failure on the Grand Ol' Opry would leave a bad taste in Elvis's mouth for years to come. The Louisiana Hayride on the other hand was almost a stepchild to the Opry. It was a nice show, but nothing that could ever be too important to a performer's career.

Sam Phillips: When he went on and he started on "That's All Right Mama," this guy was still in his little cocoon. You know, before that butterfly comes on out. And Elvis Presley tore them up alive.

Dixie Locke-Emmons: It seems to me that the whole attitude was different at the Louisiana Hayride, and I don't know if it was or maybe they were a little more forgiving or excepting than Opry was at that time. But now I think he enjoyed the trips to the Louisiana Hayride. In fact, people in Memphis instinctively knew, you know, that he was destined for greatness and – and I don't think anybody in Memphis – I never heard an unkind word or anybody that wasn't excited about him.

Ray Manzarek: The first time I heard Elvis Presley was on Al Benson's Show in Chicago, a blues – a rhythm and blues station. I grew up on the south side of Chicago. It was an all black station, of course. It just gave me life and hope and desire to make music. Then one day, Al Benson said, "We've got this new guy, Eldin Priestly. Called "Mystery Train." "Train, train coming down the line." And it was different from any of the Chicago blues. I didn't know he was a white guy.

It's just that people were talking about it and it had that beat. And only later when I saw him on TV did I realize Elvis Presley was in fact Eldin Priestly of "Mystery Train."

Elvis's success on the Hayride led to a one-year contract to appear on the show every Saturday. Now a full-time musician, Elvis returned home and quit his job as a truck driver spurning the advice he had received at the Opry.

The Hayride also introduced Elvis to a new friend who would have a profound effect on the life of the King of Rock 'n' Roll. He was a Dutch immigrant and former carnival barker named Andreas Van Kuijk. But his friends just called him Colonel.

Eddy Arnold: Tom was different. See, he wasn't the Colonel when I first met him. You people call him Colonel, but when I met him he was just Tom. And that's the reason I refer to him as Tom. And we got along fine. But, oh yeah. Very good promoter.

George Klein: Colonel Parker at that time managed an act named Hank Snow. And Elvis was an extra-added attraction. That's what it said on the poster cards, and Elvis was getting pretty popular in Arkansas, Mississippi, Tennessee, Kentucky, Texas, and Oklahoma. So Colonel Parker picked up Elvis to open up the show or maybe be second on the bill or third on the bill.

Well, Colonel Parker saw what was happening. He knew something was happening, but he couldn't place his finger on it because every show that Elvis went on he stole the show. That the other acts they could've given up and gone home because after Elvis had left, they kept hollering, "We want Elvis. We want Elvis." So Colonel Parker told Hank Snow, they had an agency together over at Nashville. He said, "Hank, why don't you go down to Memphis and talk to Elvis's parents, Gladys and Vernon, and give them a sell job and tell them what I've done for you. They'll be impressed by you because you're a big country star, and help us get Elvis in this agency." And Hank Snow gave Colonel Parker a great recommendation and told him how much Colonel had helped his career along. And while he was out on the road, he read in the trade magazines, Billboard and Variety, that Elvis had signed with Colonel Tom Parker. So as soon as Hank Snow got off the road, he said he went into Colonel Parker's office and he said, "Hey Colonel, I see where we got that Elvis Presley kid." And Colonel Parker said, "What do you mean 'we', Hank?"

D.J. Fontana: Colonel saw it I guess. I mean he's not my favorite person, we didn't get along, but I didn't have to get along with the Colonel. If I needed something, I'd go see Elvis. You know, he worked 150% for Elvis, period. That's all he knew about it. He didn't care what anybody's concern was about or anything. He could care less. As long as he was working for Elvis, he was happy.

Pat Broeske: Let's face it. He was an old carney huckster. He wasn't interested in art. He was interested in showy glitter and colors and things that happened quickly and things that made money. I mean this is a guy that used to stand outside of Elvis's early concerts selling 8 x 10 glossies of Elvis for 10 cents, and he stood there himself hawking them.

PAT BROESKE
AUTHOR

Joe Esposito: Colonel Parker once told him that you have a million dollar's worth of talent. And he said by the end of the year, you'll have a million dollars. And I believe he would say that. I mean that's the way the Colonel was, and he always thought ahead. And when he said something, he really came through and he did.

JOE ESPOSITO
ROAD MANAGER & FRIEND

Dixie Locke-Emmons: By the time of my junior prom in '55, he was of course on the road a lot, but I'll always remember that because he was in Texas, and I was so afraid the he wasn't gonna get back in town for my prom. And his mom and I had actually been shopping, and she had bought my dress. And Bob Neal's wife had ordered my flowers, which Elvis got kind of upset about that because he ordered flowers himself, and he was kind of bothered that they thought that he wouldn't remember to order my corsage. So – so I left the one that Ms. Neal ordered in the refrigerator, of course. But he came in just in time, and in fact, I went to my 45th class reunion a few years ago. And it was funny. So many of the people that were in school said you know, "Boy, I remember when Elvis came over and picked you up, and I remember y'all doin this, and I remember when you all walked in at the prom." You know, it's a lot of fun memories.

DIXIE LOCKE-EMMONS
HIGH SCHOOL GIRLFRIEND

With Colonel Parker's promise fresh in his mind, Elvis's career began a rapid acceleration unmatched in the history of entertainment. He began to get bookings all over the country, still knocking them dead with that Presley Performance style. But this time, he had the promotional powers of Colonel Tom behind him as well as a new sound courtesy of the latest addition to the band... drummer D.J. Fontana.

Although the Colonel appreciated all that Sam Phillips had done to get Elvis started, he felt that Sun, with its limited influence, could only take Presley so far, and Parker had bigger plans for the performer he now called "his boy". He also didn't want anyone else around to influence Elvis's thinking when it came to business decisions.

On November 20th, 1955, Elvis signed with recording giant RCA in a deal that was reportedly the biggest in the history of the music industry to date. Presley also began appearing on television, a blossoming medium with growing power and influence over the American way of life.

Arthur Godfrey's talent show had auditioned Elvis in New York for a spot on the program but decided he just wasn't good enough for their "quality" show. Thanks to his appearances on the Dorsey Brother's Stage Show, Presley was rapidly becoming something of a curiosity to the teenagers who had been raised on Frank Sinatra and Perry Como.

Dixie Locke-Emmons: Everything he did from then on was just like, you know, wow, look where he's at now. It was just a steady progression of popularity and his visibility on television was – it was exciting of course.

Elvis and I talked about getting married almost from the time we started dating probably until early '56. We remained friends forever and ever. In fact, we were still friends even when we knew that we did not have a future together because his career was going a totally different way. We knew that he would never have a 9 to 5 job, and we both had a good cry about it. And then, uh, he went his way, and I went mine.

But it was his appearance on the Milton Berle Show that changed the way people looked at Elvis Presley and Rock 'n' Roll.

EXCERPT FROM THE MILTON BERLE SHOW

Milton Berle: Uh, I want to tell you something. Incidentally ladies and gentlemen, I don't think that I'm revealing any secrets when I say – when I say that – that Elvis Presley is the fastest rising young singer in the entertainment industry today.

Some were outraged by what they saw as the blatant sexual content of Elvis's gyrating hips. Others were paranoid about Elvis's voice.

EXCERPT FROM A TV NEWS BROADCAST

Preacher: We set up a 20-man committee to do away with this vulgar animal-istic [Negro] rock 'n' roll bop. Our committee will check with restaurant owners and the cafés to see what Presley records is on their machines and then ask them to do away with it.

EXCERPT FROM NEWS FOOTAGE

FAN: No. It just all depends – I mean on how you look at it. I guess if you want to think its nasty or sexy, you could. But to me its just –

Reporter: Well, the two things are not necessary the same.

FAN: Yeah, well, you know, it's just so limber and loose. I mean it's really marvelous.

FAN: Well, he just feels the rhythm. He Digs it the most.

Reporter: You don't see anything wrong with it?

FAN: No.

EXCERPT FROM NEWS FOOTAGE

Commentator: The obscenity and vulgarity of the Rock 'n' Roll music is obviously a means by which the white man and his children can be driven to the level with the [Negroes]. It is obviously [Negro] music.

In an attempt to head off criticism, Elvis agreed to perform his hit "Hound Dog" to an actual Basset hound, while wearing a tuxedo on The Steve Allen Show. He hated every minute of it.

Elvis Presley: I did the Steve Allen Show, and they had me dress in a tuxedo on the Steve Allen show and stand perfectly still, and I couldn't move. I was standing like this. And singing to a dog man. There was a dog here, you know. And I'm singing, "You aint nothing but a hound dog." And the dog's looking at me like what are you doing, calling me names?

On CBS, The Ed Sullivan Show was ordered to film Elvis only from the waist up to avoid touching off the same firestorm that the Berle show had caused.

DIXIE LOCKE-EMMONS
HIGH SCHOOL

Dixie Locke-Emmons: To ourselves, we thought it was funny because those of us who had known him forever knew that that's what he did all the time. When he sat down, one of the first comments my mother made was, well, cannot – can he not be still. You know, because he was always just moving, moving, moving. So when people started to make a big deal out of it, we – we really thought it was funny 'cause it was like hey that's not – I mean that's just him. He's is not putting that on.

So it was kind of then a shock for people to make references to "Elvis the pelvis" and that kind of thing because – and try to make something off-color about it because he would have never in his wildest imagination done anything that would have been offensive to anybody.

EXCERPT FROM AN INTERVIEW

Reporter: What about the name "Elvis the pelvis"?

ELVIS: I mean it's one of the most childish expressions I've ever heard of. I don't like to be called "Elvis the pelvis", but if they want to call me that I mean there's nothing I can do about it.

Soon after, Elvis became the nation's foremost celebrity and the unwitting recipient of an enormous outpouring of emotion from the youth of America. Though Elvis would remain unaware of his overall impact on the music business and popular culture, his new found success gave him a chance to change his life in ways he had never imagined.

Presley's escalating income allowed him to fully develop the roll of caretaker to his family – something he had already begun in a switch on the traditional roles of parent and child.

Dixie Locke-Emmons: Elvis and his mother had a very special relationship. There's something special about a son and his mom, and Elvis and his mother had that. He totally adored her, and she did him. But Elvis and Vernon – this is a hard question for me to answer. I guess this is the only way I can say this. Elvis was almost the father figure.

I don't know that Vernon ever assumed his role as the father figure. Not to say that Elvis didn't love him, he loved his father. But most of the decision-making and things of importance were mostly discussed between Elvis and Gladys, and I think a lot had to do from the time that Elvis got out of school. He was – he contributed financially a lot of times more than Vernon did.

Elvis's dreams were coming true at an alarming rate and like any young man flush with fame and fortune, he indulged his love affair with that all-American institution, the automobile. Elvis bought a used car from a maker that would become almost synonymous with his own name… Cadillac.

Even though Elvis's first experience with his dream car had ended in a less than storybook fashion, he purchased two more Cadillacs that same year. The first was a 1956 El Dorado that he had painted purple and drove as a symbol of his new title of the King of Rock 'n' Roll.

The second was a 1955 Fleetwood that he had painted pink and gave to his mother even though she had never learned to drive.

The '55 Fleetwood would become the most famous Cadillac in the world, a dual symbol of Rock 'n' Roll and a boy's devotion to his mother. It was the only car in his vast collection that Elvis never sold.

He also bought a Lincoln Continental Mark II. A car that was so scarce, the dealer ran ads stating that if you saw one on the highway, there was a 1 in 2000 chance it would be Elvis Presley at the wheel. This was the car he was driving when he pulled into a gas station in late 1956. A group of girls gathered around the Lincoln clamoring for autographs. As usual, Elvis was happy to oblige. But the gas station attendant was impatient and told Presley to leave.

The young singer explained he'd only be a moment, but the angry attendant struck Elvis in the head, so Presley got out of the car and decked him. This landed Elvis in court where the charges were eventually dropped.

Elvis also purchased his family's very first modern home on Audobon Drive in Memphis. It featured a pool and a carport where Elvis could park his ever-expanding collection of vehicles. There was also a small fence where he met freely with his fans once word got out that Elvis Presley had moved into the neighborhood. Gladys and Vernon watched their son's meteoric rise to super stardom on a brand new television set in the living room of that very house.

Pat Broeske: Rock 'n' Roll stars today, you know, one of the first things you have to do when you become really successful, you got to buy your mom a house. It's just an unwritten rule in the rock 'n' roll world. Elvis started that unwritten rule.

PAT BROESKE
AUTHOR

Elvis also indulged his other passion… clothing. But he continued to shop at the store that had provided him with his unique wardrobe from his high school days, Lansky Brothers on Beale Street.

Bernard Lansky: We had a big tailor shop in the city of Memphis. I mean we were in the big – all the big guys start coming in right behind Elvis. They knew where Elvis was buying his clothes. Elvis was our PR man. Anybody that had saw him, they knew what he was wearing, they'd want the same thing. They'd buy a lot silk shirts, a lot velour shirts that he was wearing. Little old jackets with the lace on the pockets, down right really sharp. And everybody that took one. Man, they liked it. Elvis was sharp.

BERNARD LANSKY
MEMPHIS CLOTHIER

George Klein: As far as his clothing, you know, he continued to dress flashy, but more classy looking flashy I guess you could say in '57. You know, we'd go to Lansky Brothers on Beale Street. He would buy nice flashy different looking stuff, and he was dynamite on stage, very hypnotic. You couldn't take your eyes off of him.

GEORGE KLEIN
MEMPHIS MAFIA/FRIEND

But Elvis's popularity was growing too large to be contained by this small suburban neighborhood. It was time to find a new house suited to his new station in life. He would find that house in early 1957 and would keep the name given to it by its former owners. They called it Graceland.

By this time, he had also found himself a new steady girlfriend, one who would not feel out of place in the circles he now traveled. Local celebrity Anita Wood now became Elvis's main female companion.

Anita Wood: I met Elvis in 1957. I was on the Top 10 Dance Party on WHPQ radio television. And it was a popular dance show that they had every Saturday afternoon. The teenagers would come and dance and he'd watch that show a lot. And one Saturday after the show, he wanted a date to see me that night. And to be honest with you, I really wasn't an Elvis fan at that time.

And so this night I got dressed and ready and when they drove up in the Cadillac, that big long black Cadillac. And then Elvis started driving around like we did on many dates that we had, just drive around Memphis. And then Elvis said, "Would you like to come out and see Graceland?" He just purchased Graceland at the time. And he proceeded to show me around.

And he'd show me all the rooms and took me and introduced me to his mother and dad. Then he began to try to get a little fresh with me. And I said, "No. No, that won't work. You know you're gonna have to take me home." So he said, "Okay." And he took me downstairs, and he took me home. He was a gentleman about it. He was very nice. But he did try to get fresh the first date, but he didn't get to first base.

Though Elvis demanded that she remain 100% faithful to him during their relationship, he himself indulged in yet another perk of his growing celebrity... feminine attention.

Anita Wood: Mrs. Presley she wanted us to get married, and she wanted us to have a little boy and to name it Elvis, Junior. And she said, "I could just see him running up and down the driveway in his little bare feet, this little blonde-headed boy, you know." We talked about things like that a lot. I remember she telling me about Natalie Wood coming to visit there. And she didn't much like that. She would talk to me about how she hoped that, you know, we would end up together that – that you're just the girl for him. You will take care of him.

His career now was taking him away more then ever before, but now he was not simply touring. Elvis had become a movie star. During the next two years, Elvis would make four movies that would be considered some of his finest acting work. He would also further cement his life in Memphis making himself more than just a celebrity who happened to call the city home.

Every year at Christmas in a ceremony that would become familiar to the denizens of the city, Elvis would hand out envelopes containing $1000 apiece to various charities at the courthouse downtown. At the same time, he would spare no expense to decorate Graceland like a winter wonderland as his visual gift to his neighbors and fans.

George Klein: Memphis was it for him. It was the real deal. I could just see him. I could just see that relaxed atmosphere in him, and he would be whispering under his breath to me, "Yeah, GK. Graceland will rock. Get some chicks out to the house tonight." You know, stuff like that.

Whenever he wasn't in Hollywood, Elvis would come home to relax by taking friends and family to familiar places around his home. Though even at this early stage in his career, it was becoming more and more difficult for Elvis to enjoy his hometown like a "normal" person. Now special arrangements would have to be made to accommodate Memphis's favorite son. If Elvis wanted to go to the fair or local amusement park, the entire park would be rented out.

Anita Wood: He always invited his fans to go with. Sometimes we would go to the fairgrounds, and he would rent it after hours, and we would stay all night long and ride everything as many times as we wanted to. Just had a wonderful time. That was a lot of fun– all night long. Here I'm getting so tired and sleepy, and they were all ready to go.

For movies, the theater would be closed to all but Elvis and his invited guests. And if the newly crowned King of Rock 'n' Roll wanted to shop, it would have to be done after hours when his hordes of fans had gone home.

And it was in Memphis at Graceland during the holiday season that Presley would receive the letter that would change his life in more ways than one. And in ways not even the Colonel could foresee. Elvis Presley was ordered by the United States Government to report for induction into the armed forces.

JOE ESPOSITO
ROAD MANAGER & FRIEND

Joe Esposito: When he did get his notice, I'm sure he was not too happy. I mean you think you're the biggest star in the world at the time and all of a sudden the army says, "Hey. We want you." I mean it can't feel too good no matter who you are. I didn't feel good, and I was a nobody when I got drafted. I wasn't too happy about it at all.

ANITA WOOD
FORMER GIRLFRIEND

Anita Wood: I can remember the day that Elvis received the draft notice, and he brought it into us and Ms. Presley and Mr. Presley and myself. And they just could not believe that he was gonna have to leave them and go in the service. He really didn't want to leave his family. I mean nobody would want to. Elvis and Mrs. Presley were very close. She was devastated. Scared. Sad.

EXCERPT FROM NEWS FOOTAGE

Military Officer: Congratulations. You are now in the Army. You are all privates. That's the way you'll be addressed from now on. Private Presley, you'll be in charge of the group.

Though it would have been easy for Elvis to get a special assignment in the Army to one of the military's entertainment units, making his stay in the Army one of performing and special privilege, he felt that it was important that he be treated like any other soldier.

The only special treatment that he requested was that he be allowed to complete his latest picture before entering the service so that in his words, "These folks will not lose so much money with all they have done so far." The government allowed the deferment, and "King Creole" was finished.

On March 24th, 1958, Elvis left Graceland, kissed his mother and girlfriend goodbye and reported to the induction center to be sworn in as a soldier in the United States Army.

Anita Wood: He hugged me last. The last thing he said to me was, "Little, I love you and I will return and don't forget me." It was hard. It was difficult. I could not – my heart was being just torn away and it was very hard to see him leave.

From here on out, the King of Rock 'n' Roll would be known as Private Elvis Aron Presley, serial number 53310761.

A FINE YOUNG MAN

"I WAS JUST IMMEDIATELY IN LOVE. I MEAN, I WAS A SMALL CHILD. BUT I KNEW, WOW, MY FIRST HORMONAL CHANGE HAPPENED RIGHT AT THAT MOMENT. I WAS ONLY LIKE FIVE."

— CASSANDRA "ELVIRA" PETERSON

When most people speak of Elvis Presley's television years, they're usually talking about "The Ed Sullivan Show."

But Elvis's appearances on the small screen actually date back a full year-and-a-half before the landmark Sullivan performances.

By late 1954, Presley's star was on the rise.

His Sun Records renditions of "That's Alright," "Blue Moon Of Kentucky" and "Good Rockin' Tonight" were getting a lot of air play but only on southern radio stations.

In October of 1954, Elvis was booked for an appearance on "The Louisiana Hayride," a live Saturday night radio show that originated in Shreveport.

LIVE RADIO BROADCAST 1956

Reporter: How did you get your start on "Louisiana Hayride?" What brought that all about?

ELVIS: I went down there as a just to try out, more or less. I went down there once, and I went back again a couple of weeks later. And the people, they seemed to kind of go for my songs a little bit. So, they gave me a job down there.

George Klein: "Louisiana Hayride" was a fun situation for Elvis. He enjoyed being on it. It was more of a looser show than the Grand Ole Oprey. By looser I mean that in Luisia they weren't as picky and as particular. And Elvis actually became a quick, a very quick popular person on "The Hayride." And it was Sam Phillips who got Elvis on "The Louisiana Hayride."

Sam Phillips: When it came time for Elvis to go on stage the first time at Shreveport, I looked out in that audience. And it was packed. The city auditorium was packed. I got my ass out there, and I found me a seat behind a bunch of old men and women. And there where kids over here, 18, 20. And I was going to be a one-man cheering section. Because we just could not fail.

And I got out there, and let me tell you something. Elvis went out on that stage, untried, unproven. I'd be the first person in this world to tell you that there's no one in the world could have been more nervous than he was. And you certainly understand why. When he went on and he started out on "That's Alright, Mama," I thought I was going to really have to stand up, you know. And here is an old woman, ah, if she's a day, then 65 years old was old, even for me. And all of a sudden, they're all on their feet.

And Elvis Presley tore them up alive. If that didn't tell me something, you know, you'd have to get a bigger blackboard and draw the picture a little bigger. It told me a lot. But I didn't have to stand up. I didn't have to do anything except sit back and enjoy the show. Man, you're talkin' about... That was just like heaven opens up and says, come on in.

The audience's enthusiastic response led to a contract for Elvis to appear on "The Louisiana Hayride" every Saturday night for a year.

Beginning Saturday, November 6, 1954, and continuing for fifty-two consecutive Saturdays, thereafter, "Hayride" also led to a fateful meeting with a drummer who would become a pivotal member of Elvis's back-up band.

D.J. FONTANA
ELVIS'S DRUMMER

D.J. Fontana: Delmer Franks was helping run the "Hayride." He called me one day, and he says, "Come on down to the office. I want you to hear this record we got." I said, "Yeah, I'd like to hear it." And I went down. It was Elvis, Scotty and Bill. I said, "Ah, that's a good record. How many pieces they got on that thing?" You know, and they said, "Oh, it's just three guys." I said, "You got to be kidding! It sounds like a six- or seven-piece band." I said, "Are we going to invite him in here? He's getting a lot of play in Louisiana, Texas, Arkansas, kind'a in the territory there."

And I said, "Yeah, he ought to do all right." Well, he come in. I said, "Let's go back to the dressing room, I want to talk about it and see what we'll do." All he had was "That's Alright, Mama." And the other tunes were all cover tunes. He'd just pull them out of the hat, and we'd do them, you know. So, that's how I kind of got started.

JOE DELANEY
CRITIC "LAS VEGAS SUN"

GLEN GLENN
SINGER/FRIEND

GEORGE KLEIN
MEMPHIS MAFIA/FRIEND

HAL KANTER
DIRECTOR LOVING YOU, BLUE HAWAII

Joe Delaney: There was a jukebox operator convention in Chicago. And I was there representing one of the record companies. And Leo called me, and he said that he'd been down in Shreveport, KWKH, "The Louisiana Hayride." And he'd seen this kid. And the quote was, "I don't know if he'll sell any records, but boy, what he does to an audience is just incredible."

Glen Glenn: They called him The Cat, you know; that young cat down in "The Hayride" is tearing em up.

George Klein: "The Hayride" was a good launching vehicle for Elvis. I think it was Hal Kanter, the director of "Loving You," went to "The Hayride" with Elvis. And if you look at "Loving You," it parallels a lot of what Elvis was doing at "The Hayride" and on tour at that time.

Hal Kanter: He was on his way to Shreveport, where I was going to accompany Elvis for his farewell concert for "The Louisiana Hayride." And that was one of the primary reasons that I went to Memphis, not only to meet Elvis himself, but also to see him in action and to learn as much about his method of operation as I possibly could. And I was awakened at about maybe 7:30 by hoards of children shouting Elvis's name and waking him up.

He opened the window in his hotel room and leaned out and said, "Please let me get some sleep, folks. I'll see you all later." And they quieted down. And I was amazed at that. I never saw anyone control a crowd so effortlessly as he did.

On March 5, 1955, in the midst of his "Hayride" radio contract, Elvis appeared on "The Louisiana Hayride" television show. Although it was only broadcast locally to the Shreveport area, it marked Elvis Presley's official television debut. In August of that year, Elvis signed another important contract making Colonel Tom Parker his personal manager. Parker's aggressive style paved the way for Presley's move from small time Sun Records to big time RCA and some higher profile television appearances.

George Klein: Once I asked Colonel Parker, I said, "Colonel Parker, did you get Elvis on 'The Hayride?'" He said, "I did better than that, George." I said, "What's that?" He said, "I got him off."

Jimmy and Tommy Dorsey were two musical brothers who had dominated the pre-rock 'n' roll era of swing. By the mid-'50s, they were hosting a weekly television series for CBS called "Stage Show" which was carried nationwide. The Colonel arranged for Elvis to make six appearances on the Dorsey Brothers' show catapulting Presley from local to national prominence.

Joe Delaney: Most people think Sullivan gave Elvis the first national television. It wasn't. It was Tommy and Jimmy Dorsey.

Now, the rest of America could finally see the revolutionary young singer who had taken the South by storm.

John O'Hara: It's real interesting when you put it in the context of what else was on TV at the time also. You know, people clicking the channels would see, you know, Perry Como or, you know, somebody juggling plates, and then there's Elvis, you know. I think it was Peter Guralnik had a great thing to say, that when he came on the stage in one of the Dorsey's shows, he looked like a guy shot out of a cannon and had the same impact.

D.J. Fontana: Of course, we were scared, you know, a bunch of hillbillies out of Tennessee and Louisiana, hadn't never been out to no big towns or anything like that, and then going to New York to do a big, you know, television show, scared the heck out of us. But we went up there and we did what we knew what to do, you know, just the tunes. And I guess it worked out real well. We did six of those shows, actually.

Ray Manzarek: I'm one of those rare individuals who saw Elvis on his very first television performance: The Tommy and Jimmy Dorsey Show, a summer replacement for Jackie Gleason. So, out comes Elvis Presley with Bill Black on bass, D.J. Fontana on drums and Scotty Moore, playing that incredible guitar.

The first song that Elvis performed on national television was "Shake, Rattle And Roll." It may have been a little off key, but nobody seemed to mind.

Johnny Tillotson: The first time I saw him on television was on The Dorsey Brothers' Show. And I wanted the sound to be better because I was used to the Scotty and Bill sound.

Glen Campbell: I thought it was just sensational. I mean, it didn't make any difference if the guitars were out of tune or in tune or anything. Elvis Presley carried the show. You could feel the rhythm. You could feel that pulse. That's why rock 'n' roll is so big.

Ray Manzarek: My mother calls out to me, "Ray-mond, you'd better come in here and take a look at this guy. You like this kind of stuff." I shot into the living room and my eyes went 'boing.' Elvis Presley live on TV, the darkest, meanest most dangerous white man ever to be on television. He's wearing a cream colored suit, black and white TV, that had a cream color to it, a dark shirt and a cream colored tie and, no doubt, blue suede shoes. It was one of the transcendent moments of my life, altered my destiny. Okay, that's what I want. White guys can do rock 'n' roll too.

America's reaction was decidedly mixed including those who accused the white singer of ripping off the original rhythm and blues artists.

Ray Manzarek: Up until that time, what it had been was Little Richard, Fats Domino and Chuck Berry. And this was like the first white man I saw do rock 'n' roll. And I said, "Rock, is for this guy." And that changed my life.

After his astonishing success on the Dorsey shows, other stars were eager to book Elvis. Milton Berle was one of the kings of TV comedy in the 1950s. In fact, one of his nicknames was "Mr. Television." On April 3, 1956, just a week after his final Dorsey Brothers appearance, Elvis guest starred on "The Milton Berle Show."

Most of Berle's shows were broadcast from ABC in Hollywood with a studio audience made up largely of older people. But his one was televised from the deck of the U.S.S. Hancock, which was anchored off the coast of San Diego.

THE MILTON BERLE SHOW, USS HANCOCK – APRIL, 1956

Show Announcer: Tonight, "The Milton Berle Show" joins forces with the navy in bringing you an hour of star-studded entertainment. And here they are, the men of the U.S.S. Hancock with their families. It is to them and to all the brave guardians of our shores, the men of the United States Navy that we dedicate our show tonight.

Milton Berle: And now, you guys and gals, all your wives and sweethearts, you're in for a real treat. This is the first time that the Hancock is going to rock 'n' roll while still at anchor. Here's a young man who in a few short months has gained tremendous popularity in the music business. His records are really going like wildfire. He's America's new singing sensation, our new RCA recording artist, here he is, a big reception for Elvis Presley.

Since the Berle program was basically a comedy show, Elvis tried his hand at a funny sketch opposite "Uncle Milty."

ELVIS: Thank you, ladies and gentlemen. And now, I got a little surprise for you. Here for his very first public appearance, I'd like you to meet my twin brother, Melvin Presley. Melvin.

Milton Berle: Hello friends of Radioland. Radioland.

ELVIS: Radioland. This is television, Milt, Melvin.

Milton Berle: Milton or Melon?

ELVIS: Melvin.

Milton Berle: Musta had another brother, too? Tele-vi-sion, what the heck is that?

ELVIS: Well, it's a little box...

Milton Berle: Yeah.

ELVIS: Got a window in it.

Milton Berle: Yeah.

ELVIS: Millions of people out there. They're looking in the little window.

Milton Berle: Yeah.

ELVIS: And they can see you, but you can't see them.

Milton Berle: Well, the dirty Peeping Toms. But Melvin, you're wonderful. And keep buying them records, will you folks. No, who – Elvis. Hot-dog. Elvis needs the money. I'll tell you, I'm sure mighty proud to be here on this ship here, the U-shun Coke and I want you to know... The U-shun Coke

ELVIS: U-shun Coke?

Milton Berle: U-shun Coke that's what it says on the side of the boat, U-S-S-H-A-N-C-O-C-K. U-shun Coke. What's the matter. I know how to spell.

ELVIS: That's U.S.S. Hancock, Melvin!

Milton Berle: Keep buying them records. I'm real proud of you, Elvis.

ELVIS: Well, Melvin, I owe it all to you.

Milton Berle: You owe everything to me.

ELVIS: You taught me everything I know.

Milton Berle: Yeah, I'm glad you told that to the folks. I did. I taught him his singing style. I used to drop grasshoppers down his pants. That's how he keep jumping around. Ask the grasshoppers. Keep buying them records. Do that for us. What are we going to do now?

ELVIS: Well, let's sing a song.

Milton Berle: Let's sing a song, let's do "The Blue Suede Shoes" half sole. Here we go. One more. Take it away.

ELVIS: Well, it's one for the money, two for the show, three to get ready, now go, cat, go...

The combination of Berle and Presley was magical. One out of every four Americans tuned in that night which translated into over 40 million viewers.

This led to a second and very controversial Berle appearance two months later, this time back at the ABC studios.

Susan Brodsky: He made a dynamic impact by just his presence and the way he performed and all this moving and shaking and, oh, especially when people see him on Milton Berle doing "Hound Dog." That was just something no one had ever really seen before, a person move that way. It was just like he was moving and shaking the world at the same time he was moving and shaking on the stage.

The show was another huge hit in the ratings. But Elvis's sexy gyrations touched off a firestorm of criticism.

EXCERPT FROM AN INTERVIEW

Reporter: A lot of people possibly don't like it.

ELVIS: I've been getting some pretty bad publicity lately, especially after the Milton Berle Show, I got quite a bit of bad publicity about my actions on the stage.

Reporter: Quite a group of people who don't sort of approve of...

ELVIS: I have to move around. I can't stand still. I've tried it. And I can't do it.

Reporter: They seem to think that it contributes to juvenile delinquency and all sorts of things.

ELVIS: I don't see how they could think that it would contribute to juvenile delinquency. If there's anything I've tried to do I've tried to live a straight, clean life and not set any kind of a bad example.

If I stood up in front of an audience and did nothing but sing. If I didn't put on a show and if I didn't act like I enjoyed what was doing, they wouldn't come out to see me the next time I went back.

It's like this, there's people regardless of who you are or what you do, there's going to be people that don't like you. There were people that didn't like Jesus Christ. They killed him. And Jesus Christ was a perfect man, you know.

There are going to be people that don't like you regardless of who you are or what you do. Because if everybody thought the same way, they'd be driving the same car. They'd be marrying the same woman. And that wouldn't work out.

Gordon Stoker: And he said, "We move when we sing. It's our way of showing love for the Lord, just the movement. And that's really..." He said, "I got those movements from singing religious songs in church." And why should they call it vulgar? First of all, he wouldn't have done anything vulgar because of his mother and dad, the love he had for them. And he certainly he would not have done it for the love he had for the people.

One popular show never had Elvis as a guest, but not necessarily because of the controversy.

Dick Clark: Colonel Parker would never let Elvis appear on "American Bandstand" certainly not for AFTRA scale. I think it was $150 or something. Unbelievable. For that amount of money, he should have been on two or three times.

Despite the controversy, one television host was hot to book Elvis for an "American Bandstand" type show called "Top Ten Dance Party."

Wink Martindale: One of the first things on his agenda was to do a charity benefit show for a charity organization called the Cynthia Milk Fund here in Memphis. So, he wanted to promote that. And of course, I was trying like the dickens to get him to come on as a guest on "Top 10 Dance Party." And he wouldn't do things like that in those days. The Colonel did not want him making free, quote on quote, "freebie appearances." He wanted Elvis to be paid for everything. Of course, we had no budget. But Dewey Phillips and George Klein, thanks to them, and my brief friendship with him, he came on and promoted the Cynthia Milk Fund thing and leaned on the jukebox. And, you know, it's kind of an interesting and a famous interview to this day.

TOP 10 DANCE PARTY, JUNE 1956

Wink Martindale: I got a big show at Westwood Park scheduled for July 4th. Bob Johnson, surely, I know, wants us to mention that. And we want to mention it. I believe the proceeds from this show go to the Cynthia Milk Fund. Is that right, Elvis?

ELVIS: Yes sir, that's right. And I'd like to say that... Let's see, what would I like to say? I'd like to say that we have a diamond ring that we're going to have as a door prize.

Wink Martindale: Uh-huh.

ELVIS: It's my initial ring. I've had it for some time. And it has 14 diamonds in it. And we're going to give it away at the door as a door prize.

Wink Martindale: I see.

ELVIS: And everything.

Wink Martindale: And all the proceeds from this particular show, this is July 4th at Westwood Park. Elvis is going to be there. He's going to sing and play. His band will be there. Many other stars will be there too. We will certainly want you to watch Bob Johnson's column in The Memphis Press Scimitar. Watch all the publicity on it and get your tickets in advance. Elvis Presley, I want to thank you again...

ELVIS: Thank you

Wink Martindale: ...because we know you're a busy man. And thanks a lot for coming by and seeing us at "Dance Party" and saying hello to all your friends here in Memphis the mid-South. Any time you're in town and want to come by, we certainly will welcome you.

ELVIS: Well, thank you very much, Wink. And I'll see you again.

Wink Martindale: Okay, thanks a lot... Elvis Presley.

Wink Martindale: And I was nervous. The kids were nervous. Everybody was... I mean, it was like that day at WHPQ Channel 13 was like magic. I mean, we had extra security there. We had... You couldn't get near the place, there were so many cars out front, because Elvis was – Elvis was Elvis in 1956. And he just got bigger from there. But it was quite a day, a day I'll never forget. It's ingrained in my memory.

But "Dance Party" was a local Memphis show. Would a popular national program still want Elvis in the wake of the continuing "Hound Dog" hysteria?

Like Milton Berle, Steve Allen was another giant of early television. He defied the squeamish NBC brass and pushed to have Elvis on his top rated Sunday night show, controversy or not. But by poking fun at Presley's image, Steverino avoided one controversy and generated another.

THE STEVE ALLEN SHOW – JULY 1956

Steve Allen: Well, you know, a couple of weeks ago on the "Milton Berle Show," our next guest, Elvis Presley received a great deal of attention which some people seem to interpret one way and some viewers interpreted it another. Naturally, it's our intention to do nothing but a good show. Somebody's barking back there. We want to do a show the whole family can watch and enjoy. And we always do. And tonight, we are presenting Elvis Presley in his, what you might call his first come back.

And at this time, it gives me extreme pleasure to introduce the new Elvis Presley. Here he is.

Elvis, I must say you look absolutely wonderful. You really do. And I think your millions of fans are really going to get a kind of a kick seeing a different side of your personality tonight.

ELVIS: Well, thank you, Mr. Allen.

Steve Allen: I'll hold your guitar here.

ELVIS: It's not too often that I get to wear the suit and tails and all that stuff.

Steve Allen: Uh-huh.

ELVIS: But I think I have a little something tonight that's not quite correct for evening wear.

Steve Allen: Not quite formal? What's that, Elvis?

ELVIS: Blue suede shoes.

Steve Allen: dOh, yes!

D.J. FONTANA
ELVIS'S DRUMMER

D.J. Fontana: Yeah, that Steve Allen show we did was… He wasn't very happy with it at all. But he didn't want to argue with Steve about it, you know. He knew that he didn't like it. And I don't think he ever forgave Steve Allen about that whole situation or not. But Steve said, "Well, we'll clean up your image and this…" you know, that garbage that Steve said, that's what he wanted to do. But it didn't do a bit of good. Elvis was going to be Elvis. You know, and the people saw what was going on. And they thought, you know – the fans, and they thought it was pretty pitiful that they would pull something on him. Like I said, he didn't want to argue with Steve or anybody else. He said, we'll do it and get it over with, you know.

Steve Allen: Oh, no, he loved it. In fact, he spent the whole week in rehearsal laughing. Some people who now see him as second only to Jesus Christ, imagined that he must be affronted. But he wasn't a superstar at that time. He was just a young kid lucky enough to be on our big show. That was it. So, he had a marvelous time.

THE STEVE ALLEN SHOW

Steve Allen: Well, Elvis, you're certainly being a really good sport about the whole thing. And now, I have a little surprise for you. Gene, can I have the surprise.

Gene Rayburn: There you are.

Steve Allen: Thank you, Gene Rayburn. This, Elvis, believe it or not, is a giant petition. It was signed by three giants out in the alley here. No, seriously. This was signed by over 18,000 of Elvis's loyal fans saying they wanted to see him again soon on television. It was sent into us just the other day by our good friend D.J. Don Wallace in Tulsa, Oklahoma. 18,000 signatures on this. Elvis, it's a fine thing.

John O'Hara: I liked Steve Allen a lot. He seems very – or was a very brilliant guy. But I don't think he got Elvis.

JOHN O'HARA
AUTHOR

As a matter of fact, he was a bit of musical snob, thought rock 'n' roll was just some passing, you know, teenage fad and obviously thought, you know, Elvis was just another teenage fad sort of thing. And, you know, the famous Elvis singing to the hound dog thing. I know Elvis didn't like that. But, you know, you got to see him in a tuxedo, and that was pretty cool.

Putting Elvis in white tie and tails was one thing. But Steve's idea of a trouble free version of "Hound Dog" was something else entirely.

EXCERPT OF 1970 INTERVIEW

ELVIS: I did "The Steve Allen Show." And they had me wear a tuxedo on "The Steve Allen Show" and stand perfectly still. I couldn't move. I was standing like this. And I had to sing it to a dog, man. There was a dog here, you know. And I'm singing, "You ain't nothing' but a hound dog." And the dog's looking at me like, you know, what are you doing, calling me names or what?

Just as he had done on "The Milton Berle Show," Elvis took part in some comedy sketches including one featuring Steve, Andy Griffith and 50's comedy queen Imogene Coca.

THE STEVE ALLEN SHOW – JULY 1956

Steve Allen: Well, this guy here is Tumbleweed Presley. Come on out Tumble. I'll tell you about this fellow. He is a trick rider. You ain't seen trick riders till you've seen Tumbleweed, right.

ELVIS: You tell them.

Steve Allen: I'm telling them. You tell me to tell them. And I'll tell em. But, you know, let me tell you.

Yesterday, he went across the range at a full gallop blindfolded. And he picked up a rattlesnake with his teeth. He jumped four fences, and he dropped that snake into a gopher hole at a full gallop. Tell them why it was so tough, Tumbleweed.

ELVIS: I didn't use no horse.

ALL: Yippie-aye-oh. Yippie-aye-ayea. Yippie-aye-oh-ayea. Tell em, Elvis.

ELVIS: Well, I got a horse, and I got a gun. And I'm going out and have some fun. I'm, a-warning you galloot, and don't step on my blue suede shoes. Yeah.

ALL: Yippie-aye-oh. Yippie-aye-ayea. Yippie-aye-oh-ayea.

Just as Elvis had to answer for the controversy following his sexy rendition of "Hound Dog" on the Berle Show, he appeared on Hy Gardner's Talk Show the very night of his talked about guest shot on Steve Allen.

HY GARDNER CALLING! JULY, 1956

ELVIS: Hello.

Hy Gardner: Did you have fun tonight on "The Steve Allen Show?"

ELVIS: Yes, sir. I really did. I really enjoyed it.

Hy Gardner: First time you ever worked in the tux or tails?

ELVIS: That's the first time I ever had one on, period.

Hy Gardner: What do you keep in mind mostly, I mean, some of the songs you're going to do or some of your plans or what?

What What goes through your mind?

ELVIS: Well, everything has happened to me so fast in the last year-and-a-half, till – I'm all mixed up, you know.

I mean, I can't keep up with everything that's happening.

Hy Gardner: I know. I tell you, it's just been swell talking with you. And you make a lot of sense.

ELVIS: Thank you, very much.

Hy Gardner: Give my best to the Colonel, now.

ELVIS: Sure will.

Hy Gardner: Bye-bye.

Steve Allen's chief competition on Sunday night was "The Ed Sullivan Show." Sullivan, a newspaper columnist, was the quirky host of this wildly popular variety program. Straight laced Ed had initially said he would never have someone like Elvis Presley on his "really big shoe." But it was becoming increasingly impossible to ignore Presley's enormous popularity. So, Sullivan changed his mind.

PAUL GONGAWARE
CONCERTS WEST ASSOCIATE

Paul Gongaware: When Elvis was really starting to break big, Ed Sullivan was pursuing him to put him on the show. And the Colonel, he knew he could get the slot, but he told Ed Sullivan that you got to pay this outrageous amount of money, whatever it is. And of course Sullivan said, "But Colonel, I mean, I've only got this budget. You know, this is the budget. You got to do it." And the Colonel said, "Well, we're not going to do it for that kind of money. Go back to you sponsors and do what you have to do. But if you want Presley, this is what it's going to cost you."

Sullivan went back. And he went back and forth. Elvis could have been on the Sullivan show a lot sooner than he was. But during this time of negotiations, this whole thing just kept building and building and building so when Presley finally went on Sullivan, it was an event.

If Ed Sullivan didn't want to stand on the same stage as Elvis Presley, he got his wish. Shortly before Elvis's first appearance in September of 1956, Ed had an automobile accident.

Pinch hitting for the ailing Sullivan was Charles Laughton the distinguished star of the classic, "Mutiny On The Bounty."

The tenderness of "Love Me Tender" won over a lot of viewers who had only seen Elvis as a vulgar rock 'n' roller. Presley's appearance generated the highest ratings for a variety show in the history of television and opened doors for other aspiring entertainers.

James Darren: Sullivan. Ed Sullivan was the first time I saw him. Yeah. I thought it was incredible. I mean, I thought here's a guy who's spearheading a whole new thing. And that's exactly what happened. I mean, he just opened up a whole new area for all other performers to come into.

Michael Ochs: Once Elvis played Ed Sullivan, it was all over. This was the essence of rock 'n' roll.

By the time Elvis made his second appearance on the Sullivan show, Ed had recovered from his fender-bender.

Gordon Stoker: Elvis was very much uptight doing those Ed Sullivan shows. That's one reason he wanted to be as close to the Jordanaires and D.J. and Scotty and Bill Black as possible is because he was a little bit insecure. And he wanted to feel secure with us as close as possible. And if you'll notice, we were right behind him. And how they got a good sound on the five of our voices with just one overhead mike. You know, now, everybody has his individual mike. And you don't have near as good a balance as we had on that show.

But a lot of viewers still didn't care for Elvis's sexy moves. So, Sullivan came up with a compromise.

Joe Delaney: Someone came up with the idea of showing Elvis only from the waist up, because they felt those gyrations were lewd. They were terrible. The outcry. The churches. And it was a very effective ploy.

CASSANDRA "ELVIRA" PETERSON
ACTRESS

Cassandra Peterson: I just remember him being shot from, you know, from the waist up. And that my parents were saying, "Oh, they can't shoot the rest of him." And I'm like, "What? What?" You know, I didn't get it. Oh, I was just immediately in love. I mean, I was a small child. But I knew, wow, my first hormonal change happened right at that moment. I was only like five. I was immediately just in love with him, the way he smiled and how sexy and how different and cool. I mean, up to then, you know, my parents biggest, favorite entertainer was Liberace, you know. So, not much going on there.

ART FEIN
PRODUCER, HOUSE OF BLUES ELVIS TRIBUTE

Art Fein: My family doesn't normally watch "The Sullivan Show" or watch "The Steve Allen Show." But that night we watched Sullivan. And I said, "Oh, my God, what is this?" And I was just a little ten-year-old kid. And I said, "Well, my past life is over. My new life is beginning." And I went down to the store where I usually bought stamps for my postage stamp collection. And they had a few records in the back too. I said, "Forget that. Give me that record called, 'Too Much' right over there."

CONNIE STEVENS
ACTRESS/GIRLFRIEND

Connie Stevens: I thought he was the handsomest guy I'd ever seen. I mean it is a toss up. Now Bobby Conrad will kill me if he hears this because he was pretty hot himself, but he was just so beautiful. He had mischievous eyes that darted around the room. So, he had the facility of talking to you, but if he darted one way or the other, that person was included big time. So, he could grab them all at the same time. And I noticed that right away. I was riveted like everybody else.

Celeste Yarnall: You know, I grew up with him. I saw his first performances on "The Ed Sullivan Show" even though my mother, who later loved Elvis, was scandalized by, you know, the "Elvis the Pelvis" nickname. When I met him, I couldn't believe how much charisma he had, how nice he was. He was so nice. He loved people. He was so warm and so kind and so generous that he was a bigger than life person.

Just as Elvis had crooned "Love Me Tender" on the first Sullivan show, he wanted to alternate the hard rocking "Too Much" with a kinder, gentler song for his third and final appearance.

Gordon Stoker: He wanted do "Peace In The Valley." And the CBS officials said, "No! In no way are we going to do a religious number." He said, "I have promised my momma that I would do 'Peace In The Valley.' And I'm going to sing it." And we did.

Kenny Rogers: I remember seeing him on "The Ed Sullivan Show." And I thought, "Well, what is all the fuss about with this guy?" And then, there's no question that he had a charisma. He had such power, because I don't think he realized how much power he had which is what made him so special. He just was what he was. And in being that, he took on this persona of something that was bigger than anybody else out there.

John O'Hara: There is a quote from Ed Sullivan. And it's one of the things that he said after Elvis's last appearance that, "So, now let's have a tremendous hand for a very nice person" which is just such a great, you know, summation of Elvis and his fans. Like people just appreciated this guy. A lot of the reason why is because he was a very nice person.

Gordon Stoker: Ed did not come to the dress rehearsal. He only came to the filming of the show. And on one of those shows, Ed walks over, do you remember, and shakes hands with Elvis and turns around and motions to us and says, "This boy's really an okay kid." That's the first time we'd met him.

EXCERPT FROM SULLIVAN SHOW

Ed Sullivan: This is a real decent, fine boy. And wherever you go, along with... The guys who accompany you over there, we want to say we've never had a pleasanter experience on our show with a big name than we've had with you. You're thoroughly all right. So now, let's have a tremendous hand for a very nice person.

Gordon Stoker: I think that Ed Sullivan was really the main show in kicking Elvis's career off. You know, Ed Sullivan was kind of like God in those days. What he said was good went, you know what I mean. He walked over and said this is an all right – this is a real nice guy and all that type of thing. And I think that influenced an awful lot of people. Because that show was the most watched of any TV show that's ever been.

As Elvis waved good-bye on January of 1957, he couldn't have known that he was also waving good-bye to his television appearances of the 1950s. Having done Sullivan, "Steverino" and "Uncle Milty," it was time for Uncle Sam.

Beginning in March of 1958, Elvis Presley served two years in the army stationed in West Germany. In March of 1960, he was finally discharged, receiving a warm welcome from 19-year-old Nancy Sinatra upon his return to the States. At a press conference in Memphis, he announced his immediate plans.

PRESS CONFERENCE

Reporter: Can you give us in detail some of your future plans?

ELVIS: Well, the first thing I have to do is to cut some records. And then after that, I have a television show with Frank Sinatra.

Sinatra's show, which aired in May of 1960, included some of his "Rat Pack" pals as well as a reunion between Elvis and Nancy.

Joe Esposito: Elvis was especially nervous, because he had been gone in the army for two years. He didn't know how he was going to be received. I mean, you know, Elvis the way he showed his nervousness, well, he'd be walking back and forth in the dressing room up in his suite or something. And he was sweating profusely. And you could tell he was nervous. He didn't talk too much. He was thinking what was going to go on in this show. But, you know, any good star that really feels what he does when he sings and performs, gets nervous, because they're always concerned about it. And he... Once it all got started and got rolling, he got back to himself again.

JOE ESPOSITO
ROAD MANAGER & FRIEND

If Elvis had vowed never to wear a tuxedo again after doing "The Steve Allen Show" in 1956, he seems to have broken that promise.

JOE ESPOSITO
ROAD MANAGER & FRIEND

Joe Esposito: I forgot if Frank Sinatra said it or not. Somebody said, "Well, you know, everybody has to wear tuxedos."

Well, Colonel Parker was in the meeting, and he said, "Really?" He says, "All the guys with Elvis?" He says, "Oh, yeah. You know, it's tuxes, it's a very formal show." Well then he called Sinatra and them over to the side. He didn't say it in front of us. He says, "Well, none of the guys have tuxedos. So, if you want them to wear tuxedos, you have to get them tuxedos." And, you know, Sinatra being the way he was anyhow, it didn't mean anything, he says, "Oh, yeah, we'll make sure we get them tuxedos." Well, they sent a tailor up to the room and measured us all out, and we all had tuxedos which were great. We got to keep the tuxedos too. I still can't fit into mine again. I don't why.

Having matured during his army days, Presley no longer looked out of character in a tuxedo even while swinging his hips to his latest hit, "Stuck On You."

MALCOLM LEO
DIRECTOR/WRITER/PRODUCER
"THIS IS ELVIS"

Malcolm Leo: When he did "Stuck On You" which is a pretty okay song but not really a killer. And I saw him do it on the Sinatra show. And he had a whole different ent groove going. I was just saying, oh, he's marching right along, you know, marching. The '50s were definitely over. But he came back and did that tune.

Joe Esposito: And it was the first time I think that Elvis had ever met Sinatra. So, he was a little nervous. He didn't know what to expect, because there were rumors about Frank saying certain things about Elvis when he first came out that he wouldn't last long. The music wasn't that great.

Pat Broeske: Yeah, Frank Sinatra was one of the people who joined the angry mob and badmouthed Elvis, as did Bing Crosby. They were cruel. Their comments were very mean.

John O'Hara: Just a few years earlier, Frank Sinatra's talking about his famous quote. And it's in Elvis And You about rock 'n' roll being a rancid aphrodisiac, you know, and Elvis being, you know, untalented. And then a couple of years later, he's, you know, singing a duet with him.

Ed McMahon: My oldest daughter, Claudia, got right into Elvis Presley, like he affected every young person in the country, in the world, for that matter. But that's where I first heard about him. And, you know, it's like a lot of times when your kids come along, you dismiss something because it's them. It's a terrible thing to do. But we all do it. You know, we say, "Well, they like that. I probably won't like it." You know, that's one of those things. But later one, I found out of all people, Sinatra, the greatest singer that ever lived, no question, in my opinion, was a big fan of Elvis Presley. And I said, like wait a minute. I'm missing something here. If Sinatra thinks he's a great guy, great singer, great performer, whatever, I'd better pay more attention.

Joe Esposito: He could charm anybody. And once somebody meets him, it's a completely different situation. So, when Frank Sinatra and Elvis met together that day, uh, you know, Frank treated him very nice. I mean, he was very nice to him, very polite like he normally would be. But I think once he was around Elvis and saw that Elvis was a nice, intelligent young man, very respectful of the stars and other people, I think Frank changed his mind about Elvis. He thought Elvis was a pretty good guy.

Pat Broeske: That was a great PR move of course as well, both for Sinatra and for Elvis Presley. Remember, the Colonel wants him to appeal to a new audience. What better way than to, you know, have him doing a duet with Frank.

FRANK SINATRA SHOW, 1960

Frank Sinatra: You do "Witchcraft." Okay. And I'll do one of the other ones. Okay. We work in the same way only in different areas.

Frank Sinatra: Love me tender. Love me sweet. Never let me go. You have made my life complete. And I love you so.

Elvis Presley: Those fingers in my hair, that come hither stare that strips my conscious bare. It's witchcraft.

Susan Brodsky: And Elvis definitely tries to adapt to a different style when he's singing Frank's song "Witchcraft," kind of tries to sing it the way Frank sings it. But Frank, on the other hand, picks up "Love Me Tender" and, if you listen, he's trying to, I think, Sinatraize by swinging it. And "Love Me Tender" is not, I don't think, meant to be sung that way. But Frank has a certain style of singing that he kind of, that's the way Frank sings.

SUSAN BRODSKY
ELVIS HISTORIAN

FRANK SINATRA SHOW, 1960

Frank Sinatra: Love me tender. Love me true. All my dreams fulfilled. For, my darling, I love you. And I always will.

Elvis Presley: It's such an ancient pitch, what matters is which. Because there's no nicer witch than witchcraft.

Frank Sinatra: I love you, and I always will.

BOTH: For my darling, I love you.

Frank Sinatra: Man, that's pretty.

BOTH: And I always will.

JOE ESPOSITO
ROAD MANAGER & FRIEND

JOHN O'HARA
AUTHOR

Joe Esposito: My memories of the show being taped were just great. I mean, it was exciting for me, first time being around this kind of a situation and seeing the reaction... You know, this is the first time I saw Elvis on stage with a live audience too. So, seeing the reactions from the audience and the people screaming and yelling and just all the excitement, it gave you goose bumps. And it was really exciting for me to see this. And I know Elvis was just beaming with joy that the reception was so warm for him.

John O'Hara: His television appearances. I think there were only 12 in the early part of his fame. And, you know, that was it. Like America just got a look at that.

After the Sinatra Special, Elvis returned to Hollywood and resumed his movie career at a dizzying pace. His appearances on the small screen were over except for two notable exceptions. In 1968, his popularity sagging, Elvis made what is commonly referred to as the "Comeback Special," which reminded everyone what an astonishing entertainer he had been and could still be.

This led to Elvis's enormous success in Las Vegas and a quick time out in 1973 for another television special "Aloha From Hawaii." This time, the show was broadcast live via satellite, reaching an estimated 1.5 billion viewers around the world.

It proved to skeptics that Elvis, at nearly 40 years of age, was still a force to be reckoned with. "Aloha From Hawaii" would prove to be the last Elvis special to be televised during his lifetime. He spent his final years playing to packed houses in Las Vegas and touring all across America.

But those early appearances that Elvis Presley made from Ed Sullivan...

...to Steve Allen...to Milton Berle...

...and, of course, the Dorsey Brothers Show that introduced him to a nationwide audience, constitute a unique legacy in the history of television and popular music.

LIGHTS, CAMERA, ELVIS

"I WASN'T READY FOR THAT TOWN, AND THEY WEREN'T READY FOR ME."

— ELVIS PRESLEY

From the moment he stepped onto his first sound-stage, until the day he walked off his last, Elvis Presley created a motion-picture legacy that will never be forgotten.

Between 1956 and 1969, he starred in 31 films.

Some Good and some...well...

Elvis's Hollywood years parallel the milestones in his private life. Sometimes what went on behind the scenes was more interesting than what was captured on celluloid, because the real Elvis Presley was a lot more compelling than the two- and sometimes one-dimensional characters he played on the big screen.

Unfortunately, Presley's enormous success at the box-office only hampered his hopes of becoming a respected dramatic actor; and that is the dark side of Elvis's Hollywood years, a story that began with infinite possibilities nearly half a century ago.

JIMMY DORSEY SHOW

Jimmy Dorsey: Well, we're going to get things started out with a young man who is making his sixth appearance on Stage Show. He's a dynamic singer of songs who incidentally leaves for Hollywood tonight for a screen test. We wish him a lot of luck. Here he is, Elvis Presley!

By the spring of 1956, Elvis's television appearances and record sales had catapulted him from total obscurity to national superstardom. So it was no surprise when Elvis left for Tinseltown to take his shot at the silver screen.

George Klein: When Elvis was in Memphis before he went out to Hollywood, he studied Hollywood in his own way. He would go see movies day in and day out. He'd watch movies, he'd go to movie theaters and he'd watch movie after movie. He was an usher in a movie theater. He got to see motion pictures over and over. And he studied; he did his homework. He noticed that Clark Gable wore his shirt open, didn't wear an undershirt. He copied that. He noticed that Brando and Jimmy Dean and Tony Curtis and those guys had dark hair, and they didn't do a lot of smiling. And actually that worked for him, because when he got to Hollywood, if you'll notice, all of his early publicity pictures he's not smiling. Because he said he felt that the guys who smiled a whole lot and had that typical Hollywood blond hair, blue eyes, smile look actually faded out quicker than the guys who had the demeanor of a Brando or a Jimmy Dean.

Elvis arrived in Hollywood and went straight to Paramount Studios, where he met with legendary producer Hal Wallis, who had arranged for a screen test. It was the beginning of a very productive relationship.

A.C. LYLES: I remember the day Elvis Presley first walked on this lot, his first motion-picture set. And he was already very well established. And one of our most prominent producers was Hal Wallis. And he saw in Elvis Presley the same thing he saw in Kirk Douglas and Charlton Heston and the other famous people that he had found. He saw a big movie star, and he brought him here on the lot.

A.C. LYLES
PARAMOUNT PRODUCER

The first half of the screen test featured Elvis lip-synching "Blue Suede Shoes" while strumming a stringless prop guitar.

SCREEN TEST EXCERPT

Director: Sound ready?

Elvis Presley: All ready.

Director: Let's make a tape. Come on, turn 'em over. Speed. Action!

Elvis Presley: It's one for the money, two for the show. Three to get ready, now go cat go... Stay off of my blue suede shoes! ♫

Director: Cut! Fine! Great!

The second half was a dramatic scene from THE RAINMAKER, which was slated to be Presley's movie debut.

Hal Kanter: I was asked by Hal Wallis to come and see a screen test that he had made of a young man named Elvis Presley. And I had heard of Elvis Presley, but I had never seen him work. And I had great trepidation about seeing that, because I didn't think that from what I had known of Elvis that he was screen material. I thought he was a passing fancy for young children, especially young girls. But I was very pleasantly surprised. As a matter of fact, my socks were knocked off seeing what I saw on the screen.

Wallis was equally impressed and, after some tough negotiations with Colonel Parker, signed Elvis to a seven-year contract.

A.C. Lyles: Colonel Parker knew about Hal Wallis, knew of his background, knew of the great things he'd done for so many stars and the variety of pictures he had made. Also, Hal Wallis, the producer, knew the importance of keeping Colonel Parker, as you say, in the loop of what was happening, because Colonel Parker really controlled Elvis. So there was a happy marriage between Hal Wallis and Colonel Parker.

Wallis put THE RAINMAKER into production, but with one minor change in the casting. As planned, Burt Lancaster and Katharine Hepburn starred in the colorful drama. But in the role that had been intended for Elvis, Hal Wallis cast newcomer Earl Holliman.

The reason Elvis dropped out was that the part of Hepburn's kid brother was just too small for the film debut of Elvis Presley.

Pat Broeske: If Elvis had done THE RAINMAKER and had done okay in the film, he might have gradually worked his way up to other parts. Who knows?

After THE RAINMAKER fell through, Hal Wallis set about trying to find a script worthy of the King. Unable to find a suitable project at Paramount, Wallis loaned Elvis to 20th Century Fox for a Civil War drama entitled THE RENO BROTHERS, co-starring Richard Egan, Debra Paget, and William Campbell.

WILLIAM CAMPBELL
CO-STAR, LOVE ME TENDER

William Campbell: One day I receive a call. They ask me to go up to a certain projection room at 20th Century Fox. They were showing wardrobe of different people, including Debra Paget. When this beautiful girl's picture came up on the screen I heard somebody behind me, and I suddenly realized it was Elvis saying, "Golly. Boy, is she a looker." He says, "Am I gonna kiss her?" And I hear Parker, the Colonel say, "Yeah, I think so. A couple of times." He says, "I can't wait." Finally, the lights went up. Richard Eagan and myself were chatting, and all of a sudden I get a touch on my shoulder. And I turn around and it's Elvis. And he said, "Mr. Campbell?" He says, "Could I talk to you?" I said, "Sure." He says, "You know, this is the first time I ever did any actin'. I want to do a good job in my first picture." He said, "And I was wondering if you'd help me out." I said, "What do you mean, help you out? Elvis," I said, "they're gonna photograph you up, down, over, under, left, right." I said, "You're going to look like one of the best actors in America."

And Elvis was doing very well, I thought, for what he was given. This was not, you know, this wasn't the greatest dialogue in the world. It was a pretty pedestrian film in the sense that it was a typical western kind of motif: the bad guy, the good guy, the morality play and all that good stuff.

The film was intended as a straight drama without songs. Presley was clearly excited about making a serious picture.

Pat Broeske: When Elvis was first signed to THE RENO BROTHERS, you know, a Confederate love story, it was a straight western. And he was really looking forward to appearing in a straight role, you know, non-singing. That was a big deal to him. But again, you know, the studio paid for Elvis Presley. And pretty soon, a few songs worked their way into the screenplay. The next thing you know, you know, he's rocking 'n' rolling out on the front porch of a Confederate homestead. It was kind of goofy.

Four songs were added, including a tune that became an instant classic – and the film's new title. Since the picture now had musical numbers, it was Campbell's turn to get advice from Elvis.

William Campbell: Bobby Webb, the director, came over and he said, "Bill." He said, "I want you to bone up on that number that Elvis sings on the porch." I went into orbit. I said, "I wasn't hired to sing with Elvis or anybody else." I said, "I'm not a singer." And I'm sitting there looking at the sheet music, and Elvis was watching this. And I had said a couple times, "I'm sorry, Elvis, the way I feel." And when it was over, he came over laughing and he said, "Bill," he said, "what I'm gonna do every day when we have some time, we'll come in here and we'll go through it. And I'll choreograph this out with you." All I had to do was clap my hands and go "boom-boom, boom-boom, boom-boom," but nobody else had anything else to do. And I did it. And I was still embarrassed, but years and years later, of course, I'm very proud of that moment, you know, being the first one to actually do that with him.

WILLIAM CAMPBELL
CO-STAR, LOVE ME TENDER

We were shooting on the back lot. I will never forget this. And he had his musicians there, and we all ate out there. And Elvis sees all these kids there. And it was supposed to be, if you remember, it was supposed to be like the county fair type thing we were at. And Elvis took his guitar, jumped on the stage, and his musicians that had been set up, they jumped up there. And he gave up his lunch to play for the people and for the kids. He had a great humanity. You know? It was really something. And he did not have a typical ego. I got to the point where I loved him. And it really worried me. And I thought to myself when Parker came to me, he said, "I'd like you to travel with Elvis." I said, "What do you mean travel with Elvis?" "I would like you to be his companion, watch over him." I said, "What are you talk– I've got a career." He says, "I promise you in every picture you will have the second lead." And I said, "Lookit, Colonel, I appreciate it. And I know that I'd make myself a bundle of bucks." But I said, "I can't do it. I've got my own career. Don't you understand?"

DEBRA PAGET TV INTERVIEW - 1956

Reporter: You just finished a picture with Elvis Presley.

Debra Paget: Yes, and Richard Egan. It's called LOVE ME TENDER.

Reporter: How'd you like working with this man, Elvis Presley?

Debra Paget: Oh, very much, Dave. He's a very nice person. He's very co-opera-tive and friendly.

Reporter: Where are you off to now in your bejeweled chariot there?

Debra Paget: I'm on my way home for a party I'm giving for the cast and crew of the picture.

On November 16th, 1956, LOVE ME TENDER premiered at the Paramount Theatre in New York. Thousands of screaming fans showed up to celebrate Elvis's motion-picture debut, a publicity stunt arranged by Colonel Parker. LOVE ME TENDER earned back its million-dollar production cost in just three days. Elvis's status as a box-office champ was established with his very first film. But reviews were as mixed as the audience's reaction to the ending.

Michael Ochs: I remember seeing LOVE ME TENDER, and it was really hysterical because when Elvis dies at the end; all the males in the audience cheered and all the girls were crying. There was a real schism between the Elvis Presley fanatics.

Barbara Leigh: I did not like LOVE ME TENDER because he died in it. And I didn't want him to die. I wanted Debra Paget to fall in love with him, and I wanted him to end up with the girl, and it didn't happen, so I was sad.

The film also made an impression on a couple of future rockers.

Ray Manzarek: Morrison was a big fan of LOVE ME TENDER. Elvis was great in his very first movie. You got to see the man raw and real. And for me also, LOVE ME TENDER, I'd say for both of us it's LOVE ME TENDER.

By now, Paramount had found a project for Presley, which began production in January of 1957. As with LOVE ME TENDER, the title tune became a big hit.

LOVING YOU was written and directed by Hollywood veteran Hal Kanter.

Hal Kanter: LOVING YOU, BLUE HAWAII,
Hal Wallis sent me to Memphis, Tennessee, to
meet Elvis in person and to talk about the show,
but also to see him in action and to learn as much
about his method of operation as I possibly could,
and eventually to incorporate some of what I had
learned into the film itself. Because I had not only
written the screenplay, I was now to direct it.

Elvis found Hal Kanter to be the sort of person who would give you the shirt off his back — literally.

Hal Kanter: I was wearing a black velour shirt that
my wife had given me just before I left to go to
Memphis. And Elvis admired the shirt. He said,
"Where'd you get that?" And I said, "Do you like
it?" He said, "Oh yeah, I like it very much." I
said, "If you got another shirt, I'll give you this
one." He couldn't believe that I had given him
that shirt. He was so proud of that black velour
shirt. When he showed up in Hollywood several
weeks later to start rehearsing the show, he was
wearing that shirt. And I said to him, "That's
a good lookin' shirt you're wearing there, Elvis.
Where'd you get that?" He said, "Oh, some fan
gave it to me." I said, "Okay."

A.C. Lyles: He was opposite a lovely young lady
that Hal Wallis had found and was under contract
to us here at Paramount, Dolores Hart. They
did two pictures together, his first picture and his
second picture, together. And you could tell on
the screen and on the set, the adulation and the
respect and perhaps love that they had for each
other. She left our business, became a nun, and
she's now I think a Mother Superior.

The LOVING YOU storyline was loosely based on Elvis's own experiences with fame, fortune, and controversy.

Michael Ochs: LOVING YOU was the essence of a great rock 'n' roll movie. I mean, he played this character Deke Rivers. This poor kid who, you know, works his way up through rock 'n' roll and then gets attacked for being too overtly sexual onstage. Then he goes on national TV to defend himself and then does the most overtly sexual number you've ever seen on camera. I mean, full bump and grind, running up and down the aisles. I mean, it was just amazing to watch.

LOVING YOU also gave Elvis's backup band a chance to appear on camera.

D.J. Fontana: He said, "You guys wanna do the movies too?" We said, "Well, yeah, I guess we can do one or two and see what happens." So we did LOVING YOU, which I thought was a good movie. I thought it had good material there.

As with LOVE ME TENDER, the film made quite an impression on another budding young rocker.

Barry Gibb: LOVING YOU is amazing. Just the way he was dressed, the bandanna around his neck ... So memorable.

Once again, the film was a huge success. Once again, reviews were mixed, with Elvis his own worst critic.

EXCERPT FROM INTERVIEW

Reporter: How do you rate yourself as an actor?

Elvis Presley: Pretty bad. I mean, that's something you learn through experience. I think that maybe I might accomplish something at it through the years.

Reporter: You think it's just the sake of acting natural? Don't you do that? In your last two pictures, I'd say you have.

Elvis Presley: In In some scenes I was pretty natural. In others I was trying to act. And when you start trying to act, you're dead.

Reporter: How did you find Hal Wallis as a producer-director?

Elvis Presley: He's a very, very, very fine gentleman.

Reporter: Did he help you out? Or who was the big help and aid in your show LOVING YOU?

Elvis Presley: Well, there's nobody that helps you out. They have a director and a producer. And as far as the actin and as far as the singing and all, you're on your own.

HY GARDNER EXCERPT

HY Gardner: They predict that Elvis Presley will be another James Dean. Now have you heard that?

Elvis Presley: I've heard something about it. But I would never compare myself in any way to James Dean, because James Dean was a genius in acting. Although I'll say that I sure would like to. I mean, I guess there's a lot of actors in Hollywood that would like to have had the ability that James Dean had. But I would never compare myself with James Dean in any way.

The Presley-Dean comparison was dismissed by Hal Wallis, who said, "We did not sign Elvis as a second Jimmy Dean. We signed him as a number one Elvis Presley." Wallis wasn't the only one of his generation to appreciate Elvis's considerable gifts. More and more of the studio brass were starting to admire Presley's talents.

Hal Kanter: He was a very unique talent. I had completely misjudged him at first. I think most people my age misjudged him.

Robert Relyea: The older people who were in the business then had their opinions set already, that this was something that was very questionable. Remembering what era that was that, "Well, isn't this the kid who moves his hips funny and isn't it vulgar?" And he disarmed 'em so fast 'cause he was very pleasant to work with. It is absolutely flatly true that there was never a guy who worked with him that didn't like him. You know, he'd hit makeup in the morning, he'd start with getting coffee for the hairdresser. Then he'd get coffee for the makeup men. Then he'd get coffee for himself. That goes a long way in this business.

A.C. Lyles: Elvis Presley was one among equals on the set. One among equals. He wasn't above anybody; he was there. And the people had that feeling. And he was so professional. God, he was so professional.

George Klein: He was there every morning at nine o'clock on the button. He was never late. He knew his lines, and the funny part about it was he knew the other people's lines too. 'Cause he had that photographic memory, you know. And he was real good with his lines, very cooperative. Didn't argue with anybody. 'Cause he was trying to let it be known in Hollywood he wanted to be a serious actor. He wasn't out there just fooling around trying to make a rock 'n' roll movie. He said he wanted to learn the trade and become a part of that Hollywood movie situation.

To make the best of that situation, Elvis tried to make the movie set feel more like home.

Gordon Stoker: We would usually go into the set and he would go in and sit down at the piano and start singing spirituals. This is a way that he got in the mood. This is a way he relaxed. It just took that for him to relax and to feel at home and to feel at ease with the people around him. And this is what he had to have to be himself.

GORDON STOKER
SINGER - JORDAINAIRES

"Being himself" also involved a little fun and games during those long periods of down-time.

Steve Stevens: One day I'm going to lunch, and as I'm walking into the commissary door, coming around the corner is this tall fellow with a pompa-dour and sideburns and a red shirt and jeans and white bucks. And I thought, wow, this is a mighty looking fellow. I had no idea who he was. Looked kinda familiar. As we walk in together, the place is packed. And a lotta people were looking over at him. I didn't know if it was because of the sideburns or they knew who he was. To make a long story short, we finished lunch. And he said, "Wanna have some fun?" Why not? I'm a 17-year-old kid. Why not have some fun? All the soundstages had these metal ladders bolted to the top of the soundstages. And he just heads on up. And he says, "Come on." And I follow him up to the top. He reaches in his pocket and he pulls out balloons. He's got all these bal-loons. So we go ahead and we fill them up and we start tossing 'em. And then look down and people are jumping and bouncing, and we're backing up, and it's like two 10-year-old kids. We are laughing. He's laughing so hard he's literally rolling on the tar paper on the roof in hysterics. Then he goes ahead and he's got this big one, and pop, he lets it go. And he bounces back, says, "I gotta go. I just wound up hitting my producer Hal Wallis on the head. I'm in trouble."

STEVE STEVENS
ACTOR/FRIEND

By the spring of 1957, Elvis's schedule was so jam-packed with concerts, recording sessions, and movie making, he barely had time to move into his new mansion, Graceland, before returning to Hollywood for his next picture, this time at prestigious MGM.

George Klein: Being in radio and television in Memphis and dreaming about Hollywood and hearing about those big soundstages and driving through the gates of MGM, and all of the fantastic things you heard about movie studios, MGM was the top of the line at that time. It was the biggest studio in Hollywood, the most famous studio in Hollywood. And as we drove through the studios that first day, I'll never forget it, we're in that limousine and the guy, the gate guard was a guy named Kenny Hollywood.

Robert Relyea: I got a call that there was a commotion at the Thalberg Gate at the front of MGM over in Culver City. And they said that Elvis Presley is coming in, and we're just overwhelmed with female workers who are trying to get at the car and everything else. And I said, "Well, take the kids and chase 'em away. You're a policeman." And they said, "No, you don't understand. It's not the kids. It's middle-aged and elderly women who've come out of the executive building."

The studio's first order of business was selecting songs from the various tracks Elvis had recorded for his new film, tentatively titled JAILHOUSE KID.

Alex Romero: The producer, Pam Berman, says, "Alex, what number of the 10 you've heard has the most production value?" And I said, "Well, there's only one. Jailhouse Rock." And he said, "Oh no no no, we can't use that. That goes over the titles." And I said, "The titles?" And he said, "Yes." And I said, "You're wasting a great number." I said, "I don't mean to be bragging, but that's a show-stopping number."

But some believe it was Elvis himself who did the choreography.

Ray Manzarek: Watch him dance in JAILHOUSE ROCK. Y'know, Elvis choreographed that routine in JAILHOUSE ROCK. So the man, you know, the man was a dancer.

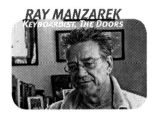

So did Elvis or Alex do the choreography? The truth is somewhere in between.

George Klein: When Alex Romero, who was the choreographer of JAILHOUSE ROCK, first presented the dance sequence for "Jailhouse Rock," Elvis shook his head and he said, "That's not me. I can't do that, Alex. I appreciate, you know, what you've done here." He wanted Elvis to do more of a Gene Nelson/Fred Astaire type. Elvis said, "It's not me. I'll try it." And Elvis being the cooperative guy, he got up and tried it. He said, "See Alex, it's not me." And that's when Alex said, "Elvis, I'll tell you what. Let me incorporate your stage act into what I wanna do, and let's see if that'll work." And he went home that night, came back the next day, and he had taken Elvis's stage act and incorporated that into a dance sequence. Elvis said, "Hey, I can do that. That's me." And in one take, right there in the rehearsal hall at MGM, Elvis had it down. And of course it became historic in being Elvis's best dance sequence in a motion-picture.

The sequence was way ahead of its time and would serve as the prototype for what would later be called the music video. Presley's enthusiasm while rehearsing the JAILHOUSE ROCK number led to a potentially catastrophic health scare.

ROBERT RELYEA
PRESIDENT OF PRODUCTION, MGM

Robert Relyea: In those days you did musical pieces that are pure music. You'd do 'em ahead of time in pre-production. And that number, "Jailhouse Rock," we did do in pre-production. And we were up on stage 27. And Elvis came over and said, "Doctor what's-his-name, the dentist, the lot dentist, is making me a cap." And he said, "He put a temporary on while it's being manufactured." I said, "Yeah?" He said, "Well, it just came off while I was swinging. And, listen to me, this is just neat." And he breathed out... And there was a whistling sound. The damn thing was in him. It was in his lung. So, they had a procedure, which was a little frightening, where they put him out and then take an instrument and go and get it. About now, Colonel Parker arrived. And if I've ever seen a man close to a coronary, it was when the doctor was saying, "Well, now Colonel, there's nothing to worry about. See, we took this instrument we have, and we just spread the vocal chords, and we go between that, right down." And Parker's face was ashen. And he said, "But we got hold of it, and then it broke. So now we had two pieces. So we just spread it some more." And of course you could see a whole career passing by.

The classic title song has added significance for one of Elvis's friends.

SHARON SHEELEY
SONGWRITER

Sharon Sheeley: I remember coming home from that movie. And it was very late at night, and there was this little drizzle out. And "Jailhouse Rock" came on the radio. And I remember Elvis stopped the car, got out of the car. It was on Fountain Avenue. And he danced the whole scene he did in the movie, in the middle of the street on Fountain Avenue. And I kept thinking if people woke up right now and looked out their windows, they'd see Elvis Presley dancing in the streets like Gene Kelly.

As with LOVING YOU, JAILHOUSE ROCK drew from Elvis's real life, only this time it was about an ex-con who makes it big in Hollywood.

Shortly after filming was completed, Elvis received some tragic news.

GEORGE KLEIN
MEMPHIS MAFIA/FRIEND

George Klein: We'd just finished completion of the shooting of JAILHOUSE ROCK. We'd been home about a week. And Elvis comes knocking on my door early in the morning. My mom says, "It's Elvis." And I go, "Elvis, what's up?" He said, "Come on, get in the car." I said, "What?" So I threw on some clothes and jumped in the car and said, "What's wrong?" He said, "You're not gonna believe what happened." I said, "Elvis, what happened." He said, "Judy Tyler just got killed in an automobile accident." I said, "What?" Judy Tyler was his co-star in JAILHOUSE ROCK. It was her big break. This was her chance to really make a name for herself in Hollywood, you know, opposite Elvis Presley, big motion picture and everything. I said, "Elvis, what happened?" He said, "Well, she and her husband were driving home, back to where they lived, I don't know whether it was Utah or wherever, and they were in a fatal accident and they both got killed." And I said, "Oh wow." He was really upset. It was one of the times that I really saw Elvis upset. And he was really seriously down and out. And we drove around for about three hours, not saying too much either, just driving around Memphis and driving around. Finally we would reminisce about something that happened on the movie set with her, tell a little story about her, or recall an incident with her in the motion-picture. And we just couldn't, so this was Elvis's way of accepting it. And we drove around Memphis, as I said, for about three or four hours. And he was really depressed that she'd passed away.

JAILHOUSE ROCK was a box-office smash when it opened in October of 1957. But opinions can change over the years.

Kenny Rogers: I loved JAILHOUSE ROCK. I mean, if I'm gonna pick one that— I saw it on television the other night, and it that movie was so bad and cool, those things become camp now when you look back on 'em.

Elvis was now the fourth-ranked box-office star in Hollywood. As 1958 began, so too did production on Elvis's next picture, which was shot in New Orleans.

Although many would consider it Presley's finest film, the project wasn't intended for Elvis.

Sharon Sheeley: KING CREOLE was being prepped for James Dean. And it was based on a book by Harold Robbins called "A Stone For Danny Fisher." James Dean got killed. It was about a fighter. And they changed it to a singer and put Elvis in it.

The director was Michael Curtiz, who had teamed with Hal Wallis to create such classics as THE ADVENTURES OF ROBIN HOOD with Errol Flynn, YANKEE DOODLE DANDY with James Cagney, and CASABLANCA with Humphrey Bogart. Could they work that same magic on a picture with Elvis Presley?

Jan Shepard: He was so good in it. He was very good in it. I think everyone was shocked. I think Walter Matthau and Paul Stuart and Dean Jagger and all the old hands were shocked at how good he was.

I was amazed at Elvis's talent. He had a great sense of timing, he was so normal, so real, so natural. And he amazed me. And he went with whatever you did. He would just fall right into it. He was wonderful.

Anita Wood: Elvis's favorite movie that I ever knew about when I was dating him was KING CREOLE. And he liked it because the story-line was good. And he liked it because the actors were serious actors that he was playing with or working with. And he would like to do more pictures like that, more dramatic pictures.

ANITA WOOD
FORMER GIRLFRIEND

Audiences were finally given a chance to see what Elvis could do with a first-rate cast and script.

A.C. Lyles: Michael Curtiz was Hungarian. And he had this thick accent. And I don't know if he ever really understood the English language, but he understood the camera and what to do. And his pictures were wonderful. And when I heard that Michael Curtiz was gonna do a picture with Elvis, someone said, "But, you know, how will they get along?" I said, "Michael Curtiz can do anything with anyone and do it well."

A.C. LYLES
PARAMOUNT PRODUCER

Jackie Joseph: He was sitting on a chair attached to a huge boom that went up and hovered over the whole dimestore set. He had what looked like a big horn that he screamed at people through. And he wasn't like being incredibly sensitive, because if he wanted somebody to move, he'd scream, "Would the old lady move outta the way? Get outta the way, you little old lady!"

JACKIE JOSEPH
CO-STAR KING CREOLE

Jerry Schilling: Michael Curtiz, he didn't want Elvis for that move in the beginning. And then he fell in love with Elvis. And I never will forget, at the end of the movie, Elvis went up to Michael Curtiz, this was his fourth movie, and said, "Thank you, Mr. Curtiz. Now I know what a director is."

JERRY SCHILLING
MEMPHIS MAFIA/FRIEND

Michael Moore: KING CREOLE was a serious picture. It wasn't like some of the others we did, on the beach, on Hawaii, getting in on a surfboard. You know, those pictures did not have the depth I think that KING CREOLE had.

A.C. Lyles: We ran it here at the studio, and I saw Elvis a couple days later and told him I'd seen the picture. And I said, "Elvis, this is the best thing you have done. It's wonderful." He said, "You know why I was so good in it?" Why? He said, "'Cause I was hiding. I was hiding behind the makeup of being someone else."

But Elvis would have to put his promising motion-picture career on hold. Shortly before filming began on KING CREOLE, he received a letter informing him that his attendance was requested in the United States Army.

George Klein: KING CREOLE was coming up right after the holidays, down in New Orleans. So Colonel Parker and his people got together with the U.S. Government and the Draft Board and all. And at that time, since there was no war going on, the United States would give you time to clear up your business if you had a project going on. So they gave him a deferment to make KING CREOLE. And he went down and he made KING CREOLE, and he wasn't very happy he was being drafted. Because here you are making millions of dollars, the biggest star in the world, living at Graceland, living in mansions, living in penthouses and suites in Beverly Hills and making motion pictures, and all of a sudden, boom, you're in the United States Army, a dog-faced soldier. Elvis was patriotic and all. But, you know, the truth be known, he wasn't very happy that he had to go in the army.

KING CREOLE premiered in July of 1958 and was another smash hit. After suffering a critical drubbing for his first three films, Elvis got the best reviews he had ever – or would ever – receive. As the Los Angeles Times put it, "Well, for heaven's sake. Elvis Presley is turning into an actor."

Just when audiences were beginning to see Elvis's real potential as a dramatic actor, he had to drop everything so he could serve his country.

PAT BROESKE
AUTHOR

Pat Broeske: While he's in the military, a lot of things happen to society, a lot of things happen to Hollywood, and things can't be the same when he gets back.

DICK CLARK
TELEVISION HOST/PRODUCER

Dick Clark: While Elvis was away, a lot of other teenage idols arose. You know, they couldn't fill his place, but little girls needed another hero. But when he came back, he took over all over again. Didn't wipe out the scene; all the other people continued, but Elvis was back, and the King had returned.

In March of 1960, Sergeant Elvis Presley was discharged from the army. His first order of business was holding a press conference to announce his plans – and hopes.

EXCERPT FROM PRESS CONFERENCE

Elvis Presley: I'd like to do a little more of a serious role, you know? Because my ambition is to progress as an actor, which takes a long time. And a lot of experience. 'Cause I have three pictures in a row to do. I hope it won't be a rock 'n' roll picture, 'cause I made four already. You can only get away with that for so long.

Ray Manzarek: I've heard stories that Elvis was– they wanted him for the movie WEST SIDE STORY and Colonel Parker said, "No no no, he's not playing a hoodlum." You know, they wanted him for Tony. They wanted Elvis for the lead. Can you imagine? The part of Tony, the Richard Beymer, part, Elvis doing that? And the Colonel said, "No, that's a hoodlum, those are gangs, we don't want Elvis associated with gangs. He's got enough of a hoodlum reputation, you know? We don't want him to be a hoodlum, with the greasy hair and all of that. No way. Zip guns? No, Elvis is not a juvenile delinquent, he's not a hoodlum. He's a good, decent, wholesome American entertainer who's gonna give you ROUST-ABOUT."

Wherever Elvis went, he was welcomed as a returning hero, including at his old stomping grounds, Paramount Studios.

Joe Esposito: The first day on the set was really different for me, but for Elvis, he was thrilled. You could see he had a big smile on his face, and everybody was welcoming him on the lot. Craft people, all the grips and assistant directors, they were all thrilled to see Elvis back at the studio.

But if Elvis expected Paramount to present him with a dramatic, non-musical film, he had another thing coming. Hal Wallis had lined up Norman Taurog and Michael Moore to direct a lightweight musical about an American soldier stationed in West Germany.

Michael Moore: Probably if he hadn't been in the service they wouldn't have done G.I. BLUES with Elvis. To be able to come back from the service and now be a part of G.I. BLUES I think was the whole idea.

Pat Broeske: I mean, it's a different kind of musical than the films he made previously. In KING CRE-OLE when he sings, he's a nightclub entertainer, there's a reason he's singing those songs. In LOV-ING YOU, same thing, he's an entertainer. Now he's gonna start making the kinda movie where you burst into song for really no apparent reason. You know, and you're wondering, where are the backup, where's the backup musicians? It's kind of signifying something to come, 'cause pretty soon there'll be a formula for these type movies that he's gonna make.

PAT BROESKE
AUTHOR

The soundtrack album to G.I. BLUES hit stores in October of 1960, quickly hitting number one and remaining on the Billboard charts for a staggering 111 weeks. It would be the most successful album of Elvis's career.

Juliet Prowse: He was fabulous. He was as you... When I was doing that particular movie with him, he was a complete teetotaler. Didn't smoke, didn't drink, didn't do anything. Except have girlfriends, lots of girlfriends. And had a wonderful sense of humor. And I remember though thinking at that time, it must be very hard to be him, 'cause he couldn't go anywhere. I mean he really couldn't. He had a suite up at the Beverly Wilshire Hotel, and he couldn't leave.

JULIET PROWSE
CO-STAR, G.I. BLUES

When the film opened the following month, it did huge business, ending up one of the top-grossing films of 1960. If Elvis had any worries about his post-army popularity, the one-two punch of the G.I. BLUES soundtrack and film immediately dispelled them. His worries about the quality of those films, however, remained undiminished. After the promising reviews for KING CREOLE two years earlier, Elvis had been counting on more challenging, dramatic roles.

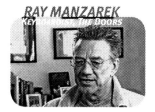

Ray Manzarek: The movies that probably were offered to Marlon Brando but Brando turned 'em down for whatever reason, could've been offered to Elvis, but I don't think Hollywood even bothered offering him those movies because they knew he wasn't gonna do it. He was gonna do light musical, musical-comedies in a way. And that's what he was gonna do, and that's what he did. And that's a tragedy.

In fact, his next film, FLAMING STAR, had been offered to Marlon Brando, who turned it down.

It was a moody western co-starring Barbara Eden in her pre- I Dream of Jeannie days.

Barbara Eden: He played an Indian in that film. And he was very concerned, very concerned about what he was doing. Whether he did it well. Because he was conscious of the fact that he wasn't schooled in this particular facet of his profession, and he wanted to learn. And he was trying to learn. I thought he was great.

Joe Esposito: This was a little different. It was more serious. He figured this was a more serious part, and he thought there weren't gonna be as many songs in it. He didn't think there were any songs in it, really, at first. But they added some songs to it.

With an eye toward lucrative soundtrack sales, the studio was eager to fill the picture with songs, including one that Elvis would have to sing on horseback.

Pat Broeske: Elvis actually had one of his rare temper tantrums on that set, 'cause he didn't wanna sing a song on horseback. And Don Siegel actually wound up getting some of those numbers out of the film. There's only a couple now.

Unfortunately, FLAMING STAR generated little heat at the box-office. Elvis's next picture was another drama, WILD IN THE COUNTRY, in which he played a would-be writer plagued by personal problems.

JOE ESPOSITO
ROAD MANAGER & FRIEND

Joe Esposito: Elvis thought it was more of a serious role for him. He got into it. I mean, he really felt and he really tried. But, you know, still again he was not too thrilled with throwing a couple songs in. There were only I think three or four songs in that whole movie. But he wished there wouldn't have been any songs in it.

WILD IN THE COUNTRY would be the last out-and-out drama Elvis Presley would make for nearly a decade. The message was clear: If the studio wanted to make lots of money, his movies needed lots of songs.

1961 would be a pivotal year in the motion-picture career of Elvis Presley. He had recently signed a new five-year contract with producer Hal Wallis. The first film under the new agreement was partially shot on location in the recently admitted 50th state... BLUE HAWAII.

Joe Esposito: One of the best movies Elvis made and enjoyed making was definitely BLUE HAWAII, because of the locations we were at. We were on Kauai, and there was a hotel called Cocoa Palms which is no longer there. Every night after we were shooting, there was a place we'd go sit outside after dinner. Everybody ate together at night in those days. Every night we sat there, we ate with all the people, the crew; well, most of it was crew people. And after that, he'd go sit in the bar. And Patti Page, the singer, was there 'cause her husband Charlie O'Curran was the choreographer on the movie.

Barbara Eden: After dinner he would go to his room, get his guitar, and some of his guys would get their instruments and come back down. And we would just sit around in the lounge there and sing. And that was fun.

Joe Esposito: Elvis and she would sit, play guitar and sing songs all evening. It was just something that was just unbelievable. It was like a movie scene. But it wasn't, it was just us having a good time. He felt great in it. And those are memories that I can remember that were just unbelievable, and he was so happy. And that was one of the happiest movies he ever made.

Patti Page had another connection to BLUE HAWAII.

Patti Page: Elvis's cousin Lamar and I, who rode in this little canoe down the lagoon, going into the wedding when they got married in BLUE HAWAII. And they didn't have enough extras to do this. And so Lamar and I offered to do it. And I remember we didn't get paid either, so we weren't members of the Extras Union, so hope nobody catches me for it after all these years. But Lamar and I took a dollar bill and we each took half of it. And he signed mine and I signed his. And I still have it.

Pat Broeske: Hawaii is, it's a new state. It's our new 50th state. There's a great deal of excitement, you know, over welcoming Hawaii to the U.S. What could be more commercial than sending Elvis Presley to Hawaii, putting him up against the lush tropical scenery, giving him an incredible bevy of beauties – including Joan Blackman. You know, they're really not his equal in many ways, but they're pretty, they're eye candy. It's got 14 songs, which means there's a soundtrack you can sell. It's got one song that's absolutely terrific, "Can't Help Falling In Love," probably one of the greatest ballads Elvis ever did, which is gonna give it lots of airplay, which is important. You know, they're gonna be able to sell records at the same time. And a plot that is sorta cute. The plot isn't offensive, it doesn't threaten you. It's got a number of gags, it's got a little romance in it. Non-threatening romance. Y'know, and pretty much you have the Elvis Presley formula. BLUE HAWAII becomes the cookie cutter for the films to come.

BLUE HAWAII opened in November of 1961 and went on to become the highest-grossing film of Elvis's career thus far. As with G.I. BLUES, the BLUE HAWAII soundtrack album was released a month before the film came out. It hit number one on the Billboard charts and stayed there for an impressive 20 weeks. Even as his popularity soared, his albums sold and his movies made a mint, Elvis's hopes of becoming a serious actor were drifting further and further beyond his grasp.

William Campbell: I told Parker, said, "I don't know why you didn't let Elvis get some training." Could've had a major performer. I mean, he was a major personality, probably the greatest personality of certainly anybody that I ever saw, including the Beatles. He was one man, the Beatles were four. I mean, you got a different dynamic going. But I said, "No one was more personable than he was." And he could really touch the public, be they old, young, middle age, it didn't make any difference. I said, "I witnessed that." And he said, "Well, Bill, I thought it was better to put him in those things that he knew best."

BARRY GIBB
THE BEE-GEES

Barry Gibb: I think the great shame here is that Elvis could've made 50 incredible movies that would've really highlighted what a good actor this guy was, working with the right people, working with the right directors. But it appeared like nobody really wanted him to do that. You know? They wanted him to dance on tables and have go-go girls behind him the whole time. I never really got that. Never understood that. But you never miss the opportunity to see it. You know. KING CREOLE was a great film. JAILHOUSE ROCK was a great film. But I think as time went on, he wasn't really – maybe he wasn't into it so much. I don't know. I don't know. But it came across like he wasn't really into it.

By 1962 Elvis Presley was one of the brightest stars in Hollywood. BLUE HAWAII had reached number two at the box office, quickly becoming the highest grossing film of Elvis's career thus far. But despite the fanfare, the dramatic recognition he yearned for was nowhere in sight.

When Elvis made KING CREOLE three years earlier, his flair for drama was undeniable. And after two years in the army, Elvis returned to Hollywood in 1960, more determined than ever to become a serious dramatic actor. But the enormous success of BLUE HAWAII showed that moviegoers were less interested in Elvis's dramatic abilities than they were in other things.

Place Presley in a colorful setting, give him a challenge to overcome, some hard hitting action, a handful of catchy tunes, and plenty of smooching with the most gorgeous girls Hollywood had to offer, and you were sure to have a box office smash.

For the most part, this formula worked brilliantly. And over the next eight years, Elvis made 23 films, most of them big money makers.

Averaging three movies a year, however, leaves little time for creative excellence. And Elvis eventually became disenchanted with the whole routine. But in 1962, things were still looking up. Presley's film career was at its peak, and some of his most memorable work was still to come.

May of 1962 marked the release of Presley's ninth motion picture, FOLLOW THAT DREAM. The film was shot entirely on location in sunny Florida, and received appropriately warm reviews.

Although Elvis strayed from his typical musical comedy character, he still managed to get the girl after a solid dose of two-fisted action.

The two fisted action carried over into his next film, KID GALAHAD.

Robert Relyea: The first thing we had to do was, train him to be a boxer. Elvis was a light heavyweight by size. So we hired the famous Mushy Callahan, to come and train him, and told Mushy that he had six weeks to work with Elvis before we'd start to shoot.

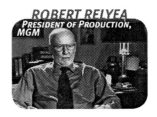

ROBERT RELYEA
PRESIDENT OF PRODUCTION, MGM

Joe Esposito: Mushy Callahan, one of the trainers hired to train Elvis for the movie, boxing. You know, said to a lot of people, you know, Elvis – if he had Elvis to train him to become a fighter he could – he could become a contender.

JOE ESPOSITO
ROAD MANAGER & FRIEND

Because I think 'cause of the karate situation. And, Elvis enjoyed it. He thought it was great. I mean, he thought he was – not Muhammad Ali at the time but, you know, he thought he was a, you know, Rocky Marciano. I mean, he really got into it.

Elvis's black belt in karate came in handy during a break in the filming of KID GALAHAD, much to the annoyance of tough guy co-star, Charles Bronson.

Robert Relyea: One day after lunch, the grips put down some bricks. And then they put a 2 by 12 – piece of 2 by 12 on the bricks. And he turned around, did the ah-ya-ya, swung his hand, and went right through the 2 by 12. And in the background, we heard, huh huh. And it was Charlie bless his heart. Charlie Bronson said. Bunch of bull. Now that's a mistake. Because then the grip said, "Oh yeah Charlie? It is? That means you can do it, right?" And Charlie said, "Of course." Elvis's saying, "Why don't we forget this and go about our business?" And, the grips were saying, "Oh no, no, no. Charlie knows what he's doin', don't you Charlie?" So Charlie goes over, doesn't do any ah-ya-ya. He just takes his doubled up fist, and he lets that thing have it. Which, of course, does nothing to the board. I thought I heard things breaking but it was not the board.

In March of 1962, Elvis returned to Hawaii for location work on his next musical romance, appropriately titled, GIRLS, GIRLS, GIRLS. Presley played a charter boat captain opposite beautiful Stella Stevens, who had a less than stellar experience.

Stella Stevens: He was not very much interested in acting as I was. He was interested in his own success and letting Colonel Parker make all the decisions for him I guess. I was actually miserable making that film, and that's the one film I've done that I have never seen in my life, nor will I ever see it. So, I hesitate to talk about it, in that it was such an unpleasant experience for me.

Joe Esposito: Stella Stevens was one of the co-stars in the movie. And I heard some comments she's made about Elvis during the making of this movie. She's the only person I've ever seen in my life that worked on an Elvis movie, that made bad comments about it. So apparently, there's something wrong here. Elvis treated everybody nice. He was really great. He was polite to everybody and, that's the way he was.

JOE ESPOSITO
ROAD MANAGER & FRIEND

But yet, he didn't care for her personality, and he just didn't care for it too much. And I think that upset her 'cause Elvis was hitting on a lot of girls in the movie. Elvis loved women and enjoyed being around them. But, he didn't care for her.

Laurel Goodwin: Stella is such sour grapes on working with Elvis. And I think that's kind of sad. First of all, she didn't work with him that long. I mean, she was on the picture a very short period of time. I had a wonderful time. It was great fun.

LAUREL GOODWIN
CO-STAR GIRLS! GIRLS! GIRLS!

The crew, the cast, the talent. I was so thrilled to work with him. Elvis was a doll. He was sweet, he was considerate, he was thoughtful, he was loyal to his friends. What more could you ask?

The stuff that you see, photographed on the sailboat, those were some of the most pleasant times. Because we got to visit and talk and rap and chat and, he was really concerned because his father had a girlfriend, whom he later married. Which everybody knows. And Elvis was very upset about that. He was very upset about it. And it was really causing a rift between him and his dad.

And I said how can you expect him to live the rest of his life alone? Because he's involved with another woman doesn't have anything to do with your mother. It doesn't have anything to do with the regard he had for your mother. You love him. You think you're enough for him. You're not. You have your own life. Lighten up.

Lance Legault: I got a call on the next picture called GIRLS, GIRLS, GIRLS, to come in with Jack Nitchie on piano and Hal Blain on drums, and they needed me to play some bass and sing "Return To Sender" with him. I mean, to mouth "Return To Sender." In the picture I played upright bass and sang along with him and, that went great.

He was the easiest cat to work with, that you can imagine. He had a memory. You didn't have to show him a thing but once, maybe twice, you know. And he had it.

Rita Rogers: When Lance would go in and do the, the dance, you know, and we'd rehearse it and rehearse it and rehearse it with Lance. And Elvis would just be there watching. And then we'd go – and in one take, he could do all the choreography with one take.

"Return to Sender" helped make the GIRLS, GIRLS, GIRLS soundtrack a smash, landing Elvis a spot in the top five. For his next film, Presley traveled to Seattle to shoot on location at the World's Fair. Dropping Elvis into the middle of a jam-packed global event was no walk in the park.

Joe Esposito: If you see any of the pictures off-camera there's thousands of people around Elvis. Every place we went. Between takes we'd have to jump into these little golf carts, and we'd go drive through the crowd and try to get to a dressing room someplace private for him, to stay away. But, Elvis was the type of guy, he had to stop and sign autographs.

And all the guys had – for security reasons we all wore these black jumpsuits like, we all dressed the same so he could see us in a crowd easier. We all wore sunglasses, like the secret service, you know. We're all lookin' around. Lookin' – we were lookin' for girls. We weren't lookin' for anybody that was gonna hurt us. So, we did the – it looked good.

Gary Lockwood: When we went on location in Seattle and it happened that the World's Fair, there were tens of thousands of people, tryin' to get in the hotel. I mean, that was a real phenomenon. It was like the Beatles.

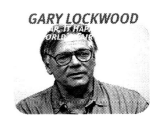

GARY LOCKWOOD

Vicky Tiu: Even to this day, I think I'm oftentimes more well known as the little girl who made the movie with Elvis Presley. I remember there was one scene that I just had great difficulty with. And it got to the point where I was so nervous that I was stuttering, stumbling over my lines. And Norman Taurog, a very big, intimidating director I think, just got really upset with me, and finally I remember Elvis stepping in and saying, "That's it. That's a take. And I'm gonna spend a little time with the little lady here." And he talked to me and he asked me, "Are you homesick?" And he was right, I mean, I was very homesick. My parents were not with me. And I started crying and telling him, pouring my heart out to him. And, that made me so much more at ease and from that point on I don't think I had much difficulty with any of the scenes.

VICKY TIU CAYETANO
Co-Star, It Happened
The World's Fair

Another young actor was also making his first screen appearance.

Vicky Tiu: I remember Kurt Russell making his debut. And he was a very excitable young man, maybe about 10 – 9, 10 years old. And I remember he was telling me, "Isn't this great? Isn't this exciting? And when I get out of school, I'm gonna go into the movie business." And sure enough, that's what he's in.

Ironically, Russell would portray Elvis himself in a TV movie some 15 years down the pike.

Dick Clark: My favorite recollection of the Elvis film that we did for television was, in the casting, we ended up casting a guy named Kurt Russell, who up until that time had worked for Mr. Disney in the FLYING RUBBER DUCK and other silly films. And the world fell on its – you got Kurt Russell? The Disney actor? You know what? Kurt did the best, most extraordinary job ever. He should've won an Emmy.

Elvis added to his resume with another display of song, romance, and virility. Not to mention an abundance of bathing beauties. Set against the exotic backdrop of Mexico, FUN IN ACAPULCO featured the voluptuous Ursula Andress, who had recently made a splash in the James Bond classic DR. NO. Self conscious about his physique, Elvis took one look at the statuesque Ursula and commented, "Her shoulders are broader than mine. I don't want to take my damn shirt off next to her."

Elvis's movies continued to be money makers, regardless of their varying quality. As producer Hal Wallis put it, a Presley picture is the only sure thing in show business. The enormous success of the soundtrack albums only added to the pressure to keep on making movies as quickly as possible.

Elvis was aware that some people wanted more out of his films.

Elvis Presley: People'd say to me all the time, why don't you do an artistic picture? Why don't you do this picture and that picture? Well that's fine. I would like to. I'd like to do something someday where I feel that I've really done a good job as an actor in a certain type role. But, I feel that it comes with time and a little living and a few years behind ya. I think that really. And I think that it will come eventually. You know, that's my goal.

Pat Broeske: Elvis Presley often spoke very hopefully about the kind of roles he would like to do. But whether Elvis Presley could have turned it around by starring in a serious role, playing a lawyer, you know, playing a private eye. You know, I, I don't know that audiences would have bought it.

Elvis understood the reasoning behind the formula, even as he felt imprisoned by it.

Elvis Presley: If I can entertain people with the things I'm doing well, I'd be a fool to tamper with it. It's ridiculous to take it on your own and say well I'm gonna change. I'm gonna apply – I'm gonna try to appeal to a different type audience – I'm gonna – because you might not. You might not. And if you goof for a few times you don't get many more chances in this business. That's the sad part about it.

Pat Broeske: Even though it's the 1960s, the country still feels culturally like the 50s. So, you know, he's, he's not the only one having to do kind of fluffy pictures. Because Hollywood was kind of – kind of feeling its way, you know, through what is going to be a cultural revolution.

The first shots of that revolution were fired in Dallas, Texas, just days before FUN IN ACAPULCO hit the theaters.

Following the assassination of President Kennedy, America found itself riding a wave of change. But for Elvis Presley, change did not come easily.

By now Elvis's influence on Hollywood extended beyond his own films. 1963's BYE BYE BIRDIE was a musical comedy about a sexy rock star, whose female fans are devastated when he gets drafted.

Ann-Margret became a star by playing the lucky fan who gets to kiss the singer on The Ed Sullivan Show. Later that year, Ann-Margret was cast opposite the real thing, Elvis Presley, in a film that was destined to become a cult classic.

George Klein: Elvis and Ann-Margret probably were the two hottest items going in Hollywood at that time. And for them to do a motion picture together was really great. There was a lot of electricity, a lot of sparks going on. And they hit it off right off the bat. They became very, very close friends right from day one. Elvis and Ann would ride motorcycles together, or they would play silly games together, or they would sing, you know, goof around. And it was real – VIVA LAS VEGAS probably was one of the most fun movies Elvis ever made.

Joe Esposito: I think it was one of Elvis's better movies and I think it had a lot to do with the chemistry between the two of them. It comes across on screen.

Ann-Margret: He had the greatest sense of humor. He just was hilarious. And he was so smart. So smart. And he would say things under his breath, I had to jab his ribs.

Lance Legault: I did the fall off the divin' board in VIVA LAS VEGAS because, again, you're not gonna let Elvis go off of that board with a guitar around the neck. If the guitar hits the water it takes part of your face off, you know –

VIVA LAS VEGAS also launched the career of a future star.

Teri Garr: I was doing CLOSE ENCOUNTERS OF THE THIRD KIND, as I told this before. And, Steven Spielberg was directing it and he – one day he's talkin' about his, his favorite movies. His favorite movie was, was VIVA LAS VEGAS. Oh Oh, I was in VIVA LAS VEGAS Mr. Spielberg. He says you were not. I said oh yes, yes I was. That was my first movie.

So Elvis Presley is the first person I worked with in a movie. It really was a big influence on me because, he's a person, I'm a person. If he can do it, I can do it. And he made you feel like that, too. You know, he made you be an equal.

Anita Mann: Well I couldn't believe I was on a stage at 18 at – in Culver City I think at MGM on a sound stage shooting a film next to Elvis Presley and I was getting paid.

1964's KISSIN' COUSINS gave audiences two Elvis's, including one with blonde hair, which was actually closer to his natural color.

Lance Legault: Every scene had to be shot twice. Because where, you know, he'd play the one character, Josh, and then he'd have to change hair and clothes and we'd have to shoot it again. It's over my shoulder on him. And then it's over my shoulder on him in the other wardrobe. It was a tremendous amount of work.

Cynthia Pepper: We were up in Big Bear and, he had to sing around a jeep. And right up – right up close to me. And, we had to stop because it was raining a bit. So we stopped and, and he said, "Cynthia?" And I said, "yes?" He said, "you know, I don't know what I'm doing here." I said, "What do you mean?" He said, "I should be driving a truck." And, that gave me chills. It kind of told a lot about Elvis. That that was his roots. That he was a country boy, simple. Not simple minded but simple and didn't put on airs. And in show business, you've been in it long enough, you realize that's a rare quality.

By now making movies had become routine, both on and off the screen. So Elvis found ways to amuse himself and his entourage, which now included a pet chimpanzee named Scatter.

Joe Esposito: Well we were shootin' a movie at Goldwyn Studios, in Hollywood. So we brought the chimp quite a few times to the set. But you couldn't keep him on the set 'cause he was too noisy. So, we had to take him over to the dressing room. You couldn't sit with him all day in the dressing room. We just left him in the dressing room one day and the chimp got out. Out through one of the windows and crawled up to the second floor, where I think Sam Goldwyn's office was, and he got in the window. And he started tearin' the place up. Throwing paper around, biting into anything soft pulling the stuffing out and having a good time. We get a phone call on the set, they said you guys better go to the dressing room quick. Alan Fortas went over there real quick, and Scatter had tore up the place and, there was a couple security guys holdin' this chimp. It was like he was arrested.

1964 saw Elvis starting opposite Hollywood heavyweight, Barbara Stanwyck, in yet another lightweight offering.

Lance Legault: Red did the fights with him. When you see Elvis fightin' a guy, most of the time it's Red, because Red and he had these things worked out. But for the most part, the guys that doubled him, were specialists in that stunt.

For example, when Leif Erickson runs Elvis off the road in ROUSTABOUT, that's Howard Curtis, that doubled Elvis.

Joe Esposito: We were doing a movie, ROUST-ABOUT. And in the scene at the beginning of the movie, Elvis is driving around on a motorcycle and he's singing. One of the producers said well, where would these voices be coming from, if you're drivin' down a highway on a motorcycle? Elvis said the same place the guitar and the drums and all the other music's coming from. If he'd have done more of that, and been tougher, he would've gotten a lot more stuff that would've been better for Elvis than what it was.

Teri Garr: ROUSTABOUT, another fabulous movie. And, oh Barbara Stanwyck was in it so it was I, I mean, I was just thrilled to be there but so we were – he's a carnie, I'm sure you've seen it, where he's a carnival barker. And so we're up there dancing our – we wear costumes that are made out of watermelons, who knows? And I, I never really fit into the chorus girl thing. I was always a little bit off and a little bit wrong. Thank God. Anyway, they'd be starting to roll this thing and they go okay action and we're rolling. Cut, cut, cut. Who is that dumb broad on the left? Honey, get it together! Okay action roll action. Cut, cut, cut. Honey – oh god that stupid bitch. And the director was just so mean to me. And he was about to fire me and Elvis said, excuse me sir, but this girl – and he defended me.

Elvis finished out 1964 with GIRL HAPPY, opposite former Miss America Mary Ann Mobley, and newcomer Chris Noel.

Mary Ann Mobley: Doing your first movie, with Elvis Presley, was a great way to start out. 'Cause Elvis was wonderful to work with. He was a gentleman. He stood up when I entered the set. He would say where's Mary Ann's chair? One of the boys said damn in front of me and he said please, never cuss in front of a lady.

Chris Noel: I never saw him ever lose his temper. Or ever, create any sort of a scene. He just was always just perfect.

And I think he was a wonderful actor. He truly was. Yes, we made very innocent films. But in the early 60s the time was still innocent.

It wasn't until the Vietnam War, and the Beatles started recording their music that things really changed.

Teri Garr: I've already done a couple movies with Elvis, and these guys that are Elvis's — I don't know whether it was Joe or whoever it was came up to me, where have you been, honey? Well I've been to — I've been to England and I've met the Beatles. You poor thing. That's what they said to me. 'Cause, of course, the Beatles were the enemy. And so it wasn't — I bet you were smokin' that pot. Well yeah, I did smoke some pot.

Mary Ann Mobley: I don't think I've ever worked on a project, that has been as much fun as HARUM SCARUM, which was directed by Gene Nelson, the dancer Gene Nelson. And, we used a set that had been done from one of these Lawrence of Arabia type movies in the past. And the set was already in existence. So they had to write a story to fit the set. Elvis was great to work with. There wasn't the, the big star ego quality that, that is sometimes prevalent today. If anybody could've had it, and probably should've had it, it was Elvis. And he had none of that. he was, he was a true southern gentleman when I worked with him.

MARY ANN MOBLEY
CO-STAR, HARUM SCARUM,
GIRL HAPPY

Billy Barty: When we did HARUM SCARUM it, it, it was a thrill. We wrote it as we went along. Or he wrote it as he went along. Now here's what we're gonna do here. Now Billy you're gonna come in with a – and you're gonna hit the guy in the head.

BILLY BARTY

Even though movies such as HARUM SCARUM and TICKLE ME continued to turn a profit, audiences noticed they were losing some of the spark of his earlier films.

James Darren: He was such a tremendous image and, as Elvis Presley, that they – he was pigeon-holed because, no one ever thought of him as doing anything else. They were taking advantage of what he did that was accepted by the public. And, these images unfortunately are created for you sometimes. That, you know, that song and dance kinda guy.

JAMES DARREN
SINGER/ACTOR

Barry Gibb: I think he understood that he was being exploited. I don't think he was, you know, this was not a silly boy. He, he knew what was goin' on.

BARRY GIBB
THE BEE-GEES

Mary Ann Mobley: He got tired of doing these movies with the songs. But a lot of people were depending upon him. He was supporting a lot of people.

Elvis's frustration continued to mount as he was handed silly role after silly role. That great dramatic part still nowhere in sight.

Julie Parrish: How awesome he made the steal, for these cheap movies. And I, you know, they, they do have a certain charm but they are pretty formula. They're different locations, different faces, but it's pretty much the same kind of stuff. And I don't know if any – a single song in our film that was memorable.

Jan Shepard: He was a little jaded at that point, as far as the type of films that he wanted to do. I don't think he was happy. He just didn't have a, a goal. I didn't see a goal. I just saw like, I'm doing this again, type of attitude. And, I think he'd done this type of picture too often.

Teri Garr: And for the moment it was good to do six movies a year and all that stuff but then, I don't think he or the Colonel ever thought about where that was gonna lead. Because it leads to – it's not good to do a bunch of bad movies in a row. For the moment it's good. You know, it's like getting drunk. For the moment it's good and then the next day it's not so good.

George Klein: Colonel Parker kept telling him, Elvis, the public wants to see you in these type of motion pictures. If we go dramatic and the bitc– and the picture bombs, it would – you don't – the old cliché if ain't broke don't fix it.

Two more Presley pictures appeared in 1966, FRANKIE AND JOHNNY, and SPINOUT in which Elvis did much of his own stunt driving.

George Barris: He would race the cars. The stunt guy would only do the spinouts, but Elvis would do the fast scenes and the drag outs and always the burn outs. He was very consistent that he wanted to be a part of each one of those scenes, not where somebody had to double him and be in the – in the spot where he was supposed to be used. When he did SPINOUT, actually the scene where he went and did the drive through, and then he had to do a spinout. He wasn't supposed to do the spinout. Even though we put the gravel on the ground and all that and I showed him how to put the braking. Actually you accelerate, you kick down the gear I said. You pull the hand brake, spin the wheel, and you'll go into a 360. Elvis goes right down that line, hits the brake, hits the – spins the wheel, accelerates. Does a beautiful 360 all the way around it and takes off again.

Charlie Hodge: Shelley Fabares I think was probably his favorite star. I mean, I, I've seen them just start a scene sometime and, Elvis would be singing. And there'd be a P in the song. And when he'd say the P in the song, her hair would go – and they got to laughin', and mister – Norman Taurog, Elvis's favorite director about then, just sent 'em home. And he said we'll shoot around you. Go home.

Diane McBain: Elvis Presley and I did a movie called SPINOUT. Which was, basically your musical about race cars.

How those two things came together I don't know. I guess because of Elvis. Anyway so, Elvis was one of my favorite people, that I ever got to meet in Hollywood. Primarily because he was so – such a gentleman.

Elvis had a lot of respect for women, and it showed. And he was – he showed that respect to all of the women that he worked with on – in our movie.

Deborah Walley: I wasn't really impressed about working with Elvis. I was more excited to do the film because of Norman Taurog, and because of the part that he had written for me which was really delightful. So, first day comes, and in comes Elvis. And, it was just absolutely amazing. I don't think I have ever met anyone, I certainly hadn't at that point and I haven't since, with that kind of charisma. I mean, he turned the room into electricity.

Diane McBain: I think that he was going through a time when he was questioning, some of the things in his life.

Deborah Walley: If he couldn't do what he wanted to do he'd rather not do it at all, than to go on doing the kind of pictures that, he had been placed in.

By 1967, the demand for Elvis movies was tapering off. Producers were hesitant to make the same expensive deals Presley had become accustomed to.

Joe Esposito: Things were dyin' off. His career was a little slower, the music was slower. The movies weren't doin' as well, either.

EASY COME, EASY GO turned out to be a prophetic title. The picture, Elvis's last for Paramount, sold precious few tickets. Two months later, MGM released DOUBLE TROUBLE, another unfortunate title since it, too, spelled trouble at the box office.

Presley's Hollywood career hit rock bottom with CLAMBAKE, his 26th motion picture.

Teri Garr: If the Colonel decided let's just call it– a word came to his head, CLAMBAKE. Let's just make this movie.

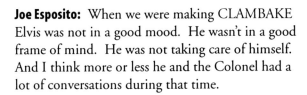

And it was a movie about nothing. But they – he didn't care. Just have – we'll have Elvis, we'll have a few dance numbers, we'll have some kissing scenes, we'll have Elvis's dance numbers, da-da-da. We said okay, we'll do it.

Pat Broeske: During the making of CLAMBAKE, Elvis probably looks worse than he does in any other movie. For the first time in his life, he's screwing up some things on, on, on a film set. He takes a bad fall at his place one night, as a result of, taking some pills. And things are getting out of hand.

Joe Esposito: When we were making CLAMBAKE Elvis was not in a good mood. He wasn't in a good frame of mind. He was not taking care of himself. And I think more or less he and the Colonel had a lot of conversations during that time.

And I think it came to a point where they decided hey, you know, it's time to make some changes here.

The most significant change came on May 1st, 1967. After seven years of courtship, Elvis and Priscilla were finally united in holy matrimony. Only a few weeks after the wedding, it was back to business as Elvis began production on another race car picture, this time opposite Nancy Sinatra.

Teri Garr: Elvis liked my roommate Carrie Foster. Let's, let's be honest. And he used to ask her out. But, for Elvis to ask someone out I wouldn't say it's like asking her out. It's just, want to come over? So, you can get yourself up here honey.

By this time, Elvis was more interested in finishing out his contract than making a quality picture. But things did begin to change for the better. In fact, his next two films, STAY AWAY JOE, and LIVE A LITTLE, LOVE A LITTLE, strayed from the typical Elvis movies.

Celeste Yarnall: The original title of the script was "Kiss My Firm But Pliant Lips." Ah, Elvis had firm but pliant lips.

The songs weren't so bad either.

Mac Davis: I had a song that I had actually written for Aretha Franklin. And it was called "A Little Less Conversation." But it fit right into the situation in the movie. You know, all Elvis's movies in those days were, situation. You know, that the situation led to the song and that's, that's all the movies were written for was for the music really.

Celeste Yarnall: Elvis looked so good. Elvis was so healthy when we did LIVE A LITTLE, LOVE A LITTLE. I mean, I'm so blessed that I knew him when he was at his best. Lisa Marie had just been born. So it, you know, was a special time and, we had a – we had lunch every day together in his dressing room, and he would say what would you like for lunch today, Celeste? And I'd say, I'll just have whatever you have.

And they had him on a diet. They had him on a very strict diet so we'd get this cremated hamburger patty that looked like hockey puck. But he looked terrific. He just looked fabulous. He – I don't know if people realize how exquisitely beautiful Elvis Presley was. But, his profile, you know, looked like a Roman coin. And those royal blue eyes. He was just exquisitely beautiful, especially in 1968.

You know, I was in one of his last movies. There were only a couple after me. And he – you could tell that he was very burned out but he loved doing LIVE A LITTLE, LOVE A LITTLE. At least, I felt he did because it was one of his first comedic roles. You know, where he was – it was really a modern movie. He was playing a kind of a, you know, like a playboy magazine photographer.

It, it was a sophisticated comedy. And I think – I think he appreciated that.

LIVE A LITTLE, LOVE A LITTLE may have been a refreshing change of pace, but it did little to change the pace of Elvis's continuing decline at the box office. His next project was another western, only this time his character was darker than the typical Elvis role.

JOE ESPOSITO
ROAD MANAGER & FRIEND

Joe Esposito: He wanted to do action movies 'cause, you know, he was very into karate at the time. And he wanted to do, you know, the DIRTY HARRY-type movies. He loved DIRTY HARRY. He loved Clint Eastwood. And if you look at CHARRO he tried to look a little like Clint Eastwood. That hat and everything.

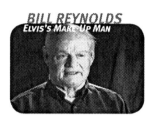

BILL REYNOLDS
ELVIS'S MAKE-UP MAN

Bill Reynolds: Yeah, that picture was totally different from the others I'd worked with him, on, 'cause it wasn't a musical. He was a, a cowboy or the bad guy in a sense. Makeup wise it was different 'cause he looked terrible and grubby. So you had to darken his skin good. But that's – I think that's the one where they threw the snake on me in the makeup room one time.

Joe Esposito: Elvis called Bill, "I need some touch up," so Bill goes in and Elvis said, "Bill, excuse me for a second. I got to go out and get somethin'." So as he left, I heard him say that. All the guys shut the door on the outside of the dressing room, and I let this snake out. Well the snake comes slithering up at Bill. And Bill is jumpin' on the couch screamin'. There was an air conditioner in the wall. He's tryin' to hang on the air conditioner. He was screamin' – and the whole trailer was shaking. The guy's gonna have a heart attack. So Elvis opened the door and Bill jumped out and he took off running.

Bill Reynolds: Oh, I went screamin' out of that trailer. That one was a – good thing I was younger then, 'cause that was heart attack time.

Joe Esposito: Bill and Elvis never got back in the dressing room after that. Said Elvis I, I need to be touched up. He said well come on out here, I'll touch you up out here.

Although Elvis's voice was heard on the theme song, CHARRO represented the first and only time in which he did not sing on camera.

Mac Davis: You live behind the eyes of other men. Da-da-da. CHARRO. Boy, I can't even remember it now. I'm sure Elvis was – they had to pretty much hog tie Elvis to get him to cut it but that was the days when, he did what the studio told him to do.

MAC DAVIS
SINGER/SONGWRITER

Elvis did sing in his 30th film, THE TROUBLE WITH GIRLS. And the songs were more fully integrated into the plot than in previous Presley pictures.

Marlyn Mason: He was the manager of this, troop called Chautauqua, which is a real – it's in fact I think they still have it today. And, the purpose of Chautauqua was to bring culture to the rural areas. And, so he played the manager, and I was this union person. I was always screaming at him, for this or for that. And I screamed at him through the whole movie. And, of course, you could tell we were both very much in love with each other but, we were never gonna tell each other that. And, I think it comes through in the film.

MARLYN MASON
CO-STAR; THE TROUBLE
WITH GIRLS

Sheree North: Elvis was a wreck about acting, and I knew how he felt, because he was still so insecure about his acting. He was so solid and secure as a – as a performer, as an entertainer. And when it came to acting, he would start telling jokes about himself, before you could – before you could put him down, he'd put himself down.

SHEREE NORTH
CO-STAR; THE TROUBLE
WITH GIRLS

Elvis finished out the socially conscious 60s with an unusual film about a ghetto doctor and a crusading nun, played by Mary Tyler Moore.

Billy Graham: I remember that she was a little bit on the prissy side. But, that was okay because she was playing a nun.

Barbara McNair: I'd heard so much about how hard it was to get to know Elvis and how he kept himself surrounded by people to keep – to keep other people away. But, I didn't find him that way at all. I found him very accessible. As a matter of fact, we used to go into his trailer when we weren't shooting, and he loved to sing to his own records. So we – every time we had a break in, in the action we'd go to his trailer and sing. At the time he just was putting out "Suspicious Minds."

During CHANGE OF HABIT, Elvis seemed more determined than ever to improve his acting skills.

Billy Graham: I found that, the he could handle humor quite well. And he could also handle a fight scene. He could do an argument. Very well, very believably. But in certain other areas like if it was a love scene or if there was some subtlety that was called for, he was a little self-conscious. So, I decided that we could do some work in that area. Well, the Colonel got wind of it. He said we make these movies, for a certain price. And they make a certain amount of money. No less and no more. So he said, don't you be goin' for no Oscar, Sonny, because we ain't got no tuxedos.

Joe Esposito: CHANGE OF HABIT, which I thought was a great movie, a great director in Billy – Billy Graham. Had a great time makin' that movie. Great actresses and a good director. It made a big difference. And, but, you know, he still felt, you know – I think he wanted to get back out in front of a crowd.

After completing CHANGE OF HABIT, Elvis was booked for a four week engagement at the new International Hotel in Las Vegas. This was the beginning of a new phase in Presley's career.

Pat Broeske: He's really gonna go on to become the ultimate stage performer. You know, over the next few years. And though he will talk to, to some of his colleagues about films he'd like to do, I think the realities of, of what he's able to do at that time are starting to diminish. For one thing, you know, he has an exhaustive concert schedule. The man is booked.

PAT BROESKE
AUTHOR

His Hollywood career seemed a thing of the past until 1975, when another superstar approached Presley to discuss a remake of A STAR IS BORN.

Myrna Smith: Barbara Streisand had brought the idea to Elvis. He – she and Jon Peters came to the dressing room one night and they were down there until about 5:00 in the morning and they were talking to Elvis. And, he was so excited.

MYRNA SMITH
SINGER, BACK-UP GROUP
SWEET INSPIRATIONS

Joe Esposito: Barbra Streisand, Jon Peters, Elvis, Jerry Schilling and myself in this little dressing room, in Las Vegas. And went through – they went through this whole story about we thought was a great idea.

JOE ESPOSITO
ROAD MANAGER & FRIEND

Kanai Seanoa: Joe and all of us probably sat up with him until 7:00 the next morning. He was so excited, about the opportunity to have a legitimate acting role like that. He thought that he could really tear it up.

KANAI SEANOA
SPIRITUAL FRIEND

Myrna Smith: Next night he came down to do the show and, and it's just like somebody had pulled the rug from under him. He was just real down. Because the Colonel had talked him out of it.

George Klein: That was one of the biggest mistakes Colonel Parker ever made, was not letting Elvis make A STAR IS BORN with Streisand. The electricity. I'm sure Elvis would've been nominated for that. And I think he would've lost weight, got back in shape. and that probably would've started him in Hollywood all over again, with more dramatic type roles.

Joe Esposito: But we don't know all the exact details why it didn't happen. A lot of meetings between Elvis and the Colonel. What went on between the two of them, I don't know. I knew there was a lot of talk about Jon Peters being the director. And, that was not a good idea because he was a hair designer at the time. And, he didn't know anything about show business and they all figured he couldn't do it. Well he never did direct it anyhow.

Jerry Schilling: I was in that walk in closet in Las Vegas when Barbra Streisand offered him A STAR IS BORN and he accepted. I think those type of roles would've brought him new life and not boredom. And, you know, I, I always think that we lost Elvis, by creative disappointment.

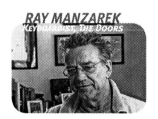

Ray Manzarek: For me, a tragedy of Elvis Presley's life, is that he didn't get to make the movies he wanted to make.

Mary Ann Mobley: He was – it's sad in a way that he never had a chance, to do what he really thought he could do. And people would say well why didn't he – why didn't he break away? Why didn't he stay out? Stand up and say, you know, I'm not gonna do this. I'm gonna do this movie with Barbra Streisand. But you have to understand how he was brought up. It would not have come into his mind, to say wait a minute.

MARY ANN MOBLEY
CO-STAR, HARUM SCARUM,
GIRL HAPPY

I'm gonna do what I want to do. What if that had been Elvis Presley, on that poster, with Barbra Streisand? What if it had been Elvis Presley, you know, doing those songs with Barbra Streisand on that screen?

JOE ESPOSITO
ROAD MANAGER & FRIEND

Joe Esposito: Kris Kristofferson did a good job. Elvis could've done a better one.

Pat Broeske: Remember, he's already had the comeback on television. The comeback in Vegas. It would've been just yet another resurrection of the King.

PAT BROESKE
AUTHOR

Charlie Hodge: Elvis, in the 60s, honest to God, kept Hollywood alive. Everyone else was shootin' their pictures outside this country. And in – and in different locations and everything, and Hollywood was hurtin', at movies. And Elvis was the only one that wasn't leavin' town. He was doin' movies right there in Hollywood.

CHARLIE HODGE
FRIEND/SINGER/GUITARIST/
MEMPHIS MAFIA

Lance Legault: Every minute, every day I ever worked with him he was special. He was the most unique, disarming, charming. Let me tell you something, this guy you – if you didn't work with him, you can't believe what a human being he was.

LANCE LEGAULT
ACTOR/FRIEND

Billy Graham: Of all the people I've ever worked with in my entire life, and I've been a director for 47 years.

Elvis was the nicest man I've ever – I've ever worked with.

Elvis's Hollywood years began with a chance at a career-making role opposite Burt Lancaster and Katherine Hepburn, and ended with a chance at a career-changing role opposite Barbra Streisand. Neither came to pass. Although he never did get that serious dramatic role he'd been hoping for, Elvis left us with 31 fun, enjoyable, and very entertaining motion pictures.

Anita Mann: I remember every day like I couldn't wait to go to work. Every single day.

Teri Garr: Me, too. Me, too. I have to say that. Even though we're getting paid peanuts for it. And then I realize now that, if Elvis was making movies that were bad movies and bad for his career, he was having fun. And sometimes fun is better than a big career and money.

Glen Campbell: Now that I look back on it I'm glad he did 'em, you know. At the time I thought they were kinda hokey, you know. But, now when you see 'em on TV I – they're, they're pretty cool.

GI SHUFFLE

"I was gettin' used to the movie star bit. You know, I had dark glasses on, you know, sittin' in the back of a Cadillac limousine sayin', "I'm a movie star. Hey, I'm a son of a bitch. Hey!" So I did that. You know, I was livin' it up, man, and then I got drafted. So overnight it was all gone, man. It was like it was a dream. You know, I was sayin', "Was that me? Did that happen?""

—Elvis Presley

In the mid-1950s a cultural explosion took place that would define the decade like nothing that had come before it, throwing young women into a frenzy and setting the world on its ear – and it had a name.

ELVIS PRESLEY

He was the world's biggest superstar, a king both in name and in lifestyle.

In 1956, when a young truck driver named Elvis Presley burst onto the rock 'n' roll map with his single, "Heartbreak Hotel," the teenagers of the world had finally found their touchstone.

A rock 'n' roll god whose mannerisms and style boys would copy for generations to come and whose suggestive eyes and rolling hips would send millions of young women into spasms of delight and their parents into a frenzy of disapproval.

Barry Gibb: That's a phenomenal thing. You know, this was as global phenomena in the way that it changed every kid's life, every boy's life – not to mention every girl's life. The idea of just looking like Elvis, whether you did or not, became very important. And your hair became his hair, you know? And if you didn't have the right hair it was not gonna happen, and whoever did; got the women, you know?

Anita Wood: There were a lot of girls and boys and men and women and they would rush him and – sure, anybody – I would be worried and concerned about that because he could get hurt. And he may have gotten hurt some of the time. I mean I think they jerked his shirts off and things like this, you know, grabbing for him.

EXCERPT FROM NEWS

Church Minister: These men come down here from New York and from Florida to find out my reasons on rock 'n' roll music and why I preach against it, and I believe with all of my heart, if you talk to the average teenager of today and you ask them what it is about rock 'n' roll music that they like, and the first thing they'll say is the beat, the beat, the beat!

Dixie Locke-Emmons: We thought he had way too many girls clamoring around at that time. The excitement of knowing that you're doing well and that people like him, it's rewarding. At the same time it's kind of okay that time is up now. Let me take him and go home now. Yeah. And that didn't happen.

But in 1958 Elvis faced an even bigger threat to his standing as the nation's foremost rebel.

EXCERPT FROM NEWS

Military Officer: Congratulations, you are now in the Army. You're all privates. That's the way you'll be addressed from now on.

The United States Government had seen fit to embrace Elvis Presley in the only way it could, by drafting him into its army.

Anita Wood: We all saw him off and his mom was there and his dad. Some other fans were there and he hugged me last. And I was trying not to cry because I did not want him to see me leave crying. You know, I was trying to smile. It was hard. It was difficult. I could not – my heart was being just torn away and it was very hard to see him leave.

Joe Esposito: When he did get his notice, I'm sure he was not too happy. I mean when you think you're the biggest star in the world at the time and all of a sudden the Army says, "Hey, we want you," I mean it can't feel too good.

Elvis's induction was more than just news to the American public, it was prime time entertainment.

In the days before his induction, as parents all over the country looked on gleefully at the process that would take away their children's idol for the next two years, that idol was readying himself for what was to be one of the most traumatic days in his young life. He had already decided to rob the press and public alike of at least one vicarious thrill associated with his new status as America's foremost draftee – the shearing of the famous greasy Presley locks into a regulation Army crew cut.

Joe Esposito: I don't know if he had his hair cut before going in the Army 'cause I didn't know him before then, okay? But it looked like he did. Knowing him, he probably had a nice, clean little shorter haircut than normal, than having to cut so much off from one extreme to another so much. And he probably did that, knowing Elvis. He thought about those kinds of things. He knew he was gonna be filmed. He had to make sure he looked good on camera.

JOE ESPOSITO
ROAD MANAGER & FRIEND

Elvis spent the three days after his formal induction at Fort Chaffee, Arkansas, where he was given his various inoculations, his uniform and duffel bag, his Army aptitude test, and most importantly, his eagerly awaited and long-dreaded 65-cent haircut. He also gave his first-ever salute to a battery of cameras that had been allowed to follow him through the induction process due to the arrangements of Colonel Tom Parker.

Joe Esposito: Elvis being drafted, I thought it was very unusual because, you know, I figured a big star like him would never get drafted into the service. But he did, and I think Colonel was smart in saying, "Hey, go do your two years. I'll keep your name out there and interest in you and don't do special services 'cause they're gonna come after you if you do special service. Just serve your two years." And it was a great move.

JOE ESPOSITO
ROAD MANAGER & FRIEND

From Arkansas, Elvis was transported to Fort Hood, Texas, where he began his basic training with A Company, 2nd Tank Battalion, 2nd Armored Division. Though Elvis was taking all of this in decidedly good public humor, behind closed doors and away from the press he was truly miserable. He had gone from the sumptuous confines and safe haven of Graceland to a numbered bunk in a barracks with dozens of other faceless and nameless recruits. Though his array of cars would be waiting for him in the civilian world, he now had to make due with a regulation Army jeep. And as for his obsession with clothes, the Army would see to it that he would be dressed in the finest olive drab that money could buy. Though Elvis's transformation from worldwide superstar to buck private was not fun for the young rock 'n' roller, it was tolerable. There was, however, at least one person upon whom the entire affair would have a devastating effect. Gladys Presley had always been her son's number one fan, friend and confidant in the years leading up to his emergence as the most powerful performer the world had ever seen, and the prospect of being separated from him for two long years was more than she could bear. With Elvis gone, first to his career demands and now to his Army training, Gladys increasingly relied on alcohol as a means of coping with this latest crisis in her life. Though most people would have seen Graceland as the culmination of a lifelong dream, to Gladys Presley it was a gilded prison that removed her from the places and people she found most familiar, by creating a social wall around her which would be impossible to climb. While Elvis's hordes of fans desperately longed to enter the gates of the antebellum mansion, Gladys wanted nothing more than to leave them and Elvis's fame behind her forever. As her sister Lillian later put it, "A woman from the hills of Mississippi is only interested in going so far."

JOE ESPOSITO
ROAD MANAGER & FRIEND

Joe Esposito: Most of the people don't realize that Elvis was not a drinker. He did not like alcohol. In fact, when I first went to work for him there was no alcohol allowed in the house. I mean no wine, no hard booze, no beer. And I come to find out over the years that it was because apparently a lot of his mother's – Gladys – the Smith side, lotta drinkers, and he just didn't like that, didn't like people drunk.

For Elvis's part, he threw himself into this new endeavor with a zeal that few would have thought possible, given his status as the lightning rod of rock 'n' roll rebellion. His scores on the preliminary aptitude tests earned him a place in the 5th Army's coveted tank corps, known as "Hell on Wheels." This was largely due to the advice of Colonel Tom Parker, who had told his young charge early on that the world would be watching his every move, and that the best way to insure his status upon leaving the service was to be the most gung ho spit and polish draftee the Army had ever seen. The Army, however, was still fighting to have Elvis placed in one of its special services units, where his skills as an entertainer could be maximized to the Army's benefit. The fight went on until the 11th hour, with the Pentagon threatening to do as it pleased with its new recruit and the Colonel stubbornly resisting the military at every turn. The battle over Private Presley finally ended when the Colonel pre-emptively released photos and news information about Elvis's assignment to the Hell on Wheels battalion, stressing that Elvis was reveling in his new job. That effectively stopped the Army dead in its tracks, for it could not afford the outcry that would ensue if Presley were assigned to a cushy entertainment job after the banner headlines announcing his normal soldier status. And the Pentagon's top brass had to admit that they had been outmaneuvered by an honorary colonel in a straw hat and Hawaiian shirt. The first eight weeks of Elvis's Army hitch began, as for all soldiers, with basic training. Once again, Elvis showed the world and the Army what he was made of by enduring the daily five-mile hikes and various physical and mental challenges so well that by the end of it all he had been lifted to the post of acting sergeant, the highest honor a draftee could receive during training.

Charlie Hodge: That's how I met Elvis. It was at Fort Hood, and I went over and I said, "I'm Charlie Hodge. I was the lead singer with the Foggy River Boys." And he said, "Hey, man. I used to watch you every Saturday night on TV!" You know. And I think our friendship was a natural friendship, 'cause when we met there at Fort Hood and got on a ship going to Europe, we knew the same people in the gospel field. We knew the same people in the country field. You know, like Wanda Jackson was on our show and she was Miss Rockabilly, and Elvis always wanted to date her, you know, and so we had a lot to talk about.

CHARLIE HODGE
FRIEND/SINGER/GUITARIST/
MEMPHIS MAFIA

Due to the rigorous training he was now undergoing, Elvis had not yet moved his friends and family out to Texas to join him, but he was not alone in the Lone Star State. Eddie Fadal, a Texas sports announcer who had emceed one of Presley's concerts in the mid-'50s, now opened his home as a safe haven for America's most famous draftee.

Janice Fadal: Daddy reacquainted himself with Elvis. A few months later here in Waco, Texas, when Elvis played a concert at the Heart of Texas Coliseum and he went backstage to meet him, and he said, "Do you remember me?" And lo and behold, Elvis had remembered him. And my father was always very generous, and he said kind of off the cuff, "Come visit me sometime in my home. I'd love to have you. My wife would cook for you. We'd love to have you in our family" and it was just a standing offer. And in 1958 when Elvis became stationed at Killeen, Texas, he did just that. He would come visit our family on the weekends and to show up unexpectedly. He would never call first. He would just drop in. He would bring his friends, his entourage, his girlfriend at the time, Anita Wood, and pile in the house. And my mother, who, you know, would be running around in her robe and her house shoes or whatever, would suddenly run and go back and put a dress on and start cooking. There was never a dull moment at that time.

JANICE FADAL
EDDIE'S DAUGHTER

With his initial training complete, Elvis was now free to move his entourage into the home he had rented for them in nearby Killeen. True to form, Elvis reshaped his surroundings to suit his own individual tastes and needs. This meant that his favorite foods had to be on hand at any given hour, that entire rooms would have to be altered to resemble those in Graceland and that the family atmosphere, which was so important to him, would have to be maintained. His off-base life now comfortable, Elvis set about the task of becoming a tank gunner, blasting his way to the top of his class and earning the right to be an instructor, a rare honor for a mere private. His happiness would be short-lived, however. After moving into the home in Killeen, Gladys Presley's health took an immediate turn for the worse. Though she had felt isolated within the columned splendor of Graceland, the flat, barren wasteland of south central Texas and the lonely hours away from Elvis only exacerbated her feelings of dread and despair. The Army had finally managed to sever what rock 'n' roll could not – the umbilical cord between mother and son had begun to disintegrate, leaving Elvis a man and Gladys an emotional wreck. Vernon's personality did nothing to help her in her time of crisis, so Mrs. Presley turned to alcohol, drinking straight vodka to assuage her suffering. She had also begun to take high doses of amphetamines, which in conjunction with her drinking, began to take a terrible toll on her health, both mentally and physically. She had long suspected that Vernon was seeing other women, and one night in a drunken rage she knocked him unconscious with an iron skillet. The emotional outburst caused her to collapse on her bed, where Elvis's friend Lamar Fike found her, her skin turning yellow, a sure sign of liver damage.

After informing bodyguard Red West of the situation, the two then sat Elvis down to try and get him to transport his mother back to Memphis for treatment. Elvis refused. He had seen his mother in this state before. He had even found her drunk on more than one occasion. It was, he said, nothing new. And besides, he needed mama in Texas. Gladys' health would soon cause even Elvis to rethink this idea. In early August, 1958, Mrs. Presley's body could no longer take the strain it was being subjected to. She could no longer stand without assistance. Her skin took on a grayish-yellow tinge, and she was retaining so much fluid that it was causing unbearable pain in her right side. After seeing a local doctor, Gladys, accompanied by Vernon, was transported by train to Memphis, where she entered Methodist Hospital. Doctors drained a gallon and a half of fluid from her abdomen, an indicator that her liver and kidneys were no longer functioning due to the damage caused by her heavy drinking. Back in Killeen, Elvis, who had not been able to secure a weekend pass, was wracked with guilt over his apparent lack of interest in his mother's health and his enthusiastic pursuit of tank training. By August 11th, Gladys was drifting in and out of consciousness, repeatedly asking for Elvis. Elvis had requested an emergency leave, but in a callous move, the officer of the day denied that request on the grounds that Presley's mother wasn't dead – yet. This sent Elvis into a frenzy, and he told his sergeant that he would go AWOL to get to his mother's side. Having wisely and calmly advised Elvis that the Army would likely jail him for his offense, his sergeant then told Elvis to have his mother's doctor call the base commander. Within two hours he was on a plane to Memphis, while the officer who had denied his leave was disciplined. Elvis arrived at Memphis Methodist at 7:45 p.m. that night. His mother brightened up at the sight of her only son, as they conversed in a baby talk language, with Gladys referring to Elvis as her wittle itty-bitty and Elvis referring to his mother as his satnin. This form of communication was one that they had always shared and one that entirely excluded Vernon. Late that evening, Gladys ordered Elvis to go home and get some sleep. He protested, but his father agreed with his mother, and Elvis was sent home to rest. Elvis returned to Graceland and slipped out of his uniform and into bed, falling into a fitful sleep. At three a.m. the phone rang. Elvis knew what it was before his cousin Billy Smith took the call. Gladys Love Presley, the one person he could not live without, was gone. Her funeral would be one of the most traumatic events in Elvis's life. He grieved loudly, wailing over her lifeless body in the hospital, and later openly crying on the steps of Graceland with his father, in full view of the ever-present media. When her body was laid out in its coffin inside the stately mansion, Elvis spent hours massaging her feet, which he called her sooties, continuing their private language even in death. The day of her burial, Elvis repeatedly said, "Everything I have is gone."

Dixie Locke-Emmons: He was devastated when his mother died. I just can see him at the funeral home that day. He was just absolutely devastated. I've never seen anybody go through a death in the family that took it any harder than he did. And I'm sure he felt that he had lost his best friend, which she had been all of his life.

After his 30-day leave, Presley returned to Fort Hood, a noticeably changed man. Though he had never been a boisterous soldier, he had always been gregarious, but his mother's death left him silent and withdrawn. Soon enough, he was ordered to ship out to Germany, where he would be stationed at the Army's base in Friedberg, with Company D, 1st Battalion, 32nd Armored Division. It was a different Elvis Presley that faced the cameras on the eve of his departure.

INTERVIEW EXCERPT

Reporter: Elvis, do the other soldiers give you a rough time because you're famous?

Elvis Presley: No, sir. I was very surprised. I've never met a better group of boys in my life. They probably would have if it'd been like everybody thought. I mean everybody thought I wouldn't have to work and I would be given special treatment and this and that. But when they looked around and saw I was on KP and I was pulling guard and everything just like they were, well, they figured, "Well, he's just like us."

Reporter: Elvis, you don't get out of the Army until 1960. If rock 'n' roll should diminish in popularity or even disappear, what would you do?

Elvis Presley: Well, I would probably try acting. I mean, you know, I would try to make good as an actor. I know it's a tough field to break into, acting, 'cause you've got so much competition.

Reporter: Elvis, what do you think about going to Germany?

Elvis Presley: Well, sir, I'm kinda lookin' forward to it. I mean just before I came in the Army we were planning a tour of Europe. And I get quite a bit of mail from over there and everything, you know, and I'm kinda looking forward to it, really.

CHARLIE HODGE
FRIEND/SINGER/GUITARIST/
MEMPHIS MAFIA

Charlie Hodge: On the way over to Germany on the ship at night I could hear Elvis start grieving sometimes at night, and I'd get out of my bunk and sit down and start talking to him and maybe joking with him a little bit, get him in a little better mood, then he'd drift off to sleep. And he said years later, he said, "Charlie," he said, "if it hadn't been for you," he said, "you kept me sane all the way across the ocean."

Sheree North: He said when he went in the Army he – I think he said he was on a ship and he could not show his feelings in front of the other guys. And he said at night after everybody – he made sure everybody was asleep, he'd put all the pillows over his head and cry for the loss of his mom, 'cause that was a very painful thing for him.

SHEREE NORTH
CO-STAR TROUBLE WITH GIRLS

Upon his arrival in Germany, Elvis was greeted by the same pandemonium that had been his steady companion since 1956. Sixteen-year-old Karl Heinz almost snagged the first European autograph from Presley on the gangplank of the troop ship. Though Elvis gamely tried to oblige, the duffel bag he carried was just too cumbersome, leaving him trying to write with his left hand. Presley and his fellow soldiers were whisked away as rapidly as possible by a troop train that would take them directly into the base. But Private Presley was still no normal soldier. Normal soldiers didn't require armed guards to get them to their barracks. In a replay of the firestorm of coverage that greeted his induction, the European media and fans now took their turn, not even allowing him the time to lie down on his bunk without it being cause for a photo op. Once again, Elvis handled the attention with the good humor he displayed back in the States. And once again, he transported his family and friends to his post to make himself feel as at home as possible.

Dick Clark: Colonel Parker would never let Elvis appear on "American Bandstand," certainly not for AFTRA scale. I think it was $150.00 or something. Unbelievable. For that amount of money he should have been on two or three times. But he did allow us to talk to him on the phone because he wanted to keep his audience aware of the fact that Elvis was recording and his music would be available. So we talked to him in Germany.

DICK CLARK
TELEVISION HOST/PRODUCER

AMERICAN BANDSTAND INTERVIEW

Dick Clark: Hello, Elvis?

Elvis Presley: Hello, Dick. How are ya?

Dick Clark: Fine, thank you.

Elvis Presley: Okay.

Dick Clark: Where on earth are you at this minute?

Elvis Presley: I'm in a place called Germany.

Dick Clark: Tell me a little bit about your activities. What did you do say, today, for instance?

Elvis Presley: Mostly classroom work, studying in, uh…

Dick Clark: What are you studying?

Elvis Presley: Map reading and then uh, greased my jeep and so forth. You know just the regular routine.

Dick Clark: Do you have any time for music anymore?

Elvis Presley: Only at night. You see, I get off work at 5:00 in the afternoon and…I have a guitar up here in my room and I sit around and…Ya know, up here…I don't wanna get out of practice, you know, if I can help it.

Dick Clark: I should hope not. Let me tell you some good news. I know by now you know why we're calling. In the annual "American Bandstand" popularity poll you walked away once again with a couple of honors this year. The favorite male vocalist award and the favorite record of 1958 award. The kids voted you —

AMERICAN BANDSTAND INTERVIEW CONTINUED

Elvis Presley: Well that's sure tremendous Dick.

Dick Clark: – top man all-around.

Elvis Presley: That's really great, boy.

Dick Clark: How about it, do you miss home?

Elvis Presley: Oh, boy. You, you, you. I can't hardly talk.

Dick Clark: Well, Elvis, there's one thing and I guess maybe our poll is an indication of it, the folks at home certainly haven't forgotten you. If anything, they're more and more interested in your activities and the things that you're doing and anxiously await your return.

Elvis Presley: Well, that's really great, Dick...Believe me, that is the big thing that I'm looking forward to...You'll never know how happy I'll be...I mean I'm glad that I could come in the army and do my part, you know, but...but you'll never know how happy I'll be, boy, when I can return to the entertainment world ...because once you get a taste for show business there's nothing like it.

Dick Clark: You know it. Elvis, thank you ever so much for talking to us. We look forward to your return. We'll see you just as quick as we can all get together.

Elvis Presley: Well, thank you very much Dick. I'd like to say one more thing before you go. If you have the time.

Dick Clark: Sure. Please do.

Elvis Presley: Uh, (laughs). Boy, I'm so excited I can't hardly talk, you know.

AMERICAN BANDSTAND INTERVIEW CONTINUED

Dick Clark: Take your time. We got all the time in the world.

Elvis Presley: Uh, Uh…I'd just like to tell all those, those wonderful kids…

…they'll never know how happy they've made me, and…

… just longing for the time where I can come back out and entertain them again and…

…travel around and make movies and records and things like that, you know...

Well that's about it.

Elvis next went through a press conference that one reporter said would be a shade smaller than President Eisenhower might expect to see if he came to Germany.

PRESS CONFERENCE OF ELVIS ARRIVING IN GERMANY: EXCERPT

Elvis Presley: I was very surprised at the reception. I wasn't expecting anything quite that big, and I only regret that I didn't have more time to stay there with the. But maybe someday I can come back when my Army tour is up as an entertainer and then I'll have more time and I'll have an opportunity to try and make myself at home over here.

Reporter: Thank you very much, Mr. Presley, and we wish you a pleasant stay in Germany.

Elvis Presley: Thank you very much. Arrivederci! No, that's Italian, isn't it?

Soon afterward, Elvis was given permission to live off-base with his family, who had been staying at a nearby hotel. With him in Germany were his father, Vernon, his grandmother Minnie Mae, whom he called Dodger, and his perennial buddies Red and Lamar. The motley group now found themselves thrust into a foreign culture, though none of them was particularly worldly.

This would lead to problems during Elvis's stay in Europe. He and his entourage first stayed at a local hotel, until they were thrown out due to Red and Lamar's pranks, which included setting paper on fire and shoving it under Elvis's door.

CHARLIE HODGE
FRIEND/SINGER/GUITARIST/
MEMPHIS MAFIA

Charlie Hodge: We had a few parties and things there and almost burnt down our hotel. One time Elvis – we were playing a game and Elvis went in his bedroom and locked the door and we piled up paper out there and set it on fire. We were gonna burn him outta there. And so anyway, that's what got him outta that hotel.

They ultimately wound up in a house at 14 Goethestrasse, paying almost triple the usual rent for the relatively small house, once Frau Pieper, the landlady, discovered just who her tenant would be. Frau Pieper also refused to leave the premises, preferring instead to stay in the top floor of the house, much to the chagrin of Elvis's grandmother, who also had to share a kitchen with the cantankerous hausfrau. Though Elvis was still an All-American boy, he now began to acclimate himself to his new, distinctly European surroundings. He also learned a new German word, probably the most important one he would learn during his stay there – fraulein – and there were plenty of them for him to choose from. His German fans turned out to be no less obsessive than their American counterparts when it came to trying to meet their idol.

AMERICAN BANDSTAND INTERVIEW

Dick Clark: Elvis, I know probably you don't have too much time to yourself, but when you go out amongst the German people what is the thing that strikes you as most interesting? Are they very different?

Elvis Presley: Uh no, the difference is naturally the language barrier there. It's kinda hard to talk to most of them, especially older ones, because a lot of them don't speak English at all and I don't speak any German, ya know?

Dick Clark: How do you find the reaction of young people toward you, mainly the girls? Do they know who you are?

Elvis Presley: Well, everyday when I finish work and I come in there's always a lot of people at the gate from all over Germany, you know, and they bring their families. Especially on weekends I have a lot visitors here from all over Europe in fact. They come here, you know, and take pictures and everything.

Dick Clark: Elvis, I did wanna thank you very much for calling on this day. As you probably know, this is our special anniversary day.

Elvis Presley: Oh, well, congratulations.

Dick Clark: Many, many thanks, and we all look forward to your return.
Elvis Presley: Well thank you very much. You don't know how I'm looking forward to my return.

Dick Clark: Thank you for calling and bye bye.

Elvis Presley: Bye bye Dick.

It was at this time that Elvis made a friend who would be with him for the rest of his life through the best and worst of times, a young soldier named Joe Esposito.

Joe Esposito: I would have never thought I'd meet Elvis. You know, there's millions of guys in the service, but it just so happened he came to the same base I was. I didn't meet him for the first like, six, seven, months, but I saw him around base.

In the morning he'd drive by in this little BMW sports car that BMW let him use while he was over there, and he'd always be running late. He'd always come in late as roll call was going on. And a friend of mine, Wes Daniels, the base photographer, was assigned to take pictures of Elvis for the Army. And one day he said, "Joe, listen. We play football on the weekends and we need some more players this weekend. You wanna come over and play football with Elvis and us guys?" I said, "Yeah, I'd love to" and that's how I met Elvis.

Then in the midst of it all, Private Elvis Aaron Presley was killed when his Mercedes crashed on the Autobahn. At least that's what the press reported. In fact, what had happened was that Vernon, in true form, had wrecked the car while driving Elvis's German secretary on an errand. Both ultimately recovered from their minor injuries, but it had left Elvis in the position of having to explain that the rumors of his death had been greatly exaggerated. And this wasn't Vernon's first mishap with the new Mercedes. Three weeks before he had almost caused an accident while trying to outrun reporters. In an attempt to cut them off from his son, he had inadvertently trapped the car on a railroad crossing with Elvis and Red in the passenger seats. Somehow the train missed them, as can be seen in the photos the reporters took that day. Private Presley also had to deal with the growing war at his rented house between Frau Pieper and his grandmother over the use of the kitchen. It ended when Minnie Mae whacked Frau Pieper with a broom. The women soon got drunk together and all was forgiven.

Though Elvis was having domestic difficulties and had to deal with being on the front lines of the Cold War in Europe, there was time for him to have fun. He managed to get away for a night to be reunited with an old friend and rival, Bill Haley, at the Comets' performance in Frankfurt.

CHARLIE HODGE
(FRIEND/SINGER/GUITARIST/
MEMPHIS MAFIA)

Charlie Hodge: We 'd been to some show and a guy stopped and he said, "I'd just like to tell you –" because Elvis always wore his uniform. Said, "I'd like to tell you that it's nice to see young men that will stay in the Army and be in the military for their country." He said, "I think that's wonderful." He said, "Yes." Said, "Thank you very much." And he gave Elvis his hand and said, "My name is so and so." And Elvis said, "And my name's Elvis Presley." And the guy took him by the hand and pulled him out in the light and said, "By God, you are!"

Elvis also managed to get out and enjoy European nightlife and all it had to offer. He went on a mini-tour of the continent, starting first at the Moulin Rouge, the French-style nightclub in Munich. The pictures from one of those nights leave no doubt that it was good to be the King – or even to be just a friend of the King. The girls who were entertained by Elvis and his buddies were usually the entertainment. They were strippers. The Presley contingent made its way to Paris for some high level carousing and nightclubbing, minus one member. Red West was sent back to the States due to his propensity for getting into brawls with the European locals.

JOE ESPOSITO
ROAD MANAGER & FRIEND

Joe Esposito: Red had a short temper, and if you say something wrong Red would just punch you out. Red got in a fight with this guy over there at this bar. It was bad and it got back to Elvis, you know, and he said, "This guy's causing a lotta problems. You know, he's gonna be arrested and thrown in jail." So he went back home for that reason. That's why he wasn't on the trip to Paris.

The rest, however, wound up enjoying a somewhat debauched two weeks sampling all that Paris had to offer on a never-ending party at clubs like the Carousel, the Follies Bergere, the Crazy Horse, the Moulin Rouge and the Lido. Like any American soldier on leave, Elvis and his friends enjoyed the company of the women who were available. This included those of the "professional" variety.

Joe Esposito: We all hung out at this nightclub. All the showgirls would meet us there, and we invited a lot of them to the hotel in the evening and – what can I tell you? You know, we did what young men would do at that age with beautiful ladies. But one of the guys was not having too much luck. So we were talking about it one day with Elvis. Said, "Well, let's get him a hooker." So I called out to the bellman and I said, "Listen," you know, I told him the story. He said, "Okay, Mr. Esposito, no problem." So we're there sitting around talking, having a good time, and knock on the door comes and this beautiful, beautiful blonde lady was at the door. She saw Elvis and she ran over and just jumped all over him. Elvis said, "No, no, no. You're not here for me. You're for him." She looked over and she says, "Oh No No No he is too fett, you I want you." Well, we couldn't get her off of Elvis, so we had to ease her out the door. So our plan didn't work out.

JOE ESPOSITO
ROAD MANAGER & FRIEND

Charlie Hodge: We really had a lot of fun. We had one incident where we were dating some of the showgirls in the Lido de Paris. And we was up in the suite one afternoon and we got a call from the guy at the Lido and said, "Listen," said, "you mind sending the girls over here?" Said, "We gotta start the show in a few minutes."

CHARLIE HODGE
FRIEND/SINGER/GUITARIST/
MEMPHIS MAFIA

Upon his return to Germany, Elvis took up where he had left off. He went through his duties as he always did, diligently and carefully. Elvis also kept up his charitable work with one of his favorite charities, the March of Dimes.

EXCERPT FROM THE MARCH OF DIMES

Elvis Presley: You know, so many kids and adults too have got just about one of the roughest breaks that can happen to a person.

I'm talking about polio. Sure, we're on the way to conquering it thanks to the Salk vaccine, but take it from me, it sure isn't licked yet. Join the 1957 March of Dimes. Please, it's very urgent.

And as he would throughout his life, he made sure he took care of his fans' desire to see him in person. Each day he would come out of the front of the house and pose for photos with the girls, boys, parents, soldiers and even pets that congregated there in anticipation of his arrival. He also signed hundreds, if not thousands of autographs. Frau Pieper even managed to make a side business out of his fans' desire to see and touch anything related to Presley, although Elvis did tell her to please stop selling his clothes, as he would most likely be in need of them. He even introduced his German fans to American football by playing pickup games that included both soldiers and locals. But it was a fan from the United States whom Elvis met in Germany who was destined to have more impact on his life than any single person other than his beloved mother. Her name was Priscilla. Though she could not know it at the time, Anita Wood, whose faithfulness to her man was even put on record and released as a single on the Sun label, now had competition. Elvis also began indulging in two things during this time that would have alternating effects on his life and career. The first was karate, something he had been exposed to in his Army training and that had intrigued him on a mental and physical level. Presley continued studying the ancient art in Germany and began reading up on Eastern philosophy in an attempt to better understand the esoteric nature behind its disciplines. Eventually, Elvis would reach the level of 8th degree black belt and would continue his studies until his death. The second indulgence would have far darker consequences for the young superstar. He began taking Dexedrine, a powerful stimulant, to help him stay awake while on maneuvers and to boost his energy on nights out with his buddies.

Joe Esposito: Elvis was getting tired and he asked – I forgot who it was, one of his sergeants. He says, you know, "Man, I'm tired." And the guy said, "Here, take this little white pill. It'll keep you awake." So he took it and it woke him up.

JOE ESPOSITO
ROAD MANAGER & FRIEND

And if you ever take something like that, you'll understand. It really wakes you up. I mean you get all this energy and everything. So he said, "This is great. It's a prescription. It's a drug." It's not a off the street kinda drug, so he started taking those little by little. And as time went on, you know, probably told somebody, say, "Listen, can you –" I don't know who it was – "Do you – can you get me some of those pills? I'd like to have them with me in case I get tired and wanna take them." "Sure," they gave him a bottle. It's a good feeling and we'd go out partying and we'd go to Paris and he took them. "Hey, try one of these, you'll stay up all night. Take one of these." It was no big deal. It was not like we were taking something illegal or something that was gonna hurt us. That's how it all started.

The combination of amphetamines and the chronic insomnia that had plagued him since childhood were to wreak havoc on both his physical and mental health for the rest of Elvis's life. Presley also had a new crisis to deal with, which typically was once again the product of Vernon's actions. His father had started a love affair with a woman named Dee Stanley, an affair that flew in the face of Elvis's still raw grief over the death of his mother. To make matters worse, Stanley was a married woman with three children, whose husband was a sergeant stationed in Germany. Sergeant Bill Stanley was a decorated war hero who had stormed the beaches at Normandy during D-Day and had served as General George S. Patton's personal bodyguard, facts which made Elvis all the more uncomfortable with his father's current flame. He told his father as much, but to no avail. When Vernon asked for his son's blessing to marry Dee, Elvis begrudgingly gave it, but things would never be the same. On top of all the pressures he was already dealing with, Hollywood now came calling to make sure that Elvis's return to the fold would be profitable for all involved. Producer Hal Wallis had come to Germany to film location footage for Elvis's first post-Army picture, "G.I. BLUES." Elvis found himself once again facing the criticism that he was getting special treatment due to his stature as an entertainer. He was also suffering from a bout of tonsillitis. With any other soldier, the painfully inflamed tonsils would be removed and that would be the end of it, but with Elvis Presley it was decided that the risk of damaging his million-dollar voice was one that the Army would not be willing to take on his behalf. He therefore had to tough it out and allow his tonsillitis to run its course. So much for special treatment. After his recovery, he and his friends managed to get to France to enjoy the nightlife of the Paris clubs one last time. Naturally, Elvis footed the bill. He could afford it. The Army had just announced that Elvis Presley had been promoted to sergeant, giving him a pay raise of $22.94 in the process.

CHARLIE HODGE
FRIEND/SINGER/GUITARIST/
MEMPHIS MAFIA

Charlie Hodge: We stayed at the Ponce de Galle hotel, and there was one time when one of the soldiers was talking to this girl, but one of the people that was in the show come over and said, "That soldier, that's not a girl he's with, that's a man in drag." And so Elvis went over and said, "Look, now don't get excited. Let's just get up and leave." Said, "That's not a girl you're having a drink with, that's a man." And so he said, "Really, Elvis?" He said, "Yeah." Said, "Don't cause a scene, just get up and leave." And Elvis went back and sat down and the guy got up and left.

Things were beginning to wind down for Elvis as his stay in Germany was coming to an end. He took part in what was to be his last military exercise as the commander of his three-man team for Operation Winter Shield. He also began to prepare for what was to be a long and arduous journey back home. First he had to say good-bye to the various friends and fans that continued to gather at his rented home.

AMERICAN BANDSTAND INTERVIEW

Dick Clark: Hello, Elvis?

Elvis Presley: Hello.

Dick Clark: Hi. We had no idea we could catch a hold of you today.

Elvis Presley: Oh, I just came in the door, Dick.

Dick Clark: What is the situation regarding your release from the Army? Do you have any word on it?

Elvis Presley: Not anything definite, Dick. The way it stands now it's somewhere between the...20th of February and the 2nd of March.

Dick Clark: When you come back I understand you've got a television show with Frank Sinatra and a few movies to make. How you gonna squeeze 'em all in?

Elvis Presley: Well...Well, I'm sure Tom Parker will have everything arranged...Uh, I know the first picture I know is "G.I. Blues," and...but I don't know exactly when the television show will be.

Dick Clark: Elvis, I wanna thank you very, very much for taking the time out from your busy schedule and reassure you once again that we're all awaiting your arrival back home and on this day to wish you a happy birthday.

Elvis Presley: Thanks a lot Dick. And tell everybody hello for me.

Dick Clark: Will do. Bye bye.

The press also had their turn with Sergeant Presley at a press conference arranged by the Army.

There was no way they were going to miss an opportunity to get their most successful marketing tool ever in front of the cameras one last time.

EXCERPT FROM INTERVIEW

News Broadcaster: When asked by an Army interviewer if his military experience has been beneficial to him in any way, Elvis said —

Elvis Presley: It's been a big help in both my career and in my personal life, because I've learned a lot, I've made a lotta friends that I never would have made otherwise, and I've had a lotta good experiences and some bad ones, I have to admit.

But it's good to rough it and to put yourself to a test to see if you can take it, see if you can stand it.

Army Reporter: Another thing we hear a lot about in the Army, especially here, is that we are not only soldiers, but good will ambassadors. How do you feel about that?

Elvis Presley: Well, it's definitely true. It stands to reason because we are in a foreign country and what we do here will reflect on America and our way of life.

Ironically, he ran into his old supporter from Sun Records, Marion Kesker, who was herself serving in the Air Force at this time.

MARION KESKER-McGUINESS

Marion Kesker-McGuiness: The one thing that every G.I. has is the right to bitch. You gotta complain all the time or you're not a real G.I. Elvis couldn't do this because if Elvis had one single word about even ordinary run of the mill complaint, which from his best buddy would have been acceptable and expected, somebody would have sure gotten it to the press.

After 18 months away, Elvis now waited to board a plane that would carry him back to civilian life. As he strode up the steps looking resplendent in his dress uniform, a clutch of fans and friends waved good-bye. For some it would be the last time they would see their idol in the flesh. For one, it was only the beginning of the story. The plane touched down at Fort Dix, New Jersey, and Elvis emerged into a snowstorm, both literally and figuratively. The photographers clicked away as Nancy Sinatra welcomed Elvis home on behalf of her father, and as Elvis was handed his discharge papers and his mustering out pay of $109.54. He also went through yet another press conference.

DISCHARGE PRESS CONFERENCE

Reporter: Elvis, do you feel that you're a little old for the teenagers now?

Elvis Presley: That's the first time I've been asked that one. I don't know. I don't feel too old. I can still move around pretty good.

Reporter: Are you apprehensive about what must be a comeback?

Elvis Presley: Uh Yes, I am. I mean I have my doubts, you know? I'm not gonna commit myself in saying that I'm gonna do this or I'm gonna do that, because I don't know, actually. The only thing I can say is that I'm gonna try. I'll be in there fighting.

Reporter: Now that you're about to be discharged from the Army, Elvis, have two years of sobering Army life changed your mind about rock 'n' roll?

Elvis Presley: Sobering Army life. No, it hasn't. It hasn't changed my mind, because I was in tanks for a long time, you see, and they rock 'n' rolled quite a bit.

And then suddenly Elvis Aaron Presley was once again a civilian. He left that day with Colonel Tom Parker to board a train that would take him back to Memphis. At each stop along the way he was greeted by throngs of fans in an outpouring of emotion that made him feel more secure about his future in the entertainment industry. Colonel Parker had done his job well.

Joe Esposito: It helped his image tremendously being in the Army. Before Elvis went in the service the adults were putting Elvis down. You know, all the goody two shoe people out there were saying how evil Elvis was and the devil's music. But after he come out it all changed. He served his two years like any other G.I. who was out there in the field, in the mud, and he got a lotta respect after that.

As the train pulled into Memphis, the fans were once again waiting. Elvis leapt off the train and into the waiting crowd, signing autographs and chatting with the girls. Soon he was whisked away in a police car with sirens blaring.

The world that Presley found was a different one than he had left. Buddy Holly, Richie Valens and the Big Bopper had died in a plane crash. Jerry Lee Lewis had married his cousin and wrecked his career. Chuck Berry was in jail on a sex charge.

And Little Richard had become a Baptist preacher railing against the devil's music. For his part, Elvis was to do a welcome home special with Frank Sinatra and the Rat Pack in Miami.

As the police convoy approached Graceland, the gates swung open, enfolding the King of Rock 'n' Roll as he entered his palace, once again a free man. The '50s were over.

THE MEMPHIS MAFIA

"THERE'S A LOT OF PEOPLE THAT WROTE STORIES ABOUT ALL OF US. WE DIDN'T HELP ELVIS IN HIS LIFE AND, WE WERE ALL JUST THESE SPONGES TAKING THINGS AWAY FROM HIM. WELL THOSE PEOPLE DON'T KNOW WHAT THEY'RE TALKIN' ABOUT. THEY WEREN'T THERE."

— JOE ESPOSITO

They knew Elvis better than anyone. A small group of friends, relatives, and employees known affectionately as The Memphis Mafia. And Elvis started recruiting members long before he hit the big time.

Jerry Schilling: I grew up in North Memphis where Elvis did. And one day I went to the local playground. I went over to try to get up a game. And, there were five older boys, trying to put together a football game. This is 1954. That's how unpopular Elvis was in 1954. He couldn't get together six people. And Red West knew my older brother and he knew I played grade school football. So he said Jerry, you want to play with us? And I said sure. I didn't know who, you know, who the other guys were but, little kid always wants to play with the older boys.

One of those older boys, Red West, would be with Elvis for years, as would his cousin Sonny. When Elvis went to Germany he would form some of his most enduring and loyal friendships.

Joe Esposito: I was drafted into the army the same time he was in 1958. I went to Fort Hood, Texas. Did basic training there. I didn't meet him there. I saw him around base once in awhile, but the post was too big. I went over to Germany about a month before he did. And the only reason he didn't come over the same I went over is because his mother passed away before he left for Germany. So he went to Memphis and took care of all the funeral arrangements there. And so I went over.

Charlie Hodge: On the ship goin' over, they put him in sergeant quarters so that other soldiers wouldn't bother him for autographs all the time. So, he requested that I be up there, with him. And I said well I just can't go up there. I said, you got to ask the commander. And the commander told him said well after everybody's settled yeah, he can move up there. So I moved into the sergeant's quarters with Elvis.

Pat Broeske: He's away from the United States. He's living on his own, with some family members, and the hangers on that he picks up in the military who will come to be known as the Memphis Mafia, his buddies. They will become lifelong buddies after that.

Joe Esposito: He had a house he rented over there for his grandmother and his father. And went there, went to his house, and Wes introduced me to him. And Elvis walked up to me and he said "Hi, I'm Elvis Presley." And I introduced myself. And, that's a moment that really sticks out in my mind quite a bit. When Elvis smiled at you he had this little grin on his face.

It really made you feel good. I mean, he had that certain aura about him that really relaxed you.

Charlie Hodge: On Sundays he wanted to go play touch football, and a bunch of the guys would come over. And, you know, guys that were in his outfit there. I never did play 'cause I was too little. I'd get hurt.

Joe Esposito: He said, "Joe, you're on my team today." I said "Fine, let's go." So went to this little field not too far from the house and had a great football game.

Another friend from Memphis, Lamar Fike, tried to enlist but was rejected because of his weight. He went to Germany anyway, and lived with Elvis's family.

Charlie Hodge: Lamar Fike called me. And he said Elvis is gettin' a 15 day leave. He says can you – can you get a 15 day leave, Charles? And I said yeah, I think I could. I'll go see. So I went and asked my sergeant and he said yeah, you can have one. I told him that Elvis wanted me to go Paris with him.

Joe Esposito: We went on leave to Paris, France, in January of 1960 before he got out of the service. His dad, Vernon, he and I became friends and he said, "Joe, here I want to give you the money. You keep track of all the money when we get back so I know what happens 'cause usually nobody ever gives us, you know, they take the money, spend it, never get receipts back."

Charlie Hodge: And Joe did somethin' that no one had ever done for Elvis. And that's when they'd pay a bill or somethin' Joe would get all the receipts. And, Elvis said why are you doin' that? And Joe said, well you can count this off from your income taxes. Well nobody had ever done that for Elvis. I mean, all his friends, the hangs on, whatever, just spend the money and enjoy it, you know. And so he saw a man of value there.

Joe Esposito: When we came back, I gave Vernon all the receipts for all the money and paid the hotel bills, paid all the bills.

And, he was just thrilled. He had something to show him where the money went. And I, I don't know for sure but I'm sure he and his dad talked about it and before we left the service, Elvis and I took a ride in the car. Drove around Bad Nauheim.

And he asked what I was gonna do when I got out of the service. Go back to Chicago, get a job like I had before. And, he said, "Why don't you come to work for me?" And, that was a shock and that's how it all happened. From that time on I was with him.

While Joe earned the respect of Elvis and Vernon Presley almost immediately, it would take a little longer to win over Elvis's manager, Colonel Tom Parker.

Joe Esposito: When I first met the Colonel, you know, I was the only Yankee, Italian guy from Chicago, that joined the organization. Before that it was all cousins and friends that Elvis went to school with. Red West, his cousin Gene Smith, Lamar Fike. They were all from the South. And I came along, and I think Colonel didn't know me. You know, he'd never met me before and all of a sudden I'm workin' for Elvis. So, he had his concerns about me. I mean, he didn't know me that well and, you know, what is this guy doin' here from Chicago? And, all of a sudden he's sort of in charge of things and, we had a few dis– misunderstandings, in the first few months. But I think after he got to know me and I got to know him a little better, 'cause I was a little frightened of him, too. We became very good friends and we socialized quite a bit.

His army hitch over, Elvis quickly found his way back to Hollywood, but not before stopping off in Memphis to pick up a few things, and a few friends.

Charlie Hodge: Elvis was goin' to Hollywood to do GI BLUES. I was down at the train station. I, I even left my clothes at his house. And I was down there and Elvis looked down he said, you want to go to Hollywood? I said why not? I said but I don't have my clothes here. I said they're all at your house. Said we'll buy you some out there. Let's get on the train. And so that's how it started.

The new decade marked a new beginning for Elvis and his crew, as they settled into their glamorous new jobs and their fancy new digs.

Joe Esposito: We stayed at the Beverly Wilshire Hotel. Great hotel, probably the nicest hotel in Beverly Hills at that time. Had a nice suite, penthouse on the top. And then we had this other suite on the 8th floor that Elvis lived in and myself and Gene.

Charlie Hodge: And there were some residents who lived in that hotel. And we used to get into little water battles. And we'd start out with water guns, and that wouldn't be enough. Then we'd get glasses of water to throw on each other. And then we started puttin' heads on it with shaving cream. You know, just any wild idea. And we'd get – I think one time we came in, water was drippin' from the ceiling. And somebody ran down the hall and somebody had givin' Elvis an old cheap guitar and he threw it down the hall. And the lady looked out and ducked back in because went right by her head and broke it all to pieces when it hit down there. Well not long after that we begin lookin' for a house.

Joe Esposito: What Elvis liked about the house was that it was very spacious. It felt better than a hotel room, which naturally I think it would anyhow. And the pool. We'd go sit around the pool. Elvis worked out. His karate in the backyard. And, had a lot of friends over there and pool parties, swimming. And, it was much more private.

Richard Davis: Well here, here's two little country boys. We'd never been anywhere in our life. We walk in the door, and here's this big beautiful mansion. Big chande – crystal chandelier, marble hallways, stairways goin' up both sides. We walk in the house, and I know my eyes are real big. Jimmy's is big and here's all these beautiful girls walkin' around. Everyone 'em looked like a movie star. I mean, oh my gosh. You know, we've made it now. We have – we have actually made it.

Elvis inducted one member of the Memphis Mafia who stood out from the rest of the guys, because she wasn't a guy at all.

Patty Parry: I first met Elvis in November of 1960. I was 17 years old and I was with a girlfriend driving down Santa Monica Boulevard and we saw a big black Rolls Royce. And we went drove – drove up to it, to see who was in it. And it was Elvis Presley. I couldn't believe it was Elvis Presley. And we pretended like we didn't know who he was, just to be different.

PATTY PARRY
FRIEND/MEMPHIS MAFIA

And he rolled down the window and I said gee, you look familiar. Do I know you from somewhere? And he laughed 'cause he knew we, we knew who he was and we – he was going to Radio Recorders actually to record "Flaming Star," the song from FLAMING STAR.

The movie had just finished. And they gave his phone number and said come up to the house. We have parties at the house.

JOE ESPOSITO
ROAD MANAGER & FRIEND

Joe Esposito: So after awhile she was around so much she was just one of the guys. And so we didn't hide anything from her.

Patty Parry: In 17 years I have to listen to all their girlfriend problems. All their marital problems. All their sex lives. No nothing was censored. Nothing was censored. I was – they called me one of the guys, you know. But they were like my big brothers so, I mean, you don't censor from your sister, you know.

PATTY PARRY
FRIEND/MEMPHIS MAFIA

Richard Davis: We all got along great together. Well you had to or you couldn't stay in this group. Because Elvis would not have anybody workin' for him that couldn't get along with everybody else and, and fit in into the inner circle.

RICHARD DAVIS
MEMPHIS MAFIA/FRIEND

Charlie Hodge: When he started back shooting again, in movies and everything, he wanted all the fellas to become extras so they could be in the scenes.

And then, then he could look out and see a sympathetic face 'cause there was his friends out there. But we, we learned them tricks, too. And that was not let your face be seen, on camera. That way you could work every day. 'Cause once they saw you, you couldn't work no more see?

Teri Garr: They'd work as actors. They'd work as extras. They'd work as stunt men. They were his pals and there really, to be honest, wasn't that much for them to do.

Not entirely true, says Joe Esposito, especially after he took charge.

Joe Esposito: Before I came into the picture, nobody had a specific job. He took his friends with him, his relatives on tour in Hollywood. So nobody had a specific job, but when we got out of the service, he became a little more organized himself, bein' in the army. So he needed somebody to oversee everybody's specific job and that was my job to make sure people had a certain job to do. Make sure it got done. Went out – Elvis had to tell one guy one thing. He'd tell me and I would tell all of them. And basically that's what it was. I became as like – they called me the foreman. That's what it was.

Richard Davis: So when I first started with Elvis, in 1961, my capacity was basically a gofer I guess you'd say. But, I became his wardrobe manager. Which means that I, I bought all of his clothes for him, his personal clothes wardrobe. Or he – or had 'em custom made for him, or whatever. And, I was his one of his bodyguards. And I was his movie stand in, in 23 movies. So I had my hands full right there.

Patty Parry: I used to cut the guys' hair and, you know, Elvis didn't like to miss out on anything so he said to me one day he said would you come and give me a haircut? Well I panic, you know, it's Elvis Presley. I got to cut his hair. We go upstairs. He's got this fabulous barber chair. And I cut his hair. And he gave $750 for the first time. For my first hair cut, $750. I said thank you. That's great. But after that I would never take his money. I'd throw it back at him because I lived there practically, you know. He, he bought beautiful gifts. I'd eat there, you know, I mean, he took care of me. I, I couldn't take his money.

Teri Garr: And then at time Elvis was making about six movies a year, around MGM or whatever the heck he was making. And each time, they would have dancers in it. They would call us up and Elvis would send – I don't know if Joe was one of the people but all of his Memphis Mafia guys would come and watch the girls audition. And they would tell the ones that, that he wanted picked. Elvis would like her. Elvis worked with her before. So we all got hired again. I mean, not that we didn't deserve to get hired. We were also very good but it was a little bit of a, little boost in the right direction. So, which was very nice, you know. He, he was comfortable and he was loyal to his friends. Obviously he was loyal to the guys that he brought from Memphis. And, so it was very nice to be in his inner circle.

Richard Davis: Making movies with Elvis was not a job. It was a pleasure. Every day was like a holiday. Every day was fun. Now, we probably drove a lot of directors and producers to drinking, taking drugs, and having grey hair. Because we cut up on the sets more than we did any time, in any place. From the time we got there in the morning till the time we left, there was practical jokes. It could be anything from water gun fights, firecrackers, whip cream fights, you name it. Anything that could go on, we did it.

BILL REYNOLDS
ELVIS'S MAKE-UP MAN

KATHY BLONDELL
ELVIS'S MAKE-UP PERSON

JOE ESPOSITO
ROAD MANAGER & FRIEND

Bill Reynolds: Those guys always had somethin' crazy goin' on to get you during the down times, you know. The other reason – lightin' the set or whatever. And, they blew up my makeup case one time and, oh. It's just you never knew. Oh we had roman candles. I remember roman candle fights. Gol-lee. It's crazy we wouldn't get hurt, you know, with them stupid fireballs comin' at you.

Kathy Blondell: Bill had decided that we'd had enough of the fireworks and the firecrackers and everything during this particular job. So he called over to the wardrobe people and he said now look, he said, we're gonna get some pies here.

Joe Esposito: So the last day of the shoot, Bill said we got to do somethin'. We've got to get Elvis at the end of this shoot.

Bill Reynolds: The prop guys we all got together and met and we had all these pies made up. And then we had, half a dozen of the crew all lined up.

Kathy Blondell: So I remember we all kind of lined up with our pies, tryin' to hide 'em and everything and they were doin' this scene.

Joe Esposito: So the director yelled, "All right, it's a wrap."

Kathy Blondell: Pies flew from everywhere.

Joe Esposito: They all attacked Elvis. He had this blue suit on and they all just hit him with these pies.

Kathy Blondell: We were waiting man. We just buried those guys.

Joe Esposito: And they got back at him, and Elvis didn't know what to do. He was covered in pie and whip cream and stuff so, but Bill got back at him.

Bill Reynolds: Oh, that was a great one. That was over at MGM, yeah.

Joe Esposito: But, it wasn't over. So that evening, at the end of the shoot a lot of the guys would go to this little bar right around the corner from the studio and have a drink, a beer after.

So we all got together. Elvis said, "Okay, get some pies. We're gonna go over and get Bill." So we snuck around. We knew he was there. We all went in the back door, and we got him right in the bar. We just plastered him with pies. So Elvis got back at Bill Reynolds.

Pat Broeske: And it was during this period that a little bit of rivalry popped up between Elvis and his buddies, and Sinatra and his buddies. You know, they were the Rat Pack, and Elvis had, of course, the Memphis Mafia. And there actually were a few magazine spreads at the time and things like, you know, the movie magazines of the time, about is there a feud going on between these two, you know, Hollywood gangs.

Joe Esposito: The newspapers were tryin' to make a rival thing between Frank Sinatra and the Rat Pack and Elvis and the Memphis Mafia. There never was. The only time we actually were with all the Rat Pack at one time is when Elvis did the TV special in 1960 when he came back from the service. Otherwise, you know, we saw Mr. Sinatra's shows. We – Sammy Davis was a good friend of Elvis's. Dean Martin, Elvis loved Dean Martin. So there was never ever a rivalry between Rat Pack and Memphis Mafia. We were all friends.

Legend has it that the name, The Memphis Mafia, was coined by veteran entertainment reporter, Rona Barrett.

Rona Barrett: They were always around him. Dressed very nattily. And well they had to protect them. And it always reminded me of men, that we always associated with the Mafia, who were always there again around the dons. And Elvis was the don and these guys were his, his men. And because they came from Memphis, we just attached the name Mafia Memphis to them.

But I don't know if I was the very first one who did it. I do know that I used the expression, on many an occasion.

Joe Esposito: The Memphis Mafia. That title was given to us by I don't know if it was a Las Vegas reporter, 'cause we used to do that a lot in Las Vegas. We'd all pull up in a limousine or big Rolls Royce limousine, and we'd all have black suits on and black shirts and white ties or the opposite, white shirt and white tie. You know, whatever. We looked like the mob. And with sunglasses, and Elvis liked that because he was intrigued with, with the mob and he liked to be different. And so, that's what we did. Mohair suits and somebody would say, Elvis and The Memphis Mafia showed up in town tonight. Now, we never had that name and never thought of it, and we thought it was funny. We enjoyed it. It was a big kick. And I – Rona didn't come up with that name. I'm sure she, she wrote it in her articles and stuff but, no she never came up with the idea, for the Memphis Mafia.

Sandy Basset: It was very important for him to have people that he knew around him because he couldn't go out. And do things like you and I could. Because of him being so famous.

William Campbell: He couldn't even go for a hamburger in the drugstore. I mentioned, I said doesn't this disturb you that you don't have real freedom of movement? And he said oh yeah. He said, I often think that if I weren't young, I don't know if I could take this. He said, of course, I have my cousin and then we always meet somebody and the girlfriends come up and we, we eat and they send out for food for me. Anything I want. But, it is very difficult.

Sharon Sheeley: He took us to the movies. The guys would call ahead. We'd time it 10 minutes after it started.

Sandy Ferra-Martindale: Joe Esposito got out and went and bought all the tickets. And then came back. And then we waited till the movie just started and it was dark in the theater. And then we all went in and, like a, an army, you know. We took the – like one of the last rows. And we just took up the whole row with Elvis and all the guys and they all had dates.

Sharon Sheeley: I think we saw, a half an hour of it, before that whole theater started buzzing. Elvis – he, he was electric. You just knew he was there. and the whole theater – nobody was watching the movie it was just Elvis Presley's here, Elvis Presley's here. You could hear the whole theater. And he'd give that signal, which meant everybody get up, and run for it.

Sandy Ferra-Martindale: So he just stood up, snapped his fingers. The whole row got up and we left. So then I had to have my mother take me back so I could see the end of the movie.

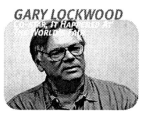

Julie Parrish: It was hard to really get close to him. Because when you would start talking to him, his gang, the Memphis Mafia, I don't know – I suspect it was set up that way, would distract him.

Anita Wood: That's one reason why I could never have married Elvis when you really get down to it because you're not alone very often. There were very few times in our life that we were totally alone. They were always there. They live with him. They took care of him. They did everything he said. And they were always there, and they were always gonna be there.

Richard Davis: We did everything together. When Elvis slept we slept. When Elvis partied, we partied. When Elvis worked, we worked. We did everything together.

Gary Lockwood: Those guys, they were from the south. They were different. I was a California guy. I'd been an athlete. I ended up playing quarterback on his football team on occasion. But, I mean, you know, they're southern guys. They're, they were tough, you know, redneck guys. What I mean by that is, I mean, you know, they were men. They, they came out here and, you know, they weren't from the theater. Or they were, you know, they were redneck boys. They wore funny little cuffs and things like that. But, you know, they were a helluv– they were good guys. I liked 'em.

Pat Broeske: The Hollywood community viewed him as an outsider. A little bit of a hillbilly, you know, surrounded by those, those guys, his Memphis Mafia buddies and stuff. And as a result of shutting him out, Elvis Presley sort of created his own kingdom in Hollywood. You know, at his bachelor pads, which became a little bit notorious for their swinging parties and that whole scene.

Joe Esposito: We had a lot of parties. But our parties were very tame. Really. They were sittin' around talking, drinking sodas. We didn't have alcohol in the house in the early 60s. He didn't care for any – no beer cans or booze.

And, we went along with it, you know. We just had fun.

Teri Garr: We went up to his house. And, I think, this is no party. This is Elvis and the guys, and they're watching TV. Or playing pool or something. He just wants to have people around him. But, you know, we're here so we'll see. You know, there's no chips and dips. There's no – it's no party.

Patty Parry: The parties were really just a lot of women there and, what we ever did was watch television most of the time. And, sometimes and my favorite times were when the guys would get together and sing gospel. I would say I'm the only Jewish girl that knows every gospel song there is. But it was mostly just socializing. And the, the funny part is that, to see who would get to sit closest to Elvis. If one girl would get up another girl would run and sit next to Elvis. And then she'd get up and go to the bathroom, another girl would sit down there. Just like – that was – that was the enjoyment of watching the entertainment.

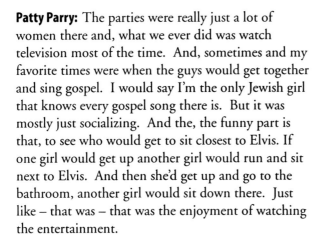

Pauline Sayers: But there was an unspoken rule. If Elvis was sat on the couch, and there was a – there was a binder at the side of him, you didn't sit there because he was either expecting somebody or having somebody come, or he didn't want anybody sitting there, for that particular night and that's what happened.

Even with all the parties, the guys would sometimes complain about being bored. To liven things up, Elvis brought a new member into their fold, a mischievous chimpanzee named –

Richard Davis: Scatter. That monkey caused more trouble than you could ever believe.

Patty Parry: And this chimpanzee was a little bastard. And he used to run up to the girls with his hands up in the air and started screeching and he – and he'd, he'd drink all the drinks that were left on the tables. And then he'd lift up the girls' dresses.

Richard Davis: He would steal the jewelry off of girls' fingers and rings and stuff. And, and he had a little – like a little pack rat. He had a lot of jewelry hid under the piano.

Patty Parry: And he liked to bite. So I was going, this was on Bellagio I believe. And I came into the den one day, and he came running up to me with his hands in the air with that screeching. Well I thought he was gonna bite me so I give him a right hook. And he flew across the room. And Elvis fell off the couch laughing. But that chimpanzee never came near me again, ever. It was funny.

Richard Davis: One night he got loose, in Bel Air. And our next door neighbors were having a party. And, Scatter got loose and, somehow made his way down to their backyard party. And he's right in this middle of this party backyard and, and he's screaming and ravin– raisin' his arms and hollerin'. And people are just runnin' everywhere. So, we, we got him – me and Alan got him we brought him back to the house. And we apologized to the people we're sorry and we didn't mean for him to get out. Well, the next day, we get a letter from the Bel Air Association. The monkey has to go or we got to go. So Elvis says okay guys, let's send him back to Memphis. So we sent him back to Memphis.

Primates aside, not everyone who knew Elvis liked the Memphis Mafia or thought it was a good idea that they were always around. Mac Davis remembers one night at the movies.

MAC DAVIS
SINGER/SONGWRITER

Mac Davis: I went out to use the bathroom and one of the gang around him came back and says, you know, I hate to tell you this, Mr. Davis but, you're not supposed to sittin' next to Elvis. I said, tell me if I'm wrong but was, was it Elvis that invited me to come down and go to the movies? He said yeah but nobody sits. He says you notice, Sonny and Red West don't even sit with him. Joe sits behind him. Everybody sits back in the back. I said well where was I supposed to sit? And he said well, with the invited guests back in – there was a row back in the back for all the, the local people. And boy I got hot. He says no, no, don't get upset. I said I am upset. I am thoroughly upset. And there was a big deal about it. The movie was lettin' out and Elvis came up. He said what's the matter? He says you look upset. And I told him what had happened. He says who said that? And I said ah, I don't want to get anybody in trouble. I just said, you know, I just think you ought to know that this is – this goes on around you all the time. I don't see how you can have a life.

SHECKY GREENE
COMEDIAN/FRIEND

Shecky Greene: I think there was – there were – he had too many people with him. When you build an entourage like that you sort of lose yourself. Everybody catering to you. Everybody saying yes. Everybody doin' this. Everybody, you know, worshipping because of the money. Everything was the – the cars that he gave to the people. The gifts he gave to people.

The watches. You know. That's wonderful but it's not natural. It's, you don't buy your friendships.

Joe Esposito: That's the way he shows appreciation. Instead of sittin' there sayin', "Listen, I thank you very much for doin' a great job for me. You're the best I need ya and all that." He'd give you a gift. That's the way he showed his appreciation.

Sam Thompson: Elvis bought a house for me. Elvis bought a couple of Cadillacs for me. Elvis bought my parents a house. He bought them a car.

George Klein: He walks over and says stick your hand out. I stuck my hand out. He drops the keys in and he says, Merry Christmas. And he said that's your gi– your Christmas gift. I said Elvis, you mean that car is for me for Christmas? And he said yep, it's yours. Merry Christmas, GK. And you could've knocked me over with a feather and I said Elvis, I'm, I'm flabbergasted. I don't – I'm, I don't – I've lost the words. I don't know what to say. And he put his arm around me he said GK, he says what is fame and fortune, if you can't share it with your friends. That kinda really blew me away.

Sheree North: You gotta have some friends that have nothing to gain by knowing you other than, your friendship. And that care about you, you care about them, you know. That kind of thing. And I don't feel that he ever had that on a quality basis.

Even Colonel Parker voiced concern about some of those close friends and their motives.

Joe Esposito: The Colonel had his suspicions about everybody that came around Elvis. He didn't know if they were takin' advantage of Elvis or what. If they were doin' the job correctly. And there were some people that did not like the Colonel.

Pat Broeske: The Colonel sees the Memphis Mafia as a threat. He sees some other Elvis hanger ons as kind of a threat.

You know, Elvis is tied in with some folks who espouse different kind of – we'd call 'em new age religious beliefs. Things like that. That's starting to kind of get on the Colonel's nerves.

Rona Barrett: I didn't understand why he always had to have these guys around him. Even to this day I've never really quite understood, because we've had many a super star in Hollywood. And none of them ever really seem to need an entourage, but Elvis did.

Joe Esposito: He didn't need all the guys around him, but he wanted them around him. He felt comfortable because, he knew them first and then hired 'em secondly. In other words they, they understood him, so he felt more comfortable with us around him.

Teri Garr: He wanted his friends around. I understand that. I want my friends around, too. Especially, you know, the, the more lonely you get the more out there in stardom. I mean, it must've been scary for him, this guy from Tupelo, Mississippi. All of a sudden having icons and Frank Sinatra and kings and queens bowing down to him. He's like, I want my friends with me from my – from Memphis, okay? I'll think of somethin' for them to do. I mean, I love him for that.

And Elvis kept his friends around as the 1960s marched on, and his Hollywood days gave way to the Vegas nights.

Joe Esposito: When Elvis played Vegas, we'd go in two weeks before opening night. Just to have a good time. And we went and saw all the other stars in town, you know. We'd go see the Sinatras, Dean Martin, the Sammy Davises, and all the big stars. 'Cause Elvis loved shows, too. He loved entertainers. Go to the lounge acts, see all the lounge acts.

Patty Parry: Last Vegas I think was his happiest time. When he got on the stage, I mean, he became Elvis Presley. It was like, there was like there's two different Elvises. The one at home is different. When he got on the stage he blew it all out man. He loved entertaining. He had the women in his hands. He had the men in his – in his hands. He just – he had the best time. He had a blast up there.

Joe Esposito: Elvis loved Vegas. He liked it because it was a 24-hour-a-day place, you know. No clocks. He didn't care what time of day it was. Didn't mean anything except when you had to work.

But even the life of a superstar can become routine.

Patty Parry: Well the life in Las Vegas was like, eat sleep and entertain. We didn't do anything really. A couple of nights we went out just to see some gospel singers. But mostly in the suite, for the whole month.

Joe Esposito: Order some food, sit down and eat, and watch TV. Elvis had a piano up there and sit and play gospel music.

Sing with all the, the musicians and the backup singers. We would do that till daylight. Then we'd all run in our rooms and close the blackout drapes and go to sleep like vampires. And that's the way it was. It went that way for 30 days. Sometimes we never saw the daylight. That's how bad it was. We looked like ghosts when we came out of that for 30 days. Didn't see the sun.

Las Vegas was the setting for one of the happiest days of Elvis Presley's life. It was there on May 1, 1967, that Elvis married Priscilla Beaulieu at the Aladdin Hotel.

George Klein: I was one of 14 people at Elvis's wedding. I was a groomsmen. It was a – it was a magical moment for me. I was very impressed and taken back and, so proud that he wanted me at his – at his wedding. And, I'll never forget it the rest of my life. It was really a moment that will go down in, in my memory bank forever.

Only two other members of the Memphis Mafia were at the wedding. And oddly enough, they ended up sharing the title of best man.

Joe Esposito: Elvis asked Marty Lacker to be his best man before he asked me. And, that was fine. I had no problems with that. A few weeks later, Elvis and I were alone. And he said Joe, you know, I changed my mind. I'd rather have you as my best man. I said well you can't very well do that. You know, you can't kick Marty out of it. I mean, you asked him. I mean, that'd be terrible. You know, we have to work together. And I said, you know, why don't we just both be best men for it? And basically that's what happened.

But there were still some ruffled feathers that day.

CHARLIE HODGE
FRIEND/SINGER/GUITARIST/
MEMPHIS MAFIA

Charlie Hodge: They had set up one room, to be it, and there was just room enough for the immediate family. And, and Joe and Marty, as best men. And I – it didn't bother me but the rest of the guys really got upset. Because they thought they was all gonna get to be at the wedding. But, but they were all at the wedding breakfast, which I thought was fine, you know.

I knew couldn't everybody be in there, but some of the people really got upset. I'm sorry they did, because it wasn't meant to upset anyone. It was just him doing – Colonel doing what he always tried to do with Elvis, and that was keeping something like that, a wedding, from becoming a circus.

Las Vegas may have been the site of Elvis's wedding and many of his triumphant concert appearances, but it was never home. Elvis always returned to the place he loved best.

PATTY PARRY
FRIEND/MEMPHIS MAFIA

Patty Parry: Memphis was where I think he was most comfortable. He had a good time in Memphis. He had – he was home, you know.

JOE ESPOSITO
ROAD MANAGER & FRIEND

Joe Esposito: When we were at Graceland, we would often go to the fairgrounds and stay all night. Elvis would invite about 100 people. Naturally, everything was compliments of Elvis. And we'd just ride till daylight. Any ride you wanted to do.

We had a ball. It was fun. The roller rink was the same thing. Movies. Elvis loved movies. You know, he wanted to see some movies and we'd call the movie theater and say we're gonna come in after it, you know, it closed at 11:30. We'd be there at 12:00. Sit there and just watch it and have a good time.

Patty Parry: The first time I got there he, he took me on a complete tour. He took me to Humes High. He took me to show me where he grew up. He took me to see Sun Records. He took me to his mom's grave. I mean, I mean, it was really, really special for me, you know. But I think he was really happy there. He was very comfortable there.

And he, he liked, you know, he – we – he liked to play, you know. We all – we all played together. It was really fun.

Richard Davis: Every 4th of July and every New Year's we'd have firework fights at Graceland. And, these became real battles. And I'm serious now. These, these were real battles.

Charlie Hodge: And we'd start out lightin' a roman candle and shootin' 'em to each other.

Richard Davis: Elvis came out with his football helmet on and his glasses. And I had a roman candle. And, I kept poppin' him in the ear with a roman candle. And it burnt his ear to almost like a piece of bacon.

Charlie Hodge: And Elvis would run away from me and I went choonk. And it went right up through the middle of his hair. And then we'd get – we'd get – we started getting like one in each hand.

Richard Davis: And then Elvis went up, and popped me in the eye with a roman candle, which almost blinded me. And I fell on the ground and I was holdin' my eyes. And I said, that's enough I stop, I stop, I stop. I quit, I quit. And he just kept poppin' me in the butt with this roman candle, 'cause he thought I was fakin', but I was really hurt.

CHARLIE HODGE
FRIEND/SINGER/GUITARIST/
MEMPHIS MAFIA

RICHARD DAVIS
MEMPHIS MAFIA/FRIEND

GEORGE KLEIN
MEMPHIS MAFIA/FRIEND

Charlie Hodge: And we learned over the years to wear gloves, snow mobile masks, you know.

Richard Davis: Too many of us started gettin' hurt so we stopped it, you know. It was fun for awhile.

George Klein: It was Christmas time, and we were all up at Graceland. And usually, the day before Christmas Elvis gave out bonuses to the guys who worked for him, and to close relatives. So just happened to be around. Of course, I wasn't working for Elvis at the time so I expected nothing. Elvis is walking around, and he's passing out and everybody thought it was their Christmas bonus. They open it up and they look at it. They look at Elvis and then make a funny face. And I opened up and I looked at it. And I looked at Elvis. And I could tell he was biting his lip to keep from laughing. And what it was was, it was a McDonald gift certificate, for two free hamburgers at McDonald's. And I said Elvis! And he said, and he – and he busted out laughin'. And everybody else was a little nervous 'cause they thought that was their bonus. And then, of course, he reached in his – in his – in his pocket of his suit and pulled out the real bonuses and passed 'em around. And then they start laughin' and clappin' hands, you know, givin' him a high five. But it, it was a fun situation.

PAT BROESKE
AUTHOR
ELVIS

Pat Broeske: There was an incident once at Graceland where Elvis caught some of the guys in his entourage, you know, looking at the video monitor, you know, which showed the fans clustered outside the Graceland gates. And they were choosing the most beautiful fans to get to come on into the house. They were choosing, you know, beautiful slim blondes and gorgeous redheads. And, you know, and they were making comments about, about the women's figures and faces and things like that.

And, Elvis came in and saw them doing this and said, wait a minute, wait a minute, wait a minute. Don't do that. Don't be that way. And he just pointed to some of the, you know, the average people standing in line. Overweight, imperfect people standing in line, clustered around. He said, bring them in. Bring them into – please don't ever do that, to people.

Joe Esposito: Nah, we never did things like that. We used to go down to the gate, yes, of course we did. We went down to the gate once in awhile, you know, if nobody had a date that night and take a walk, out of the gate and look around and see who's there. And you see a pretty girl you talk to some and you say, what are you doin' tonight, you know? And, you'd had to be a little cool about it. You just couldn't say, you know, come on up 'cause all the other people would get their feelings hurt. You know, you could say hey listen, you know, why don't you meet me down the – down the street at the coffee shop or wherever it was. And, I'll be over there in an hour and we'll have a cup of coffee and then I can bring 'em back.

Just drive in the house with 'em. And a lot of the guys did that.

Linda Thompson: Joe. We used to lovingly refer to him as Gentleman Joe, because he always was a perfect and true gentleman.

He was very loving. He was very kind. He was always very devoted to Elvis, and always had Elvis's best interests at heart.

Linda Thompson was Elvis's girlfriend from 1972 until 1976. She knew somebody who'd be just perfect for the Memphis Mafia.

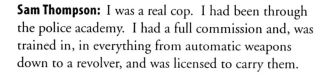

Sam Thompson: I was a real cop. I had been through the police academy. I had a full commission and, was trained in, in everything from automatic weapons down to a revolver, and was licensed to carry them.

Linda Thompson: With Elvis, everything was a family experience, you know. Elvis embraced his family wholeheartedly and with open arms. He embraced the men who worked for him as if they were family. They all traveled together, played together, shared holidays together. So he was a very familial person. And it just seemed very natural that my only sibling, a brother, who was in law enforcement in Memphis at the time, was hired by Elvis to be one of his bodyguards.

Sam Thompson: He was really crazy about law enforcement and he, he told me many times, and I'm sure he told other people this too that, that if he hadn't done what he did, that he would've liked to have been a cop.

Elvis's fascination with law enforcement made him that much more appreciative of his bodyguards.

But sometimes Elvis gave his bodyguards headaches, like the time he went AWOL from Graceland. Nobody knew where he was for several hours, until a phone rang on the other side of the country.

Jerry Schilling: And I got this call late at night. And I said who is this? And he says it's me. So I said, Elvis. Where are ya? And I forgot where I thought he said. I think he said he was in Dallas changing planes. Would you meet me at the airport? And I said well who's with you? Of course I'll meet you but who, you know, he said nobody. I said nobody? This was unheard of. Never. And it's the only time it ever happened. And he said Jerry, I don't want anybody to know where I am.

Elvis also wanted Jerry to fly with him to Washington, D.C., so he could hand deliver a letter to the White House.

Jerry Schilling: And we get there. Elvis kinda jumps out of the back of the limo. And he's got the cane. And, he wouldn't recognize him 'cause it was – it was dusk. So I jumped out the limousine and I said, you know, this is Mr. Presley. He just wanted to drop off the letter to the President. And they really warmed up when they found out it was Elvis Presley.

JERRY SCHILLING
MEMPHIS MAFIA/FRIEND

In the meantime, Sonny West had flown up from Memphis to join Elvis and Jerry. Together the three of them headed for the White House.

Jerry Schilling: They took Elvis into the Oval Room and said that Sonny and I could not go. And, we said well, you know, Elvis is pretty hard to say no to.

A few minutes later the phone rings and the President wants to see Mr. Presley's friends. And the White House aides said, you know, I've seen people leave their mothers, grandmothers. He was really impressed that Elvis had gotten us in there.

As soon as that door opened, and Elvis said come on in and I was – I, I was kind of frozen. 'Cause, it is an oval office and down at the end, I saw Nixon. He was at his desk signing something. And I, I just thought, all this stuff that's gone on in this room. And Elvis pushes me. He said don't be afraid, you know.

And so Nixon and, and Elvis both went back over to the, the President's drawers and fumbling around for stuff to – for us to take home.

Elvis had a gift for the President, too: A World War One pistol from Presley's own collection.

Jerry Schilling: Both of these men did not want this meeting exploited. And, you know, it didn't come out for like another year when the Washington Post got it. Which is amazing that, you know, we were at the White House, you know, for a few hours. And, the fact that the press did not get out for a year was amazing.

What did get out were stories about Elvis's drug use. After being fired in a cost-cutting move, Red and Sonny West bit the hand that had fed them for two decades. Along with Dave Hebler they wrote "Elvis What Happened?"

Joe Esposito: While it was being written, we were getting chapters, of it, and that's what made it worse because we knew where they were goin' with it. And that's what affected him more than anything. I think it really, personally inside, really hurt him tremendously. And, instead of, tryin' to do somethin' about it, it only made it worse. So, instead of tryin' to clean his act up he became more and more depressed.

The book was published on August 1, 1977. Two weeks later, Rona Barrett was discussing it on Good Morning America.

Rona Barrett: I had just come off the air. And, got a phone call. That they had just discovered Elvis's body and he was dead. I was in shock. Total shock. I thought for a fast moment, that we had contributed. Not meaning to but by being the first person to review this book, that laid it all out. And, people knowing that I don't make up stories. And reaching the kind of audience that I reached on Good Morning America. I thought maybe we had sent Elvis over the edge. That he thought there was no way of coming back. I will never know.

NEWS EXCERPT AUGUST, 16 1977

Reporter: What's been the reaction of the family to the allegations which have been made that the death was caused by an overdose of drugs?

Joe Esposito: It wouldn't surprise me because it always comes up with something different.

Reporter: Is there any truth?

Joe Esposito: No, no, no truth whatsoever. They come up with that report before the autopsy was even out. They, they made a statement like that. I don't know how the press does that.

Joe was then asked about the infamous book.

Joe Esposito: My reaction to them, I hope they have to live what they – what they wrote. That's all I can tell you. You have to believe what you want to believe. If you read that kind of book, that's fine.

Over the years, you know, I've been told that, you know, they – Red and – wanted to get a point to Elvis, you know, to try to clean up your life. You know, what are you doin' to yourself? And I understand that, you know. 'Cause Red, really loved Elvis.

Patty Parry: I think Red West will never forgive himself for writing that book about Elvis, because they were really, really close friends.

Almost 30 years after Elvis's death, several members of the Memphis Mafia remain close, sharing a special bond with each other, and with Elvis Presley; a friend, indeed a family member, who will never be forgotten.

Richard Davis: And the love between Elvis when we were together, you, you couldn't be – you could feel the vibes, in the group. You could feel that.

Joe Esposito: One time a guy told me, that some idiot professor did a – he saw this interview on something he says, we killed Elvis. The guys around Elvis killed him, you know, 'cause we sheltered him or whatever it was. And if I would've saw that, I think it was about four years ago. If I would have seen that I would've turned around and sued him for slander, but it's too late now. But, he was a total stranger, never knew Elvis Presley, never met him. He just assumed the guys around him were just a bunch of leeches and all we cared about was ourselves and not Elvis. That's not true. We all loved Elvis, and we were there for him, 24 hours a day. And that I want to make sure gets clear.

Patty Parry: This was the most incredible person. He was a, a wonderful boy. He was a wonderful man. He was a fantastic friend. And I was really lucky to be a part of his life. And to be part of his legacy. And I'm really proud of it, you know. I mean, it's wonderful and, and it, it's – he made me a different kind of person. He changed my life completely. And I miss him terribly.

Jerry Schilling: I'd like the fans to know, and I know they know that, he was a human being. Very special human being, but he was a human being. You know, I would like for them to have the good fortune that I had, of knowing him. In all instances, would be the guy, that they think he is. He wasn't perfect but, he was the best man I've ever known.

THE KING AND HIS QUEEN

"He said, "She's everything I've ever looked for in a woman."

— Charlie Hodge

Elvis and Priscilla. To the world, it seemed like a love story pulled right from the pages of a fairy tale. A love story only imaginable in a dream.

But every fairy tale has a dark side, and every dream can become a nightmare.

At the height of Elvis Presley's young career, he was drafted into the U.S. Army and sent to Germany.

His family, his films and his music were thousands of miles away. Just as it had at the beginning of his career, his life changed before his very eyes. But Elvis would see one more change before he was out of the army – a change that would affect the rest of his life. Just a few towns over from where he was stationed, 14-year-old Priscilla Beaulieu and her family had just moved in.

Joe Esposito: Elvis first met Priscilla in Germany. Her father was stationed in Wiesbaden, Germany. Her dad, Colonel Beaulieu, he was Major Beaulieu at that time, was there with his family, and Priscilla was there. Curry Grant, his name was Curry, not Cary Grant, Curry Grant was this– he was in the Air Force. And Curry knew Priscilla from the base. And he told Elvis he wanted to bring this young lady to meet him. So, one evening, I happened to be there, Curry brings in Priscilla. A beautiful dark-haired young lady in this like little sailor dress. I mean, she was shocked when she walked in the door, a house with all these men, just a couple girls. Anybody when they first meet Elvis Presley is in awe anyhow of him, so it's understandable.

Charlie Hodge: He went over and said, "Hello, I'm Elvis Presley." I swear, that's what he'd do when somebody new came in. You know, he was always friendly.

Joe Esposito: They talked a little bit, and he took her to the side and they sat down and visited, the two of them, for a little while. And, you know, we sorta left 'em alone because, you know, I mean she had to be nervous. I mean, none of us knew she was 14 years old at the time, because she looked maybe 16.

Charlie Hodge: That first meeting with Priscilla was something else. Like I said, he was just enraptured. And when she left that evening after it was over, he looked at me and he said, "Charlie, did you see the structure of her face?" He said, "It's like almost everything I've ever looked for in a woman."

Joe Esposito: Curry took her home that evening and asked Elvis would he like to see her again. And they communicated back and forth, yeah, and she'd come over and visit once in a while. Somebody would go down and pick her up and bring her back and visit and hang out and go to movies.

Charlie Hodge: Her father allowed it as long as she was brought over there at a certain time and brought home by a certain time.

Pat Broeske: I believe that Priscilla Beaulieu came along at a very important period in Elvis Presley's life. His mother had recently died. You know, there's a huge hole in his life and a hole in his heart. And along comes this beautiful young woman who does bear a bit of a resemblance to the young Gladys Presley. I don't think there's any question about that.

Joe Esposito: Elvis and Priscilla spent a lot of time after he met her in Germany. I mean, not all the time, because he was still in the Army. And during the week it was tough. On weekends, she would come over, hang out with Elvis, and the two of them would spend a lot of time alone. So in the Army days it was getting to know her more or less, getting to understand her. And, like I say, she was only 14, so what went on between the two of them alone together, I don't know because I wasn't there at the time. But they got to know each other a little better.

By March of 1960, Elvis's army days were over. As he prepared for his return to the United States, Priscilla begged Elvis to consummate their love the night before he left, but Elvis declined, saying, "Someday we will, Priscilla, but not now." He gave her his sergeant's stripes and combat jacket to fill his absence.

Joe Esposito: They did not have real sex until their honeymoon night. And I would believe that. Elvis was an old-fashioned type of guy. He didn't believe in that before he got married. And that's my story from the other half. Never asked Elvis that, but that's what Priscilla told me and I believe it.

The day Elvis left Germany, reporters caught Priscilla's emotional farewell to the King, sparking rumors that shot back to the States before Elvis even arrived. No one was more surprised by the rumors than Anita Wood, Elvis's girlfriend in Memphis.

ANITA WOOD
FORMER GIRLFRIEND

JOE ESPOSITO
ROAD MANAGER & FRIEND

Anita Wood: I had read a little bit about Priscilla in the papers, and he assured me that this was a child. A 14-year-old child that was the daughter of an army officer.

Joe Esposito: Anita saw the article in the paper about Priscilla saying goodbye to Elvis as he left and, you know, naturally she asked him about it. And he said, "Oh, no, just a young lady that I knew over there." And he sorta, you know, got away from it.

Elvis tried his best to quiet the gossip about his personal affairs in Germany, but it did little good.

EXCERPT FROM INTERVIEW AT GRACELAND

Reporter: There have been a lot of rumors about your love life. Did you meet anyone special in Germany?

Elvis Presley: Not any special one. Uh There was a little girl that I was seeing quite often over there. Her father was in the Air Force. Actually they only got over there about two months before I left. I was seeing her, and she was at the airport when I left. And there were some pictures made of her. But it was no big, it was no big romance. I mean, the stories came out, "The girl he left behind" and all that. It wasn't like that. I mean... I have to be careful when I answer questions like that .

Joe Esposito: He missed Priscilla. I mean, he really did. And they talked back and forth from Germany and Memphis. And I think it's like anything, when you're away from someone, you miss them more than when you see 'em all the time.

Elvis secretly began planning his future with Priscilla while continuing to date Anita Wood. It wasn't until Anita found a letter from Priscilla that she realized the innocent, teenage crush was actually a full-fledged love affair.

Anita Wood: And in the letter it said, "Please call my dad. I want to come over there, and if you call my dad, I know he will let me come. He will listen to you. I miss you. I wanna come bad." Just kept on like that. So when he came in, I said, "What is this letter? Who is this, this Priscilla? You said she was just a child." I didn't want to talk to him, I didn't want to talk. But he kept calling, and I remember when he got me on the phone, "Little, please don't tell anybody about this. This girl, she's just a 14-year-old child. It means absolutely nothing." You know, oh boy! And "She just wants to visit. It means nothing. And if you told anybody, I'd get in a lot of trouble, she's so young."

ANITA WOOD
FORMER GIRLFRIEND

In 1962, nearly two years after Elvis left Germany, Priscilla finally got her chance to see the King again. After producing a daily itinerary and a first-class ticket, Priscilla's parents approved a two-week visit to stay with Elvis over Christmas.

Patty Parry: He was going with Anita actually when I first met him. But she was in Memphis, you know, and he was in California. And Priscilla came over, and I was there. She came in, and Elvis asked me to take her upstairs and help her, show her the bathroom, help fix her hair and stuff.

PATTY PARRY
FRIEND/MEMPHIS MAFIA

Charlie Hodge: The women he was with over the years, he was really a one-woman man. 'Cause there was Anita Wood. And then he wanted Priscilla comin' over there, and when that started happening, Anita was out and nobody else.

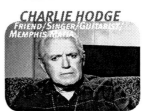
CHARLIE HODGE
FRIEND/SINGER/GUITARIST/
MEMPHIS MAFIA

George Barris: This young man brought this wonderful girl that he really loved in from overseas, and we went to the party he had up in his home in Bel Air. And all the gang was there, all the rock 'n' rollers and everything like that, but he was so respectful of her, he said, "Now I don't want you staying here with me. I would like to have you go with my dear friends Shirley and George Barris and stay with him when you're here in town. And when I get ready to go to dinner and things like that, I'll come over and pick you up with the limousine." And that's just what he did. He was that kind of a person. He was truly thoughtful and considerate of people and people around him, and mostly of Priscilla, that she was in good care.

Patty Parry: Elvis had all of the girls that used to hang out at the house, you know, the regulars. And they would sit down in the den and he said, "Look, I met this little girl in Germany, and I'm bringing her over here. And I'm really serious. And the parties are gonna stop." And the parties did stop, actually.

After a slew of late-night social bashes, a near overdose from Elvis's sleeping pills, and then a drunken New Year's Eve party, 16-year-old Priscilla returned to Germany, more in love with Elvis than ever. They still had not made love, by any traditional standard, and Priscilla began to suspect that Elvis was not as faithful as he insisted.

Joe Esposito: Elvis was still seeing other ladies too, at the time, okay? Elvis was – we all know, loved women, to be around women as companionship. Not necessarily just for sexual things or anything like that. Just he loved being around women.

Sandy Ferra-Martindale: He liked a certain kind of a girl. And in a lot of ways we were alike. We were both kinda quiet and demure sort of, in a way, back then. I'm not now; I'm a bigmouth, I talk a lot. But I was very quiet then and kinda shy. And he liked that. And we were about the same age, and we were built kinda the same. And he said some things earlier on, when Priscilla was in Germany, he said some things to my mom in regards to, you know, the wanting me to move in. And he said some things that leads you to believe– I mean, he didn't want me to go to college 'cause he didn't want a girl to be smarter than him. But ultimately, Priscilla was cuter and she got him, so what can I tell you?

SANDY FERRA-
MARTINDALE
GIRLFRIEND

Elvis and Priscilla maintained their relationship over the phone for several months, until Elvis realized he could no longer live without her. He called Priscilla's parents and begged them to let her move to Memphis under his guidance. They reluctantly agreed.

Charlie Hodge: She was still very young. And so the deal was that she would stay with Elvis's parents. And he would see that she went to school, which she did. She got a good education. And I don't believe he ever touched her till they were married.

CHARLIE HODGE
FRIEND/SINGER/GUITARIST
MEMPHIS MAFIA

Joe Esposito: When she first came to Graceland and she was living with Elvis's father and stepmother, she didn't come in and move right into Graceland. But as time went on little by little, she started moving her stuff in there. But it was trying to kept down, not make a big thing out of it, 'cause she was young. And little by little, you know, they were seen together, they traveled together, we did things together, and it was fine.

JOE ESPOSITO
ROAD MANAGER & FRIEND

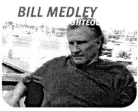

Sandy Basset: We had such wonderful times there, going to the theaters, going to the amusement park. I mean it was all late at night. But he had no choice, he had no other choice to enjoy life but to do it with his intimate friends. And we used to have these great New Years parties that were so fun. New Years Eve parties. Yeah, we'd all go down and then Elvis and Priscilla would come down to the club, you know, and celebrate with us.

Bill Medley: I was at Graceland for a couple days, and I walked in and I think Priscilla opened the door. Her hair was light brown, I believe, and up in a bun or something. And I just had never seen anybody that gorgeous. She just was absolutely stunning.

Sandy Ferra-Martindale: I don't know, I figured when she moved in there, that's a pretty good anchor. You know, that's kinda like staking your territory and laying your claim.

Priscilla eventually graduated from Immaculate Conception, a Catholic all-girls school, and her relationship with Elvis grew into more of an adult love. They attempted to lead a normal life between his films, but dating Elvis proved anything but normal.

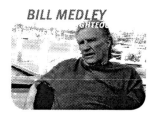

Bill Medley: Elvis used to rent the theater to see movies that he wanted to see. So he said, "Bill, we're going down, you know, to see some movies." I said, "Well, cool." And so we get out to the limousine, he said, "Bill, you get in the back."

I said, "O Well, okay." And Elvis and Priscilla got in the front. And we drove out, down to the front gate, and there was like, I don't know, 75, 150 people. They see that limousine come, they start screaming. And everybody looked in the back, thinking Elvis was gonna be in the back. And it's me in there, and I'm waving at 'em, and nobody looked in the front. We just drove right off to the theater.

George Barris: We had some great, great stories about Elvis, about all the gang got together, Chief and Joe and all, and they said, "Well, this is Christmas time." Elvis said, "Well, what can I give them, my guys, for Christmas?" And they all said, "Well, let's vote on all having El Dorado convertibles." So here I am out there searching for about seven or eight El Dorado convertibles, and then I had to ask everybody, "Well, what color do you want? Do you want red, you want green, you want blue?" Well, Priscilla, she got into the groove. She liked pink. So the motorcycle we created for her was pink with pearl and different pinstriping, and her initials in the right way, and same way with her car. So she got involved with the car action and motorcycles with him just as much, to show you how much she appreciated being a part of his life too.

Sandy Basset: Priscilla and I used to go horseback riding in Memphis. We'd go to the stables and rent horses with, you know, some of her friends. A bunch of us would go down and rent horses, and so we had a common bond there where we loved horses.

Jerry Schilling: You know, that whole thing started, it was around Christmas time, and he said he wanted to get Priscilla a horse for Christmas, and would I mind if he bought Sandy a horse and they could ride together. And I said, "No, man, she'd love it." So he said, "Okay, let's go out and look for horses."

Sandy Basset: He bought Priscilla a horse and myself a horse, and had it waiting outside, you know, the back gate of the pasture. And he said, "I have a surprise for you," and he had Cilla's Domino, she named him Domino. And then my horse. And because of those two horses, it started his love and his desire to get horses for everybody. I mean it started something that was just incredible. It went from Graceland with two horses...

Jerry Schilling: And then he and I got one, and that was the first four horses. And then of course we wound up with 37 horses and a ranch. It was a real great camaraderie type of thing, you know. Not just to ride the horses but, even though it was in the back of Graceland, it seemed like another world. And nailing up, you know, he had everybody's name on their stall, and the horse's name.

Charlie Hodge: He said, "Daddy's." He didn't say "Vernon's", put "Daddy's." "Priscilla's." "Mine."

Sandy Basset: We used to come to Hawaii and stayed in Kailua at a house that he rented. It was a dead-end street, and Elvis rented a house right up the dead-end of that street. But being in Hawaii with everybody, we just hung out at the beach. We didn't do much of anything except stay there, enjoy the beach and the swimming pool, and I don't believe we really ventured out much to go sightseeing. We just hung out on Kalaka Street, that's what it was. Priscilla and I were real good friends. We spent a lot of time together. I mean, she was a sweetheart. And I really believe that she and Elvis were made for one another. Yeah, they had a special relationship.

Elvis styled Priscilla's hair the way he wanted, dressed her in the colors and clothes he chose, and even did her makeup the way he liked. She became Elvis's doll for him to show off by his side. She started tagging along with him when he went to Los Angeles to begin a new film, partly out of loneliness and partly to keep an eye on him around certain female co-stars about whom rumors began to arise.

George Klein: Before they start a motion-picture in Hollywood, usually the stars meet and they go over a few things. Then they do the wardrobe test, then they do the still-picture test. And at that meeting, Elvis and Ann-Margret became very friendly. But while they were making the movie VIVA LAS VEGAS, they were very very close, if you know what I mean.

Danny Striepeke: It was VIVA LAS VEGAS with Ann-Margret. And, boy, what a hot pair. And I said to Elvis one morning, in fact at the Sahara Hotel, I used to go up to the room and wake him up, and I said, "That's a match for you." And I don't know whether I should say this or not, he said, he said, "Well," he said, "Wait till you meet Priscilla."

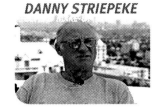

DANNY STRIEPEKE

Charlie Hodge: He told me, he said, "You know why I stopped going with Ann?" I said, "No, why?" He said, "Because I knew I was gonna marry Priscilla." So he broke it off himself. You see, he was beginning to feel things for her. And like I said, he knew he was going to marry Priscilla, so he just broke it off before it could go any farther.

CHARLIE HODGE
FRIEND/SINGER/GUITARIST/
MEMPHIS MAFIA

Elvis's film career and record sales began slipping during the mid-'60s. Poor reviews, coupled with turning 30, caused Elvis to start doubting himself, questioning the very talent that had brought him this far. His arguments with Priscilla grew more heated as a result. He even helped her pack once when she threatened to leave. Priscilla's parents began urging him to finally marry their daughter, as if to complete some contract.

Joe Esposito: I think that came more or less from Priscilla's parents, saying, "Hey, you know, she's been with you long enough, it's time to get married." And Elvis had no bones about that. He was very happy to.

JOE ESPOSITO
ROAD MANAGER & FRIEND

Lance Legault: Elvis told me on the set of SPEED-WAY that he and Priscilla were gonna get married. And I said, "Oh man, don't tell me no secrets." And I laughed, you know, it was a joke, but I said, "Don't tell me any secrets. You know, if it gets out, it could be me you think, or somebody thinks, so don't tell me no secrets!" So we finished the day's work, and I'm on the San Diego Freeway and I'm going home, it's about 6:15, and it comes on the radio, the announcement that Elvis and Priscilla are gonna get married pretty soon. And I said, "Oh geez, don't tell me," but it was alright 'cause Colonel Parker had called a press conference.

LANCE LEGAULT
ACTOR/FRIEND

It was official. Elvis, at 32 years of age, would take Priscilla, now 21, to be his wife in a private ceremony on May 1st, 1967, at the Aladdin Hotel in Las Vegas. So private, in fact, that most of the Memphis Mafia were excluded.

Stan Brosette: By Friday I guess we were told on Saturday a car will pick you up at your home at a certain hour. And the car picks us up, takes us to the airport, and only when we get to the airport and are given tickets do we know we're going to Las Vegas. And someone, one of the other young people around, said, "Oh, you know, I just have a feeling Elvis is getting married." And I said, "Oh no. No way." So we got there, we went to the back entrance of the Aladdin. At that point I did not know there were hundreds of press inside, you know, camping out on the floors, 'cause word had gotten out.

Charlie Hodge: I knew about it, because I was driving the Colonel to Palm Springs. And a lot of the guys thought I was going to Palm Springs, and we really were going to Vegas. The Colonel set that up at the Aladdin Hotel. They'd set up one room to be in, and it was just room enough for the immediate family. And Joe and Marty as best men.

Joe Esposito: They weren't allowed to come into the ceremony itself because the apartment was not big enough. And some of them were very much offended that they couldn't come in for the ceremony.

Matt Cimber: Actually I was a drop-in guest. My ex-wife and I were in Vegas and we saw the Colonel the night before, and he said, "Come on over to the Aladdin tomorrow, we're having a bash. Elvis is getting married." But the astounding thing that I remember about the wedding was that many of the people that were there had never really seen Priscilla in person. And when she entered and came down the aisle and she turned toward Elvis, she lifted her veil and they were both side view of the two looking at each other. And what was amazing was that they looked exactly alike. It looked like he was marrying a mirror image of himself.

MATT CIMBER
PRODUCER

Cassandra "Elvira" Peterson: I sometimes look at that picture of her for their wedding and think, man, she looks like Elvira. She's got the eye thing going on there and, you know, the black makeup on the eyes, and the hair, and I think I'm turning into her.

CASSANDRA "ELVIRA"
PETERSON
ACTRESS

Phyllis McGuire: Such a beautiful, beautiful couple. They were just stunning. When they walked in, I mean, everything stopped.

PHYLLIS McGUIRE
SINGER/GIRLFRIEND

George Klein: I thought Priscilla Presley was perfect for Elvis. I thought Priscilla Presley was the most gorgeous thing in the world at that time. I just thought they made a beautiful couple. You couldn't have had a more perfect couple than Elvis and Priscilla Presley.

GEORGE KLEIN
MEMPHIS MAFIA/FRIEND

Stan Brosette: There were hundreds and hundreds of photographers and correspondents camped out. And they were having the wedding reception. Only a handful of people went to the wedding, but there were 200 people or something invited to the reception, the RCA people and the William Morris Agency people and the MGM people and the Paramount people. Finally the Colonel went out of those doors into the lobby where all these press people were coming and he said, "If you're willing to leave your cameras and your notebooks, your pads and pencils outside, you can come in and be guests of Elvis and the Colonel."

Rona Barrett: So many people know that I was the one who broke the story about Elvis really gonna get married to Priscilla, and this time it wasn't a joke. I noticed that people were coming in and out, and the Memphis Mafia had new shirts, new suits, ties, things that I had never seen before them do in such a flurry. And I said to one of my staff members, I said, "This is the weekend he's going to get married. I just know it." And the next thing I knew is that there was a lot of flurry at the house in Palm Springs.

Stan Brosette: I believe that she broke the story that they were going to be married. I know that when they did get married, she was camped out in Palm Springs, because her information– Colonel was good at getting a lot of misinformation out. So Rona Barrett I think was in Palm Springs during the wedding, thinking she was going to get an exclusive there.

A week later, Elvis and Priscilla held a second ceremony in Memphis for their family and friends to attend. The movies and the music were on hold, and Mr. and Mrs. Presley tried, as best they could, to lead a normal marriage.

Charlie Hodge: Elvis had taken, he and Priscilla into riding horses a lot. And he only had like 13 acres there at Graceland.

And they would ride around on 'em. So he started looking for a place. And they found this place just across the state line down there, it was 165 acres. And this guy was willing to sell it. And Elvis bought it so he could have his horses down there and have 165 acres to ride on. But that was where we had an awful lot of fun, 'cause it was down there Elvis loved to get out, he'd wear a big ol' jacket, western jacket and his cowboy hat.

Stan Brosette: It had a beautiful lake with a huge white cross on it over the lake. And it was with red Santa Grachudis cows all over. You know, the ranch had a little house there.

Jerry Schilling: There was a little house, beautiful little cottage that had been in some magazines. Not very big but really nice, looked great on the property. And that's where Elvis and Priscilla stayed originally. And then he bought trailers for the rest of us guys.

Charlie Hodge: Elvis had bought all the guys trailers and had put cement slabs would be on out there all along the fence. And he bought himself a trailer. And one for his grandmother. And Alan Fortas, who he made like kinda foreman of the ranch, he let him and his wife live in that hundred-year-old house that had been restored and everything. He lived in a trailer. That's where Lisa Marie was conceived.

Joe Esposito: If you see a lot of pictures during that period of time, you'll see they're very happy, they're smiling, they're having a good time. And then when she became pregnant, that even made it better, 'cause Elvis loved animals and kids. He loved kids. And he just adored 'em, 'cause I know when I had my two daughters, he was very close to them. And so he was happy. I mean, he was smiling all the time, you know, they were having a great time. We had the ranch in Mississippi, and it was like a whole new little group thing happening.

Dr. Lester Hoffman: She seemed to develop more of a personality as she got older. But when I knew her, she was just a young lady just as– matter of fact, I knew her before she married Elvis and I knew her after the wedding, we were invited to the wedding reception. And she seemed to develop after the wedding much more so. She was just a young girl before that. Young pretty girl.

Stan Brosette: When Elvis and Priscilla were expecting, they had me bring Vernon Scott out and broke the news. Told him so he could break the news and release the story.

But the honeymoon had to end sometime. Just when Elvis was finally enjoying his new, quiet life on the ranch, Hollywood called, and he reluctantly returned to the studios to begin yet another film.

Jerry Schilling: I think, number one, he didn't want to go back and do a mediocre movie. And that's what was next on line. He was just enjoying being there with everybody. He had just gotten married. Elvis and Priscilla were very happy at this time. And he wasn't ready to go back, and then the pressure started about, you know, time to go to work, time to get back to Hollywood.

During Priscilla's seventh month of pregnancy, apparently from out of nowhere, Elvis suggested a trial separation. He packed some things and left, only to return two days later with an apology. His films were now laughably being booked as second-features. It was a long, dark cloud that was only lifted by the birth of Lisa Marie on February 1st, 1968 – nine months to the very day of their wedding.

Charlie Hodge: I never will forget when we was going to the hospital, when she felt she had to go and have the baby, and Jerry Schilling, I said, "Now Jerry, where are we going?" He said, "Methodist Hospital." I said, "No Jerry, Baptist." He said, "Charlie, I swear, I thought –" I said, "Jerry, let me be wrong. You drive to the Baptist Hospital."

Jerry Schilling: We had done a trial run to the Methodist Hospital. Nobody told me anything different. Somehow, through some meeting, they changed to the Baptist Hospital. So I'm driving to the Methodist Hospital and Charlie's sitting beside me, and Charlie said, "No no, it's the Baptist." I said, "Charlie, I did the trial run. You weren't even here." And then Elvis said, "No no, Jerry, I forgot to tell you we changed it."

Charlie Hodge: And then on the way there to the hospital, we had a phone in the car, and– Was Johnny with me? I can't remember. But whoever was there, I said, "Call Joe." And so, "Call Joe." He was in Los Angeles.

Joe Esposito: I got a phone call when I heard Priscilla was on the way to the hospital to have Lisa Marie. So I told, I forgot who called me, it was either Jerry or Charlie, I said, "Tell her to hold on till I get there." So I got the first plane out, I flew from California to Memphis, and somebody picked me up at the airport and took me right to the hospital. I got there before Lisa Marie was born. So she did hold out for me. She kept her legs crossed.

Jerry Schilling: Elvis is this big iconic figure to everybody. And, you know, to us guys and family and whatever, I mean, here's the guy that we sat in the waiting room with while he's waiting for the birth of his daughter. Here's the guy we laughed with, we cried with. We were all like brothers, you know.

Sandy Bassett: When Lisa Marie was born, it was a very special time for all of us, because here this little baby was gonna be coming home to Graceland in a little while. I mean, we'd all been waiting for this special moment, Elvis's and Priscilla's first little baby, you know.

Joe Esposito: Well, after Elvis and Priscilla did get married, things changed a little bit. And after Lisa was born – this has been talked about before, but I think Elvis had this thing about Oedipus complex or something like that, I don't know what it is. It's like they're making love to their mother type thing. And I mean, I can't say for sure, but that's my feeling.

I think their, their passionate life together wasn't as well as it was before Lisa was born. I mean, it hurt the relationship, very much so.

Elvis soon realized that although he was a superstar, a husband, and now a father, he was also going broke. He sold the Circle G Ranch, returned to Hollywood, and filmed what would be the last of his movies.

Elvis Presley: When you get right down to the nitty-gritty, isn't it a pity that next big city. Not one little bitty man let me coulda been a little bit wrong.

Marlyn Mason: I remember him bringing a picture of Priscilla and the baby, and she was on the floor with the baby, she was kinda on her side like this, and the baby was laying right in front of her. And I remember Lisa didn't have any clothes on. It was just a beautiful mother and daughter picture. And I couldn't get over how beautiful Priscilla was, because I'd always seen her with the big hairdos. And her hair was just straight and loose, and she was absolutely stunning. She was as beautiful as he was handsome. And I thought what a couple they make. She never came to the set, however. I asked him one day, I said, "Does Priscilla ever visit?" And he said, "No."

MARLYN MASON
CO-STAR, THE TROUBLE WITH GIRLS

Pat Broeske: He expected her to, you know, be locked up within the gates of Graceland while he went out and cavorted around the world. And, you know, she became, you know, like many women in the 1960s and 1970s, more assured, more independent, fiercely independent, and found out she could do some things on her own. She's a pretty savvy businesswoman in her own right.

PAT BROESKE
AUTHOR

Priscilla enrolled in dance classes in Los Angeles, where she fell into a brief affair with her teacher. She was crying out for attention, but Elvis was too far away to hear.

Joe Esposito: We were hearing little rumors around that Priscilla was dating her dance instructor. And we couldn't believe it.

A lot of the guys, "Oh, that's not true, that's just stories and all that." But we didn't talk about it too much 'cause when I heard it was happening, I didn't believe it. Said, "No, there's no way." Come to find out it was happening.

JOE ESPOSITO
ROAD MANAGER & FRIEND

Mary Lou Ferra: She wanted to be a star. He found out that she was taking lessons in Graceland. She had a coach come in and give her lessons, you know. And yeah, she wanted to be a star. You could tell. That's why she married him, to get up there too.

MARY LOU FERRA
FRIEND/OWNER, RED VELVET LOUNGE

Priscilla's requests for more passion and affection from Elvis slowly became a hindrance to what would be the rebirth of his career.

JOE ESPOSITO
ROAD MANAGER & FRIEND

Joe Esposito: He was happy, she was happy, and we did a lot of vacations, traveled to Hawaii, Colorado, up into Vail, Aspen. I mean, there was a lot of great times. They enjoyed the company, had a lotta good times together. But then, it started to change. And Elvis went back on the road, '69. Before that, we were in Hollywood making movies, we were together a lot more, so it was a little more normal at that time. But then when we hit the road, it completely changed again. Now we were traveling a lot, so we weren't making movies anymore and we were just gone 250 days a year. And that's tough. And we didn't bring any of the wives together on the tours. Once in a while, but we were too busy. You know, when we're on tour we did a show every night, a different city every night. It's not like you had to drag along the wife, because it's too hectic at the time. So we didn't bring 'em along.

SANDY BASSET

Sandy Bassett: When the guys were away on tour, the girls were the ones who — we did fun things together, whether it was going to the movies or shopping or just hanging out at home. You know, but we did things together and we — she welcomed all of us. I mean, we were all her friends.

PAT BROESKE
AUTHOR

Pat Broeske: I think the realities of what he's able to do at that time are starting to diminish, for one thing. You know, he has an exhaustive concert schedule. And you have to remember, he's not just playing Vegas, you know, one weekend every six months. He's playing it for months at a time. You know, the man is booked.

MADISON SQUARE GARDEN PRESS CONFERENCE

Reporter: Are you satisfied with the image you've established?

Elvis Presley: Well, the image is one thing, and human being is another. You know. So...

Reporter: How close do they come? How close does the image come to the man you are?

Elvis Presley: It's very hard to live up to an image. Put it that way.

Elvis proved himself to be the King of Rock 'n' Roll once again, but it was difficult to return to the lifestyle of loving husband and humble father when the crowds were again shouting his name.

Patty Parry: He was a wonderful father. But, you know, you also have to realize that his lifestyle was not conducive to having children. You know, he was up all night and slept all day. So he'd play with her late in the afternoon. He was a great father. He lavished her with fur coats and stuff when she was like three. But he loved her, he did, he really loved his daughter.

PATTY PARRY
FRIEND/MEMPHIS MAFIA

Charlie Hodge: She had some children her own age to play with. And Elvis slept all day. She just more or less ran wild.

CHARLIE HODGE
FRIEND/SINGER/GUITARIST/
MEMPHIS MAFIA

Jerry Schilling: Lisa would get by with stuff that nobody else could get by with. And, yeah, she's kinda got that personality like her dad.

JERRY SCHILLING
MEMPHIS MAFIA/FRIEND

JOE ESPOSITO
ROAD MANAGER & FRIEND

Joe Esposito: Things were getting tough. We were always traveling all the time. Even off the road. When we got back home, we'd all take off. All the guys would go to Palm Springs, say, "We've gotta get away, we're working hard," and left them. Left obviously Priscilla, and she would be home. They knew that we were out fooling around. My ex-wife, all the other guys' wives and girlfriends, I mean, we were a wild bunch of young guys with this life we were leading. And it was getting to her.

She got a little more held back and they had more fights, but not out in front of us. I think she had too much respect for Elvis to get in a big fight in front of the guys. So I mean, I did hear some screaming and yelling in the bedroom once in a while. Couldn't hear completely what it was about, but I'm sure it was about not giving her enough time and attention for her that she deserved.

That's a tough life. And, you know, and us being around, all the guys around all the time, his buddies, I mean it's not a way to have a good married life. Somebody there all the time, no intimate times to themselves, not that often.

There were times that, you know, just the two of them would be around. But it changed. It got harder for her.

Between tours, Elvis and Priscilla tried working their problems out. She knew Elvis was having affairs on the road, but he would never admit to it. They decided to take a vacation, hoping to patch things up, but the events that unraveled from there would eventually sour the rest of their marriage.

Joe Esposito: We were on vacation in Hawaii one time, Elvis, Priscilla and all of us. And there was a karate tournament going on in Hawaii. Ed Parker was having this karate tournament over there, and we went to see this thing 'cause Elvis was very much into karate at the time. And there was a fighter in this tournament, his name was Mike Stone. Great fighter. Probably one of the best karate people there ever was. I mean, he was great, he was fast, he was quick. Elvis thought he was wonderful, and we all did. So we said hello to him, met him after the show, and that was it. But then we were in Las Vegas, Elvis was performing there, and Phil Spector, the record producer, came to see Elvis's show. And he came backstage, and it just so happened his bodyguard happened to be Mike Stone, the karate guy that we saw in Hawaii.

JOE ESPOSITO
ROAD MANAGER & FRIEND

And Elvis was more interested in Mike Stone than he was in Phil Spector, so they started talking, you know, and talking about karate, and Mike said, "I'm teaching karate in Los Angeles" and all that. And he said, "Priscilla, you should take karate from this guy. He's great." So that's what really happened. She started taking karate lessons from Mike Stone in Los Angeles when we were out of town. And as time went on, little by little, they started dating, on the side naturally. And I didn't know about it, nobody knew about it, and then rumors were starting to get around. And somebody said something to me about "Did you know that Priscilla and Mike are dating?" I said, "No, come on. No way. It wouldn't happen. I know Priscilla. She would never do that." And lo and behold, later on we find out that she was.

Sheila Ryan: I mean, what's a man gonna say? His wife runs off with somebody. He's living a double standard, like anyone in his position would then and still does now. Not maybe as much, but... You know, it was okay for him to be with anybody and everybody that he felt like being with, but when she became independent and fell in love with someone else, it killed him.

Joe Esposito: Priscilla was upset, you know, that Elvis was never home, out running around the country, dating different women.

And she confronted Elvis with it. She told Elvis about it. She came to Las Vegas, we were performing there, and took Elvis into the room and they talked. And she told him about it. She said, "I'm dating Mike Stone and I want a divorce." So Elvis wanted to find a Hit Man to have him killed and started lookin around.

One day Red went and in and told him, he said, "Okay, I found somebody to do this." And Elvis thought about it, "Well, okay, I'll let you know." Because he would never have done that. I mean, Elvis was mad and upset but he would never have somebody killed.

Priscilla and Lisa Marie permanently moved to their Los Angeles house, where she continued to date Mike Stone during his divorce from his current wife. Elvis, although saddened and heartbroken, continued on with his touring, falling deeper and deeper into the arms of prescribed drugs and other lovers.

Linda Thompson: He had been deeply, deeply hurt by what he perceived as Priscilla's betrayal of him, and having another man involved was all the more painful. It would've been one thing if she'd said, "I don't like your lifestyle," but having another man involved was tremendously destructive to his ego and to his perception of relationships and marriage.

Patty Parry: When I heard Priscilla was divorcing Elvis, I could understand it completely. You have to realize, a girl that gets married to Elvis and she's living in a house with eight other guys, with their wives, with their girlfriends, it's not conducive to a happy life.

Sheila Ryan: He would say that he didn't love her, that he kind of made a promise when she was very young and he kept his promises and so he married her. But yet he had a certain sense of ownership that I think, you know, destroyed him. And the fact that she would go on without him, his ego could not handle that. So he had mixed feelings. I mean, I don't know that he was honest with himself if he was saying that he didn't love her. You know. But he did say that.

Patty Parry: I think he loved Priscilla, and he always found girls that looked like her afterwards. But I don't think marriage was the right thing for Elvis. You know, he loved women too much.

Even though Elvis and Priscilla rekindled their friendship some time after, the love they once shared for one another had truly ended. Elvis filed for a divorce on January 8th, his birthday. It was the gift that kept on giving, as you'll hear in this live performance from 1974.

Elvis Presley: The thing I'm trying to get across is, we're the very best of friends and we always have been. Our divorce came about not because of other men or another woman but because of the circumstances involving my career. And it was just an agreement that I didn't think it was fair to her. So therefore, we just made an agreement to always be friends and be close and care. Well, after that, I got her a mink coat. She got me – listen to this – a 42-thousand-dollar white Rolls Royce. That's the type of relationship that we have, you know. It's not a bad setup, is it, fellas?

Christina Ferra: I know that he wanted very much to have a special marriage. He had an idealistic view of what his marriage would be like. And he very much wanted to have a woman who was his wife who was a virgin, who was just in love with him. When his marriage failed and that family fell apart and his child, you know, wasn't with him all the time anymore, I think that really took a lot of his steam away.

Shecky Greene: I don't know Priscilla, but I just, from the things that I watched and I perceived about this girl, I think it would've been nice if he woulda stayed with her. I don't know what their problem was. But I could've settled it. I would've called her Mademoiselle Goulatwash and they would just – everything would've been fine.

Elvis immersed himself in his concerts, substituting his adoring audience for the loss of his marriage. Priscilla continued raising Lisa Marie in Los Angeles, introducing her to a lifestyle that didn't primarily consist of over-indulgence and pampering. Lisa alternated between the sane and the surreal, by living with Priscilla then staying with Elvis.

Myrna Smith: Lisa Marie. She was a doll. But she was... She could maneuver us pretty well. 'Cause she was so cute. She walked on her tippy-toes and she would come into our dressing room and hang out. And we formed a little club, and she was our treasurer. And we'd put a quarter in at every meeting and she would hold the money. And we'd never see it again.

In the early afternoon of August the 16th, 1977, as Lisa Marie waited for her father to awaken to say goodbye, a horrifying discovery was made. Elvis Aron Presley, at the age of 42, was found dead in his Graceland bathroom.

Elvis Presley left his father Vernon to act as executor of his estate until Lisa Marie reached the age of 25.

Vernon, while in ill health, made a surprising decision that would forever alter the course of the Elvis Presley estate. He chose Priscilla to succeed him as executor, and handed over the entire Presley fortune to her. When Elvis died, a new Priscilla was born.

PAT BROESKE
AUTHOR

Pat Broeske: Were it not for Priscilla Presley, for all we know, Graceland would've been torn down by now. You know, and all that Elvis memorabilia, you know, reflecting his life and times, for all we know, parts of Graceland would be offered on Ebay or something. Instead, you know, she turned it into a thriving – you know, it's a tourist mecca. And in many ways, I see Graceland as a symbol of an astounding American success story.

Priscilla's business sense was only part of her blossoming rebirth. After trying her hand at modeling, she ventured into acting, something she had always wanted to do. The television show "Dallas" would be her start.

After five years in television came Priscilla's film debut in the blockbuster "NAKED GUN." It may have been destiny that brought Elvis and Priscilla together in 1958, and it may have been fate that divided them in 1973, but the absolute love they shared for one another will forever reunite them in the hearts of millions... for eternity.

MY BOY

"THE COLOR OF TRUTH IS GREY"

— ANDRE GIDE

Colonel Tom Parker wasn't really a Colonel, his first name wasn't really Tom, and his last name wasn't really Parker. Other than that, much of what you've heard about this colorful character is also shrouded in mystery.

Joe Esposito: He never really talked too much about his early years. I never even knew he changed his name till I read it in a book or I saw it in a newspaper someplace. Somebody said, you know, he was Van something. I don't even know the name. I just know him as Colonel Tom Parker.

Although he claimed to have been born in Huntington, West Virginia, Andreas Cornelius Van Kujik came into this world on June 26th, 1909, in Breda, Holland.

Loanne Parker: When the Colonel was a young man, he was always big for his age, he said. Tall. He was six feet tall. Although in later years he became a bit stooped. But he was about six feet tall. And when he was a young man in Holland, one of his jobs was carrying big rounds of cheese from the factory on to the barges.

When he was 20, Andreas stowed away onboard an ocean liner and entered the United States an illegal alien. He immediately joined the U.S. Army and set aside his Dutch heritage to take the name of his commanding officer, Thomas Parker.

Paul Gongaware: It all seemed, you know, it all seemed kind of, you know, strange that he felt the way he did, that maybe somehow he didn't belong here or somehow in the end it wasn't totally legal for him to be here. I never understood that part of it, but that was part of the Colonel.

Joe Esposito: I asked the Colonel sometime after Elvis passed away, I said, "I never knew you were a non-citizen." He said, "Well, Joe, I served in the army for two years. And that made me a citizen 'cause I served in the Army of the United States." And he says, "Nobody ever asked me." He said, "If somebody had asked me if I was a U.S. citizen, I would've said no."

After leaving the Army in 1932, Parker was hired as a barker with a traveling carnival called the Johnny J. Jones Exposition. It was a job that would have a far-reaching influence on the rest of his life.

A.C. Lyles: He was like the barker in a circus, y'know, the barker in the circus say, "Step right up, folks, the big show is on the inside."

A.C. LYLES
PARAMOUNT PRODUCER

Joe Esposito: Oh, Colonel loved to talk about the carnival days. I mean, he felt very proud about that. He was more or less the P.R. guy for the carnivals that he worked with. But he did everything. He was a barker, he did the games, he sold hot dogs. And there's a famous story about the canaries. He had these sparrows and they would spray 'em yellow and sell 'em as canaries. Canaries were too expensive, but sparrows were free. So that's what they'd do, they'd spray 'em and sell 'em. Then the dancing chickens, another famous story.

JOE ESPOSITO
ROAD MANAGER & FRIEND

Paul Gongaware: They would throw down some chicken feed on this hot-plate, and the chickens would like – it was hot, and they were dancing around, they were trying to eat the chicken feed at the same time.

PAUL GONGAWARE
CONCERTS WEST ASSOCIATE

Joe Esposito: They'd be jumping all around. Those are funny to us.

JOE ESPOSITO
ROAD MANAGER & FRIEND

Julie Parrish: He was a con man. He was a man who wasn't even here legally in this country. He was a man who did a carny show by putting, he had a dancing chicken act, he put this chicken on a hot stove and made it jump around. And he called it the dancing chicken. What else can you say?

JULIE PARRISH
CO-STAR PARADISE HAWAIIAN STYLE

By now, Parker had married Marie Mott Ross, whom he'd met while working with the carnival in Florida. One legend that dogged Parker all his life had to do with a patent medicine of questionable repute known as Hadacol.

PHYLLIS McGUIRE
SINGER/ELVIS'S GIRLFRIEND

Phyllis McGuire: We first became aware of Colonel Parker when we were touring Texas. And we looked on the billboards, and throughout Texas there were these huge signs "Drink Hadacol." My uncle, who was an ordained minister, said to my mother, "You know, I feel so much better lately because I have started drinking Hadacol. It really makes me feel great." So we found out later that Hadacol had a high percentage of alcohol. I thought that was funny. But, oh, Colonel Parker was at my house with his lovely wife, and I said, "Oh, here we go. I have to tell ya, I always think of you as the Hadacol man." And you know something? He didn't really wanna hear that. He bristled a bit.

GLEN CAMPBELL
SINGER/ELVIS'S FRIEND

Glen Campbell: After selling Hadacol, I guess he figured he could sell anything.

JOE ESPOSITO
ROAD MANAGER & FRIEND

Joe Esposito: Colonel Parker had nothing whatsoever to do with Hadacol. He told me many times, "Joe, I don't know where they come up with these stories. I know nothing about Hadacol. I never had a bottle in my hand."

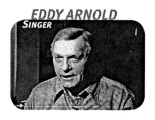

EDDY ARNOLD
SINGER

Eddy Arnold: He had nothing to do with Hadacol. The reason I'm saying that, they tried to hire me. He wouldn't let them have me as a performer.

By the early '40s, Parker had begun a new career as a manager for up-and-coming singers, another job that would have far-reaching consequences.

JOE ESPOSITO
ROAD MANAGER & FRIEND

Joe Esposito: He managed Gene Austin, country singer, very famous country singer back in the '40s. And then he handled Eddy Arnold and he managed him.

Eddy Arnold: When we'd be in a town and there'd be a circus or whatever it happened to be, he'd take me and introduce me to these people. I met people that I never thought about meeting that was in the circus business. Because he was an old carny. And they help one another. They really do. They help one another. And he did.

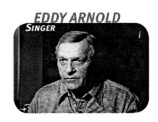

In 1948, the Governor of Louisiana bestowed on Parker an honorary military title. Parker immediately announced to his assistant, "From now on, see to it that everyone addresses me as the Colonel." In 1953, Eddy Arnold, in a move still shrouded in mystery, sent the Colonel a telegram, informing him that his services were no longer required.

Joe Esposito: I don't know how Eddy and the Colonel split. All I know is they remained friends till Colonel passed away.

Eddy Arnold: Yes, I did the eulogy for him, and would do it again today.

Around this time, a young singer from Tupelo, Mississippi, was just starting to make a name for himself down South.

His manager was a young disc jockey named Bob Neal.

George Klein: Bob Neal was still managing Elvis at that time. He was a Memphis disc jockey. And he got Elvis on these shows because Elvis was making some noise in the South.

Joe Esposito: Now I think Bob knew though that he couldn't handle him, 'cause he didn't know what to do with him. He didn't know where to go with him. And I think he realized Colonel Parker could take him to far better places than he could've.

In 1955, the Colonel's assistant, Oscar Davis, informed his boss that this Presley fellow was worth taking a look at.

Joe Esposito: When Elvis came along, Colonel was not managing anybody. Okay? He more or less had shows, he put country shows around, Hank Snow and stuff like that. He was booking shows around the United States. And if I'm not mistaken, somebody mentioned to him, I can't think of who it was, about "I saw this kid at this club one time. You've gotta see this kid. You should book him on one of your shows." So Colonel Said, "Okay, we'll try him out." So he booked him, and Colonel didn't even see him. Then he went to the show and he saw the reaction.

George Klein: Elvis sometimes had to come back for two and three encores because they just wouldn't leave. Finally, at the end of those tours, they put Elvis on last.

Joe Esposito: And eventually he had to be the closing act because even Hank Snow got mad about that, when Elvis had to open a show for him, and then eventually he was opening the show for Elvis.

George Klein: But he knew that the reaction from the audiences was pretty strong, so he did his homework, did his research, and found out that Elvis's contract was coming up pretty soon.

Joe Esposito: He worked on Elvis about becoming his manager. And that's basically what happened.

By early 1956, the Colonel, who wasn't even Elvis's official manager succeeded in switching Presley from the relatively obscure Sun Records label to more prestigious RCA and arranged for him to make his national television debut.

Elvis Presley: Last year, in '55, my manager was Bob Neal, who's a disc jockey in Memphis. And we organized Elvis Presley Enterprises and had an office. But when I signed up with Colonel Tom Parker in Nashville, we didn't figure we needed the office anymore, so he's handling everything out of Nashville.

On the Ides of March, 1956, Colonel Tom Parker signed Elvis Presley as his one and only client, although "signed" might not be the right word.

Richard Davis: There was never a contract signed between the two men. It was a conversation, a gentleman's agreement, and a handshake. And throughout all the years that they were together, they both honored that contract.

George Klein: It was more, much more than manager and artist. It was like surrogate father, best big brother, uncle, or something to that effect. Colonel Parker actually got pretty close to Elvis. And so Elvis really went along with almost everything Colonel Parker suggested, because Colonel Parker had gotten him to the top, kept Elvis on top. So he more or less followed the direction of Colonel Tom Parker. And they were very good friends in addition to Colonel Parker being his manager.

Having conquered records, radio, and television, for which he received 25 percent of Elvis's earnings, Parker arranged for Presley to take on Hollywood, once again using his persuasive managerial style to swing an unprecedented deal with the studios.

Joe Esposito: Before Elvis Presley, nobody ever got a piece of a movie. They got a salary and that was it. Colonel was the only man that started where artists got a piece of the picture. So that changed how a lot of other managers and agents started doing that with other stars. Colonel was always very tough when it came to money. "I want my money up front," because he knows by the end, that when he goes through all the bookkeeping in Hollywood, you never get a dime on the percentage you got coming. So he always said, "I want it up front." That's why Elvis Presley was the first man to get a million dollars a picture, plus a piece of the movie.

Rona Barrett: If I ever saw the Colonel – and I saw a lot of the Colonel in Palm Springs – I would always ask him about something, and he'd say, "Ma'am, I don't know anything about the other side of Elvis's life. You wanna talk to me a little bit about the business life, I can tell you everything about the business life. And please know that I have 50 percent of everything he makes."

Pat Broeske: The deal was outrageous. The deal was outrageous. In fact, it's outrageous back when Elvis was getting 50 percent of the profits for his movies. 'Cause Elvis of course is not really getting 50 percent of the profits for those pictures because of the way his deal is structured with the Colonel. The Colonel is becoming fabulously wealthy.

Loanne Parker: Colonel Parker never took 50 percent of Elvis earnings. Never.

Rona Barrett: The Colonel always was bringing him movies in which there was a great deal of music and singing, and I'm quite sure it was all for financial reasons, because it was either publishing that they could own or there were records that they were involved with that could make money from. And the Colonel was always interested on one level from the financial point of view.

Joe Esposito: Well, Elvis, everybody blames everything on everybody else, but ultimately it's Elvis, it's Elvis Presley. He makes the decisions. I'm sure he did not make a lot of right decisions in his life either, but he's the one that could've made the change. Nobody else could make the changes. Even Colonel Parker couldn't make changes. 'Cause if Elvis stood his ground, Colonel had no choice.

Glen Campbell: He should've let Elvis do what Elvis wanted to do, because Elvis knew what he wanted to do and that was play and sing.

Paul Gongaware: He always let Elvis make the creative decisions. He would present him with opportunities and Elvis would say yes or would say no. "Do you wanna do this movie, do you wanna do this script, do you wanna do these songs?" All those creative choices were Elvis's.

A.C. Lyles: Elvis had finished a picture, and I said, "What do you do next, Elvis?" And he said, "I don't know, the Colonel hasn't told me yet."

Loanne Parker: He never interfered with the creative part of Elvis. He said, "Elvis is the star. He knows exactly what he's doing. I'm not gonna tell him what to sing or how to dress or how to act. He knows how to do those things. I just do the business part."

STAN BROSSETTE
PUBLICIST, MGM STUDIOS

Stan Brossette: The Colonel was Elvis. If you wanted to pay respects to Elvis, you paid respects to the Colonel, and that was it.

The Colonel was a great buffer. If the Colonel approved of you, everything was cool.

PAUL GONGAWARE
CONCERTS WEST ASSOCIATE

Paul Gongaware: Oh yeah, there were always people that wanted to meet Elvis, all these dignitaries and politicians that wanted to meet Elvis. Colonel just had a simple answer: No.

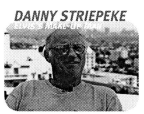

DANNY STRIEPEKE
ELVIS'S MAKE-UP MAN

Dan Striepeke: The guy was – you know, he played the homespun part; he was so far from that, of course, as we know. He was brilliant.

Hal Kanter: He was one of the sharpest con men that I've ever run across.

HAL KANTER
DIRECTOR, LOVING YOU,
BLUE HAWAII

A.C. Lyles: Every time you'd see Colonel Parker, he'd be reaching in his pocket and sticking things in your pocket. He'd be putting a button on your lapel.

Red Robinson: I noticed that on one side of the ground, fairground, it's "I like Elvis" buttons, and the other side it's "I hate Elvis" buttons. And what do you think of that, Elvis? He said, "Well, everyone's got an opinion." But did you look at the back? And one of the guys turned over and said, "Oh, for crying out loud. Elvis Presley Enterprises. On both of them."

A.C. LYLES
PARAMOUNT PRODUCER

By the late '60s, Elvis's popularity as a box-office draw was slipping, causing the studio brass to rethink his contract.

RED ROBINSON
HALL-OF-FAME DJ/FAN

Hugh O'Brian: Colonel Parker thought for a moment, he said, "You know," he said, "you're absolutely right. My boy may not be around too much longer, therefore I think we oughta, since this is probably gonna be his last film, we oughta double the price." And he got it. He said, "You started the negotiation." As I understand it, Colonel Parker walked out of that meeting getting twice as much as Elvis would've gotten if he'd stayed just under the normal contract.

HUGH O'BRIAN
ACTOR/FRIEND

Joe Delaney: I was there, yes, with some of the deals that the Colonel made. He was a very shrewd bargainer. You know, he paid a lot of dues, the Colonel. Come up, you know, in the old carny days when you really had to be on your toes every second.

JOE DELANEY
CRITIC, LAS VEGAS SUN

Joe Esposito: Men did like Colonel, 'cause he was a strong individual and he did great business deals and he was very smart. He did a lot of things. And women, Colonel was not real warm with women.

JOE ESPOSITO
ROAD MANAGER & FRIEND

Marlyn Mason: Yeah, he was not an approachable person. I didn't care for him, I guess, because he wasn't a... He was just different than everybody else on that, you know, connected with the movie. He was very standoffish.

MARLYN MASON
CO-STAR, THE TROUBLE WITH GIRLS

Sheila Ryan: Elvis had a dream. And the Colonel just cashed in, didn't care about Elvis's dream. Cared about the cash, cared about the Colonel. And if a man's dream dies, then so does the man.

SHEILA RYAN
GIRLFRIEND

Valerie Allen: I was worried also about the Colonel. And he said, "Oh, my personal life is my own. The Colonel just directs my career." And of course now we see that's not true at all. He was behind everything.

VALERIE ALLEN
ACTRESS

Myrna Smith: He liked to bluff people, see how scared you'd be of him. Then when you weren't, then he said, "Oh well. This is one that won't take my bluff."

Joe Esposito: But once he got to know you, he loved kids. He loved, you know, he was very friendly to all our wives and girlfriends once he got to know them. Animals. Loved animals. So any person that loves animals and kids has gotta be, you know, have a good heart. I mean, it's true. And Elvis loved animals and kids too. But he loved women too.

Loanne Parker: Colonel Parker played practical jokes but never to hurt a person. I've never known him to do a joke that was harmful to the person. He was very sensitive about people's feelings. Colonel was a moon child. They have a great sensitivity.

Bill McKenzie: There were a number of cases when we're in the office and somebody would call, and he would answer the phone not as Colonel Parker but as an anonymous assistant.

Loanne Parker: "Is this Colonel Parker's office?" Colonel says, "Yes." "Who is this?" "This is Sam Ferguson." "Oh." And you could hear her in the background talking to her friends saying, "I've got Colonel Parker's office on the phone. Sam Ferguson answered the phone. Is Elvis there?" "No. No. But he just left. Hold on and I'll see if I can catch him before he gets to the elevator." And he puts the phone down and we're all sitting there just, our mouths are open. He picked up the phone, he says, "I'm so sorry, I just missed him. But I tried. Try later."

Red Robinson: "Howdy hi. Hi, this is the Colonel." I said, "Colonel, it's Red Robinson in Vancouver." "Oh yeah, Red, how are ya?" I said, "Well, Tom Moffat told me to call Elvis's room." "Ya just missed him." I'll never know, but to this day I think Elvis was in the room. But I recorded my conversation with the Colonel.

RED ROBINSON
HALL-OF-FAME DJ/FAN

TAPED CONVERSATION

You know, I was wondering if it would be possible to talk to Elvis. Maybe not, but he said you're the man to call.

Colonel Parker: Gosh, I wish you'd have called about 10 minutes ago. He just left.

Red Robinson: Oh, for crying out loud.

Colonel Parker: He just walked outta here.

One of the more amusing manifestations of Parker's sense of humor was a rather exclusive club he founded himself.

Steve Binder: For those that don't know, the Snowman's Club was a fictitious club that the Colonel was president of, or chief potentate I think he called himself. And it was strictly for anybody who was great at knowing how to B.S., you became a member of Colonel Parker's Snowman's Club.

STEVE BINDER
PRODUCER 1968 COMEBACK SPECIAL

Loanne Parker: Colonel was the most high potentate of the Snowman's League of America. And our slogan was "Let it snow, let it snow, let it snow." I'm sure you've heard of snow jobs.

LOANNE PARKER
COLONEL PARKER'S

Paul Gongaware: So people that he thought were good snowmen he would invite him. And he was the chief potentate of the Snowman's League of America. So there was a long period in there where we didn't even call him Colonel, we called him Potentate.

Loanne Parker: It was so much fun to see new members get their book, because they were excited about it. And they would start and they would look at the first part and they would read a few basic rules, and then they'd come to this section that was all blank pages.

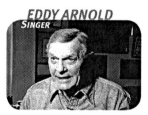

Eddy Arnold: He was promoting when he handed you a book with nothing written down on the pages. He took you. You know?

Loanne Parker: When you can read everything on every page, you're a real member. And they would give him this look, "What is this about?" And then he would say, "A real snowman reads between the lines."

In 1967, Elvis married Priscilla in Las Vegas, a city that would have great significance for both Elvis and the Colonel.

Matt Cimber: The Colonel said, "Come on," and nudged me, he said, "Come on." Where was he going? He loved roulette. And roulette was his game. And we went out, he bought about 50-thousand dollars worth of chips, which at that time I think was about 1967 it was, and 50-thousand dollars was a big buy. And while he was playing, he said, "This is the luckiest casino for me." So I always suspected that that's why he selected that one to have the wedding at, because it was a good chance for him to get out. And by the way, he lost the 50-thousand.

Although gambling would prove to be a worrisome vice, Parker had no problem avoiding other temptations.

Joe Esposito: I used to drive him sometimes from L.A. to Palm Springs to his home, we'd stop halfway down there, he'd say, "Joe, stop and get a beer." Well, I never knew the Colonel ever to drink. So I said, "Okay, so let's split a beer." We'd split a beer. Apparently, he never ever said it, maybe he was one of those guys when he was young that when he drank he was a completely different person. I had that feeling about it. So he knew that he couldn't drink. And that was the only time I ever saw him have anything with alcohol.

JOE ESPOSITO
ROAD MANAGER & FRIEND

Paul Gongaware: You know, I don't recall that the Colonel ever drank. But he did enjoy a great cigar. And we always had cigars on tour.

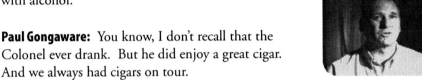

PAUL GONGAWARE
CONCERTS WEST ASSOCIATE

In 1969, Elvis began performing at the International Hotel, signifying the official start of his Vegas years.

Loanne Parker: I first met Colonel Parker in 1969, in the spring of 1969, when he came into Las Vegas to sign the contract for the opening at the International Hotel. And the hotel wasn't even opened at that time. It was still under construction.

LOANNE PARKER
COLONEL PARKER'S WIFE

The romance bloomed because Colonel and I were kindred spirits. We had a personal relationship before we had a working relationship. At that time his wife was suffering from what they now would call Alzheimer's. She didn't always even know Colonel. His life was– it was a sad life, at home.

Steve Binder: You could go to Vegas with him when Elvis was there, and he might stay up all night in a casino or just at the hotel and go get two hours sleep. And the rest of us, who were a lot younger than the Colonel, would just be dragging. And he would be full of pep.

STEVE BINDER
PRODUCER 1968 COMEBACK SPECIAL

Loanne Parker: When they were filming THAT'S THE WAY IT IS at the International Hotel, the fans from the back had started to move forward and he was about to be mobbed. And Colonel jumped up, ran up, picked up Elvis, and put him on the other side of a barrier. And I sat there, I absolutely could not believe it. He came back, sat down like nothing had happened. And I said, "Colonel, you're back. Are you alright?" And he said, "I had to help him."

With Vegas now his center of operations, the Colonel was able to indulge his vice with even more passion than in earlier years.

Joe Esposito: Colonel liked to gamble. When we first started playing Las Vegas – I mean, we didn't know this till we went to Vegas and started playing there. And I'd see him at the roulette wheel. And he said, "Joe, sit down, play." We'd play some roulette, you know. And little by little, I think he got hooked.

Shecky Greene: You know, he was gambling, and when you gamble, you'll sell your mother. I didn't sell my mother for too long.
Just two days I sold my mother. She overcame that.

Steve Rossi: Colonel Parker was a tremendous gambler. I mean, when Elvis was working at the Hilton Hotel, he lost literally millions of dollars. And that's why he booked Elvis in there a lot of times. And I don't think Elvis ever really knew how much money that was being taken from him.

EXCERPT FROM A LIVE PERFORMANCE

Elvis Presley: My manager Colonel Tom Parker, where is he? Is the Colonel around anywhere? No, he's out playing roulette. Don't kid me, I know what he's doing. Him and Cosby out there talkin' mash and drinkin' trash or whatever.

Despite Elvis's kidding, there may have been some genuine frustration behind those words.

Sandy Ferra-Martindale: If the Colonel would come in the room, I mean, it was like, you know, "Anything, you know, whatever you want."

And then as the years wore on and as the relationship deteriorated, we'd be in Vegas seeing Elvis and he would, for spite, sing the songs that the Colonel hated the most, just to make the Colonel upset. And the Colonel would be outside gambling Elvis's next paycheck.

Joe Delaney: I think the Colonel kind of boxed him in. The feeling I had about Elvis is he wanted more of a life, and he was having less of a life. They were a great match. But like all good matches, there came a time when the Colonel should've eased. And I don't think he did.

Joe Esposito: Colonel and Elvis had a big fight one time, and Colonel walked out. He said, "I'm through, I'm outta here." It was in Vegas at one time. And he said, you know, "You get somebody else." And that went on for about a week, 10 days, and I think Elvis said, "We've gotta get somebody else to manage me. And let's talk to Tom Hulett, see if Tom will handle me." And Tom was one of the concert promoters, he was Jerry Weintraub's partner in Concerts West. And Elvis liked Tom tremendously. And Elvis even talked

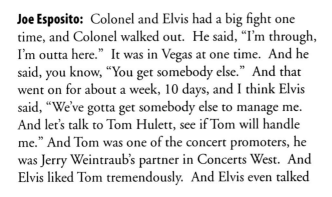

JOE ESPOSITO
ROAD MANAGER & FRIEND

to Tom Hulett about taking Colonel's place. And Tom said, you know, "You can't do that. Colonel's your best manager. He knows you and he's with you, stuck with you all those years, and he's the best guy for you."

Some members of Elvis's backup band were treated to the Colonel's special brand of eccentricity.

JERRY SCHEFF
MUSICIAN

Jerry Scheff: I was down in the dressing rooms. It was that long hallway. And we were the only two down there, and the Colonel was walking this way and I'm walking this way. And he did one of these numbers, just passed me like this. Didn't even acknowledge I was alive. And I thought, "God, what did I do? What did I say, you know?" So I asked, I think it was Red West, I asked somebody, I said, I told him what happened, and Red started laughing, he said, "Oh," he said, "they had a meeting last night, and the Colonel found out how much you were making." And he told Elvis, he said, "Boy, I could put chimpanzees on the stage with you and the people'd still love you." And he never said a word, as far as I know, I know he didn't say a word to me for five years.

One up-and-coming singer-songwriter got a first-hand taste of the Colonel's peculiar ways.

MAC DAVIS
SINGER/SONGWRITER

Mac Davis: Somebody said, "The Colonel wants to meet you." And I said, "You're kidding." And I said, "Okay." And I went over there. And he says, "You the boy that wrote this song?" I said, "Yes, sir." He said, "What's your name?" I said, "Mac Davis." He says, "Bend over here and let the Colonel rub that curly head of yours." And I said, "Excuse me?" And all the Memphis boys said, "Hey, let him do it." So I did it, and he rubbed my head and he said, "Now you can tell everybody that Colonel Parker rubbed your head. You're gonna be a star."

Steve Wynn: He was constantly calling me on the telephone and giving me advice, at the Golden Nugget and at the Mirage and at Treasure Island, and then never made it to Bellagio, but at the Mirage. And he always knew what was going on. He once called me up and said, "Steve, I want you to take out a pencil. Now you know I don't give you any bad steers. You know I can spot somebody when they're coming." I said, "Sure, I know that, Colonel." He said, "Well, I'm gonna tell you one. Now you mark this down. It's a girl. First name Celine, C-E-L-I-N-E. Last name Dion, D-I-O-N. Like the singer. Now this girl's from Canada. She's got a voice the size of the Empire State Building. She's gonna be a giant star. You figure out how to make a connection, get this girl to work at the Mirage." I never could quite convince him that I had Siegfried and Roy there, you know, that I couldn't just push 'em out.

STEVE WYNN
LAS VEGAS HOTEL OWNER/ FRIEND

Ever the savvy businessman, Parker understood the value of keeping the fans happy.

Paul Gongaware: "Put your butt in the seat." And what he was saying is, is "Look at this from the perspective of the fan. What does that fan want? What does that fan expect? That's what I want you guys thinking about and that's what I want you guys doing."

PAUL GONGAWARE
CONCERTS WEST ASSOCIATE

Loanne Parker: So many times, he would see a fan standing in line and maybe recognize the fan as being a hardcore loyal fan, and he would walk them through the line and say to the maitre d', "Where are you going to put these people?" And the maitre d' couldn't say anything but, "The best seat, Colonel." Colonel would wait to make sure they got a good seat.

LOANNE PARKER
COLONEL PARKER'S

Joe Esposito: Yeah, I remember Colonel Parker starting out selling programs, pictures, hats, different things of Elvis at the concerts. Well, a lot of other groups, managers, were saying "Ah, how could he do that, so tacky" and all that. And all of a sudden they realized there's a lot of money in that situation, and all of a sudden everybody, every concert you go to now, you got t-shirts, sweatshirts, and programs, everything you can think of. And the prices are big. You know, a t-shirt you can buy for a dollar, they're selling it for 20 bucks.

Elvis's talent and the Colonel's promotional magic succeeded in conquering Vegas, but how to bring that powerhouse combo to the rest of America?

Bill McKenzie: There was this manager named Jerry Weintraub who lived in New York that had this desire to promote Elvis Presley.

And he, it took him several years, he kept hounding Colonel Parker.

Jerry Weintraub: I used to call every morning. "Good morning, Colonel, it's Jerry Weintraub. I wanna take Elvis on tour." And every morning he said to me, "What are you ..You're crazy. Why do you keep calling here? You're wasting your money." This went on for one year. And finally one morning he said to me, I called him and he said to me, "You still wanna take my boy on tour?" I said, "Yes." He said, "Okay, you be in Vegas tomorrow at 11 o'clock with a million dollars, and we'll talk." I hung up, and I said to my wife, "You see? I told you I was gonna get Elvis Presley." She said, "Well, you got one little obstacle here, you know. You owe the bank 65-thousand dollars as it is. You know? Where are you gonna get a million dollars?"

Bill McKenzie: There was a gentleman named Steve Weiss that knew Concerts West and also knew Jerry Weintraub, and he was the one that put Jerry Weintraub together with Concerts West. And again, we had the two elements he didn't have: we had the experience and we had the money.

Jerry Weintraub: I spoke to the guy and I said, "Can you please send me the million dollars right away." He said, "Well, what am I gonna get for it?" I said, "I'll give you half of the money I make in the concert business forever."

Bill McKenzie: My boss, Lester Smith, and I went to the U.S. National Bank in Portland, Oregon, and used our line of credit to wire the funds to Las Vegas.

Jerry Weintraub: About an hour later, I had now called the Colonel and pushed my meeting to two o'clock. He said, "I'll give you till two." I said, "It's on the way, the money is on the way. I just need a little longer." And he said, "Okay, I'll give you till two." So, the money came in. And this fellow came out from the back, the president, he said, "Can you come in my office?" I went into his office. And he said to me, "There's a check here for you for a million dollars made out to Elvis Presley. I can't believe this." I said, "Well, that's what I'm waiting for. Like can I have it?" So he said, "Yes, yes. What are you gonna do with this?" I said, "I'm gonna take Elvis Presley on tour. Gonna do a tour." And he said to me, "Can you use an accountant? I'd like to leave here and go with you." So I got the money, went to the International Hotel, got to Tom Parker, and I found him – couldn't miss him – he was sitting with a cigar and his cane and his hat on and he had more chips on the table than anybody else. And I said, "I'm ready, I have the million dollars." I knew at that moment in time, and I was only a young boy, you know, I was in my twenties, I knew that my life had changed. That my life was never gonna be the same. 'Cause I now was gonna be in business with the biggest star that had ever been. The only thing Elvis Presley ever cared about, to have his fans in the first 20 rows. He said, "Don't put those big-shots in the front. Put 'em in the back."

Steve Wynn: After they had been doing the concert tour and Jerry had gone from being penniless to being a wealthy guy, he met the Colonel out west. And the tour had been going on for about six months or five months. And Jerry had a million dollars in the bank for his part. And the Colonel had two briefcases. He opened them up and they were filled with money. Money. Jammed with money. "One's mine and Elvis's, the other one's yours. Which one do you want?" Jerry says, "But Colonel, I've already been treated generously on the concert tour. The tour operator doesn't usually have anything to do with the sales of the novelties." He said, "A partner's a partner, Jerry. Which one do you want? You decide." Colonel took his cane and he hit one of 'em, closed the other one, said, "That's yours." Jerry Weintraub says that's the single greatest moment of his life.

Paul Gongaware: "Elvis! Elvis! Elvis! Live!" You know, "Bloomington, Indiana, live, Elvis! Elvis! Elvis!" It was like, it was the strangest thing. You know, it was just a guy pressing really hard. And he bought spots all the way across the board so everybody in town knew about it. He was the guy who really sort of invented the way of putting shows on sale now where you put everything out front or you put a big punch out front so people know when it's going on sale.

Loanne Parker: Colonel was totally dynamic. Colonel didn't stop thinking. He was twenty-four-seven for Elvis. He was a perfectionist.

Jim Mydlach: He was a man that expected a lot of things from you. But he was also a very very fair man.

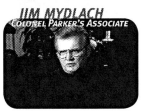

Red Robinson: Somewhere in the mid-'70s, when Elvis came back on another road tour, I went to Seattle again to see him. He never came back to Vancouver. And while I was there, there's warmup acts and then there's an intermission. And I looked down, and who's out there selling programs? Who's out there hawking stuff in the front of the stage, but Colonel Parker. So I go down and I talk to him. He said, "How you doing, Red? I'll be very happy if you buy something."

Hal Kanter: He was always trying to get me to do something for him for free. He said, "If you do my biography, you're gonna make a lotta money. It's gonna be an automatic bestseller." He said, "Immediately gonna be a bestseller." I said, "How do you know that?" He said, "Because I'm gonna sell advertising in the book." I said, "What?" He said, "Yeah, the book is gonna– I've already sold the back cover to RCA, and I'll sell the front cover to Paramount Pictures. So the book is paid for immediately, so every dime that comes in now is pure profit." And he said, "I've also got a title for it." And I said, "What's the title?" He said, "The title is How Much Does It Cost If It's For Free?" I said, "Pretty good title." And I said, "Let's talk about making a movie out of your life." He says, "I can do that." I said, "And I got the ideal guy to play your part." He said, "Who's that?" I said, "W.C. Fields." He said, "Thank you very much," and never mentioned the subject again to me.

Paul Gongaware: The Colonel was very generous. We always got a tour bonus at the end of the tour. And even if we didn't work on that tour or didn't do much or whatever, we always got a bonus at the end of every tour. The lowest guy to the top guys, he made sure that everybody was taken care of.

Glen Campbell: Well, he was a jerk, man, you know. He never let Elvis go out of the country. I mean, you don't want to talk about people, deceased people, but he couldn't go with Elvis to England, he couldn't go with Elvis out of the United States 'cause he didn't have a visa. He was here illegally. And that's why Elvis Presley never went out of the United States.

Joe Esposito: Colonel said, "There's no stadium big enough for Elvis to play there indoors." His idea, which was toward the end of Elvis's – you know, before Elvis passed away, there was talk about them going over there and doing one stadium but do it for 30 days, stay in England, and he figures there'll be people from all over Europe would fly in to see Elvis there. So there was talk about that. And he also said, "Joe, I didn't have to go with him. Tom Hulett and all those guys. I didn't have to go.

JOE ESPOSITO
ROAD MANAGER & FRIEND

Shecky Greene: I think Parker, he really had a tremendous concern at the beginning about Elvis. But I think later on it just became a piece of meat.

SHECKY GREENE
COMEDIAN/ELVIS'S FRIEND

Joe Esposito: You had to be there to understand the whole situation. It was a very unusual situation.

Loanne Parker: We were touring, and he came back to the room one night and he was crying. He said, "I've lost him. My friend is gone." It was because he went to have a meeting with Elvis and Elvis couldn't be roused for the meeting. We all have weaknesses. We all have failings. And Colonel understood those in Elvis. He tried every way he could to help Elvis overcome it, but it was not possible. I would want the fans to know that he cared about Elvis, always.

JOE ESPOSITO
ROAD MANAGER & FRIEND

LOANNE PARKER
COLONEL PARKER'S WIFE

Joe Esposito: I'm sure it was very frustrating to the Colonel too, at times, you know, seeing what was happening to Elvis and not looking as well as he should, not taking care of himself. He tried. And people don't give Colonel Parker credit for that. But Colonel never talked to anybody about that. What Colonel and Elvis talked about was between the two of them.

JOE ESPOSITO
ROAD MANAGER & FRIEND

Dick Clark: I will get into a controversy here about Colonel Parker, who was not one of my favorite people. I thought he was the epitome of a bad manager. I did not like the Colonel and I'm sorry what he did to Elvis.

On August 16th, 1977, the Colonel's only client died at the age of 42, the victim of his own excesses. Parker, like everyone else, was devastated by the news, but rebounded in the days and weeks following Elvis's passing.

Joe Esposito: Well, I mean, the whole world changed for a lotta people, Colonel Parker too, when Elvis passed away. You know, I think he figured Elvis was his one and only big star and he'll never manage another one ever again. I mean, a lotta people came to him to ask if he would handle them, and no, he didn't, he wouldn't do it. But he'd give advice to a lot of people. I mean, there was a lot of stars and different celebrities that became friends with the Colonel, and he'd give them advice. But I mean, Colonel, he talked about Elvis as being around, actually, after he passed away. You know, "We gotta make sure Elvis is taken care of, make sure people say positive things about him."

Tony Orlando: "Colonel," I said, "you okay?" He said, "No no, really, I have an idea. Now have you ever watched CBN?" I said, "Sure." He said, "Well, you see, that's a big thing, you know. You would be great on CBN." And I said, "Colonel, are you asking me to become Reverend Tony Orlando? Is that something? Am I hearing this correctly?" He said, "You got it! Precisely!" I went, "Case is closed, lunch is over, you need a doctor. Outta here." I had to leave. He said, "No no no no, really. I can see it. We'll open a church, you'll be–" I said, "Colonel..." He said, "We will sell more bibles..."

Bill McKenzie: You know, I have a lot of fond memories of Colonel Parker. He was very interested in me as an individual and concerned and, you know, so he's somebody I really cared for and actually, you know, I loved the guy.

Loanne Parker: He played Santa Claus for the children at the Christmas parties. Many times we would be eating in the restaurant and he'd see an old couple eating a very meager meal, and he would call the waitress over and say, "Tell those people I'd like to buy their dinner. Maybe they could order a little more." He was always doing things like that. He gave hundreds and thousands of dollars to charities. Always with the stipulation: no publicity.

Ken Wynn: I guess the most poignant story that I can talk about to do with, you know, the sensitive side of the Colonel is, about two years before he died – and you have to understand that at that time it was very difficult for the Colonel to walk and everything – he calls me up one day and he says, "Come on, Kenny, we're going to the circus. I got great seats." And he went down this 150 or so odd steps, a great great deal of pain and suffering to himself, to get to our seats and watch this whole thing. And then coming back up, I thought he was gonna collapse. I mean, his face was filled with beads of sweat. And he just did that out of his concern and his caring for my kids.

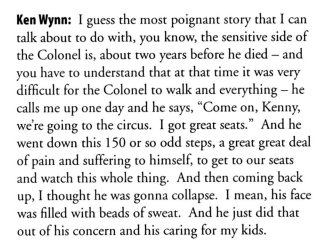

Steve Wynn: My brother became very close to Colonel Parker and stayed that way, as you know, until his death. Kenny was one of the guys that did the eulogy for Tom when he died.

Ken Wynn: A lotta times I think he felt misunderstood, particularly, you know, in the later years when he would see some of these things that were written about him, things that were written about his relationship with Elvis and, you know, the way the business of Elvis was handled.

JOE ESPOSITO
ROAD MANAGER & FRIEND

LOANNE PARKER
COLONEL PARKER'S WIFE

MATT CIMBER
PRODUCER

Joe Esposito: Well, I'll put it this way. If Colonel Parker heard all those stories about the Colonel screwing Elvis and make bad decisions as far as career goes, he never mentioned it to me. I could see the Colonel hearing about it but never doing anything about it. He would just, just let it go, because he knew, he'd been around the business long enough, they're gonna say something about you no matter what; if it's good or bad, they're always gonna talk about you.

You can't let that bother you.

Loanne Parker: Colonel was always hurt by the way the tabloids talked about him.

Matt Cimber: In his later years, he was around with the guys around the casinos, and we'd sit and have coffee and just talk. He was, at the end, he seemed very lonely and despondent.

Joe Esposito: Colonel once told me, he said, you know, he was thankful that he lived as long as he did. And he did say one thing though, he said, "If it wasn't for my wife Loanne," he said, "I would never last this long." 'Cause she really took care of him. And she inspired him and kept him happy and always took care of him well. And I think he really felt great about that. And, I mean, I miss the Colonel too. I mean, he was a character, one of the smartest people in the world, nice human being, people don't realize it. Very considerate. He loved people. I wish people could really have met him, instead of what they read about him.

On January 21st, 1997, Andreas Cornelius Van Kujik, alias Colonel Thomas Andrew Parker, died of a stroke. He was 87 years of age and had outlived his legendary client by two decades.

Red Robinson: I don't think you'll have a partnership like Colonel Parker and Elvis ever again. The world's changed. It's totally different. I mean, artists today, they burn through managers about every two weeks. That was a special association.

Steve Wynn: You know, they changed the world. And normal people can't do that.

Joe Esposito: You had to be there to understand. Elvis was not easy to handle. And Colonel Parker was the only man that could've handled him. Another manager could've handled him, but would not have done as good a job as Colonel Parker did. But I'm not saying, like I said before, Colonel made a lotta mistakes too. But overall, nobody could handle Elvis Presley better than Colonel Parker.

Ken Wynn: Elvis was "ELVIS!" in capital letters with an exclamation point because of Colonel Parker. Obviously he had a great talent, but the Colonel made it happen. And he made it happen the right way and he made it happen big. And it was because of the Colonel. I mean, some of the people that I see that manage artists today, if they were managing Elvis Presley, Elvis Presley wouldn't have been "Elvis."

Joe Esposito: It was like they were meant to be. Just Elvis and the Colonel. I couldn't see another manager with Elvis.

EXCERPT FROM MADISON SQUARE GARDEN

Colonel Parker: Thank you very much, and I'd like to say he's a nice guy. This is it, folks.

COLONEL PARKER,
THE QUIET STRENGTH BEHIND THE KING

Elvis Presley's manager stood quietly in the wings
Taking care of business, leaving Elvis to sing.
His name was Tom Parker, better known as "The Colonel",
In the first year together, their profits made The Wall Street Journal.

The Colonel was a quiet man, not one for the limelight
His whole focus was Elvis, promoting him day and night.
Content to remain behind the scenes, giving no interviews
He was a mystery to the media, misinterpreted in the news.

When it came to business, The Colonel was very tough
Some presumed that he was mean, with an attitude so gruff.
He was blamed for preventing Elvis from touring overseas,
When the obstacle was really crowd control and security.
Plans had been made for a '78 concert in Wimbledon UK
Sadly, it was not to be, for in 1977 Elvis passed away.

Those who knew The Colonel, knew the rumors were untrue
They remembered him as a kind man, with a sense of humor too.
He used to be a carny, and told a story from those days
How he made chickens dance, by placing a hot plate under the hay.
The story was made up, he was just testing peoples' response
But some believed him, and the press repeated the nonsense.

They said he was an illegal alien, could never leave the U.S.
They forgot all about the 1956 Canada tour, I guess.
Accused of cheating Elvis, stealing more than his share
A money hungry man, who did not seem to care.
In truth, Elvis and The Colonel were like father and son
Two trusting partners, a manager and his star, his only one.

The world's greatest manager, of the world's greatest star
His achievements outnumbered his mistakes, by far.
A genius when it came to negotiating skills,
Signing his boy Elvis to many first time deals.

Before Elvis and The Colonel came along
The recording companies chose the songs.
The singers were never given a choice,
But The Colonel changed that when RCA signed his boy.
Sound track albums, photo inserts, Elvis souvenirs
All of these things were Tom Parker's ideas.

When Elvis became an actor in the 1960's
No artist received an advance payment for a movie.
The Colonel worked out a deal, unheard of back then
With Elvis receiving payment before the filming began.

In '61, Colonel learned while reading the news
Of plans to build a memorial to the USS Arizona crew.
The program had been halted, due to lack of funds.
Deciding that something needed to be done,
He organized the first high profile benefit concert
Convincing the Navy Brass it was worth the effort.

Though not a real colonel, the Navy boys saluted him
As he handed out Elvis photos to all of them.
One hundred thousand dollars was raised from the concert
Elvis and The Colonel paid expenses out of their pocket.

Tom Parker proposed an Elvis show, televised live
It was the first world-wide concert, viewed via satellite.
The performance was held in Hawaii January 14th, 1973.
Viewed by over one billion people in 40 countries,
A sum of 75,000 dollars was raised from the proceeds,
Donated to the cancer fund in memory of Kui Lee.

If The Colonel was greedy for money, as some say
He would not have given thousands of dollars away
Through regular donations to his favourite charities
Which he did while insisting there be no publicity.

The Colonel sent the Vegas Hilton a giant floral bouquet
From "Elvis and The Colonel", every year on Mother's Day.
While dining out, he was known to pay the tab for a stranger's feast.
When driving, he stopped to give to the less fortunate on the street.

August 16th 1977, on receiving word that Elvis had died,
The Colonel took those who were with him aside
Saying, "Though he's gone, we're still working for him.
It will always be Elvis and The Colonel till the day I die.
I don't want to see anyone getting emotional and such,
Let us show Elvis respect, and make him proud of us."

Prepared for a concert tour, he was staying at a hotel
He had packed his touring clothes, that served him well
He never wore a suit, and he knew Elvis didn't care
About the clothes that his manager chose to wear.

He attended the funeral, without a suit and tie
His face lacked expression, no tears did he cry,
Leading to rumors that he was an uncaring man
Not knowing The Colonel, they did not understand.

Other stars wanted him to manage them, after Elvis died
Having represented the best, he politely declined.
He was asked to write an Elvis book, and to give interviews
He knew that they only wanted dirt, and so he refused.

In January 1997, at age 87, The Colonel passed away suddenly.
At the time he was working as a consultant for an Elvis movie
The bond that they had shared was eternally tied
It was "Always Elvis and The Colonel till the day he died."

by Marion Lindsay, April 4th 2006

KING OF HEARTS

"I DID LOVE ME TENDER, AND LOVING YOU, LOVING HER; LOVING ANYBODY I COULD GET MY HANDS ON AT THE TIME."

— ELVIS PRESLEY

Elvis Presley is known throughout the world as the undisputed king of rock 'n' roll. The only Elvis legend that could possibly surpass his music is that of his many loves.

At the Rainbow Roller Dome in Memphis, an unknown Elvis met 15 year old Dixie Locke. She would be his first true love.

DIXIE LOCKE-EMMONS
HIGH SCHOOL

Dixie Locke-Emmons: Elvis and I first met in, uh, January, '54. He was, of course had already graduated from school and I was in school, a sophomore at Southside. I had tried to tell my mom and dad about him, you know, that he was a little different from the other guys and, uh, but when he came, they were very, uh, leery. They weren't sure that I was even supposed to go with him that night. And my curfew that night was shortened extremely. I think we had like an hour, hour and a half before we had to be back at the house. Elvis and I talked about getting married, uh, almost from the time we started dating. We uh knew that that was what was supposed to be. And we had talked about it from the very beginning. By the time of my junior prom in '55 he was of course on the road a lot. I'll always remember that because he was in Texas I believe during Louisiana Hayride at that time.

And I was so afraid that he wasn't gonna get back in town for my prom. And his mom and I had actually been shopping and she had bought my dress. He was unknown. He wasn't – he hadn't been singing in clubs and the few people who heard his name, he was like unknown, you know. And just overnight he was there. And it was just phenomenal.

With Elvis's career taking off, it wasn't long before he ventured into motion pictures, which in turn led to romance with actresses both on and off the screen.

TAB HUNTER
ACTOR/SINGER

Tab Hunter: I was working with Natalie Wood, uh, on a number of films but on one she had met Elvis. He had met and dated quite a few very attractive gals – Stevenson and of course Natalie. And Natalie and I were in New York doing the Perry Como Show and we were walking back to her hotel. She was staying at the Essex House and I was staying at the Gotham. She was going on and on about Elvis and I was getting a little annoyed about this, a little jealous here. And the hotel sign said E S S E X House, all over

Broadway. The E S, the lights were out, so it said, "Sex House." And I said, "Don't tell me he's going to come and visit you at the Sex House. And she took her purse and went wham and just hauled off and belted me. I'll never forget that. He had some wonderful gal friends. Uh, Natalie was crazy about him. I mean he had a way, he had a magnetism, he had a charm.

TAB HUNTER
ACTOR/SINGER

While filming JAILHOUSE ROCK, Elvis demonstrated that charm to some of his co-stars.

Gloria Pall: I did my bumps and my grinds, and I moved around and I winked at him from the stage, and I did a whole dance routine. But they were not interested in my dance routine. It was a setup for Judy Tyler's entrance into the nightclub where she sits down next to Elvis. So they didn't really feature me, but they caught the bottom half of me. Right after the movie was made I understand that there was a blowup of that photograph of Elvis looking up at me through my legs, which is funny because I was always being photographed for my bosom, you know. This was the first time my – my legs were ever, became so famous. Elvis is standing there on the side and he's looking me over, checking me out. I was looking really great, you know, a 10; now I'm a 20. I'm a, what you say, my torso's a little more so but that's okay. I can handle it. So he comes over and I reach my hand out, extend my hand. He takes my hand and he brings it up to his mouth. I thought he was gonna kiss my hand. Instead he sucked every one of my fingers, sucked it very sensually, licking his tongue up and down each finger. He said, "Listen," he says, "when we go to lunch," he says, "I wanna take you to lunch." I says, "Okay, great, why not." And maybe that's the way Elvis met everybody, every woman.

GLORIA PALL
ACTRESS, JAILHOUSE ROCK

In 1957, Elvis met starlet Valerie Allen at Paramount Studios.

VALERIE ALLEN
GIRLFRIEND/ACTRESS

Valerie Allen: We had heard on the lot it was very small, it was very family like, everybody knew everybody, that Hal Wallis had signed this country singer named Elvis Presley. I'm walking into the lot, and I look over and I see the most handsome young man that I think I've ever seen in my life at that time, or maybe ever. Anyway, the set was closed, and there was a break. The red light was on and everything. And in comes Elvis on his bicycle with a cameraman, a set cameraman next to him. And he comes over and says, "I," just announces, "I wanna take your picture, honey," with me on the bicycle. And that's that picture that I showed you that I just love so much.

He came to a party one night at my apartment. I was giving a party. He came and he hardly ever went to parties, you know. It was a studio apartment. It was just absolutely jammed. And he, I spotted him coming in the door. And one of the guests had said something like, kind of derogatory, you know. And I tried to get over there to him and then he was already gone. You know, he was very sensitive. Very sensitive. We proceeded on and off with our relationship really until just about, before he went in the service. And by that time he was, well of course all these women were after him. You know, you can imagine.

There was even a point in the late '50s where Elvis not only dated burlesque dancer Tempest Storm but pinup girl Mamie Van Doren, and finally B movie queen Jeanne Carmen.

JEANNE CARMEN
ACTRESS

Jeanne Carmen: I was at a party and I had this Indian costume on and not much else, just a little thing going between the legs and no bra. And Elvis walked in and went. Uhh H E L L OOO. The photographer started shooting us and then all of a sudden his manager came along and pulled him away because he had something he wanted him to do, which made me mad that Elvis would actually walk away from me Jeanne Carmen. The first day I went to meet him in his hotel and I was sitting in a chair and he was sitting in another chair opposite me, playing the guitar. And all of sudden he stopped and said, "Are you wearing any panties?" But I'm not the only one he asked that. That was his favorite thing to ask any girl he was with. And of course I wasn't. Well, I cooked Southern fried chicken for him, just like his mother. And he brought me a present one night when I was cooking the chicken and I thought, "Oh, he's gonna give me an outfit." I opened it up and it turned out to be an apron and nothing else. Just an little French apron. So I put it on with nothing else on and everything was going great until I bent over to look to see if the chicken was done. Obviously it burnt that night.

JEANNE CARMEN
ACTRESS

While filming KING CREOLE, Elvis bedazzled June Wilkinson, a young friend of the choreographer.

June Wilkinson: There was Elvis and he came over and he started talking to me and he said, "Would you like to have dinner?" Would I like to have dinner? 17 year old girl. Of course I would like to have dinner. So he sent a car to pick me up at my hotel and he was staying at the Beverly Wilshire. And then he said, "Let me show you all the rooms." Which meant go to his bedroom. We went to his bedroom and he started kissing me, which it was okay with me. And then he wanted to make love and I was a virgin. And I said, "Oh, this is it, my — my behind is out of here in one second here when he finds I'm a virgin and intend to stay that way." And I said I was a virgin and he said, "Oh, okay." Sat me on his bed, got out his guitar and sung to me for a couple of hours. And I was so impressed because I thought, "Here's this gentleman that could have 40 million women make love to him and he knew he wasn't gonna get anyplace with me. And it didn't matter.

JUNE WILKINSON
GIRLFRIEND/PLAYBOY PLAYMATE

Sometimes even fans became intimate with the king when they were lucky enough to reach him.

Mary Jo Sheeley: I first met Elvis when I was 15, and I would have never met Elvis if it wasn't for my sister.

Sharon Sheeley: I took my younger sister Mary Jo and just told her that we were gonna go to Hollywood and we were – it was very matter of fact with me.

Mary Jo Sheeley: When she got her driver's license she came into my room and said, "Josie, come on, we're gonna go meet Elvis." And I said, "Okay, how are we gonna do that?" She said, "Never mind, I got a plan."

Sharon Sheeley: And when we arrived there there were 1,000s of girls that all had the same idea, so it wasn't quite as easy as I had planned it out to be. So I took her home and replanned and regrouped and said, "You gotta think of something better than this."

Glen Glenn: Every time you went to see Elvis up at the Knickerbocker, there would always be 200 girls or so out in front, you know, and they wouldn't let them inside. They had a special guard when Elvis was at the Knickerbocker to make sure that girls could not get inside the hotel unless they were actually staying there at the hotel. They would stand out front hoping they could see Elvis, or Elvis would come out.

Sharon Sheeley: So the following week we checked in. So I checked into the Knickerbocker Hotel. I put my hair up. I was only 16 but I put makeup on and made myself look older and actually got a room. Snuck her in because she was too young on a very lucky occasion when there was no guard on his floor. We knocked on his door and they opened the door. And the first thing I saw through the crack of the door was Elvis sitting in a chair but he was sitting backwards, straddling it like this. And I just looked into those gorgeous blue eyes of his and I couldn't believe I was staring eye to eye with Elvis Presley. And he said, "Well don't just stand there, come on in." And I walked in that room, just stride right in there, turned around, and my sister was paralyzed behind me and her legs wouldn't move. She just, and he literally got up and walked over, picked her up.

Mary Jo Sheeley: And he looked at me and he said, "Are you a goodie goodie girl?" And I said, "What's a goodie goodie girl?" And he said, "Never mind." And with that he gave me the longest most passionate rememberable kiss I've ever had. And then he looked me straight in the eyes and he said, "There, if that gets you pregnant, I'll marry you."

Sharon Sheeley: He invited us to stay that afternoon and have hamburgers with him. And then the following week, he said if we were in town to come back up again and it just became a regular thing. Every weekend we would go and hang out with Elvis Presley.

Mary Jo Sheeley: Just walking into the room he had that presence that he had on stage. I mean he was just gorgeous, kind, great sense of humor. And he used to put me on his lap and he would sing to me "You're so Young and Beautifu," which not many people can say.

At the end of 1957, Elvis was drafted into the United States Army. His popularity had even extended into West Germany where he stationed. Within a few days of his arrival, Elvis was already dating German stenographer Margit Buergin, followed by German actress and pinup girl, Vera Tschechowa. Elvis would also meet the shy teenage daughter of an air force captain. She would one day become the only Mrs. Presley. On March 5, 1960, Elvis was discharged from the military and returned home, diving right back into making movies.

While filming G.I. BLUES, Elvis romanced his Co-star, Juliet Prowse, who at the time was involved with another singer turned actor.

Pat Broeske: Elvis Presley and Juliet Prowse definitely had a – a thing going on the set of, uh, G.I. BLUES. I think it's kind of a first of his great Hollywood romances, uh, with his leading ladies.

Juliet Prowse: He had a wonderful sense of humor. And I remember though thinking at that time, "It must be very hard to be him." Because he couldn't go anywhere. I mean he really couldn't. He had to sleep at the Beverly Wilshire Hotel and he couldn't leave because the place would be surrounded by girls, you know. Girls trying to – I know of a girlfriend of mine who actually got up the back way of the stairs because she was a youngster to his suite.

Pat Broeske: They went on to make WILD IN THE COUNTRY, which is another straight film. It gives Elvis some very good scenes with Tuesday Weld. Some really nice chemistry there, another leading lady he kind of had a thing with.

Joe Esposito: The third movie I worked on with Elvis was WILD IN THE COUNTRY. This was more of a serious movie and there was not too much playing around. He wanted to really get into it. Tuesday Weld, one of the co-stars on it, Elvis and her hit it off pretty well. I mean she was very nice, uh, great personality, lot of fun. And she was known in those days as being a wild girl of Hollywood. She was great. They hit it off and they started dating.

While dating Tuesday Weld, Elvis fell in love with a young woman named Sandy Ferra.

Sandy Ferra Martindale: I had a nightclub in Panorama City called The Crossbow. When Elvis first got out of the Army he came there. Well apparently he went into my dad's office with my dad and saw my picture and called me. He wanted to meet me. And he said, "Can you come up to the club." And I said, "No, I can't." My mother wouldn't drive me up.

SANDY FERRA-MARTINDALE
GIRLFRIEND

Mary Lou Ferra: And it must of been, oh, 2:00 in the morning when he called and he wanted to see my daughter. And I said, "No, Elvis, she's only 14." But then he kept bugging. He called again and again. He kept coming to the club until the night I said, "I will bring her up."

MARY LOU FERRA
FRIEND/OWNER, RED VELVET LOUNGE

Sandy Ferra Martindale: I of course wanted to meet him so my mom then drove me up the next Thursday and he had a date with a gorgeous girl.

Mary Lou Ferra: Tuesday Weld or somebody that was there with him. But he didn't pay any attention to the girl. He was paying all attention to my daughter and I'm thinking, "Gee, she's only 14, you know, what's his problem."

Sandy Ferra Martindale: Elvis had an understanding with my mom, and so my mom came on the first date and then she actually came on the next three dates. And he loved my mom.

Mary Lou Ferra: A few days later we went to the Beverly Wilshire Hotel and we were there for quite a while. And then he said, "I have to talk to you. I wanna ask you something and maybe you'll do it." And I said, "Uh-Oh, I don't know what it is." So he said, "You know what, I would like for you and my dau- you and your daughter to move to Graceland." I said, "You're kidding. Why?" He said, "Well you said you wanna be with her. I'd like to have her at Graceland." And I said, "Well she's too young right now, Elvis." He said, "That's all right, I'm not gonna do anything. I just want to raise her. I want her to be there as my wife." So then I went home and I told my husband and, oh, boy, he raised the roof. He went crazy. Cursing and yelling and, you know. And I said, "That's all right, I'm against it too."

Sandy Ferra Martindale: Elvis dated a lot of people but the girls that were, that he was dating, like we weren't supposed to date anybody else but that was never really like spoken because he knew that I knew that he was dating other girls. So, uh, I met, uh, Wayne Newton in Las Vegas. The next night I had a date with Elvis and he pulled this article out and he said, "Who's this Fig Newton person." He was really upset. Yes, he was very upset about that. When they met, he went to the set, one of the sets where Elvis was doing a movie and they met, one of them said, "Well, you know, we're both dating the same girl." And so I don't know which one of them came up with the idea. They both stopped dating me at the same time. It was gonna be like a joke. But neither one of them stopped dating me, so I don't know who – who the joke was on really, but I continued to date both of them for a very long time. We had a six year romance. It was great. He was the best kisser. I tell my husband, my husband's the best husband but Elvis was the best kisser. We would kiss for hours and dance for hours and watch television and would sit at the piano and just sing. And it was, we had an awful lot of fun. And then I danced in a lot of his movies. I'm in VIVA LAS VEGAS, THE TROUBLE WITH GIRLS, GIRL HAPPY, DOUBLE TROUBLE that I danced in. But I would go on the dance auditions just so that I could be there with him. And a lot of days, you know, we'd just, I'd get paid for sitting there and having lunch with Elvis. I mean what a great life for a young girl.

Elvis even dabbled in politics. When the governor of Tennessee rewarded him for his support, Elvis showed his appreciation by hitting on his teenage daughter.

ANN ELLINGTON WAGNER
TENNESSEE GOVERNOR'S DAUGHTER

Ann Ellington Wagner: I was in college, about 30 miles west of here, Middle Tennessee State University. So I skipped classes that day. It had been all over the newspapers, television that he was coming to make an appearance. The appearance was to applaud for all the work he had done. There were people everywhere. The whole Capital Hill was filled with cars and people standing outside, waiting to get a glance of his car pulling in and the Elvis Presley getting out of the car. So about that time, the door opened and here, this entity was standing in the doorway, this black suit on and every hair immaculately combed. And there was absolutely dead silence in the room. It was just like somebody had sucked all of the air out of it. And he came in and stood behind the chair. And Dad got up and walked around and shook hands with him and he sat down at the end of the table. And when the Sergeant of Arms says, "Okay, time to go," he says, "You're goin', aren't you?" And I said, "No, I'm not gonna be a part of this." And he says, "Yeah, I need for you to go." And I said, "I don't think I'm supposed to go. There's not seats arranged up there for me." And seats were a premium, believe me. And he says, "Yeah, you got to go." He grabs my hand and dad gives the nod, it's okay, go ahead, you know. And here we go, out through the crowd, down the hallway, up the steps and then into the opening. And the speaker of the house announced that Elvis Presley would be presented to the House of Representatives. We came back to the governor's residence and stayed there for a while and had some refreshments and talked. And I think it was a little kinda awkward, you know, first time being in the governor's residence and that kind of thing. And then he turned and said goodbye and headed off to Memphis. There was just an aura about him that for an instant he just absolutely consumed the area that he was in and everybody that was in it. It

ANN ELLINGTON WAGNER
TENNESSEE GOVERNOR'S DAUGHTER

was a look, it was a demeanor about him, the way he held himself, the way he would look at you eye to eye when he talked to you. He made you feel like that you were the most important person in the world for that moment. And you walked away with that feeling. I always knew that if I ever needed him at any point in time that all I had to do was pick up the phone and call.

The 1960s became a whirlwind of making movies, most of them back to back. Elvis found it increasingly difficult to maintain an ordinary lifestyle and his relationships seemed to shift from film to film.

Around this time, Elvis was introduced to actress Connie Stevens.

CONNIE STEVENS
ACTRESS/GIRLFRIEND

Connie Stevens: I think we saw each other on and off I think about two years, I think, two years. And I never spoke about him. I denied it. It gave him a comfort level that he knew that there was – I took pride in it, that there was gonna be one girl who had nothing to say but nice things because I really cared about him. I cared what happened to his life. He was just so beautiful. He had eyes, mischievous eyes that darted around the room. So we finally went, he, you know, listened to me long enough and I we went to Grauman's Chinese and I thought, "I'll never put this guy through this again." I remember Joe giving him some money, put money in his pocket and he was nervous as hell.

JOE ESPOSITO
ROAD MANAGER & FRIEND

Joe Esposito: Elvis never carried money. I carried the money. That's normal for Elvis. I mean he never carried a dime in his pocket no matter where he went.

Connie Stevens: And we went out to the car, and he wore his favorite cap. And we ran out of gas too, by the way. He was just panic stricken. He said, "Don't worry, we'll push this car." We pushed the car into the gas station, and we missed the beginning of the picture because there were too many people who recognized him going in. We missed the end of the picture. And sure enough we got out and we got into the car and we were going home, laughing about the whole night and everything. And he went to reach for his favorite cap, and it was gone. So, it was typical of, you know, people wanting a piece of him all the time. And those of us who didn't want a piece him, we wanted a part of his heart, you know, a part of him. And one of the things I knew instinctively was he probably couldn't be captured and shouldn't be captured because he was so special that he needed to be in the world and that I was just one of many that were gonna come along to love him. And that's probably why I haven't spoken, is because I was content to be, have that little part of his heart that was real when there were just so many.

CONNIE STEVENS
ACTRESS/GIRLFRIEND

Dr. Joyce Brothers: I don't think there is a particular woman that he's attracted to that I've been able to see. Uh, he seems to go from woman to woman. But all of us have a kind of map in our heads which is related to mom. Mom sets the love map in our heads, and we go from woman to woman comparing what this woman is like with the love map of mom's personality. So the woman will be sort of similar but not identical.

Elvis's love map brought him closer to more of his co-stars.

Sandy Giles: It was great doing the film. We got to know Elvis pretty well. We had a few dates. And he was very nice. It was on the set when I was introduced, and he said to one of his men, he said, "Would you get up and give Miss Giles your chair." Which is a little unusual because usually the man gets up, gives you his chair. We'd go out to the Steak Pit and have dinner because you only – you had to know the owner, Little Joe, to get in. It was a very quiet place. And we'd just talk. He wasn't, he really wasn't pushy. He really didn't try and make out."

While in Las Vegas, Elvis charmed Phyllis McGuire of the McGuire Sisters who were performing at the Desert Inn.

Phyllis McGuire: We were rather attracted to each other. We dated for a few times. We had a few dates. It was nice. The nights in Las Vegas were quite beautiful, and I was so impressed with this car because I had never ridden in a Rolls Royce. I remember that he took, he opened the glove compartment and there was this gun, a beautiful beautiful gun. He always did everything to the fullest. It was out in the desert and he shot the gun. And I giggled and laughed and I thought it was the greatest thing. So let's, you asked me how we bonded. We bonded in more ways than one, but don't take that out of context.

During the filming of KISSIN' COUSINS, Elvis could have used a real life twin while acquainting himself with a bevy of dancers and actresses on the set.

Gail Ganley Steele: He introduced himself to me. He had a blond wig on because he was playing the part of twins in KISSIN' COUSINS. And said, "Hello there," in his beautiful low voice, "I'm Elvis Presley, what's your name?" And I just sort of was taken back by his candor. Before you know it, by the second week of the shooting, Elvis made it known to me that he was very interested and he wanted me to go out with him.

Cynthia Pepper: I remember going to my dressing room, and I had met him and I remember he was very very tall and blue eyes. And I'm short, so it looked like I was standing in a hole. He just looked at me. He was very sweet. And I went to my dressing room and in my dressing room were roses. And it said, "To Cynthia from, love from EP." And being very naïve I thought, "He's got a crush on me," not knowing that he was very kind to all his leading ladies and this is what he did.

Gail Ganley Steele: Elvis made me feel like I was a queen, like I was a very very special person. And we spoke and we cried I think all night the first night we were together. We spoke about our lives and our family, and we spoke about commitments. And I think I started right immediately falling in love with Elvis. I didn't think it would take me such a short time to forget about my other situation.

Cynthia Pepper: The director used to kid with me and Elvis, I don't know if he liked it or not, he used to kid me that I was with him the night before or something. The director would make a joke about it in front of everybody and I would die. And I think he said, "You better stop that," you know, very protective of me.

Gail Ganley Steele: I had to ask Elvis at one point, you know, about other ladies in his life. And he said, "Well, I don't wanna talk about that now because there is nobody right now." He said, "There was somebody." He said, "There is somewhat of a commitment down the road. I don't know if I could keep it." But he said, "Right now we are dating each other and there's nobody in my life."

But sometimes life is just a relative term, especially in Elvis's vocabulary.

Rita Rogers: Those were the, some of the happiest days in my life, the '60s. I mean everybody was crazy out there but I was, you know, every day working on some movie with him because there was nine movies all together.

Joe Esposito: Rita Rogers worked on a lot of our movies. She was a dancer, an extra in a lot of pictures. And we kept picking her at the casting sessions for extras and we'd say, "Oh, make sure you get Rita on this show."

Rita Rogers: We like talked with our eyes, you know. We stared into each other's eyes forever. And when he was working he would turn around and I would turn too and we would catch each other's eyes. All the time we did that.

By the late '60s, Elvis had devised a variety of approaches at welcoming his co-stars.

Julie Parrish: One day on the set in Hawaii, I got very sick. My body said, "This is too much and my body said this is too much, and I went AAAch, and my right side was in a lot of pain. And we'd been standing for hours and hours and hours all day in a scene doing it over and over , it was a musical number and when my side started to hurt really bad. And so when I said I couldn't go on, Elvis picked me up in his arms and carried me. If I'd known this when I was 13 that this was gonna happen to me I would have died of heart failure. He carried me in his arms into his dressing room and laid me on cot there. And at that time he was into laying on of hands as healing. This may sound really weird, and some people may have taken advantage of it, but Elvis was really trying to heal me. He had his hands out over me.

Deborah Walley: He took my hand, and he told me what a pleasure it was to be working with me because he was a big fan of mine, and he'd seen all my films. Well, you know, I was just wrapped right around his little finger from that point on. As I got to know him, you know, I mean, the first was like, you know, getting in with a tidal wave of charisma and charm. But then as we worked together, you know, a friendship developed between us. I had lunch with him in his trailer every day, unless he had a meeting or something like that. I'd go to the house. You know, one of the boys would pick me up and take me over there, the house in Bel Air, at night and we'd talk there. I don't think I have every met anyone, I certainly hadn't at that point and I haven't since, with that kind of charisma.

DEBORAH WALLEY
CO-STAR

While making his 28th film, Elvis turned his attention to co-star Susan Henning.

Susan Henning: I first met Elvis in, it was probably '67, and I was topless and the bottom half of me was a mermaid. Everything he did, he enjoyed life. And he was certainly fun to work with and certainly very, made you feel very comfortable in what you were doing. If you were to err, he would laugh. And he's a very real person. I'm attracted to people that aren't fake. And he seemed just down home and comfortable to be with.

SUSAN HENNING
GIRLFRIEND/DANCER

Joe Esposito: And Elvis started dating her and he dated her for a while. Not too many people know about that. She never told anybody about it. She was very quiet about it and we spent a lot of time together during the movie and rehearsals.

JOE ESPOSITO
ROAD MANAGER & FRIEND

Susan Henning: And when I walked into the room, we were to practice and rehearse the dance. He had his back to me, and he had his little macho pose, and I think I had a pair of short shorts on. And I thought, "Oh, well there's Elvis, we're gonna have fun." So I remember walking up and sticking my leg between his leg and kind of doing a little cancan. And his favorite slogan was, he'd look down at me and said – my boy, my boy.

Joe Esposito: They clicked for a while and you could see it in their eyes.

Susan Henning: I met him in, one time in Arizona, we went. And I think a lot of his fun, since he was so much out, was just to be in. And we would really just stay in the room. And that sounds all perverted, but I mean we can have a lot of fun in the room besides doing what people might think. I mean just talking and he loved to get into deep thoughts of – of – he loved to eat. One of my greatest, fun times was to comb his hair and do it in different ways that he had never worn it. And he thought that was so funny that I would comb his hair in bangs or part it down the center make a butler. Or, and we just played with each other. You could do fun things. I think he had a multitude of women and I think I was one of, I don't know, one of many probably.

Before LIVE A LITTLE, LOVE A LITTLE was finished shooting, Elvis lived a little and loved a little more when he met another of the film's co-stars – Celeste Yarnall.

Celeste Yarnall: Elvis looked so good. Elvis was so healthy when we did LIVE A LITTLE, LOVE A LITTLE. I'm so blessed that I knew him when he was at his best. He just looked fabulous. He, I don't know if people realize how exquisitely beautiful Elvis Presley was. The original title of the script was "Kiss My Firm But Pliant Lips." Oh, Elvis had firm but pliant lips. My first day, they brought me down to meet Elvis, like a wardrobe test or a day before I was supposed to film. And I really couldn't believe I was gonna get the opportunity to meet him. I just thought, "Oh, yeah, sure, Elvis wants to meet me, right, uh-huh." We go back to his dressing room to have lunch and the Martin Luther King funeral is on television, and he sobbed in my arms like a baby because he was so-so devastated by Martin Luther King's assassination. His warmth and sincerity and I think the incredible back story of his struggle that, you know, it came, it came through. It was in his music, it was in his eyes, it was in his heart. It was, he touched me deeply.

CELESTE YARNALL
CO-STAR, LIVE A LITTLE, LOVE A LITTLE

And then Elvis touched others.

MARLYN MASON
CO-STAR, THE TROUBLE WITH GIRLS

Marlyn Mason: I felt very close to him. I know that he liked me very much, and I liked him very much. It was a very sweet relationship. We hit it off immediately. I think when you're in tune with somebody it's like you get a, you sense things.

And I could be sitting 50 feet from him, and I'd get a – I'd just get a feeling and I would turn and he'd be looking at me.

You could ad lib with him. We'd do a lot of that. If the director was doing a close up on Elvis and he wanted a certain reaction, he would come to me and he'd say something like, "I don't care what you do but this is the reaction I need from him." So I remember one time I was out of camera, and it was a close up on him and I was supposedly deep seated. So his look was looking down at me. And I started slowly unbuttoning his shirt and taking his belt off very quietly. And he was just giving me these looks. Well that was what the director wanted. And he just responded. He didn't stop and say, "What is she doing?" He just rolled with the punches. It was great. He was great to work with.

He turned his attention to fellow musician Jackie DeShannon.

Jackie DeShannon: I was lucky enough to first meet Elvis at his house in Bel Air. And he used to invite different artists, singers and musicians to come and jam with him at his house. Just played records and sang together and just had a great time.

Joe Esposito: He loved her singing, her personality, Southern girl. And she was great. She was just a nice, nice individual.

Jackie DeShannon: Before I went up to the house, uh, he said, "I'm gonna send you know one of the guys down to pick you up." And I said, "Well I don't think that's gonna work." I come from a background where no matter who you are, you come to the door and you say, you know, "Is Jackie home or whatever." You know, those little screen doors. And I said to my mother, "This is Elvis Presley. He will not be coming to the door."

Joe Esposito: Elvis would talk to her, give her advice about her career and her music and they jammed a lot. They'd sit and sing and play guitar and just talk. And they became very good friends.

Jackie DeShannon: He would call and track me down and say, "Come on up, we're gonna sing tonight." Or, "I'm sending so and so tonight." I said, "Elvis, I can't come, my mother will not have it." And I was living at home. And this went on for several months. And so finally I came home from ballet class one night and there is Elvis, talking to my mother with a huge pink dog, bigger than I was. And from then on, you know, my mother didn't care how I got there.

As the '60s drew to a close, Elvis's film career took a back burner to his newly rediscovered love of performing in front of a live audience. Long gone were the greased pompadours and satin jackets. The world would see an entirely new Elvis in an entirely new era – the 1970s.

Cassandra "Elvira" Peterson: I was a showgirl at the Dunes Hotel in Las Vegas. I met Elvis actually through Joe Esposito who was a friend of one of the showgirls. He invited us. He invited her to come along, to come to a party. I got to come along. So that was the way I got to meet him, was at his suite at the International Hilton, which is where he was playing at the time.

CASSANDRA "ELVIRA" PETERSON
ACTRESS

He was very kind and naïve. I got the feeling he was completely genuine, completely very innocent person. I mean really amazing – a lot different than most people would think about him. They had a party at the International Hotel, and Elvis and all his friends, you know, Sonny and Red and everybody. They were all there. And they invited a lot of other performers, a lot of people from Vegas. Uh, I went to the party, and Elvis came over and immediately started talking to me. I was, you know, almost in shock. And we talked and we talked and we talked and we talked. I mean just ended up spending the entire evening, the rest of the party, until the next morning. I just remember, you know, kissing him goodbye and I don't, everybody said, "Oh, how did he kiss?" I said, "I can't remember." I was so busy in my head thinking about telling people that I kissed Elvis that I just wasn't there. It was like an out of body experience.

In Las Vegas when 21-year-old Patricia Parker claimed Elvis did a lot more than just kiss her after a concert, she didn't just tell her friends about it. She sued, claiming Elvis was the father of her unborn child.

> **Elvis Presley:** About that Paternity suit, it turned out to be a complete conspiracy and hoax, man. And there's just no way. I had a picture made with that chick and that's all. I mean she got pregnant with a camera, a Polaroid or something. But you know what she did; boy she goofed up. She named the night, and the night she named, my wife was with me in the audience. And no way I was gonna fool around with her out there. You kiddin' me?

The case was later thrown out of court, but legal situations like this presumably caused Elvis to add a new clause to his last will and testament, providing for the care of not only Lisa Marie, his only known daughter, but any other lawful children that he may or may not know about, with proof this time of course. With the legalities behind him, Elvis was free to peruse once more.

REECA GOSSAN
GIRLFRIEND

Reeca Gossan: I was 14 when I met Elvis. It was in September of 1974. And I saw him off and on over a period of about six months. I knew Ricky Stanley. He was Elvis's stepbrother, and Ricky had told Elvis about me, and Elvis was very interested to meet me. Well, a little while later, up pulled a white Cadillac and we go out to the car. And the man behind the front seat looked in the rearview mirror and said, "Hi, I'm Elvis. You must be Reeca, the girl I've been hearing about." We would go to movies. He would close down the Memphian, and we'd all go see a movie at the Memphian. Or we would just go to his house, sit down in the TV room, watch TV, hang out there. And I would wear this coat with this big fur. It looked like a lion all the time. I would come over in that. And he just, he would call me his little lioness. And what really left a strong impression on me is that me being just as young as I was, a 14 year old, a young little girl, a nobody, you know, he being who he was, he always made sure he treated me like a princess and treated me so special and made me feel like I was the important one, not just him. He surprised me with a Trans Am. I was 14. He had me cover my eyes. And I opened them and there sat that silver Trans Am, my favorite sports car. He was a perfect, perfect, true Southern gentleman. He never took advantage of me. Everybody would think, you know, he would. Now, he is a great kisser. Best kiss I've ever had but that was as far as he would take it. And he was, like I said, a true Southern gentleman. And to me that left a strong impact too. You know, even at my age, he still could have taken advantage of me.

Myrna Smith: We were having a little party, a little get together and drinks at the bar and stuff. Elvis came up to me and said, "You wanna dance?" It was a slow record. I said, "OOOh kay." I didn't think that Elvis had ever danced with a black woman before because as he started dancing with me, his whole body was trembling. He was shy anyway. All these girls, you know, that he'd been around; and he's this macho lover, whatever, and he was just a little boy then.

MYRNA SMITH
SINGER/BACK-UP GROUP,
SWEET INSPIRATIONS

Kanai Seanoa: I was invited to Graceland that summer after school, and I got to spend a month there. I had a lot of interesting things I would never dream would ever happen in my life, like going to the mall at midnight, going to the theater at midnight, three wheeling and doing all kinds of fun things. There was a pureness about him. He was everyone's family member. Everyone that met him or, they'd never seen him even. I think probably that he was every mother's son. He was, he could be your brother. He was personal to people. He was real. And he was family. I had a piece of paper that I saved for a long time that he wrote out for me. And on the top it had L O V E. And he said this was the bottom line. And I don't know if I should say this but he said, "It's not religion. It's L O V E. And that's where we should work from always."

KANAI SEANOA
SPIRITUAL FRIEND

Love. There's no way to measure how much one can have or how much one can give. And although the women who loved Elvis knew his heart could never be captured by one single woman, they still adored him and loved him and will continue to do so for the rest of their lives.

Connie Stevens: He's one of the loves of my life. I could have spent a lifetime with him. And I knew it was never to be.

CONNIE STEVENS
ACTRESS/GIRLFRIEND

Celeste Yarnall: I'll never forget being with Elvis and being part of that camaraderie. It was so, so special. He was a very dear, precious person.

Kanai Seanoa: I consider myself very blessed to have the opportunity to come across that human being in this big world.

Jackie DeShannon: I'm really proud to have known him. And he was generous with his spirit, generous with his talent and wore his crown very well.

Deborah Walley: He's one of the most important people in my life. I loved him very dearly. I miss him but I feel that he watches over me. I am absolutely sure of that. And I feel him around me often. See, I told you you'd make me cry.

It could have been their smile or the way they laughed or maybe just their fortunate location when Elvis first glanced in their direction, introduced himself and loved them like no other.

Although Elvis married only once in his life, there were several intimate relationships, both before and after that marriage, not to mention during. Relationships with the few women who were sometimes referred to as, the lifers.

At a time when the world was shackled in mediocrity, Elvis Presley came along to transform not only the face of music, but the times themselves. He was the king. And every king needed his queen.

Anita Wood: I met Elvis in 1957. I was on Top 10 Dance Party, WHPQ radio television, in Memphis at the time. And it was a popular dance show that they had every Saturday afternoon. The teenagers would come and dance and, Wink Martindale and I would introduce the, the songs and the people and, children the teenagers that were there. And, he watched that show a lot. And one Saturday after the show, he had Lamar Fike call me on the phone. And, he wanted a date to see me that night.

ANITA WOOD
FORMER GIRLFRIEND

He'd just made LOVING YOU when I met him. And he had this shirt on, these black trousers and I think he had a, like a motorcycle cap on and he, he, he was very handsome. I mean, I have to say that Elvis was the most handsome man I've ever seen, before or after. I've never seen anybody as handsome as he. He, he was just very good looking, you know. And then as I got to meet him, and know him, he had a very good personality. Funny, pullin' pranks and laughin'. When they drove up in the Cadillac, they had a big long Cadillac. And Elvis was driving. So I got in the car and sat on my side of the seat because, in those days that's what you did. And so, then Elvis started drivin' around. And, after awhile he said, are you tryin' to knock that door out over there? And I said no so I scooted over just a little bit. Not very far, but just a little bit. And, we would go to his house many times, and we would watch TV, listen to music. He would invite the people up from down at the gate, which were a bunch of fans and crazy girls, you know. And here I was up here his date and these girls would just, man they were falling all over him wantin' to sit in his lap and everything. I really did not like that because, I was his date. I had a hard time with that. He was so secretive back in those days. And he always said it was because of Colonel Tom Parker, you know. He didn't want us to take any pictures and if I was ever with him and there was a picture made I would look down or try to look away, you know, from the camera and not appear to be too happy. Because he didn't want everybody to know our real relationship, you know, that we really cared for one another. He wanted it to be more like well we're just girlfriend and boyfriend. We're just dating. And then he would always come to me he'd say but Little, you know, that's not really true. You're just the only one for me. You know, these are just publicity stunts that don't mean anything. You're the only one I care anything about and he had a way, that he could convince you, that that's true!

I'm telling you. On the grounds at Graceland, they would have roman candle fights in the backyard, that were just scary as everything, at each other. I mean, they had no fear. Elvis included, right in the middle of 'em. Oh man, and we sat and watched this, fighting with each other, at each other, you know, with these roman candles. Right at each other. man.

Sometimes we would get on the motorcycle, just Elvis and I, and ride through Memphis. These were things we did here. And then when he went to New Orleans with KING CREOLE, you know, he would always invite me down there for a spell and in California, for a spell. The first time I went out there, he was staying at the Beverly Wilshire Hotel I believe. And I remember Ricky Nelson came up one night. And some other people. I do remember him. But, even in California, we did a lot of drivin' around. It was wild. He thought, as I thought that, things that went on out there, were things that went on in hell. I mean, really it was just the wildest place we'd ever seen. He wanted his family and his friends around him. He felt a stranger. He just loved Memphis better. He liked bein' at Graceland.

1957 was a pivotal year for Elvis Presley. In April, "All Shook Up" reached number one on Billboard's Top 100 Chart. In October, JAILHOUSE ROCK premiered in Memphis to a sold out crowd.

And in December, Elvis received his draft notice from the United States Army. It was a change that would jeopardize his career, and affect his life forever. No one took that news harder than Elvis's mother, Gladys.

ANITA WOOD
FORMER GIRLFRIEND

Anita Wood: I remember them getting the notice, and I remember his mother's reaction. She was devastated, scared, sad. Many weekends when Elvis would have time away from Fort Hood, we would drive over to Eddie Fadal's house in Waco, Texas.

And, they were so nice and they just loved Elvis, and they just had a room there that they dedicated to him. And, that he could go and just do anything he wanted to do, and I remember one time we went there and, they had a birthday cake. I think it might've been my birthday. It was in May. And they sang this song, and I got him to dance with me. You know, he didn't like to dance. But, he was singing that song Happy Birthday, Baby, Happy Birthday.

They would always fix good food for us to eat and things that Elvis liked. It was just a, a place to get away. Away from the army.

During his fifth month in the army, Elvis learned that his mother had died. It was a shock that would echo loudly throughout his life. The first woman he ever truly loved, and the only person he ever really trusted, was gone.

Elvis spent the remainder of his military service in West Germany, where he met and fell in love with Priscilla Ann Beaulieu, the 14-year-old daughter of an air force captain.

Pat Broeske: Once he met Priscilla, it sort of was all over for Anita Wood. And, Anita did hear through the grapevine and by reading other publications. It's, it's my understanding, you know, that he was seeing somebody else out in Germany.

Joe Esposito: When he got back home after the service he, Anita was there waitin' for him and they were back together again. But as time went on, I think Anita realized that, things were changin'.

Charlie Hodge: Anita Wood was the first lady that I met that Elvis was dating. When we got out of military and, and I went first to Graceland there. And, Elvis liked her but, you know Elvis.

Joe Esposito: She saw the article in the paper about, Priscilla saying goodbye to Elvis as he left and naturally she asked him about it and he says oh no, just a young lady I knew over there and he sorta got away from it.

Elvis started to breathe life back into his dormant career, by returning to Hollywood to film GI BLUES.

While visiting Elvis at his hotel, Anita stumbled across a memento from Germany.

Anita Wood: I found one letter when I was in California. And it was pressed in a book in the library outside of his bedroom. And when he came home, from the set that day, then that's when I asked him about the letter. And in the letter it said, please call my dad. I want to come over there. And if you call my dad, I know he will let me come. He will listen to you. I miss you. I want to come bad!. It just kept on like that. You know? So when he came in I said, what is this letter? Who is this? This Priscilla? You said she was just a child. He got so mad because I found the letter. He took me, and he shoved me up against the closet. So mad at me, just livid. And as I was coming down the backstairs into the kitchen...I heard Elvis say, I'm having the hardest time making up my mind between the two. And so, I just marched my little self right down those stairs. And Elvis took me into the dining room. And we sat down at the table and I said, I'm gonna make that decision for you. I heard what you said, and I am leaving. And, I remember that I started crying. It was a very difficult decision to make. And I was crying and Elvis was crying. And, he just said, I pray to God I'm doin' the right thing, by letting you go.

ANITA WOOD
FORMER GIRLFRIEND

Elvis submerged himself in film after film and fling after fling, until he finally met his celluloid match, his VIVA LAS VEGAS co-star, Ann-Margret.

Joe Esposito: Well when we got ready to do VIVA LAS VEGAS, Ann-Margret got signed to be his co-star. And, we knew a lot about Ann-Margret. We'd never met her before and at that time she was considered the female Elvis Presley.

JOE ESPOSITO
ROAD MANAGER & FRIEND

Ann-Margret: The first meeting with EP was, in a room, with a lot of people. A pianist. We went over some of the songs that we were going to do.

Joe Esposito: When they met at the studio, there was like a chemistry between the two of them, and they really hit it off as friends. They spent a lot of time together alone and they had a ball. During the making of that movie, the two of them were having a great time.

ANN-MARGRET
ACTRESS/CO-STAR, VIVA LAS VEGAS

Rita Rogers: I could see the, the spark those two had with each other. And we were always, you know, all the extras and stuff talking about that.

RITA ROGERS
ACTRESS/FRIEND

DANNY STRIEPEKE

GEORGE KLEIN
MEMPHIS MAFIA/FRIEND

ANN-MARGRET

GLEN CAMPBELL
SINGER/FRIEND

CHARLIE HODGE
FRIEND/SINGER/GUITARIST/
MEMPHIS MAFIA

Dan Striepeke: Boy, what a hot pair. Honest to God. I'm tellin' ya. That, that couple you put them together in front of the camera and it just – sparks were – flames were sizzling. I mean, it was unbelievable. Incredible.

George Klein: Elvis and Ann-Margret, probably were the two hottest items going in Hollywood at that time. And for them to do a motion picture together was really great. There was a lot of electrify. A lot of sparks going on. And they hit it off right off the bat.

Ann-Margret: We were very much alike. Funny, generous, giving, kind, loving. Gifted, so talented.

Glen Campbell: We was doin' the session and when Ann-Margret came in to do, whatever it was she was doin' there. And then, all attention all of a sudden, all eyes went to Ann-Margret, you know.

Charlie Hodge: Ann-Margret and Elvis had gone in their bedroom. And I don't think you're gonna use this, but I'll tell you anyway. I had a phone call I had to make. And I come back, and sat down and took the phone and started to dial, and I heard the El–the, the head of Elvis's bed was right behind me. And I heard MOANS. And I said goddam. And I got to laughin' and hung the phone up and left. You're not gonna use that, see. You know you're not.

Rumors of Elvis and Ann-Margret secretly marrying began to circulate. Shortly after the gossip dissipated, they ended their one year relationship.

JOE ESPOSITO
ROAD MANAGER & FRIEND

Joe Esposito: Oh I think, Ann-Margret and Elvis were definitely in love.

Mary Lou Ferra: Ann-Margret was a nice girl. Nice person. But see Elvis didn't want another celebrity in the family he'd say. He didn't – that's why he didn't want to – he didn't go with her. Because she was a star. He could've gotten any star but he didn't want a star.

MARY LOU FERRA
FRIEND/OWNER, RED VELVET
LOUNGE

Millions of hearts shattered in 1967, when Elvis officially acknowledged Priscilla as the only love in his life, and took her to be his wife. The news promptly spread around the world, finally giving life to the longtime rumors. But Lady Love had other plans for the king. Only a few years after his marriage to Priscilla, Elvis met and fell in love with actress Barbara Leigh.

Barbara Leigh: I met Elvis in Las Vegas at the Hilton, with Jim Aubrey. Jim Aubrey was the president of MGM Studios and he was my boyfriend at the time. And they had done the movie THAT'S THE WAY IT IS, with Elvis. So he took me up to see Elvis's show.

BARBARA LEIGH
GIRLFRIEND

Joe Esposito: When she came in I, I saw how stunning she was and I went back Elvis was getting dressed. I went in the dressing room I said Elvis, wait till you come outside and see this gorgeous girl that James Aubrey's with. So, sure enough, he came out of the dressing room after he got all dressed up and walked over. And I walked out and he walked over to Mr. Aubrey and introduced himself. And, he introduced him to Barbara. And he looked and, he looked over at me and, nodded his head like I was right.

JOE ESPOSITO
ROAD MANAGER & FRIEND

Barbara Leigh: The first meeting was, in the dressing room with a lot of people around. And, he had a table, that was kind of centered in the center of the room. And I was sitting in this table talking to Chris Nelson, Ricky Nelson's wife. And I felt the presence, and then kind of turned around and there he was, sitting and staring me in the eyes. And he complimented me. And then he asked me if I'd like to come back and see his show. And I said, of course. So he handed me under the table a little pad and pencil, skinny little pencil. He was all prepared.

JOE ESPOSITO
ROAD MANAGER & FRIEND

BARBARA LEIGH
GIRLFRIEND

Joe Esposito: He kept lookin' at Barbara, talkin' to Barbara little by little and, before that evening was over, Elvis had Barbara Leigh's phone number. And, that was the start of a long romance together.

Barbara Leigh: I went into s– for what I thought was one night, because I had plans for the weekend. But, when I got there, my plans changed. Elvis talked me into staying for the whole weekend. We did become romantic. Who wouldn't, right? He was just gorgeous. That's when he was thin and he was beautiful and handsome. And, he had his – like you say he was very spiritual and, charisma. He was the king, you know? He was sexy. Great kisser.

Joe Esposito: Elvis was very enchanted by Barbara Leigh. She was very striking, very beautiful lady, dark hair, beautiful face, beautiful figure. She was a very sexy lady.

Barbara Leigh: In the back of my mind I knew he was a married man. So, I didn't think about that really. Elvis had a soul, and it just came out in his performances, and his singing, and in his everyday life. The way he dealt with people. He was the most giving, kindest person, that I'd ever known. He bought me a car, a Mercedes. Guess timing is everything. I happened to be around when he was buying Mercedes, and so I got one. He bought me guns and jewelry and things like that, clothes. He had a great sense of humor. And he liked to joke all the time, make fun and, he was a lot of fun. One funny experience that I had with him, was I brought a girlfriend to see him, to meet him Palm Springs. And when I walked in the door he was there and I thought hmm, he looks – he looks different. But I couldn't put my finger on it. And he started doing his karate exhibit. He put on his gi with the guys, with Charlie. And he was doing, you know, really getting into it and hi– this wig went flying off. And everybody just stopped, 'cause no one knew how to handle it quite. They didn't want to laugh, until he laughed. And he basically laughed, picked it up and put it back on his head. And then everybody laughed and he just continued with the exhibit. Exhibition. He was magic. And everything about him was magic. When he was performing, he gave everything to the audience. And I think that people, identified with, his soul and the tenderness and the loving part of him. He was a true gentleman, southern gentleman.

BARBARA LEIGH
GIRLFRIEND

By 1972, Elvis's heavy touring schedule and amorous affairs began to strain his marriage to Priscilla, who took Lisa Marie and moved out of Graceland for good. Sensing his heartache, George Klein, one of Elvis's closest friends, introduced the new bachelor to Linda Thompson, the reigning Miss Tennessee.

Linda Thompson: I met Elvis on July 6, 1972 not to be too specific. It was after midnight. He used to lease out the Memphian Theater when the theater would close, because he was Elvis and he couldn't go into a normal theater. So he would lease out the theater, and run movies all night. Elvis did not ask to sit next to me, or nor did he ask me to come and sit next to him. George Klein had sat next to me in the theater. And George got up, to go get popcorn I thought. But when he came back, it wasn't George Klein anymore it was Elvis. So Elvis came and plopped down next to me and, you know, started doin' the old stretchy yawn thing, put the arm around me. And I was under the assumption that he was still married so I was very unfriendly and he finally said honey, you know, I'm not married anymore, don't you? And I said, no, I didn't know that as my arm went over too.

LINDA THOMPSON
ELVIS'S GIRLFRIEND

George Klein: She had this offbeat comedy about her. She had a great sense of humor, and I think that's what really Elvis liked and Elvis, liked the fact that she was attractive. And that she was a local girl. She was a Memphis girl. And he liked that.

GEORGE KLEIN
MEMPHIS MAFIA/FRIEND

Linda Thompson: We really knew each other, right away. The moment I met him, it's like okay, I've known this person for a long time. 'Cause I was raised the same way he wa– was. And so we shared a, a real tight bond right away.

Pat Broeske: Linda Thompson was kind of a professional beauty queen. She was gorgeous. She was blonde. She was dazzling. She also had a great sense of humor. Elvis really like women who, who laughed a lot. And she was also kind of a take charge woman. And, it's funny. Elvis really couldn't accept that in Priscilla, but he was willing to accept it in Linda Thompson.

Elvis and Priscilla finalized their separation by divorcing in 1973, nearly a year after Elvis learned of Priscilla's affair with her karate teacher, Mike Stone.

Linda Thompson: He had been deeply, deeply hurt, by what he'd perceived as Priscilla's betrayal of him. And having another man involved was all the more painful. It would've been one thing if she'd said I don't like your lifestyle. But having another man involved was, tremendously destructive to his ego. And, to his perception of relationships and marriage. And I think the, the next person who comes in, typically suffers the consequences of the prior person's actions. I don't think that he was bitter about women and about relationships in general. I mean, he was a very romantic, loving, nurturing, affectionate person. And naïve in many ways. So I think he still believed in marriage. In the years that I was with Elvis, particularly the first year, I feel as if I, I was with him 24 hours a day, seven days a week. I feel that way because basically I was. I mean, I, I slept with him. I ate breakfast with him. I ate lunch with him and I ate dinner with him. I traveled with him, I went to every show that he performed. I sometimes went to the bathroom with him, you know, if he showered I was in there. We were together though for almost four and a half years and there were periods, in that four and a half years, where we would talk about getting married, having babies. What we would name our children. If we'd like to have a boy or a girl. How many of each. And that kind of thing. So, you know, when you're with someone and you live with someone that long, certainly the subject comes up.

Pat Broeske: He was doing the whole Vegas thing which is a rough life. Vegas and Tahoe and that kind of stuff. And Linda was kind of there to keep him together during it all. And she sort of basked in the in, in the spotlight herself during that era.

Linda Thompson: When we were together in, that four and a half year period as, has been said before, that kind of encompassed 20 years of living a normal life with another human being. With a regular spouse that would go to work and, you know, you would have spaces in your togetherness. We didn't. I mean, we were together just solidly.

Charlie Hodge: Linda wa– was a, I think good for Elvis. She spent too much money I think which, which Elvis even said that. He said, but it was his fault. He spoiled her. But Linda did take care of him.

Linda Thompson: When he had his face-lift I went into the hospital with him. When he went to the hospital twice, and he was there for two weeks, I had a hospital bed brought into the room, and I was adjacent to his bed. I mean, he insisted that I be there with him. And if he elevated his bed, guess what? My bed was elevated, too. I was aware, of the fact that, if Elvis were not with me, there was a darn good chance he was gonna be with somebody else because he did not like to be alone.

PATTY PARRY
FRIEND/MEMPHIS MAFIA

LINDA THOMPSON
ELVIS'S GIRLFRIEND

Patty Parry: Elvis loved women, you know. He loved women. I mean, he used to – there would be one upstairs coming in and one downstairs going out. He said he'd keep 'em in a holding pattern.

Linda Thompson: The first year we were together, that was not the case. We were together literally 365 days. I mean, 24 hours a day, seven days a week. I mean, it – the hours that he – that he wasn't sleeping, that I wasn't sleeping, I had my eye on him so I know he couldn't have been with anyone else. But after that first year, I think he grew a little restless.

And, it was very difficult to reconcile that in my mind, and because I was very faithful to him and, you know, had saved myself for this kind of relationship. And, to see the person that you love that deeply and devotedly, wander off and you know they're gonna be with someone else, was very hurtful.

While touring in Las Vegas, Elvis did meet someone else. Her name was Sheila Ryan.

SHEILA RYAN
GIRLFRIEND

Sheila Ryan: I had moved to Las Vegas. I'd left home when I was about 18 and I had moved to Las Vegas because a couple of friends of mind lived there. And the I met Joe Esposito, and Joe Esposito brought me backstage. And, Elvis threw a grape at me and, hit me in the forehead and, had – and then he had to come over and say hello.

It was kind of an out of body experience to begin with. What Elvis? Hello, you know. It was a strange thing. I mean, how do you end up dating Elvis? I mean, it's so surreal. So the fact that there's another girl what am I gonna complain? You know, coming from where I came, no, I didn't. Now Linda on the other hand, she did plenty of complaining. She was a Miss America or a Miss Tennessee or whatever and she had parents that nurtured her and, and so she had a sense of herself. Whereas I was just a little bit of a free spirit and not too demanding.

When he would meet a girl there was, you know, I mean, there was a consensus among the guys that worked for him. I think they did like a score from one to 10. And I rated high.

Well, you know, and it was like stepping up the girlfriend ladder. You know, it was prestigious, in, in that world. In Elvis's world. And, and yeah, you know, you want to be number one, you know, you want to be the number one girl. And I was almost there.

Joe Esposito: I don't think Linda knew that Elvis was seeing other women, tell you the truth. I mean, maybe she did in the back of her head that she – 'cause she knew how Elvis was, too. And, she never asked any of us. Linda was not the type of person to ask hey, is he datin' anybody? She would never do that to us. Put us in that position.

JOE ESPOSITO
ROAD MANAGER & FRIEND

Linda Thompson: He would come back to me after having been with another girl, and oftentimes, it was just to have the company. He didn't always sleep with these girls. He didn't always have sex with them. In fact, very often he didn't.

LINDA THOMPSON
ELVIS'S GIRLFRIEND

Sheila Ryan: Some things were a little bit unusual, because there were things that, kept him from a, a normal through line, of action, in, in sex. He had phobias and fears of getting women pregnant. And, so, you know, that would inhibit the lovemaking, somewhat. Joe and I had become very good friends because, when Elvis had to have Linda there, because Linda and I dated him at the same time. It was sort of like Joe's job to take me to Hawaii or, what not.

SHEILA RYAN
GIRLFRIEND

To keep up with the incredible number of concert performances in the mid 1970s, Elvis found it increasingly difficult to survive without his prescription drugs. His attitude and his appearance began to slowly change for the worse.

Linda Thompson: We were about to go to bed and I looked on the nightstand and, and there was all this medication. And I said have you been ill? And he says why do you ask? And I said well there's a lot of prescription medicine here. Are you sick? And he said oh, no yeah, yeah I had a little – I had a little bout with the flu but, you know, and he made up some story.

Sheila Ryan: He used a lot of drugs to sleep and a lot of drugs to put him out right away so that he could rest before a show. And then drugs to wake him up right away so that he can get busy before a show. But he still had sexual drive. It was not that fun for me because it had to be, spontaneous for him but it wasn't spontaneous for me. And so it was like okay, Sheila you're on. Boom. And I'm like, you know, when I've been traveling, I've been on the road, I was exhausted, I didn't have 15 people taking care of me. So, you know, it wasn't always fun.

Linda Thompson: I noticed that his behavior, you know, was a little strange, in the evening. Like he would get groggy and I thought, is he just really tired? I was – I was so stupidly naïve, that it took me a, you know, a couple of weeks to catch onto what was really happening. That he was taking prescription medication to sleep. And then more prescription medication to wake up. And it had become a vicious cycle.

Sheila Ryan: The most important job was, to watch him sleep. When he got his food it was late at night. And he had already taken his meds for, for sleep. And so he would tend to fall asleep while he was eating. So you would have to make sure that, he didn't fall asleep with a mouthful of food. Marriage was not something that I considered or was even looking for. I know Linda wanted to marry him, and my father wanted me to marry him. You know, because he was interested in the financial aspects and, the fame and all of that. But he wasn't up all night, losing sleep and, breaking out in hives and, you know, watching a man die.

Even with Linda Thompson residing mostly at Graceland, and Sheila Ryan acting as a lover and a nurse, Elvis still found time to fall in love again. This time with a young lady from Los Angeles, named Mindi Miller.

Mindi Miller: I met Elvis in 1974, through a mutual friend of ours, who had wanted to introduce me to him. He had recently broken up with another lady. And said that he liked a certain type of girl. And, that he would maybe like to meet me and it was very hard for him, I'm sure, to go out and just meet people. You know, it's not like you can go to a party and say hey I'm Elvis. Would you like to go out? I drove to his home in Bel Air. And, I was late. I was told that I was going to a party. And, it turned out that there was no party. I was the party. So I remember all of a sudden, this, this large figure to my right sort of appeared in the doorway. And it's Elvis and he's standing there, larger than life. And he said well honey, sorry I'm late, but so were you. And I don't know why that hit me, but I just cracked up. And I don't know he, he was just so funny right away I liked him immediately. He was the kind of man I think who really cared, in his heart, about a lot of people. But I think he always had one special person, you know. And even though he had that one special person, he still dated other people.

LINDA THOMPSON
ELVIS'S GIRLFRIEND

SHEILA RYAN
GIRLFRIEND

MINDI MILLER
GIRLFRIEND

Linda Thompson: He would always come back and say, honey nobody can compare to you. I, I met this girl and you might hear about it later but I want you to hear it from me first. You know, 'cause nothing happened. And, I don't feel about her the way I feel about you. I love you and, and there's nobody else.

Sheila Ryan: Right from the beginning, you know, it was a new car and a new wardrobe, in week one. And I don't think that that happened with every girl. As, as a matter of fact, I'm sure that it didn't.

Mindi Miller: Oh, and I forgot too he had offered to buy me a car that night, which was amazing.

Linda Thompson: I finally came to terms with it and, understood that, you know, he is Elvis. He is sequestered, in this little tight knit group of people. He never sees people from the outside. He's with me all the time. He's got to get a little restless and bored.

Mindi Miller: He said here's 5000 dollars and I want you to, to take care of everything you need to take care of. You're gonna be here. And he goes, you're gonna go on tour. And he says I won't be seeing you every day and all that because I'm gone and I'm here and I'm there and you're in LA. He said but I will see you. And I said well you understand that I'm here now for you. I said I'm staying here for you. But at, at the same time I understood I'm not gonna just like move in or something. And, you know, I'm sure at the time he was still seeing other girls because that was Elvis.

Linda Thompson: You know, there's a part of him that was very sincere and loved me as he loved no other. But he did love other people, too.

When a girlfriend was asked to stay at Graceland, it was an indication that Elvis wanted a relationship to go further, the unwritten rule that all of his lovers knew.

Sheila Ryan: Nobody got to go to Graceland, unless you were then the number one girl. So I guess Linda got down to the number two slot. I, I don't know if that was her doing. You know, I – we didn't talk a lot about that. I, I didn't talk a lot about Linda, at all. You know, what happened with them. It wasn't a conversation that happened, you know. I just did what I was told and, when he req– requested I be there I was there.

Mindi Miller: And I remember we had gone to Graceland and I – it was really wonderful to see his home. I mean, that was a joy, to relay see where he lived and how he lived and to meet, some of the people that were left in his family. And, you know, and, and, meet his little girl. Because Lisa Marie was only three at the time.

Sheila Ryan: I actually didn't live there but I, I got there, which was a big deal. Because Linda lived there. And he had to move her out before I could come to visit. And it was a strange experience. I, you know, I expected Graceland to be Graceland and instead it was Graceland.

Barbara Leigh: I went to all of his homes. And, it was a lot of fun. He liked to do fun things at Graceland. More at Graceland than anywhere else.

Mindi Miller: We're supposed to think we're the only ones, you know, until you learn well, you're not the only one.

Patty Parry: Well I learned very early in the game because one of the girlfriends did ask me, and I wasn't – I wasn't sure how to – how to deal with it and I said something about another woman. And, she went back to Elvis and Elvis took me to his room he said, deny everything. That was his thing. Deny everything – he says don't ever talk to the girls about other women 'cause they will pump you to death.

JOE ESPOSITO
ROAD MANAGER & FRIEND

MINDI MILLER
GIRLFRIEND

Joe Esposito: We were good at keeping women from running into each other. We were very well organized.

Mindi Miller: His bodyguards called and they would say, okay we're in Georgia or we're in Florida and we want you to get on a plane and Elvis wants to see you. So it wasn't very often that he would call on his own or they'd put him on. They were well, you know, E wants to talk to you. Everything was E. So E wants to say hi. E wants to talk to you. And, then he'd make arrangements and fly you out to where he was and, meet up with him on tour and, and do the rest of the tour with him. And then sometimes go back to Graceland with him and, but it was very exciting I have to say.

In 1976, at the age of 41, Elvis's career was at an all time high, but his personal life had nearly hit rock bottom. His weight had ballooned to over 200 pounds, and his health was declining. His young lovers, tired of having to care for an aging rock star, slowly began to disappear. Some had been waiting for marriage proposals. Others just couldn't handle watching the king's descent.

Mindi Miller: Everybody knew him in a different way and in a different light. And everybody has their own synopsis of him and – their own – their own way of remembering him. So he's not gonna be the same with every single person.

LINDA THOMPSON
ELVIS'S GIRLFRIEND

Linda Thompson: My relationship with Elvis ended kind of slowly. As I grew up, as I matured, as I became wiser to the ways of the world and to the way so his world particularly, you know, I, I came to realize, I didn't want to live that way for the rest of my life. I didn't want to have a child with someone who slept all day, and was awake at night like a vampire's existence. It became depressing to me. He was also self destructive. The last time I saw him alive, I left him in San Francisco. Trite as it may sound, left my heart in San Francisco, but it's true. He was about to play the Cow Palace, and he had brought in Ginger

Alden, the girl that he would date after I left. And he had begun to date her already, and I knew she was there, because I wasn't stupid. And he was saying goodbye to me, and I was going back to Memphis. And he said now honey, no matter what you ever hear, no matter what anybody ever tells you, there is nobody but you in my life and in my heart. And I love you and nobody else.

Linda Thompson: When you love someone that much, it's very, very difficult to sit by and watch them self destruct. And more than the other women, more than the lifestyle, more than anything else I think that's what propelled me away from him because I, I, I didn't want to be there. And, I didn't want to wake up and find him dead.

LINDA THOMPSON
ELVIS'S GIRLFRIEND

Charlie Hodge: I believe that if Linda had been there that morning he might not have died. She would've heard him fall 'cause she didn't take sleeping pills, and would've gone over and, and moved him over on his back, and he might possibly be alive today.

CHARLIE HODGE
FRIEND/SINGER/GUITARIST/
MEMPHIS MAFIA

Mindi Miller: By the time I met him, it was more toward the end of his life, you see, than it was at the beginning. So I didn't know him in his 20s and 30s. I knew him in his early 40s and, you know, late 30s early 40s. And so for him, no— none of us knowing that this was toward the end of his life.

MINDI MILLER
GIRLFRIEND

Sheila Ryan: When he would get up to go to the bathroom, I would be at the bathroom door with my ear to the door. You know, and that was – that was part of the deal. You know, sometimes we would try to fill some of the capsules with sugar and make him think he was getting a sleep med, when in fact it was a placebo. And, so, you know, it was all a game. Let's pretend Elvis isn't dying, you know. We didn't really talk about how serious it was. But it was.

SHEILA RYAN
GIRLFRIEND

Mindi Miller: I think he was really missing the true companionship of, of someone who really understood him. And I think he was so much larger than life and he knew it. But yet inside, he knew who he was and where he came from, and he never lost sight of that. And he was still extremely very humble. But yet he could really get on his high horse and, you know, he knew that he had the power. If he wanted to say something or get something done, he knew people jumped.

Sheila Ryan: The first time I turned him down, it was because I had fallen in love with someone else. My husband to be, Jimmy Caan and I were staying at Hefner's mansion. And, I mean, I was seriously lookin' for a helicop– helicopters because, you know, if he couldn't find me, that was never anything that happened. I was always accessible. So I went and spent the night at my apartment, and he called at 4:00 in the morning. And said, you know, you know, you've got your horse at Graceland and, there's no more Linda. It's just you and I. And, you know, and just, you know, promised me the world, which was what, you know, I had kind of wanted, all along, but it was too late.

Barbara Leigh: The last time I saw Elvis was the last time I saw Lisa Marie. And we spent the evening in his bed. And he was reading the Bible to me. And just talking about life and, catching up on what I had been doing. And basically didn't come out of the room. I went and got him some dinner and we sat on the bed. And, just kinda caught up on things.

Linda Thompson: I was able to leave with still a good feeling. I loved him. He loved me. And there was someone else in the wings that he was gonna see and I felt, I was hoping he'd be okay.

At a time when Elvis needed someone most, he pushed his lovers further away. And it was then that he discovered what would be the last intimate love of his life. The woman that he came to refer to as Gingerbread. The woman some think almost became the next Mrs. Presley.

Myrna Smith: She wasn't naïve at all. She may have been young, but she wasn't naïve.

MYRNA SMITH
SINGER/BACK-UP GROUP, SWEET INSPIRATIONS

Pat Broeske: Ginger Alden was very young, very, very beautiful. And I think, pretty impressionable. You know, she was a teenager when she met Elvis Presley. And, and by then he was a much older man.

PAT BROESKE
AUTHOR

Charlie Hodge: He just developed a thing for her and, I think that, that probably, was a part of his life that was unhappy because he wasn't getting from her what he needed from a woman. So he, you know, it wasn't the thing that he needed for someone to stay with him. And be with him. And, he had decided he wasn't going to marry her.

CHARLIE HODGE
FRIEND/SINGER/GUITARIST/
MEMPHIS MAFIA

George Klein: I also introduced Ginger Alden to Elvis. And I personally got along with Ginger very well. I think the situation with Ginger was, Elvis was 42, and Ginger was like about 21 or 20.

JOE ESPOSITO
ROAD MANAGER & FRIEND

Joe Esposito: Ginger was a beautiful lady. But, if you look at her real close, she looks like a young Priscilla in a way or even like Elvis's mother. Dark hair, beautiful eyes, deep set. And, and I think that's what attracted Elvis, first and foremost.

GEORGE KLEIN
MEMPHIS MAFIA/FR...

George Klein: If you look at some of her pictures today, she looked like a Priscilla Presley with brown eyes but a little taller.

PAT BROESKE
AUTHOR

Pat Broeske: I think it was kind of a hard life on her, because Elvis is not in real good condition. This is 1976, 1977. It's the groggy Elvis Presley. He's not in his prime during all of his concerts. He, he can't wake up the way he should. There's some increasing medication problems. And Ginger was a very young girl to have to deal with this kind of stuff.

George Klein: I think some of the guys in the group had a problem with Ginger, but I didn't. I, I think they didn't understand that she was – really young, and was taken back by the situation. And was just learning how to cope with it when, when Elvis passed away.

Joe Esposito: Ginger was never – not very outgoing. And I can understand why because her mother was around quite a bit, and her mother would answer for her. You know, I mean, Elvis would ask Ginger a question and her mother would answer.

DR. LESTER
HOFFMAN
ELVIS'S DENTIST

Dr. Lester Hoffman: Well the last time I saw Elvis it was just a routine visit to check him over. He was preparing a tour. And he had Ginger Alden with him. And we went up, and we fixed his tooth as I said. And when we finished, he said would you mind talkin' to Ginger? He said, I got to get ready for the tour he said I'll be with you in a minute. Well I'm 60 some odd years old. I don't have much in common with an 18 year old girl. But we sat there we talked for about a half hour, and Elvis came back he says I'm, I'm not ready yet. He says go ahead he says I'll be back in a little bit. And he was gone for another half hour and Ginger and I kept talking. And this went on till about 11:00 at night.

Elvis began canceling concert appearances and spending more time recuperating in his Graceland bed. During this low point, Alden claims that Elvis proposed marriage to her.

Charlie Hodge: At first he wanted to marry her, and then I remember we were at the fairgrounds and he said look at that. 'Cause she wasn't with him, she was over there with her sisters. He says if I marry her I'll marry the whole damn family. And, he said I'm, I'm not gonna marry her.

CHARLIE HODGE
FRIEND/SINGER/GUITARIST/
MEMPHIS MAFIA

Joe Esposito: I don't think it was a big hot romantic love affair. I mean, Elvis was a lot older than her. And, a beautiful 19 year old girl. Elvis was seein' other women when he was seein' her, too.

JOE ESPOSITO
ROAD MANAGER & FRIEND

Myrna Smith: No, he wasn't serious about her. But, his ego was bruised when she didn't do what he wanted her to because, it – he was so used to – if he tells you, I'd like you to come to Nashville with me, then you went to Nashville with him. He says, how dare you tell me no.

MYRNA SMITH
SINGER/BACK-UP GROUP,
SWEET INSPIRATIONS

Pat Broeske: I think it was the classic case of a guy trying to recapture his youth, in some ways. Recapture, you know, what was lost.

PAT BROESKE
AUTHOR

ELVIS

On August 16, 1977, Ginger Alden awoke to find herself alone in bed at Graceland. After knocking on the bathroom door several times, Ginger walked in and found Elvis dead. He was 42 years old. Everyone has their own memories of the king. But only a precious few were fortunate enough to live those memories with him.

Mindi Miller: He was very much a loner. I mean, he loved people. But I remember the private talks we had. He would really open up and he would really say, you know, nobody really understands me. And I remember he would say, you know, he'd say honey, it's very lonely at the top of the mountain.

MINDI MILLER
GIRLFRIEND

Barbara Leigh: I think that he just had a wonderful spirit, that will live forever. That he was kind and besides having the most beautiful voice. It's just – even today it's hard to beat his voice. He was magic.

Ann-Margret: Funny. Generous, giving, kind, loving. Gifted, so talented.

Anita Wood: And I fell in love with him, Elvis the man. Not Elvis the star. And the minute he'd walk in a room he just lit it up, you know.

Linda Thompson: He was very much a little child at heart, which was, you know, accountable for his charm. I mean, he, he was the most adorable, endearing, vulnerable soul in many, many ways.

Sheila Ryan: He loved women. And he was wonderful, and sweet and kind and giving and, I don't think that I have, and ever will meet anybody as kind and generous and loving as he was to women.

COMEBACK OF THE GUITAR MAN

"He had an edge to him that was dangerous in his performing. You could feel it. You know, just sparks would happen, just dangerous."

– Earl Brown

America was undergoing a great change during the 1960s. Rock 'n' roll had acquired a British accent and now sang of peace and love and understanding. Elvis Presley seemed just a memory, a distant recollection of gyrating hips and a greased pompadour, an obsolete idol in a new world. But the King of Rock 'n' Roll would no longer be passed by and drift gently into history. He would return to take back his throne. He would be reborn in black leather and challenge the world once again, and he would do it his way.

Between 1960 and early 1968 Elvis made 24 films…

…But only performed twice to a live audience. Music had changed dramatically during his absence from the concert scene. The world had changed dramatically. But it was all about to change once again with one televised show, the '68 comeback.

Steve Binder: I remember telling him that in my opinion, if he didn't mind my bluntness, but to me he hadn't had a hit record in years, he wasn't making any movies, so what was really making him this superstar was just Colonel Parker and his publicity machine.

Pat Broeske: You know, up to that time he'd been kind of languishing in these movies. They were getting a little increasingly goofier.

John O'Hara: That's Elvis taking control of his career again. That's where he just had enough of the movies. And, you know, it's funny, television was always very important in
his career,

Steve Binder: But television was a way to either instantly the next day become the biggest star in the world, or vice versa. You might do the television special and fall on your ass and that be the end of your career, other than the memory of what you used to do. We set up a meeting and Elvis came out with, you know, the gang.

Chris Beard: He walked down a hallway and he was like, this caged panther, you know? He was surrounded by people, and yet I could see that he was wanting something to happen. He had gotten into this other Elvis. He had gone from one Elvis to another Elvis at this time, and he was so electric and so on and so different than obviously what he was in the movies that he had regained his stardom before he even did the special.

Steve Binder: And we went into our office, and we left everybody outside and it was just the Colonel, myself, Bones, Allan Bly and Chris Beard, who wrote the special.

STEVE BINDER
PRODUCER 1968-COMEBACK
SPECIAL

Chris Beard: I thought Elvis looks like he's got a great sense of humor, and even if he doesn't, I'm gonna take myself in hand here and try and get to a place where I can discover if he's where I think he is, okay? So we were all introducing each other to each other, and I don't know if Joe Esposito remembers this, but I said, "Elvis, I really like your work." And then I turned to the Colonel and I said, "Colonel, I like your work too, but more than that, I like your chicken," you see. It was a stupid joke. And of course Elvis, how dare anybody talk to the Colonel like this and he thought that was hysterical.

CHRIS BEARD
WRITER, 1968 COMEBACK
SPECIAL

So he started laughing, and of course when he laughed the guys that were around him laughed because that was their job, more or less. Next minute I'm looking at him and he's looking at me and we're going, "Okay, we're gonna do business here."

Joe Esposito: Colonel Parker came to Elvis with this idea, Elvis's TV special. But Elvis was a little concerned, he was a little nervous. He had never done a TV special on his own. He'd been on a couple shows, but never his TV special. And, you know, when NBC did the deal with Colonel Parker, it was also including a movie, too, which was "CHANGE OF HABIT."

JOE ESPOSITO
ROAD MANAGER & FRIEND

Chris Beard: Singer was the sponsor of the show, and, you know, we were these young Turks in those days. You know, Steve Binder, we were the people who had done all this angry television, and I don't know how we got to actually be chosen to do this, but I think Bob Finkel, who is a brilliant producer, said, "I'm gonna get Steve Binder because he's an angry young

CHRIS BEARD
WRITER, 1968 COMEBACK
SPECIAL

man, and then I'm gonna get two guys who know comedy and know music and know production, and I'll put all these people together, and I think it's gonna work." And of course that's what happened. We wrote a killer special with killer stuff that gets played every year now, and it is the classic Elvis.

But there were still many obstacles that lay ahead. Elvis's manager, Colonel Tom Parker, and the director of the comeback special, Steve Binder, each wanted the show to go in different directions. It was time for Elvis to decide his own future.

STEVE BINDER
PRODUCER 1968 COMEBACK SPECIAL

Steve Binder: Well, Colonel Parker had a lot of pre-conceived ideas, but my experience from the very beginning of my career to the present is that, you know, let creative people create and let business people do their business.

BOB FINKEL
PRODUCER, 1968 COMEBACK SPECIAL

Bob Finkel: The only problem we had was with the Colonel. The Colonel had definitive ideas about what he wanted Elvis to do, which in many cases Elvis was not happy with, although he didn't fight him on a lot of them.

CHARLIE HODGE
FRIEND/SINGER/GUITARIST/MEMPHIS MAFIA

Charlie Hodge: The Colonel wanted that to be a Christmas show.

JOHN O'HARA
AUTHOR

John O'Hara: He wanted Elvis to come out and sing some Christmas carols and then say good night and that would be it. And he was lucky enough to have been hooked up with some very good producers, Steve Binder, and they really nailed the essence of Elvis, you know, Elvis in front of a small audience just being Elvis.

Steve Binder: I just heard all of the talk of this is going to be a Christmas special, this is gonna have 26 Christmas songs in it, and to be really honest with you, it never fazed me and it never entered my mind that that was what we were going to do.

STEVE BINDER
PRODUCER 1968 COMEBACK
SPECIAL

Chris Beard: Well, first of all we had to get Elvis on our side, and of course that came when we went by ourselves in a room with him and we all said to each other, "We aren't gonna do this United Nations shit. We're just not gonna do it." So he says, "Well, I don't wanna do that, either." And we said, "Well, do you wanna do what we wanna do?" And we all said, "Yeah, we wanna do rock 'n' roll. We wanna get a 32-piece orchestra, we wanna get out there, we wanna rock. We wanna do 'Hound Dog,'" you know? So he says, "Oh, fantastic! Yeah." So we went back in the room and the Colonel looked at all of us and he's going, "Something happened in there. I don't know what they were talking about, but this isn't the same Elvis that went in," 'cause Elvis was like, he was stoked, he was like, he was getting ready to go "Ah ah" very loudly.

CHRIS BEARD
WRITER, 1968 COMEBACK
SPECIAL

Pat Broeske: There was like, a little war between Steve Binder and the Colonel and Elvis. The Colonel wanted Elvis to end the show singing a Christmas song.

PAT BROESKE
AUTHOR

ELVIS

Steve Binder: So he called me in one day with Elvis and the three of us were in this little water closet that he called an office, and he said, "Well, Elvis wants a Christmas song in the show, don't you, Elvis?" And Elvis sort of had his head down and his eyes lowered, and he said, "Yes, sir." And I said, "Fine. If Elvis wants a Christmas song in the show we'll put a Christmas song in the show." And I won't use an expletive, but we walked out of the Colonel's office thinking it was resolved, and Elvis jabbed me in the ribs and he said, you know, "Blank him." "We're not gonna worry about that."

STEVE BINDER
PRODUCER 1968 COMEBACK
SPECIAL

Chris Beard: We didn't know more or less what we wanted to do, except we now knew that we had changed their minds, and they were gonna do a rock 'n' roll show.

Steve Binder: We had a whole stack of his albums, every movie he ever made, every recording he ever made, etc., which is how we basically tailor made the show. What I told Elvis when he went to Hawaii is that we would make him a show that nobody else could do, only him. Like making a tailor made suit, it would be made for him.

Pat Broeske: The day of the first taping the Colonel had taken care of tickets, supposedly. He told Steve Binder, "Oh, no, don't worry about it, don't worry about it. I'll take care of this thing."

Chris Beard: Right before we were gonna go out there and put him in front of the audience, like maybe a couple of hours before, we found out that somebody had canceled the audience. The Colonel got on the phone and called up all the local dee jays in L.A. and said, "Hey, get down to NBC, there's gonna be an Elvis Presley live performance." And of course they had four security guards and there was a riot, but they definitely got a bunch of people down there quick.

Pat Broeske: They also sent runners over to the Bob's Big Boy in the valley, who went up and down the aisles begging people to leave their lunches and to go over to NBC to see this show. And every NBC exec who had a wife or a daughter called them on the phone and said, "You have to get down to the studio today. Get dressed up, you're gonna go to a concert."

Chris Beard: Everybody was so shocked by seeing him in this new role of like, killer rock 'n' roll singer again, you know, and the image of all those movies, even though they were still being played, I don't think still to this day is the strongest single image of him looking in the camera at the beginning of that special and saying, "If you're looking for trouble –"

CHRIS BEARD
WRITER, 1968 COMEBACK SPECIAL

ELVIS: You came to the right place

Chris Beard: And then the camera pulls back and there's a hundred people dressed as Elvis in the, uh, background.

Pat Broeske: And suddenly Elvis emerges, you know, head to toe in this black leather outfit, and he sort of reignited the flames again. It was like the old Elvis.

SUSAN BRODSKY
ELVIS HISTORIAN

Susan Brodsky: No man on earth ever looked as good as he did in 1968 in that black leather, and he sounded fantastic.

Kenny Rogers: I thought that was when he looked his best as well. I mean he was really a handsome, handsome guy at that period in his life.

KENNY ROGERS
SINGER/SONGWRITER

Steve Binder: He was awesome-looking. I mean I'm heterosexual, I'm straight as an arrow and I gotta tell you, you stop whether you're male or female to look at him. He was that good-looking.

STEVE BINDER
PRODUCER 1968 COMEBACK SPECIAL

Bill Medley: Boy, he looked phenomenal, you know. I would have had his children.

JACKIE DeSHANNON
SINGER/FRIEND

Jackie DeShannon: I just sat down like a three-year-old when I saw Elvis do his special. I just sat there mesmerized. I didn't get up. I didn't move. I was just, "Oh, my God. It's never –" you know, nothing ever changed. He always had that magic.

Chris Beard: This was the first time he had performed in front of a live audience that wasn't paid like in the movies to just come out and perform.

Bill Belew: When I looked at Elvis I said, "He's the one person that I could do the Napoleonic collar with, because it'll frame his face." And like a lotta things that you do for women when you're designing their clothes, is to draw your attention to their face. And I thought, "Well, if I have the collar up there people will notice his face."

Chris Beard: This is quite an amazing thing, what happened to him. You know, he put on that black leather, you know, and the first time he had that black leather on it was like – I think it was like a football player when a football player puts on a uniform, you know? Now it's the duty. "I've gotta go out there and I've gotta be me."

Anita Mann: My favorite thing is him sitting around – I mean as much as I love the dance numbers and love dancing – but him sitting around with the guys and doing that concert to me is a classic and will always be a classic.

Bill Medley: Him and the guys, you know, up on that little stage, and without all the fanfare there, you know, you really got a good shot at who Elvis was as a guy and who he was musically. It was terrific.

Chris Beard: The brilliance of the idea of using his old cronies from Memphis, his old musicians and friends from Memphis was it naturally relaxed him totally, and so he was able to be very loose.

D.J. Fontana: The first one or two tunes, if you've seen the film at all, you can tell he's a little nervous. He was a little bit shaky, scared. But then he got the kids screaming and hollering, you know, telling him he was fine. You could hear them talking. He's sitting just within a few inches of all of them, you know. And after that he just got relaxed and done what he was supposed to do.

Charlie Hodge: The sit-down portion in the circle, when we first did that they had us out there by ourselves, and the fans were back about 30 yards there or something like that. Elvis just talking softly, you know, he said, "Man, I don't like this, being this far from the audience." I said, "Well, it's your show. Ask them if they wanna come down here." And Elvis stood up and said, "Y'all wanna come sit down around here?" And the director said, "No!" It was too late. They were all down around there.

Lance Legault: The sit-down part of it was originally I believe supposed to be about ten minutes of the original show, and now it became such a thing it's its own special now, "One Night With You," and that's the real Elvis.

Steve Stevens: I loved it because there again it didn't separate Elvis from his fans. It was small, okay? Even the guys off to the side and the audience was close. You know, it was like, "Hey, come on over to the house and I'm gonna entertain for you guys."

Trent Carlini: I think it was great the way they captured Elvis's down to earth nature in that setting. Very powerful and very raw, it was great.

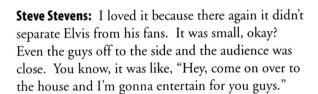
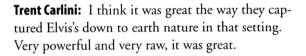

When he took the stage by himself, Elvis finally proved that he was no longer living in the shadow of who he once was.

Elvis Presley: Well, it's one for the money –

It had been nearly a decade since he had felt the excitement, the fear, the joy of standing on a stage and facing the audience literally one on one.

Chris Beard: He was nervous, but it was not nervous scared, it was nervous energy, right? It was like Elvis energy, pent up, pent up, pent up for all these years. Here he was going to sing, you know, in front of an audience for the first time.

And I don't think it was nerves, I think it was just sheer, unadulterated excitement and energy and nervous energy, but not "I'm scared to do this," it's "I want to do this."

Charlie Hodge: When we first did the '68 comeback we had the full orchestra and a choir in the same room. Elvis said, "Charlie, I can't read music. I don't know when to come in." I said, "Don't worry." I said, "I'll tell Billy to turn to you when it's time to come in." And I said, "After you do that a few times you'll feel when it's natural to come in."

And he – "Okay," he said. He trusted me on it. And I told Billy. And so when it come time for him to start singing on like, the first thing, Billy turned to him like that, and after that Elvis was home free.

James Darren: I thought that was a great show. I thought it was a perfect show. I thought it was just a wonderful reintroduction of Elvis to the people. It was intimate, you know, and I assume he really had a good time doing that.

Linda Thompson: He really got what he had done, that he set the world back on its heels, that he changed fashion and sexual mores and music, you know, that he just kinda revolutionized all aspects of our culture when he came on the scene.

LINDA THOMPSON
Elvis's Girlfriend

Ray Manzarek: He moved like a sex machine. Those hips, the gyration of those hips promised orgasm. Licentiousness and orgasm. Elvis in a way promised all women in America a good orgasm. And he would deliver.

RAY MANZAREK
Keyboards, The Doors

Susan Brodsky: He seems to be the quintessential performer. It's like he's singing directly to you. And he puts so much energy and feeling into every song that he sings, he's just an amazing performer, and it just really came across in '68.

SUSAN BRODSKY
Elvis Historian

Steve Stevens: I think and believe that what the live audience felt – the television audience felt. That's why it was so special. There again, it's not putting that certain something in between the entertainer, star, superstar, and the audience fans.

STEVE STEVENS
Actor/Friend

Earl Brown: I think he knew something great was happening for him. I mean God knows he'd done so much, so many movies that it wasn't anything new for him, but it was different somehow. The whorehouse number was unbelievable. The first version that went on the air, they didn't show that. They cut that out.

EARL BROWN
Songwriter/1968 Comeback Special

Steve Binder: First thing was the bordello sequence where he leaves his hometown and he goes and the first encounter he has is he walks into a bordello, and then there's this virgin innocent girl who's never even worked one day. And she looks at Elvis and he looks at her, and just as they're about to get together the place gets raided and they jump out the window and he's on the road again.

STEVE BINDER
Producer 1968 Comeback Special

SUSAN HENNING
GIRLFRIEND/DANCER

MARLYN MASON
CO-STAR, THE TROUBLE WITH GIRLS

CHRIS BEARD
WRITER, 1968 COMEBACK SPECIAL

Susan Henning: The '68 special, that was the second time I saw Elvis, and I don't know that he knew I had just interviewed at NBC and got the part as the little virgin, the virgin girl of the night, I guess to say it politely. I think it was little cameo shots that were going to be played in between the bordello scene. And sure, we had fun. I remember we had some grapes and he's a great tease and he's fun to play with.

Marlyn Mason: I was stunned. I really fell in love with him as a performer when I saw that. That was probably one of the all-time great specials I think ever.

Chris Beard: He was like a caged tiger. He just ate the stage. He ate the audience. He ate everything. He ate the studio. It was like, it was unbelievable.

Not only had Elvis matured with time, his music had grown up as well. Along with playing all of his original hits, Elvis added a few new songs to his growing resume of stage favorites.

MAC DAVIS
SINGER/SONGWRITER

CHRIS BEARD
WRITER, 1968 COMEBACK SPECIAL

Mac Davis: There was a chance for me to write one song – which everybody remembers of course, the section where Elvis sat in his black leather outfit and sang the old hits from the Sun days – they asked me to write a song bookending that, you know, about looking back over the years. Started writing about 6:00 in the evening, and 8:00 the next morning I had written "Memories."

Chris Beard: And we were looking at everything he'd done and we couldn't find anything that really fitted the way we wanted to express his feelings at the end of the show. And so we said to Earl Brown, who is our lyric writer, "Why don't you write a song for Elvis?" And we said, "Elvis, is that okay?" And he says, "Yeah."

Earl Brown: Something told me Elvis is not gonna like what I'm gonna write anyway, so I'll write something with Aretha Franklin in mind or somebody like that, and I'll write the music myself. So the next day I went in, we played the song for Bob Finkel and Steve Binder, and from the other room I heard Colonel Parker's voice say, "That ain't Elvis's kinda song." But behind me I heard, "I'd like to try it, man," and Elvis was behind me. I never knew he was there in the doorway listening to it.

EARL BROWN
SONGWRITER/1968 COMEBACK SPECIAL

Pat Broeske: Elvis startled everybody, by the way, during that number when it came down to laying down the tracks for "If I Can Dream," because he came into a recording studio, and, you know, there's like, an orchestra there and everything to accompany him, and he laid down on the floor and held the microphone and sang in a fetal position, kinda weeping as he sang.

PAT BROESKE
AUTHOR

Chris Beard: Elvis was very emotional when he sang that song, because he knew it was at the end of the show. And I got a sneaking suspicion he didn't want the show to end because he was having the best time of his life and here was this big, powerful song with a big, powerful lyric about him.

CHRIS BEARD
WRITER, 1968 COMEBACK SPECIAL

Elvis Presley: But as long as a man has the strength to dream he can redeem his soul and fly.

Elvis had tasted greatness once again, but his televised special was only the start of his renaissance. The biggest comeback of his life lay just around the corner and 400 miles to the east.

Joe Esposito: What really inspired Elvis to go back onstage again is when we did the '68 special, doing a little live performance and the improv section and getting the feel of the fans and the audience. He was missing that.

JOE ESPOSITO
ROAD MANAGER & FRIEND

> **Elvis Presley:** I just missed it. I missed the closeness of an audience, of a live audience.

JOE ESPOSITO
ROAD MANAGER & FRIEND

MARLYN MASON
CO-STAR, THE TROUBLE WITH GIRLS

MYRNA SMITH
SINGER/BACK-UP GROUP, SWEET INSPIRATIONS

JACKIE KAHANE
COMEDIAN/ELVIS'S OPENING ACT

SONNY KING
COMEDIAN/FRIEND

Joe Esposito: And then as we all know the Colonel's approach about playing Las Vegas at the International Hotel, and when the Colonel sat down with him to talk about doing that I think he realized, "Hey, this is what I wanna do. I wanna go back to performing on stage," and that's what started it. And from that time on that's all we did.

Marlyn Mason: He was so thrilled. He was like a little kid. He was just so, "I'm gonna play Vegas!" You know? I mean there was an innocence to him that was – I think that was part of his IT, the thing that made him so charming. There was a vulnerability to him.

Myrna Smith: I remember Elvis being very, very nervous, and I remember thinking, "Gee, I hope he has a good crowd," because I mean I knew he hadn't performed live on stage like that for a number of years, I think ten years.

Jackie Kahane: As I'm walking downstairs having introduced him, he walks by me. He says, "Are you nervous?" I said, "Yeah." He says, "I'm scared shit-less."

Sonny King: He almost threw up every time they introduced him, but once he hit that spotlight, forget about it. He didn't stammer or stutter or anything. That voice would come out, that beautiful voice, you know. And he would get out there and you knew by the look in his eyes that the fear was gone.

Joe Esposito: Well, I remember opening night in 1969 in Las Vegas at the International Hotel. Elvis was a nervous wreck. But when he walked out on that stage and that audience jumped up, standing ovation, and he was just flying. I mean you could tell he was nervous the first song. The second song he got into it and that was it. That show flew by.

JOE ESPOSITO
ROAD MANAGER & FRIEND

Johnny Tillotson: I had a chance to see the first performance of Elvis in Las Vegas. That's when he had the karate outfit. And it was just such an exciting – his shows were always exciting and they were spontaneous and they were in the moment and he sang great and he had so much fun.

JOHNNY TILLOTSON
SINGER/SONGWRITER

Emilio Micelli: The excitement was unbelievable. Since the first day that it opened…it opened the door for Elvis Presley over there. Lotta people from all over the country. I had fans from Japan, they used to come over from Tokyo to Las Vegas and saw every performance since July 31, 1969, and the last time he performed at the International.

EMILIO MICELLI
MAITRE D' LAS VEGAS HILTON

Rona Barrett: I saw Elvis perform in Las Vegas on several occasions, including the big comeback. And before that actually, from the first time he went to Vegas I was there. And he was very exciting as a performer on stage. He had so much charisma, and he had a splendid instrument in his voice. And his feelings and the way he would move and he was just really exciting. I thought he was thrilling, really thrilling.

RONA BARRETT
TELEVISION HOST / COLUMNIST

Elvis played two shows a night for 30 nights at the International Hotel before taking his show on the road. Next stop: the Houston Astrodome.

INTERVIEW EXCERPT

Reporter: The attire is not one that we're familiar seeing on you.

Elvis Presley: It was taken from a karate suit, just a regular karate type outfit. Are they coming to get me, is that it? Well, I think the most important thing is the inspiration that I get from a live audience. I was missing that.

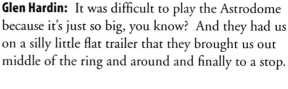

Glen Hardin: It was difficult to play the Astrodome because it's just so big, you know? And they had us on a silly little flat trailer that they brought us out middle of the ring and around and finally to a stop.

Charlie Hodge: We went into the Astrodome and it was almost like a rehearsal show because here we are out in the middle of the arena on this stage that keeps turning. And, you know, you say something and it would take I think 15, 20 seconds to get to the people, and then 15, 20 seconds for their response to get back to you. So the only thing you could do, just do straight through your show and don't stop.

Elvis Presley: I'd like to thank you very much. I'd like to tell you something else. This is the largest audience that I've ever sang to, so it makes one a wee bit nervous, I'll tell you.

Joe Esposito: Once we played Vegas and a little short tour after Vegas with the Astrodome and a couple other cities, Elvis knew that's where he wanted to be. That's what Elvis loved to do more than anything in the world, is perform live on stage.

James Darren: On the road you're really performing for absolute die hard fans – not that they weren't in Vegas, but it's a whole different thing.

As Elvis continued touring he performed for each crowd as if it would be his last. He had become a polished and precise entertainer, making the audience part of the show.

Shecky Greene: He really was a student, though, of performing. He really was. I mean I watched his growth and I saw this getting the confidence, I saw him becoming a better performer, playing with an audience.

SHECKY GREENE
COMEDIAN/FRIEND

Myrna Smith: He was very playful with the audience, and I think he really cared about his fans. He wanted to give them a good show.

MYRNA SMITH
SINGER/BACK-UP GROUP,
SWEET INSPIRATIONS

Shecky Greene: I saw the audience going crazy. They waited in lines and they did – and I love the way he played with people. He got to the point where he played with people and he got that wonderful feeling on stage.

CHARLIE HODGE
FRIEND/SINGER/GUITARIST/
MEMPHIS MAFIA

Charlie Hodge: He could play with the audience, which he liked doing. They enjoyed it, too. But he knew how far to push the audience as far as exciting them before he'd do some humorous things like that to break it up, and he'd stop there. I mean he was a master at that. My goodness. He just knew how to handle himself on stage. And he was always alert. He always walked sideways to the audience. That's in case somebody pulled him, he could use his leverage he had to not let them pull him into the audience.

HENRY YOUNG
FAN

Henry Young: Most of the time he'd sing what songs were in at that time, and as he got larger than that he wouldn't sing as much. He'd talk a little more. He actually was funny a lotta times.

Henry Young: He just didn't sing every song and that, he would talk to the audience, communicate. He'd stroll up and down the stage.

Every performance was different. I never saw two alike.

Elvis Presley: Thank you very much. Good evening, ladies and gentlemen. I'm event number eight.

Elvis never forgot the city that had welcomed him back with open arms at the beginning of his return. Las Vegas became his kingdom, and he would return there to perform as often as possible.

Joe Esposito: They would get in line. At 2:00 in the afternoon, the show didn't start til eight. In those days there were no reserved seats. Now there are reserved seats. There'd be a line all the way through to the casino all the way out past the registration desk. The hotel couldn't believe it.

Cassandra "Elvira" Peterson: I took my parents – my family came to Vegas to visit, and we got a table and we got close down the front, and I saw him perform, and it was heavy, you know. It was great. I did see him perform. I had seen him before that and after that.

Did he do two or three shows in Vegas?

Yeah, two, and I went to both of them and I got seats down in front. I used all the pull I had as a showgirl to get great seats.

Joe Delaney: Elvis filled the largest showroom we had by some – it was anywhere from about 700 seats larger than any other showroom, and he filled it consistently two shows a night, 14 shows a week.

JOE DELANEY
CRITIC "LAS VEGAS SUN"

Barbara Leigh: Everything about him was magic. When he was performing he gave everything to the audience. And I think that people identified with his soul and the tenderness and the loving part of him.

BARBARA LEIGH
GIRLFRIEND

Linda Thompson: He was the most adorable, endearing, vulnerable soul in many, many ways. And then to see him on stage, you saw this powerhouse, this dynamo, you know, this sexy, god-like being when his show was on.

LINDA THOMPSON
ELVIS'S GIRLFRIEND

Robin Rosaaen: February of 1970 we drove from Los Gatos all the way to Las Vegas, stayed in some cheap flophouse motel and went and saw Elvis for one show. That's all I could afford in those days. And didn't have the best seating, but when Elvis came out on stage I was just mesmerized by his presence, his vocal singing ability and just all these people in the showroom that came from all over the world just to see this one man entertain.

ROBIN ROSAAEN
AUTHOR/FAN

Henry Young: All excited, couldn't wait til he got on the stage. The music started playing, you got goose bumps and stuff. And I thought, "Wow, here he comes" and that music played and he walked on that stage. It was the awesome-est experience I ever had.

HENRY YOUNG
FAN

Earl Brown: He had an edge to him that was dangerous in his performing. You could feel it. You know, just sparks would happen, just dangerous.

EARL BROWN
SONGWRITER/1968 COMEBACK SPECIAL

Mac Davis: Flabbergasted, jaw dropped. Hero, you know, all that stuff. All the above. You know, he was like nothing I'd ever seen before.

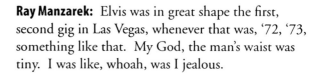

Ray Manzarek: Elvis was in great shape the first, second gig in Las Vegas, whenever that was, '72, '73, something like that. My God, the man's waist was tiny. I was like, whoah, was I jealous.

Johnny Tillotson: Because his live performances were the – there's no words to describe them. And then his record performances were always so honest. And he had a – he used his voice like an instrument, just like a musical instrument.

Elvis had conquered the west coast, now it was time to reclaim the east – New York City.

Jerry Weintraub: I went to sleep one night, and I got up in the middle of the night, 3:00 in the morning. I was living in New York on 54th Street between 5th and 6th Avenue. And I got up, and I said to my wife, "I just had this crazy dream. I saw a sign in front of Madison Square Garden that said, 'Jerry Weintraub presents Elvis.'" I went to Elvis and I said, "Let's play New York City," and he said to me, "I don't really wanna go to New York City. I'm not a New York City kinda artist. You know, they're not gonna like me in New York City. They like me in Alabama and Georgia and Tennessee, but I don't wanna go to New York City, Jerry." He said – I said, "Elvis, you're the biggest star in the world. They're gonna like you, they're gonna love you."

Joe Esposito: Elvis was a little concerned because New York's famous for tough audiences. I remember Tom Hulett and Jerry Weintraub saying, "Elvis, don't worry about it. New York's gonna love you." He was concerned about it. But then when they sold out five shows overnight, he was excited.

Elvis Presley: Man, I was tame compared to what they do now, you kidding? I I didn't do anything but just jiggle, you know.

Joe Guercio: Madison Square Garden. When he came out there were so many flashbulbs went off that the arena, there was moments when the arena was lit. And we come out in a blackout.

Jerry Weintraub: They came and slept outside Madison Square Garden for two weeks to get tickets. It was absolutely amazing.

For the next leg of his tour Elvis helped design an expensive new series of jumpsuits based on 19th century Victorian fashions that he'd seen in a book. They became his trademark throughout the 1970s.

Dick Clark: When he appeared on the stage in those magnificent outfits it was extraordinary.

Bill Belew: And we found that the color that worked the best was white. It allowed them to change the colors on him, whereas black would absorb all the color, and it was hard to highlight him. And we experimented with blue, which was one of his favorite colors, red, but it just ended up that white was the best thing.

Christina Ferra: I remember he was asking my mom – he did one of his take my mom into the back room things and ask her, "What color do you think I oughta wear?" 'Cause he had all these different outfits, different colors. He asked my mother, "What do you think?" And she said, "I think you look better in white." And I remember the next show he had white on. And he did, he looked awesome in the white jumpsuit.

Mac Davis: You know, if you look at my early pictures performing on stage in Vegas, you'll see I've got on one of those Bill Belew suits with the sequins and stuff. Of course it was never as nice as Elvis's, 'cause Bill Belew would have lost his gig if he'd have made me one as nice as Elvis's.

Bill Belew: The last thing I was working on, and we had actually done a prototype of it, it was called a laser suit. And what we did, there were certain points and it had very large stones that would tell him where he could puncture himself and that's where the laser would shoot. And we had these strategically placed on the suit, and as I say, you know, whenever he would touch himself then the laser beams would shoot out.

Sadly, the laser suit never panned out, but Elvis continued on with his tour, playing to sold out arenas and stadiums across the United States.

Joe Esposito: Well, Elvis played to audiences no matter what, big or small. Any entertainer, to perform in front of a live audience would tell you there's no feeling in the world like it. And Elvis has said it many times. You feel the love from the audience, you feel the electricity. It makes you come alive and that's why he said that's his favorite thing to do and that's why he would always do it.

Elvis Presley: A live concert to me is exciting because of all the electricity that's generated in the crowd and on stage.

Mindi Miller: And you would see this mass, mass of people and you would look as far as your eye could see and then you couldn't see anything anymore, and you knew that there were just still people out there. And you'd watch him, knowing that you knew him, and watch this human being on stage and then watch the people and it was, it was – I can't even describe the feeling.

Robin Rosaaen: Mostly in Las Vegas I would go twice a year, January/February and August and September, so that stared 1970 through '76. The last two shows I saw there in December. And then I would go to Lake Tahoe when he'd be there at the Sahara Tahoe. I also saw him at the Oakland Coliseum and the San Francisco Cow Palace.

Charlie Hodge: The reason for the first scarf was Elvis, working the way he did, perspiration would run down into his eyes. And after a lot of shows, after so much perspiration his eyes would be so red, you know. And Joe and guys like that put eye drops in there 'cause of the salt from his body. So he got the scarf so he could, you know, get some of the sweat out of his eyes and everything. And this went along and everything was working fine, then one night somebody asked for the scarf so he gave it to them. And next night he said, "Charlie, you better bring up another scarf in case somebody else want one." So brought up another scarf to lay on the piano, and it escalated.

Henry Young: Elvis would be singing and stuff, and then the Hilton, they had long tables that they sat you in rows. And they'd serve cocktails and stuff and girls would take their shoes off and walk on that stage knocking the glasses over to get up to Elvis. You know, not just hundreds of them, but a few would get that – and he'd tell them, "No, now, you can't do that or you're gonna hurt yourself." He'd usually give them a scarf and try to get them down, and that happened a lotta times.

Mindi Miller: But it was almost as if he was like, blessing each person. You know, he'd take this scarf out wrap it around their neck, kiss them.

CHARLIE HODGE
FRIEND/SINGER/GUITARIST/
MEMPHIS M...

Charlie Hodge: When we'd go on tour a lotta times Elvis and the Colonel would be down at the end of the big arena, and no one could see from behind like that. And the Colonel and them would buy those seats and give it to a home for somebody, a group of people that were able to come in, and they could sit back there and it wouldn't cost them anything. They could hear Elvis and everything. And Elvis goes back there and he throws up his scarf. It just come floating down. And he throws it up again. It just comes floating down. So he went around to the other side. Meanwhile Joe called me over to the side and told me what it was. So I went back over, and he did it a couple times over there, and then he turned around and started back up that way. And I said, "Elvis!" and he leaned over 'cause – I didn't say, "Elvis." He could tell I was gonna tell him something, so he leaned over and I said, "It's the home for the blind." He said, "Phew! I thought I'd lost it!" .

By the early '70s Elvis had achieved the rank of 8th degree black belt in karate and his surreal punches and wild kicks became as much a part of his concert performances as his jumpsuits.

Elvis Presley: After 16 years of doing this art every day for 16 years, I was awarded the 8th degree, which carries – let me see, 8th degree – there's only ten degrees of black. So the 8th degree I just got this week. The 9th degree carries senior master of the art, the next one, and the 10th, the senior grand master of the art. So that's where I gotta strive to go to, which takes quite a while, you know.

Houston Press conference reporter: What do you do for relaxation?

Elvis Presley: Karate. If you can relax doing this, I don't know.

Steve Wynn: Elvis asked me how I liked the show and I said, "In particular I really like when you finish 'Kentucky Rain' and you do that karate stuff. That sure is fun to watch."

Sheila Ryan: And he'd go into his kind of karate mode, you know, and he would go up and down his body. Wow.

Steve Wynn: Elvis drops down on the floor and starts doing these maneuvers, these exercises, and go and the legs were flying. And, you know, he was in such great shape, you know, he was agile like a gymnast.

Henry Young: One time he was singing and doing some of his karate moves and he goes, "Oh! Oh, no!" and he ripped his pants all in the back. So he just didn't leave the stage. They dropped the curtain around him and went and got him a pair of pants.

Charlie Hodge: And Richard put another pair on, zipped it up and he walked back out . But that necessitated the jumpsuits that would stretch and started that really great look, man. I always thought that Elvis was the only one that could dress like that.

Bill Belew: When we went to Vegas I contacted Ice Capades, and I talked to some friends of mine there and I said, you know, "Would you all be interested in making Elvis Presley's clothes for Vegas," because I would like to use what is known for ice skaters as stretch gab, or gabardine and it allows skaters to do their splits, their turns and everything. And I thought it would be great for Elvis because the one thing he said that he wanted to incorporate in his act was his karate.

On January 14, 1973, Elvis finally reached the pinnacle of his mighty comeback. He played in front of the entire world. His live concert, "Elvis: Aloha from Hawaii," beamed via satellite to an audience of one billion people in 40 countries around the world.

ALOHA FROM HAWAII PRESS CONFERENCE

Elvis Presley: Wheww, It's so very hard to comprehend it, because in 15 years it's hard to comprehend that happening. All the countries all over the world via satellite. It's very difficult to comprehend. But it's my favorite part of the business, is the live concert.

Reporter: How do you pace yourself?

Elvis Presley: I exercise every day. I vocalize every day. I practice if I'm working or not.

John O'Hara: In the "Aloha from Hawaii," you know, no one had ever done anything like that before. More people watched the "Aloha" concert than watched Neil Armstrong walk on the moon.

Myrna Smith: He looked absolutely stunning on that show. He was down to good weight. He was down to the weight that he was when I first met him in 1969.

Linda Thompson: When I saw Elvis on stage, yeah, it was the same man I knew in private at moments, you know, and, no, it was like, "Wow, where'd that come from?"

Christine Dashner: When you saw Elvis he was mesmerizing. He just – you didn't wanna blink because you might miss something, and it was just incredible.

CHRISTINE DASHNER
ELVIS FAN CLUB PRESIDENT

Charlie Hodge: They had 67% of all of the TVs in Japan tuned in to that show and almost the same amount on the rerun a few months later.

CHARLIE HODGE
FRIEND/SINGER/GUITARIST/
MEMPHIS MAFIA

That's where Elvis and Jack Lord became good friends. The night of the actual filming Jack Lord was there. And one of the greatest compliments another actor gave another in stage work is to stand up and whistle real loud. They said at the end of that show Jack Lord was standing on his chair whistling, you know, and said, "Get up!" and everybody was standing up giving Elvis an ovation.

Gordon Stoker: There's no way that I could explain the joy that it was to be on the stage with 25 and in Hawaii 50,000 people screaming and hollering. Elvis always said the show is in the audience not on stage. One time when they were screaming so much, as they always did, he said – he told us before he did it – "I think I'll take my coat off and throw it out in the audience," and he did. And they tore that coat – it was like throwing a pound of meat out to a bunch of hungry dogs. They tore that coat into a jillion pieces. After all was said and done, Elvis left Hawaii a million dollars richer and a billion fans stronger. He finished out 1973 by touring from Arizona to Georgia, his fan base growing larger and more intimate every day.

GORDON STOKER
SINGER - JORDAINAIRES

Emilio Micelli: The feelings that he created between him and the public, in his fans, fans that were crazy about him and, you know, out of their mind about this man, to see him, to touch him, to be close to him. No performance, no entertainer ever created that feeling, and I've worked with Sinatra, I worked with Dean Martin and Jerry Lewis. I worked with Perry Como, I've worked with big female stars, Lena Horne, even the Jackson Brothers when they were together. Nobody ever created that feeling, that I know, that was between the fans and Elvis Presley.

June Sayers: But then there was this time, he really did forget the words of "Bridge Over Troubled Water," you know?

Pauline Sayers: It was beautiful. And I have a tape of it, too.

June Sayers: And she's got it. And he came right over

Pauline Sayers: Give me a word.

June Sayers: – to us and he went –

Pauline Sayers: Give me a word.

June Sayers: Give me a word. What's next? Well, we started singing it. Like a bridge over troubled water.

Pauline Sayers: – troubled water – and then the tables started singing.

June Sayers: And then the next table.

Pauline Sayers: And then half the hall was singing and Elvis just stood there like this.

June Sayers: He just stood there. And then the other half started applauding.

Pauline Sayers: Going like this and Elvis just stood there and he said, "That's right." He said, "You did good. You did good." And then he started up again.

Ben Weisman: When Elvis loves his audience you can tell. It's like a romance. You know, when he got on the stage he seemed to just – he could relate to them, that's why people loved him. He just could relate. It was like a love affair between him and the audience.

BEN WEISMAN
SONGWRITER

Shirley Dieu: And he was only one of the most talented entertainers on this earth. God, what a – he was so gifted, his voice. Oh, God blessed him. When someone's that good, you know, they can sing that well, you can't take that away from him. He'll go on for generations and generations.

SHIRLEY DIEU
JOE ESPOSITO'S FORMER
GIRLFRIEND

Jackie DeShannon: You'd catch his eye or he would take a look or something, it was very, very personal, and that generosity was given to the audience. He had that generosity and he gave everything that he had. He did not hold back anything.

JACKIE DeSHANNON
SINGER/FRIEND

It was the greatest comeback of all time, a comeback that lasted nearly nine years. Elvis had resurrected his career by returning to what he loved most, the music.

LIVE AND ON STAGE

"WHEN HE CAME OUT, THERE WERE SO MANY FLASHBULBS THAT WENT OFF, THERE WERE MOMENTS WHEN THE ARENA WAS LIT."

— JOE GUERCIO

In 1969, Elvis Presley made the decision to return to live performing. The venue would be the International Hotel in Las Vegas, a city that Elvis had difficulty conquering 13 years earlier even though the build up to that 1956 show had been done in Colonel Tom Parker's signature style.

Shecky Greene: I remember the first time that I drove into the Frontier Hotel, or driving towards the Frontier Hotel coming from Los Angeles, and we saw this big 75-foot cut-out of this kid. And a guy we heard maybe on the radio "Blue Suede Shoes" or "Hound Dog." Those were the two most important of his songs at that time. And I said what is this. I mean, I'm – I'm in that show. And is this kid over me? Because we had Freddy Martin's band, myself and Elvis. When I went in there and they told me, "Well, you'll go on before him. Or we haven't decided, you'll go on before him or you'll go on after him." And then they watched the rehearsal and everything, and they said, "All right, you'll go on after." the people just didn't take to him. They just didn't know, you know, anything about him.

Elvis Presley: First night, especially I was absolutely scared stiff. Afterwards, I got a little more relaxed. But was strictly an adult audience, mostly elderly people.

Gloria Paul: April '56 at the Frontier Hotel. He was a total unknown. There was a 100-foot blow-up of him outside. And I went to see the show. And I sat with Rory Calhoun and his wife, Rita Barron and Danny from Danny's Hideaway, we sat ringside. And when he came out and started gyrating and rocking 'n' rolling and twisting and tossing, we all looked at each other. What is with him?

Joe Delaney: I think it was too soon. There's something that happens. When an artist gets hot with a hit record, before that record gets through to the average public, it may take a year. That record is already on the downward trend when the public becomes aware of it.

Shecky Greene: There was all kinds of rumors that he was bombing, and he was doing this, and he was doing that. But he's just going along, and then finally Parker got a brilliant idea of going to the high schools and getting the kids and having them do afternoon things. Well, you couldn't get near there. He did afternoon things, and you couldn't near the front door. I mean, you couldn't get near the strip. Our engagement was for four weeks. And he was gone after three weeks. But he only had a three-week engagement.Mine was four weeks. Freddy Martin was four weeks. So, everybody wrote up that he was canceled. He was never canceled. But I did say at the time, I told Parker and I told him, I think you got to change your style of clothing. They went to see Liberace. And Liberace got together with them. And that's when they started forming this thing about his dress. He would have special things made at everything, which gave him another charisma.

SHECKY GREENE
COMEDIAN/FRIEND

Joe Delaney: Elvis wasn't ready for Vegas, and I don't think Vegas was ready for Elvis.

JOE DELANEY
CRITIC, LAS VEGAS SUN

Many thought Presley's inability to connect with the older Las Vegas audience during his '56 appearance was proof that Elvis was nothing more than a fad, something to be worshipped by teenagers and discarded after its usefulness.

Presley believed he could better make a name for himself as a respected actor in the mold of his movie heroes Marlon Brando and James Dean. Though he had made a promising start in his movie career with LOVE ME TENDER, LOVING YOU, JAILHOUSE ROCK AND KING CREOLE.

Elvis's goal of becoming an accomplished actor was interrupted by a letter from Uncle Sam drafting him into the army. When he returned from the military, he attempted to pick up where had left off two years earlier. Sadly, although he worked hard and his movies performed well at the box office, the formulaic films did little to enhance his reputation. Though Elvis was now in Hollywood for most of the year, his mind was still in the city where he had met his one and only professional failure. Only now, he had no interest in performing in Las Vegas. But performing wasn't all the city had to offer.

Joe Esposito: Elvis loved Vegas because in those days, all the hotels had great entertainers and the big rooms. And every lounge act had great singers, you know, like Billy Ward And The Dominos, Fats Domino, Dela Reese, had all these great talents just in the lounge. It was wonderful. So, we'd hang out there, go there for a week and end up staying five weeks just to play, just go out and see a show every night, see different entertainers and stay up all night and sleep during the day and start over the next day. I don't think he ever thought about playing Vegas again because that one experience he had in the '50s.

Pat Broeske: Colonel Parker's decision to have Elvis perform in Vegas was a very shrewd decision on the Colonel's part. In many ways, it marked the reinvention of Elvis Presley.

Joe Delaney: I think the Colonel was very wise going to Hollywood and making all those films and creating such a fuss. When he came back here, they were ready for him.

Getting Elvis in front of a live audience again meant finding a venue that would be worthy of "The King Of Rock 'n' Roll." For the second time in his storied career, Las Vegas beckoned Elvis Presley.

Joe Esposito: They wanted Elvis to do the grand opening, the biggest star in the world to open the hotel. Well, Colonel said, "No, we don't want to open it. We'll be the second." And everyone said, "Why, why wouldn't you want him..." Well, Colonel thought about it, and he says, "Wait a minute. This hotel is going to open up." All hotels in Las Vegas, any hotel, there's a lot of kinks and problems going on. Something's not finished. They open way ahead of time. And he figured, well, let somebody else open the hotel. That's the reason Barbra Streisand opened the hotel. And she had to go through all the problems. He signed a contract to play at the International Hotel. And it was two times a year. Usually it was in January and August. Two shows a night, 8:00, 1200, nonstop, no days off, not like today. You just did it.

> **Elvis Presley:** So, just as soon as I got out of the movie contracts, I started to do live performances again.

Elvis would not be alone in this new undertaking. In 1956 when he had played the New Frontier Hotel, he had been backed up by a small three-man combo, appropriate in the sense that his rock-a-billy roots demanded no more than that to produce the sound generated on his early records. But Elvis's music had grown more complex, and he now required something much more elaborate in the way of back-up.

Joe Esposito: Well, when Elvis got ready to go back on the road again, he had to get a band together. So, we got a hold of James Burton. James was doing a lot of Elvis's sessions.

James Burton: When I got on the phone, and Joe said James, this is Joe Esposito. I'm looking forward to seeing you in a couple of weeks. I thought it was a bit strange. I didn't know what it was about, you know. So, then Elvis got on the phone, and we talked about three hours. And Elvis told me that he watched The Ozzie and Harriet Show just to see and watch me play the guitar at the end of the show. And Ricky would sing my song. It was great. I mean, we just talked about the type of music, what he wanted to do. He wanted to do his type of stuff, but he wanted to go even bigger. He wanted to have an orchestra.

Jerry Scheff: I had done an album with James. And he remembered me fortunately. So, he called me and asked me if I wanted to do it. I wasn't an Elvis fan at the time.

Ronnie Tutt: I got a call on Friday and said man, we've... This was a few weeks later. And they'd been auditioning drummers. And my friend Larry says, "Man, they're just... You know, we're only going to have one more night. So, can you come in tomorrow night?"

Jerry Scheff: There were a couple of drummers there the first night that I played. And one of the drummers, he was a really fine drummer named Gene Pelo.

Ronnie Tutt: This other drummer comes in and knew everybody. He had been an established player there in L.A. And they'd play a song.

Jerry Scheff: Oh, yeah, Gene was it, you know. Because he was flashy, and he had a lot of chops. And he was real good.

Ronnie Tutt: And I'm sinking lower and lower in the seat thinking I'm not even going to get a chance to play or meet him or any of that stuff.

Jerry Scheff: Larry Muhoberac the piano player, said well, you know Ronnie Tutt's sitting over there in the corner. And he just flew out here with his drums from Dallas. And of course, Elvis immediately, being the kind of person he was, said, "Ronnie, come on, man. Set your drums up, and we'll wait for you, and then we'll play."

Ronnie Tutt: Elvis said to everybody, "Hey, we got one more guy we'd like to play a song with."

Jerry Scheff: The minute Ronnie started playing we knew that, Ronnie was just perfect for the band.

Ronnie Tutt: We immediately had a rapport, you know, a real musical rapport, a real interpersonal contact between each other, shall I say. You know, we had a great thing that kinda lasted.

Joe Guercio: We were surrounded by the best. We had Ronnie Tutt, none better, Jerry Scheff was none better. The whole front line, James Burton, Glen D. Hardin. Elvis just appreciated the talent they had, and he knew what they could do.

James Burton: You know, each individual in their own right, they're just, you know – they're fantastic. And when Elvis called me and asked me to put this band together, it was really an honor to do it for him.

Joe Guercio: I was never an Elvis fan before I met Elvis. That was difficult for him. I came out of a whole other world in music. I was not a rock 'n' roller at all. And at the time, I said, well, the charisma was just mind blowingly overwhelming. And by the time we got through the first rehearsal, I was truly amazed that he sang that good.

Jerry Scheff: I went home that night, and I told my ex-wife, Libia, and I said, "You got to come hear this guy." And she said, "Ah, come on. You got to be kidding." I said, Nah, tomorrow night you come down and hear this guy." And so, she came down. And we both became fans.

Joe Delaney: I think it was The International when he first played it, and then later became The Hilton. When he came back here, they were ready for him. And the Colonel did a masterful job. He tied up every billboard in the city. He had posters all over the Hilton. I mean, the Colonel was an old carney man. He knew how to promote.

Mike Morris: The place was a carnival. I mean, it was Elvis now. The dealers wore the straw hats. He had banners out in front of the hotel, balloons. I mean, the marquee, "Elvis now."

Sammy Shore: Signs of Elvis, and you could see balloons and confetti. And I kept looking around. Where's my name? I know I'm on the show.

Jackie Kahane: And you were sold out.

Sammy Shore: I was sold out, yeah.

Jackie Kahane: That was your billing: Sold Out

Sammy Shore: My billing?

Jackie Kahane: Sure.

Sammy Shore: I thought you had that billing.

Jackie Kahane: No, yours sold out.

Joe Esposito: Well, I remember opening night in 1969, Las Vegas, at the International Hotel. Elvis was a nervous wreck. Elvis was always nervous before any show that he did. But he was particularly nervous because a lot of invited guests. And people in show business know that invited guests are a little harder to perform in front of than just fans. And he was, like I said many times, like a cat just prancing back and forth.

Ronnie Tutt: He was so nervous. He was like a caged panther, you know, ready to get let out, you know, to go to the show, so to speak. And we all were very, very nervous.

Myrna Smith: I knew he hadn't performed live on stage like that for a number of years, I think ten years. So, I was just hoping that... I hope he has a good Show...I had butterflies for him.

James Burton: He came up to me, you know, back stage and said, "James I'm so nervous I'm climbing the walls."

Jerry Scheff: That first night was amazing because, you know, Elvis wasn't really quite sure how the fans would receive him, you know.

Ronnie Tutt: He just had a lot to prove to himself and to the world that he still had it.

Joe Esposito: He walked out, and the spotlight hit him. You could just feel everybody the excitement, they just jumped up and started applauding before he started singing, because he had been gone for so long off the stage and just appreciated it so much. And the show just took off.

Jerry Scheff: When the curtains opened and he came out, he had a certain look on his face, you know. And it reflected his concern, you know. I remember as I was watching him, you know. And the crowd just went crazy. And you could just see his face just transform, you know, from sort of this doubtful look to this, oh yeah, okay. I remember this, you know. And he just went... And it was, from there, it was just great.

Joe Esposito: That show flew by. And Elvis was just, couldn't help see all those fans and the celebrities like Cary Grant, Sammy Davis and all those people giving him standing ovations after every song.

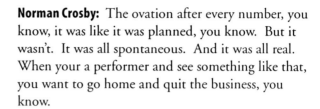

Norman Crosby: The ovation after every number, you know, it was like it was planned, you know. But it wasn't. It was all spontaneous. And it was all real. When your a performer and see something like that, you want to go home and quit the business, you know.

Rona Barrett: He was very exciting as a performer on stage. He had so much charisma.

Teri Garr: I remember telling someone, look, I'm going to Vegas this weekend to see Elvis. He invited us up. My friends said Yeah, sure. Elvis invited you up. Oh, he really did.

Joe Esposito: You could just see that he was on cloud nine. He was off the ground. Tears in his eyes from the excitement. And Colonel Parker came back to the dressing room afterwards. He had tears in his eyes. It was the first time I'd seen Colonel Parker have tears in his eyes, just so excited for Elvis. And it was just probably one of the biggest highlights of my life with Elvis to see that it was such a great success.

Joe Delaney: I was impressed because to me Elvis was such a natural. And the audience response. I saw the letters when they would announce that Elvis was coming into the Hilton. There were letters from all over the world. There were checks for $10,000, $15,000 to tie up a suite for the length of Elvis's stay here.

Jackie DeShannon: When Elvis was in Vegas, the buzz was, "How do you get in? How do I get a ticket? Who do I know? What can I do?" That was the buzz. And everybody just stopped what they were doing and focused on that.

Emilio Micelli: Fans used to start to line up at 8 o'clock in the morning for the first show at 8 o'clock in the night. You know, a lot of people don't believe it, but that's the truth.

EMILIO MICELLI
MAITRE D'— LAS VEGAS HILTON

Stan Brosette: That's what I remember most is the lines of people were winding all through the casino from all over the world. You could find someone from Mexico and a couple from Holland and a couple from Africa. And they would all be done up like Elvis and Priscilla.

STAN BROSETTE
ELVIS'S PUBLICIST/MGM PICTURES

Dick Clark: When I first saw Elvis at the International Hotel, the Hilton Hotel these days, it was an extraordinary occasion. The lines went on forever.

DICK CLARK
TELEVISION HOST/PRODUCER

Emilio Micelli: They used to offer me money, send me roses , gifts. No, young lady wants to come over to see the show in Las Vegas and sit in the back of the room so they would use heavy tricks to get ringside.

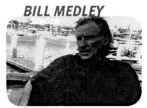

BILL MEDLEY

Bill Medley: I would show up at the show and say I'm Bill Medley. Elvis made a reservation for me. Said, yeah, come to... And this place was just wall to wall ya' all, you know. You couldn't move. And so, they walked me and they walked me. And they walked me right to the front. I'm here and the stage is here and Elvis is right up there in front of me.

Dick Clark: It was wall to wall people of all ages. And you could feel a lot of love in that room. And when he appeared on the stage in those magnificent outfits.

Bill Medley: Well, I loved the show. And I loved seeing him. But I just remembered that I had to go to the bathroom so bad. And there was no way I could go. I almost... I swear to God, I almost said, "Elvis, can I use your head."

JOE ESPOSITO
ROAD MANAGER & FRIEND

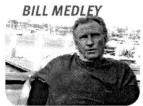

BILL MEDLEY

Joe Esposito: Bill became a good friend. Bill, I would say, is one of the nicest guys in the business. And so, Elvis one time, he says, "Okay, let's go over and give Bill a shock." He says, "Let's go see Bill's show." And we would walk across the stage, not say a word. I'm going to walk ahead. You guys walk behind me, walk just right across the stage.

Bill Medley: So, I'm doing "Lovin Feelin." You never close your eyes... And I'm right at the place where it's...

Joe Esposito: Bill is out there singing one of those big songs. And all of the sudden, people are just in shock. And he didn't know what was going on, because he didn't see us.

Bill Medley: ...And here comes Elvis. And he walks right by me, in front of me, hits me on the arm and says, "Hi, Bill" and keeps right on walking.

Joe Esposito: We all walked by. And Bill didn't know what to do. He didn't know how to act. Well, the place went crazy, went crazy. And it was great. Bill said, "Oh, well" and started singing again. Elvis did it again, walked back the other way.

Bill Medley: So, I had another show at 2:00. And I go on stage. And, I mean, the place is packed to the wall, not that it wasn't always packed to the wall. But it was mobbed. They all show up to see if he was going to come on stage again. And obviously he's not. I mean, it was a... So, I go, Baby, baby, I'd get down on my ... And here he comes again. And he walks right in front of me, and he hits my on the arm and says, "Hi, Bill."

Joe Esposito: He did that a few times with Bill and, you know, just to break the monotony.

Bill Medley: I finished the song. They finally quiet down, and I looked at the audience, and I said, "I don't know who he is, but he's now starting to piss me off."

BILL MEDLEY

Joe Esposito: One time Kenny Rogers and The First Edition, great acts, Ike and Tina Turner in the lounge, they were in there the same time we were playing the hotel. And Elvis would go see these guys all the time. And they didn't even know it half the time. He'd go in the back after the show starts and watch the show. We'd all see it and then leave. And they would come and see Elvis's shows.

JOE ESPOSITO
ROAD MANAGER & FRIEND

Kenny Rogers: I didn't realize this, but I used to work with The First Edition. And we were in the lounge here. And Elvis used to come and sit in the back of the room and watch our show. And so someone told me that one night. And I went and sat in the audience for his show. And during the middle of the show, he introduced me as, "Say hello to Kenny Rogers, my friend." And I thought, "Well, this is pretty cool. I'm Elvis's friend."

KENNY ROGERS
SINGER/SONGWRITER

Elvis's wardrobe during this time period became almost as famous and recognizable as the star who wore it.

Though it paid tribute to his past, which was rooted squarely in the 1950s era of flash and excess, his new stage persona was decidedly modern and even flashier.

Kenny Rogers: But his outfits were always... I remember the blue, the aqua one that had the bat wings on it. So, and in the Hawaii show that he did, he wore the white jumpsuit with the big stand-up collar.

Kenny Rogers: He was so far ahead of his time as far as clothing. I mean, the rest of the world was, you know, wearing jeans and shirts and stuff. And here he comes with all his rhinestones and stuff.

Bill Belew: The progression of Elvis's costumes were really dictated by the fans. I know he liked the dragon suit. I know he liked the peacock. He liked the leopard. And of course, I think possibly his favorite was always the Aloha Hawaii suit, the American Eagle. But the one thing that I never, in all the period I designed for Elvis, I never wanted any mention of his masculinity to be brought up by, oh, you know, why is he wearing this or why is he doing that?

Chris Beard: He said, "What did you think of the show?" I said, "Fantastic." I said, "I think the costumes are a little faggy. But, you know, you look great even as a fag" I think I said to him. And which he laughed at, of course.

Everything about Elvis was scrutinized by the press and public alike. His clothes...

Bernard Lansky: I made him eight coats in 1970 in the super fly time, you know, when all the movies were fly movies. Like all that stuff with mink collars, the pink coat with the mink. Just some things like that.

...his cars...

George Barris: You want it red? You want it green? You want it blue? And, of course, he gave everyone an Eldorado convertible for Christmas.

...his friends and even the feeling he would invoke when he was in town.

Dick Clark: The whole town was ablaze that Elvis was in town. There was no way to describe it.

Glen Campbell: I'd follow Elvis into Vegas, or he'd follow me in. And we were at the International then. That was back in the late '60s. It was great fun. Because I'd tell the organizers to book my performances either before Elvis was to appear in town or right after.

And I'd go hang out. Because hanging out with them, man, was, it was tough on you. 'Cause they would stay up all night and sleep all day.

James Burton: Sometimes we'd sing all night way up into the next day. And he loved it. He would sit down and play some piano.

Glen Hardin: He'd hang out until he got bored with it. And then, he'd just go to bed. But he just... The party would go right on, you know. So, we'd watch the sun come up right there on the 30th floor. It's beautiful with those mountains back there, you know.

Mike Morris: The last show would start at midnight, was supposed to break at 1:30. I guarantee you that show never broke at 1:30. It would go to 2:00, 2:15, 2:20.

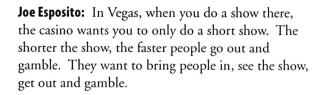

Joe Esposito: In Vegas, when you do a show there, the casino wants you to only do a short show. The shorter the show, the faster people go out and gamble. They want to bring people in, see the show, get out and gamble.

Ronnie Tutt: Many, many nights he'd say, "Oh, let's crank these guys up. Let's do an hour. Let's do an hour and 15, you know." Because they want people out there gambling, you know. And he'd do it just to spite them. Hey, these people came to see a concert. And we're going to give a good one. Let's do it.

Joe Esposito: It was tough working with Elvis, because he'd change songs right in the middle and go a different direction with it. But they were so great they could follow him no matter what he did.

Tony Brown: One night, he called out "Blueberry Hill," and when I looked at Joe Guercio and I said, "What key?" He said, "We don't do that."

Jerry Scheff: He loved to see if he could fool us. He'd started songs that we'd never played before.

Joe Guercio: It was never a set show in those days. If he would just want to pull a tune out, he would pull a tune out and sing it. And it was great because everybody behind him was his immediate group. And that was Ronnie and the rhythm section. He'd say, so-and-so. And they'd turn around, and they'd start. Well, you could say that to five guys, I'm sitting up there with 32.

Tony Brown: And, of course, Tutt and all those guys, they knew the drill. And when you got a drummer like Ronnie Tutt and a bass player like Jerry Scheff, it's just like having a locomotive behind you. You just hang on and play.

Ronnie Tutt: You never knew what he would do. And then how that related to music was the fact that he would make movements and things like that. And he expected me to be watching him at all time. The only time he'd ever really ever get upset with me in any way at all would be the fact that if he'd do something, and if I was looking away and didn't see it, you know, he'd turn around and playfully grab his scarf and, you know hit me with it...

Joe Guercio: So, it was always a scuffle. He would go, let's do this and bam, and I'd stop and they would start...

James Burton: He drove Joe Guercio nuts. Sometimes he would have to stop the orchestra.

Joe Guercio: Suddenly I'd say, "Here we go, guys." Bar twelve and I'd bring him in and I'd bring 'em in on bar twelve and we'd be locked in. And first couple of times I did that, he really turned around and acknowledged it. Because, you know, we didn't leave him out in the desert. We just jumped in the pool, a little late, but we jumped in the pool.

Stan Brosette: Shelley Fabares told me that, you know, she starred in three films. And she's very, I don't know shy is the right word. But she doesn't like any fuss made over her. She told me whenever she went to Las Vegas, Elvis would call and say come over and see the show. She would say, "Oh, yes. I want to see the show. But don't make any fuss. You have to promise me you won't introduce me or call any attention. I just want to sit at the table and enjoy the show." And he said, "I promise." And every time, the lights would come up and shoot right down on Shelley. And she would have to stand. And she would just die a thousand deaths.

JUNE & PAULINE SAYERS
FANS & FRIENDS

GLEN CAMPBELL
SINGER/FRIEND

RONA BARRETT

Pauline Sayers: When the lights went down, Liberace at the side of us. And he was just in awe of Elvis.

He stood there, and he's, ah, he's so beautiful. Ah, man, he's so beautiful. So, when the show's almost over, somebody comes up to him, "Lee, Lee, you have to go. Your show is going to start." He said, "Don't worry about a thing. I'm watching Elvis. My people will wait."

June Sayers: That's what he said.

Pauline Sayers: And he was... He loved Elvis.

Glen Campbell: I was sitting in the audience, and he said, "Ah," he said, "Campbell, I understand you're trying to do me down there." And I said, "Yeah, I'm doing you. I'm not trying to do you." And he shot back with something else. He said, "Well, you'd better stop doing me, or I'm going to get the boys after you." And I laughed, and I said, "Well, if I'm going to do you in the future, I'm going to have to gain some weight." And the audience booed me. I mean, it was just an instant boo.

Rona Barrett: God forbid whoever said anything nasty or mean about Elvis.

Glen Campbell: The band, Joe Guercio and the band, they just fell out. James Burton, I thought he was going to tinkle his britches when I said that.

Rona Barrett: They would come down on you as if a million bricks were hitting you at one time.

Glen Campbell: I wish I hadn't have said that. But boy, the band laughed, and the audience booed.

Pauline Sayers: The one kid way in the back, he starts barking like boo-woo-woo, like that. And Elvis says, "Throw that guy a fire plug."

JUNE & PAULINE SAYERS
FANS & FRIENDS

Rona Barrett: So many years since Elvis's death and about. And I don't... when was it? In the '50s, the late '50s, that he really began his career. And those who were his fans then, are still his fans to this day. And then there's a legion of brand new people who discover his music.

RONA BARRETT
TELEVISION HOST/COLUMNIST

Barbara McNair: Surprisingly to me the next generation of kids was also very interested in Elvis. You know, usually when a person is of a certain era, there is a certain age group that really relate to them. But I found with Elvis, even the younger kids related to him.

BARBARA McNAIR
CO-STAR, CHANGE OF HABIT

Gene Kilroy: He said, "In the audience tonight, we have a fellow who said he's the greatest, and he is the greatest. Muhammad Ali. Stand up." Muhammad stood up. He said, "Elvis, you're the greatest." And we went back stage. And then Elvis told us about how he does karate, and he likes to box. He'd like to get into boxing. And Muhammad told him, "No. You're too pretty." He said, "You do the singing. I'll do the boxing."

GENE KILROY
MUHAMMAD ALI'S MANAGER

Richard Davis: Muhammad Ali is in the audience. And he would like to meet you. And Elvis said, "Oh, hell yeah. Bring him on back." Because Elvis liked, you know – loved Muhammad Ali. And he said, "Yeah, bring him on back." So, Muhammad Ali comes back there. And he's got his entourage with him, and, big old guys, man, you know, big body guard guys. And we go, woo, you know. They all walked in the dressing room. We all just sat around and talked. It was great.

RICHARD DAVIS
MEMPHIS MAFIA/FRIEND

Las Vegas had become a working playground for Elvis and his friends, a place where they could not only make a healthy income, but could indulge themselves while in the company of some of the most popular and talented entertainers of their generation. But all was not fun and games in the "City Of Sin." The dark side of celebrity soon raised its ugly head in the oasis Elvis now regarded as his home away from home.

JOE ESPOSITO
ROAD MANAGER & FRIEND

Joe Esposito: Well, a couple of years into playing Vegas, my wife got a phone call from a guy. And he says, "I've been trying to reach Joe." And she said, "Who is this?" And he wouldn't say a name. He says, "I need to get a hold of him. I need to tell him somebody is out to kill Elvis." They had the police or the FBI go to my house waiting for the phone call from this person, see if they could get more information. Well, the guy never called back. There was also a time, in the showroom on one of the dinner menus there was a picture of Elvis, with a drawing of a gun shooting at his head.

JAMES BURTON
LEAD GUITAR

James Burton: Elvis thought about it, and he said, "You know, these people came, they paid good money to see me. And if something's going to happen, it's going to happen."

JOE GUERCIO
ELVIS'S MUSIC CONDUCTOR

Joe Guercio: Well, I guess I'm very happy I wasn't wearing the white jump suit. I can tell you that.

Joe Esposito: There were FBI guys in the audience for about three days.

JUNE & PAULINE SAYERS
FANS & FRIENDS

Pauline Sayers: We had two guys with us. And one of them, remember the guy who pushed Mrs. Kennedy back into the car? He sat at our table. Youngblood I think his name was. He sat with us with another guy. And I really believed that Elvis put them there to look after us. Because he was that way.

Joe Esposito: But he did tell us before he went on stage, he says, "Guys," he said, "If some guy out there, SOB, tries to kill me, if he does, you make sure you guys kill him."

JOE ESPOSITO
ROAD MANAGER & FRIEND

Most people refer to this period of Elvis's life as "The Vegas Years" due to the glitz and glamour that Elvis projected. But this is in some ways a misnomer. Vegas was not the only place that Elvis was appearing during this time. On February 27, 1970, he began a six-show engagement at the Houston Astrodome. Although the acoustics were terrible, due to the shape of the Astrodome, the concerts were an unqualified success, drawing more than 200,000 fans.

Joe Esposito: Those kind of venues are not great for performers. He wasn't too happy with it because the audience was too far away.

JAMES BURTON
LEAD GUITAR

James Burton: We had so much slap back that you couldn't listen to... You had to really pay attention to what was going on and listen to each other.

It was during this engagement that Elvis once again displayed his true character and unswerving loyalty to those around him.

Myrna Smith: There was a message sent to leave the Black girls. They didn't need the Black girls. And so, Elvis responded, "Well, if they don't come, I don't come."

MYRNA SMITH
SINGER/BACK-UP GROUP,
SWEET INSPIRATIONS

Joe Guercio: Oh, New York brought him in. And when New York wants you, they want you.

JOE GUERCIO
ELVIS'S MUSIC CONDUCTOR

On January 14, 1973, Elvis performed a live concert from Hawaii.

> **EXCERPT FROM ALOHA FROM HAWAII PRESS CONFERENCE**
>
> **Elvis Presley:** I'd just like to say before anything else that it's a great privilege to do this satellite program. And I'm going to do my best, and all of the people who work with me, to do a good show. It's just pure, you know, entertainment. No messages and no this and that, just try to make people happy for that one hour that it comes across. If we do that, then, I you know – I think we've done our job.

The program was broadcast live via satellite and watched by an audience of over one billion people, a quarter of the entire population of the world.

Joe Guercio: "Aloha From Hawaii," I said to the band before we started, I said, "This is the first time any show is going on television all over the world." I said, "We're all first on that." That was a great moment.

Ronnie Tutt: It was very well thought out. It was very well planned out. And it was very strategic in the sense that we'd only have one take at things. So, he had to feel comfortable in the songs that he was doing were the right songs for it. So, we did a lot of actual timing and rehearsing for it.

Joe Guercio: Well, the people – the Hawaiian people, knew he had done a couple of motion pictures there. They were just – the audience was just phenomenal. But the thrill of being the first... You know, I'd drop a down beat, and it's the first time you drop a down beat. And it's going all over the world on television. You know, that's a first. I mean, that's a big time first.

Charlie Hodge: Well, when we went to do the "Aloha From Hawaii" show, he told the Colonel, he said, "Let's give everybody in the show a week's vacation in Hawaii." And they did. They gave all the people that were on tour with us a week's vacation on him and the Colonel.

Though he was one of most successful people in the world for most of his life, wealth and power were not the driving force behind Elvis's ambition. He was more interested in what he could accomplish for the people around him. By the 1970s, Elvis's generosity towards friends, family and even total strangers had become legendary.

Pat Broeske: At Graceland, there's a trophy room. You can literally spend hours upon hours in that room looking at plaques from... You know, you can't count the little league teams the guy sponsored or, you know, the thank you letters from people, whose lives he touched.

George Klein: He always liked shock value when he gave things away to different people. You know, there was a lady over there once window shopping for a Cadillac. And Elvis asked her, he said, "Are you guys buying a new car?" They said, "Oh, no, Mr. Presley, we're just looking." He said, "Well, if you could buy a new car, which one would you get?" She said, "Well, we'd get that one right over there." And Elvis told the salesman, "Put it on my tab." He said, "Merry Christmas." Gave her a brand new Cadillac, a total stranger.

Mary Lou Ferra: Gee, Elvis, that's a cute table. He'd say, "Hey, Joe. Joe. Joe Esposito, Put that in Mrs. Ferra's car." I said, "No, Elvis, I don't want that." "Yeah, you want that. Put that..." I'd say, "No." So, I said, "Joe..." You know, so I was afraid to say anything nice after that, because he'd give it to me.

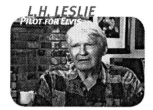

L.H. Leslie: He says, "What the hell are you going to Bangkok for?" I said, "Well, all my life I've wanted a blue star sapphire ring. And I'm going over there and get one. I hear they have some beauties over there." He said, "Did you ever see a real good one?" I says, "Yeah, I've seen good ones." And he looked at me and dug in one of his little cases there and pulled this ring out and says, "What do you think of that one?" I said, "Oh, my God, it is beautiful." He says, "does it fit?" I said, "Yeah, it fits." He said, "Keep it. It's yours." Hell, I can't take that ring. He said, "To hell you can't. You just told me you wanted one. I give it to you. Wear it."

George Klein: One time Elvis is in Colorado, and a newscaster comes on at ten o'clock, guy says, "Well, Elvis was in Denver today, and he gave away three brand new automobiles to Denver police officers. Hey Elvis, if you're watching, I could use a brand new car. I'm driving an old Volkswagen." Elvis called his road manager, Joe Esposito and said, "Joe, get him a car." Joe ran around like crazy. When the guy got off the air, sitting right in front of the television studio was a brand new automobile. The guy about fell out.

Mary Lou Ferra: My daughter still has his top of his pajama suit. She still has it. And it has Elvis on it. So, we said, "Gee, those are cute pajamas. You can meet the public in those." You know, that's the kind they were. And he said, "Oh, here, here, take it." He said, "I can't take the bottoms off, but you can have the top." So that's the one thing I took.

Bill Belew: There was this lady and she always wanted this ring. She couldn't choose it, afraid her husband would get upset if she bought it. And Elvis said, "Go and box it up and give it to her." And he said, "Really?" And he said, "Do it." So he did, went to the lady. And she said, "What's this?" And he said, "That gentleman over there, Mr. Presley, would like for you to have this ring." And she got very emotional. And she said, "No, no, you can't do this." And he said, "Anybody that wants something that bad, should have it."

Tony Brown: Elvis was like an air force. He had four planes. The Colonel had a plane. Elvis had a plane. The band had a plane. And the crew had a plane. And then all the sound guys and all the concession guys were in semi trucks and buses. So, when we hit a town, it was like you knew that Elvis was in the town, because the air force had landed, you know.

Jim Hydlach: You had the bootleggers moving. Everybody and their uncle was moving along. It was a lot of people moving all at once. Exhilarating. It was just unbelievable. Every town we went to, you would feel that electricity, especially, you know, when you heard the opening of 2001.

Tony Brown: We got a candid for the first show. And that was Elvis saying, okay, second tune is "Teddy Bear." Elvis would show me two fingers. And I would play da-da-da-da on the keyboard. Burton has the rest of it until the very end. "I Can't Help Falling In Love," you do that intro. Easy gig. Just pay attention. And so, I knew I could do it, but I must tell you after "Mystery Train," and then Elvis went... I was very, very nervous.

Late in his career, Elvis began to plan what would have been his first tour outside the United States. He had always expressed an interest in playing for his fans in Europe and other countries around the world. But one thing or another had always conspired to prevent it. This time, however, Elvis undertook the planning himself.

L.H. Leslie: The phone rang again. And I answered it. "Captain Leslie?" I said yes "This is Joe Esposito." Said, "We're sitting here with the boy" - I think he always called him "the boy" - "and some other members of the entourage. And we we're planning a world tour. And we'd like to know if you'd like to be our pilot." I said "Oh, my God. Absolutely."

Jerry Schilling: He thought he was going to be touring overseas. That's why he bought the airplanes. He was definitely considering a tour overseas.

Charlie Hodge: He wanted to go to Europe. And that would have been something he would have gotten himself in shape for.

L.H. Leslie: Before anything actually happened after that, why Elvis passed away. And that took care of that.

Glen Campbell: It's a shame that Elvis Presley didn't get to go to England and the world. And he could have went anywhere in the world. And I'm, you know, it was just... And every time that I go to these different countries and play, and, you know, that's, "How come Elvis didn't come over here?"

Gene Kilroy: Muhammad Ali was the most recognizable person on planet earth. And we traveled all over the world. And everywhere we went, people would ask him, "Did you meet Elvis? What's Elvis like?"

Elvis was destined never to tour outside of the United States. But it was in Las Vegas that he found the stage from which he would be presented to the rest of the world.

Dick Clark: There have been a few extraordinary people in entertainment. I'll try to remember some, Rudolph Valentino, Frank Sinatra, Elvis Presley. I mean, you can count them on the fingers of one hand. They have the magic that none of us can figure out. There's a mystery, a mystique. And it just gets bigger and bigger every year.

DICK CLARK
TELEVISION HOST/PRODUCER

Teri Garr: What is the thing that makes him go on forever? Is it that he died so young? Is it that he was so talented...He must have touched somebody somewhere. I mean, he's touched everybody everywhere. I don't know.

TERI GARR
FRIEND/ACTRESS

Pauline Sayers: That man was a wonderful, wonderful man, and if something went wrong later on in his life...

June Sayers: We don't know what happened with it. But, not with us. He was...

Pauline Sayers: He was wonderful with us.

June Sayers: We called him our treasured friend.

JUNE & PAULINE SAYERS
FANS & FRIENDS

Tony Brown: At the front of it all was a person that everyone who worships Elvis wishes that he was the person. He was the person. He was that guy from Tupelo that was a southerner true at heart, loved the church, loved his mom, loved his fans and was totally fascinated by being Elvis Presley himself. I think it blew him away to be Elvis Presley you know.

TONY BROWN
PRESIDENT MCA NASHVILLE
FRIEND/SINGER

Charlie Hodge: His most happy time was on stage entertaining his fans. That gave him the energy I guess to carry on doing other things.

CHARLIE HODGE
FRIEND/SINGER/GUITARIST/
MEMPHIS MAFIA

JOE GUERCIO
Elvis's Music Conductor

RONNIE TUTT
Drummer

GLEN CAMPBELL
Singer/Elvis's Friend

CONNIE STEVENS
Actress/Girlfriend

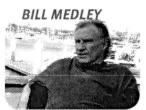

BILL MEDLEY

Joe Guercio: It's the memories. It really is, the memories and he opened me up to a lot of music. You know, here I am at my age. I'm making a living in rock 'n' roll. And, you know, I had a lot of friends that were waiting for the big bands to come back.

Ronnie Tutt: We had a rapport musically that is real hard to come by. In music, you rarely have that with good people. He was one of those guys that you definitely miss. You know, you definitely do.

Glen Campbell: I miss him as much as I miss anybody that's ever been a friend of mine. He was just a very, very special human being that graced us with his presence on this earth. He was a very special person.

Connie Stevens: I started going with, Bill Medley, one of the loves of my life, as well as Elvis at that particular time as the years went by. And we were driving around one night, and maybe Joe will remember this. And we got to talking about Elvis how much we really cared and how worried we were about his isolation and so forth. I said, "Let's go steal him."

Bill Medley: Connie and I, we dated for a while. And she was friends with Elvis and both of us was friends. Yeah, we came up to the Hilton. I think I came in to see Connie. And so, yeah, we went over there and tried to get him out.

Connie Stevens: I'll never forget Elvis's face. He walked in the room, because Joe had said, you know, "Connie's here" or something like that. And he walked out. And he was smiling. And he saw Bill. He saw me. And for a split second, he went, "Wait a minute, you know. This is kind of my territory." And then he went, "No," he said, "This is good. This is really good, you guys together. Wow, that's perfect." And so, we told him what we wanted to do. And he said, "Wow, that would be great. That's going to be fun." He never went.

Bill Medley: I think he moved, went from the living room to the dining room that about as far as we got him to move.

Connie Stevens: By the time the karate started and a thousand people just trying to get a piece of him. And when we were leaving – and we said, "We'll see you, Babe. You know, we love you." And he said. "I love you guys. I love you guys." And I never saw him again. That was pretty late in the game.

Bill Medley: Just always felt bad, you know, that, I mean, the Righteous Brothers got pretty big. We were certainly, nobody was where Elvis got and was. But if Bobby and I weren't together, I could always go walk around, you know. Maybe somebody would say, "Oh, aren't you..." And I would say, "No." And so, I always felt bad, you know, that he never, you know, that he was kind – it was the good news and the bad news, man. Good news, you're Elvis Presley. The bad news is you're Elvis Presley. You know, you can't do much out in public.

BILL MEDLEY

CONNIE STEVENS
ACTRESS/GIRLFRIEND

THE SOUL BEHIND THE MUSIC

"He made you want to put a guitar on and if you didn't have a guitar you'd make one."

— Barry Gibb

"Country music was always a part of the influence on my type of music anyway; it's a combination of country music and gospel and rhythm and blues all combined, is what it really was. As a child, I was influenced by all of that."

– Elvis Presley

Tony Orlando: Original, one-of-a-kind, no one like him, no one before or since. No one will ever be like him.

Jerry Scheff: He had a knack when he sang where the words of the song that he was singing would go up through his brain and then into his heart and then out his mouth to the people, and that's what people loved about him so much. Not a whole lot of singers are like that.

Glen Gampbell: Elvis had a charisma and he had a charm that I've never seen on a male vocalist; I've seen that charm in female vocalists, but I've never seen it in a male vocalist.

Tony Brown: He was just a regular guy, in my opinion, who grew up being a superstar, and his life was not real, it was a surreal life he lived.

Robert Relyea: On "JAILHOUSE ROCK" I remember, if we'd have a delay because the leading lady was having her make-up fixed or there was, and the crew wasn't working, he'd go get his guitar and play. It wasn't that thing about, "Oh I never do that because that's…" You know the football player who'll never throw the football between scenes. He'd get the guitar and say, you know, "This is what I do."

Patti Page: I think he brought a lot of country to the forefront. It was in the beginning of country and rock and all of that kind of meshing together. The beginning rock and Elvis was like a trailblazer along those lines because he performed like a rock star, yet he had that, down-home country quality that came from his, I think, some of his gospel music.

Elvis Presley was a man of many gifts, but above all, he was a man of music. His earliest influences were the spirituals he listened to over the radio and in church, as a young boy growing up in Tupelo and Memphis.

Deborah Walley: Elvis loved gospel more than any other kind of music, and it was part of his childhood as it was also part of my childhood. We knew a lot of the same gospel singers, we knew the songs, we'd sit around and harmonize.

Jackie DeShannon: Of course I'm from Kentucky, so that gospel soul and that tremendous spiritual quality really touched me very, very deeply, and I think Elvis had a great appreciation of gospel music and rhythm and blues obviously; he was the one that brought it to all of us.

Elvis Presley: I liked all different types of music when I was a child. Of course the Grand Ol' Opry was the first thing I ever heard probably, but I liked the blues and I liked the gospel music, gospel quartets and all that.

Gordon Stoker: This is what he wanted to be, he wanted to be a male quartet singer. You probably didn't know that he auditioned for two male quartets in Memphis and didn't pass their audition.

Ben Speer: They needed a baritone singer, and Elvis auditioned for the part, and Cecil turned him down. Elvis said all of his life that his first love was gospel music.

Gordon Stoker: I finally ran into one member of the first group he auditioned for and I said, "Do you mean Elvis didn't pass your audition?" He said, "No Gordon, to tell you the truth, the boy sang good, but you'd give him a part and before you knew it, he was singing another part; you see, when you're in a quartet, you've got to sing one part and stay on that one part."

Elvis's natural attraction to music crossed racial lines. He didn't care if the singers were black or white, so long as they were good.

KENNY ROGERS
SINGER/SONGWRITER

BILL MEDLEY

RED ROBINSON
HALL-OF-FAME DJ/FAN

TERI GARR
ACTRESS

MICHAEL OCHS
ROCK 'N' ROLL HISTORIAN

Kenny Rogers: His influences, of course, were really the black community. No one had ever done that before. It was kind of a taboo issue.

Bill Medley: Bobby and I, the Righteous Brothers, had a lot of trouble getting our music played; they wouldn't play, they said it was too rock 'n' roll, too hard rock 'n' roll, but what they were really saying was "It sounds black and we can't play it."

Red Robinson: First time I heard him, I didn't know if it was a black singer doing country or a country singer trying to sound black; I couldn't figure that out.

Teri Garr: We all went around scratching our head and went "What has this guy got? What is he doing?" Well he's doing the black music that's so fabulous.

Michael Ochs: A lot of people in retrospect attack Elvis for stealing the black music and making it white. I mean basically Elvis Presley had a black soul with a white face.

Bill Medley: He just knocked down doors for all of us other guys to walk through and work and still have a career; he was the first white palatable guy; in the early 60s there were still white stations that wouldn't play black music, you know, black artists and Elvis snuck through and parents maybe reluctantly said "Okay, you can listen to him," and then slowly but surely the walls broke down and a lot of stuff he was doing was Little Richard and some of that stuff.

In 1954, Elvis's racially ambiguous sound came to the attention of Sam Phillips, the founder of Sun Records in Memphis, Tennessee. Phillips had his own ideas about the role race played in the records he was producing.

SAM PHILLIPS
FOUNDER OF SUN RECORDS

Sam Phillips: I didn't want to do what the other R&B labels – they were doing some great stuff – I wanted to do some gutbucket stuff, and I wanted to get that black and white in there, cause black people and white people in the South, outside of the masters that ran the plantations, we were double first cousins; the skin was just a different color. Man, I just knew that there ought to be some kind of a coherent approach to where we could get the best of both hued into a beautiful thing called music, in a groove, and expose it to the people and let them make their decision.

In addition to Elvis, Phillips signed a young rockabilly singer named Roy Orbison, who enjoyed the casual, seat-of-your-pants atmosphere at Sun.

ROY ORBISON

Roy Orbison: It was a great workshop to go in because you didn't have a lot of help, there were no musicians, and if you didn't have guys in your band, you had no musicians...so it was sort of "You're on your own, do it if you've got the goods, you know, If you can make it, why go ahead." But we had a great time, because I'd finish a session or be hanging' around... and Elvis would walk in and some of the guys come in, we'd start talking and having a good time. Of course he was, by then, making films and things and coming in from Los Angeles, but then we'd wind up going maybe to Elvis's house or somebody's house and have a party.

Another Sun Records discovery was Carl Perkins, who wrote the rockabilly songs he sang. His best-remembered tune was released shortly before a nearly fatal auto accident that put Carl in the hospital. One day, he happened to catch his friendly rival singing that very song on TV. It was a little something Perkins liked to call "Blue Suede Shoes."

Carl Perkins: I watched Elvis do his first network show from my hospital bed, and they had me in a cast, and he said, "I'm going to do my new record" and he said "One for the money..."... And I nearly broke out of the cast, I said, "Oh, there it goes," but I found out, after Elvis died, that they wanted Elvis to cut that song, "they" being RCA-Victor, right after my record came out and he said, "That's my friend, he's got a hit and I'll cut it, I'll do it later, I love the song;" I never knew that till Elvis was dead.

By now, Elvis's skyrocketing popularity had allowed him to switch from the intimacy of Sun Records to a markedly more prestigious label – RCA.

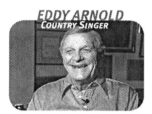

Eddy Arnold: When he got with RCA it began to happen, and you know what I mean when I say, "He began to happen," he got hot.

Even though RCA was a big step up from Sun, Elvis's new record producers appreciated the sound Sam Phillips had been able to capture, and figured if it wasn't broke, don't fix it.

George Klein: The thing that Elvis liked, I think, there was the fact that the musicians were so good and the sound was good; they had a lot of trouble trying to capture that Sun sound early on; they used a lot of tape echo, but they didn't have the right method; if you listen to "Heartbreak Hotel" and those early RCA records, you can tell they were trying to capture the Sun sound.

One particularly morbid piece of news ended up inspiring songwriter Mae Axton to compose one of Elvis's earliest RCA hits.

Buddy Killen: Mae had read a newspaper article about a guy who had committed suicide and he'd left a note saying' "I walk a lonely street." That's where she got the idea for "Heartbreak Hotel."

BUDDY KILLEN

Tony Orlando: I remember clearly the very first time I ever heard an Elvis Presley record. It was "Heartbreak Hotel."

TONY ORLANDO
SINGER

I remember hearing this amazing soul and this amazing voice. There was something about that record; there was a hauntingness about Elvis's voice that still, to this day, has never left me on "Heartbreak Hotel."

Ray Manzarek: The charisma, he had the charisma. He had Jim Morrison, he was Jim Morrison of his day.

RAY MANZAREK
KEYBOARDIST, THE DOORS

You know he had that kind of charisma. He was just a sex bomb. Sexy man who had a great voice. Didn't that man have a great voice? I mean he could sing, you know, and the rhythmic arrangements were profound. The little band, that little band behind him. Without that trio behind Elvis Presley playing the way they played. Ooh God, that music was absolutely phenomenal. The arrangements were great, the tightness of that band, that walking bass. They were right on top of it. So Elvis had all the charisma.

Phyllis McGuire: When we started it was rhythm and blues; Elvis changed that, it became sort of rockabilly...

PHYLLIS McGUIRE
SINGER/GIRLFRIEND

...And then rock 'n' roll; he changed the whole thing.

Elvis's embracing of rock 'n' roll had a chilling effect on the music that had once inspired him.

BUDDY KILLEN

Buddy Killen: Elvis almost single-handedly killed country music for a moment…you had all that rock 'n' roll stuff beginning to happen, and when Elvis took off, it was like that's the kind of music everybody wanted.

ROY ORBISON

Roy Orbison: We were pioneers and all, but and we were also caught up in it; it was brand new for us just like it was everybody else and really exciting; it was the only music we wanted to make, back then and even now.

Elvis wanted to combine the hard-driving sound of rock 'n' roll with the sweet harmony of gospel quartets. One such foursome was appearing with another singer, country music legend Eddy Arnold.

EDDY ARNOLD
COUNTRY SINGER

Eddy Arnold: I had an act on the bill with me by the name of the Jordanaires, and Elvis came to the theatre and introduced himself, and I learned later that he was really interested in the Jordanaires because he loved their four-point harmony.

GORDON STOKER
SINGER - JORDANAIRES

Gordon Stoker: You would've thought he would've come back behind stage to meet Eddy Arnold, but he didn't; he came back behind stage to meet us, and that was in 1955 and he said, "If I ever get a major recording contract, I want the Jordanaires to work with me."

RAY WALKER
SINGER - JORDAINAIRES

Ray Walker: The Jordanaires also got put down at first for being with him, and I'm sure he was complimented to a point for being with us, but I think it gave all of our fans a different perspective of both of us, the group and Elvis.

Gordon Stoker: The first session we did with the four Jordanaires was "Don't Be Cruel," "Anyway You Want Me" and "You Ain't Nothin' But a Hound Dog."

There was a lot more going on inside the studios of RCA than just turning out hit songs.

Bob Moore: Well usually we'd go in, we'd fool around for an hour or two, piddling and getting loosened up, and usually Elvis would go over; after awhile he'd sit down at the piano; now he was not a piano player, but he did know chords and he'd start singing things like "How Great Thou Art" or whatever, and he'd holler at the guys and say "Hey guys, come help me," so we'd all get into a little jam session doing kind of the gospel thing; the Jordanaires would come over and they knew all the lyrics of course, you know, 'cause they came from that background; we'd do an hour or two of that before we ever really started the recording process.

Ray Walker: He was always honest with his work; when he had to warm up a lot or sit and play the piano, we'd sing spirituals, we'd sing whatever; he was getting ready, physically, to sing.

Gordon Stoker: He just had a good attitude about everything and he would get you in a good frame of mind before you recorded and I think that's the reason these recordings have been around as long as they've been.

Even though he didn't have any formal musical training, Elvis had a natural appreciation for the amazing range of the human voice.

Connie Stevens: One thing that he did tell me was he just loved the sound of somebody's voice that could get a bass timbre.

Ray Walker: He started doing this song and he said, "Can you do this down an octave?" and I think I found out later he didn't know what an octave was, he just meant, "Can you do this lower?" I said, "Well yeah, I can," so I was doing it with the other guys on the other mike, "Now and then, there's a fool such as I," and did it several times like that; then he asked me to come over on his mike and I think he didn't want them to be able to cut me out in New York, he'd had a little problem with that, you know.

Musicians knew what to expect when Elvis showed up at the recording studio – once he got around to showing up.

Tony Brown: A lot of waiting; musicians getting there at, say, whatever, seven or eight o'clock, whenever they were called, then Elvis finally showing up hours later, but it doesn't matter because he's Elvis Presley.

Reggie Young: He wouldn't get there until late in the evening and it was usually daylight whenever we left; not necessarily just playing music; there was a lot of sitting around talking and laughing and storytelling and stuff, but yeah – it was pretty much an all nighter.

Despite all the horsing around, Elvis knew instinctively what sort of sound he wanted and how to get it.

Ray Walker: I remember one time in the studio at RCA, they said, "Elvis, would you step into the microphone? The band and the Jordanaires are leaking into your microphone;" well he was standing about six feet back; and he said, "You just handle the knobs, I'll handle the singing;" he didn't want to be any closer to that microphone; he had an uncanny ear and feel for what he wanted on that record, and he was going to get it.

Joe Esposito: Elvis complained to us about certain things about the level of music on some of the recordings he did. He felt that they brought his voice out too far; we don't know for sure who did it, if the Colonel did it or if the RCA people did it; there's rumors the Colonel said, "No, Elvis has to be brought out a little further so we can hear him more than being buried in with the music," but Elvis wanted it combined with the music and he should've really complained to RCA about it; I mean he talked to the Colonel about it, he talked to us about it.

Elvis did complain about the extracurricular activities of his backup singers when movie heartthrob Tab Hunter decided to make a record.

Tab Hunter: Randy Wood, who was a great guy and a great producer, said "I'm going to get a terrific group to back you up, the Jordanaires; they back up Elvis;" well, I was thrilled to death; so the Jordanaires backed me up and Elvis got really pissed over the fact that the Jordanaires who backed him up, backed me up, and we knocked him out of the #1 slot.

Despite all the frustrations, Elvis always managed to keep a smile on his face.

Ray Walker: He loved to laugh and when he'd get tickled, you just couldn't stop him; so many people said "You know, I wasn't a fan of Elvis Presley 'til I heard him laugh, and when I heard that laugh, I knew what kind of man he was." Well, of course we were with him and when we heard him laugh, that was the heart of the man; he laughed the best of anybody I've ever seen.

Elvis's recording misadventures continued into his later years, when he switched from state-of-the-art RCA studios in Hollywood to the somewhat more "rustic" American Studios in Memphis.

Bobby Wood: American Studios was located in really a bad section of town because people all around us was getting robbed and everything; it was not a great section of town, and I remember we had had a rat infestation in the studio; I mean rats were falling out of the ceiling…

Reggie Young: They were all up in the rafters; every now and then you'd hear em and you'd look up and here goes a rat I mean, not a mouse, a rat going across the room!

Bobby Wood: I believe it was the first night Elvis walked in there was a rat fell off of the roof right in front of him and man, he jumped about three feet and I never forgot that.

Some of Elvis's most memorable experiences in the recording studio involved celebrities other than himself.

Jerry Schilling: We were rehearsing at RCA studios in Hollywood for Vegas. You know there's always security at that point. This big guy just walks in and everybody's kind of shocked, you know, who is this guy? Nobody knew who he was and how did he get in here. Elvis was really upset that somebody could just walk in like that. So the guy says "Hey Elvis, I'm Brian. You know we're recording over in the next studio," and Elvis said, "Yeah, I'll come over." We were all like what's going on here? We went over. One of the guards said, "That was Brian Wilson;" I never will forget, Brian played him something at the playback and said "Elvis, you think we got anything here?" and Elvis said "No." But see that was the intuitive thing about Elvis – he didn't know who Brian was at that point cause Brian had gained a lot of weight, and they'd never met before anyway, but he knew there was something special about the guy.

Elvis's search for just the right sound extended beyond the confines of the studio.

Ronnie Tutt: He invited us up to his room when we were recording there, and he played us a recording of some group or something that he liked the sound of and he says, "Now why don't my records sound like that?"

Elvis Presley: What's interesting about music and about all the people here, they find new sounds and they do things differently themselves, so it's like a new experience every day; the guy on the guitar will find a new lick, the guy on the piano will find something or the voices will add something and I hear all this and it inspires me.

By the early sixties, that "inspiration" was coming from a variety of places – including Liverpool, England.

It was inevitable that the Fab Four and the King of Rock 'n' Roll would eventually cross paths.

Joe Esposito: The Beatles first came to the United States, I think, in '64; they wanted to meet Elvis and it never worked out; so in '65 when they came back again, Brian Epstein and the Colonel got together, talked about seeing if they could arrange a meeting.

Richard Davis: The night they were supposed to come, Colonel had gave strict orders, Don't nobody leak this out. Don't nobody say nothing, don't nobody tell nothing about this happening. This is top secret. Ok fine Colonel, yes sir Colonel. The night it's supposed to happen…probably a thousand girls outside the house. Now we didn't tell nobody. You know who told somebody? Had to be the Colonel.

Joe Esposito: We got there and there's thousands of kids hanging all over the walls, climbing up trees, reporters. And we pull in into the driveway. Elvis was there to greet them. Now some people say Elvis wasn't there, but Elvis was standing there from what I remember and all the other guys remember. Elvis and Priscilla were there to meet the guys, and they were introduced, and Brian Epstein and we all walked into the living room.

Richard Davis: He says all right let's bring some stuff out. So we went and got some stuff, brought it out and set it up and everything. Next thing I know is the Beatles and Elvis are jamming together. This went on for an hour and a half, two hours. Elvis was on the piano, and he's singing Beatles songs, and they're jamming with him and harmonizing with him, and it's like they're doing Elvis songs, and he's playin' the piano and singing along with them, and it's like this was an opportunity that only an idiot wouldn't take advantage of. So call me an idiot. I should have turned a tape recorder on because I wouldn't have to be working for a living right now. I'd be a multi-millionaire.

Jerry Schilling: You could walk down Perugia Way Street and you could feel the vibration from Elvis's bass playing; he always thought the bass player was the coolest guy onstage, and Paul McCartney later said, "Man, when I saw Elvis sitting there playing the bass, I knew I was in."

Richard Davis: The Beatles were telling Elvis how much he influenced their music and how much he influenced them getting started in the music business and how much they liked his music and him; and Elvis was telling them basically the same thing, "Well hey, you know, you guys are good; I like you, too; there's a lot of songs you've done that I like and one day I'm probably going to record some of them" which he did.

Joe Esposito: Elvis loved the Beatles' music; I mean let's face it, he recorded three of their songs; Elvis believed in songs with a lot of good words and meaning with something behind them, like "Michelle" and "Yesterday" and "Hey Jude," but he didn't say anything bad about the Beatles. There's all these stories about him putting the Beatles down. He respected them.

There was one memorable postscript to that historic jam session the following morning.

Jerry Schilling: John said, "Jerry, would you do me a favor?" and I said "Sure;" I mean I was a Beatle fan, he said "I didn't have the courage to tell Elvis this last night, but he said "You see these sideburns? You know, I almost got kicked out of high school because I wanted to look like Elvis, and if it hadn't have been for him," he said "I wouldn't have been anything; it wouldn't have happened" I think is how he worded it.

Even though Elvis was the King of Rock 'n' Roll, Hollywood gave him the chance to become a ballad singer with his very first film, LOVE ME TENDER.

Johnny Tillotson: Up until that point, people weren't convinced that, it's weird, they didn't think he – they weren't sure he could sing ballads, remember? I mean they knew he could do all the other stuff but he could, always sang real.

Stan Brosette: I love the simplicity of "Love Me Tender;" if I remember, there's very little music behind him. It sounds to me like a – just like a choirboy, not like a great singer, just like somebody's son, somebody's brother, you know, just singing a sweet song.

Other films led to other classic ballads.

Pat Broeske: I think BLUE HAWAII is a few notches above the standard Elvis formula musical and I'll tell you why: I mean he gets to sing "Can't Help Falling In Love," which is one of the great ballads.

Tab Hunter: I was never a great Elvis fan; I love some of the tunes; I love some of the slow ballads he sang; I thought they were really quite wonderful.

Ben Weisman: I studied all his albums and I kinda got into his head, what he wanted to hear.

So the songs that I wrote tried to stretch him a little bit. Instead of the typical rock 'n' roll things. He loved ballads. He loved singers like Perry Como and Dean Martin. So I wrote songs that could fit in that style and he like them. He recorded most of them.

Donovan: When Elvis sang that ballad or that song, it brought all women and all men together and Elvis's great legacy is that, I think.

Eddy Arnold: I thought he was pretty good, I really did. Yeah I thought he was pretty good. Me being a ballad singer, but I noticed, you know, he could do those rhythm songs and he could really do them very, very, very well.

Sonny King: Elvis lasted as long as he did, because he went into every era… He had gospel…he could sing jazz…he could sing anything 'cause he was a lover of music; he sang honky-tonk songs…he sang ballads…He captured all the audiences; whatever they liked to hear.

SONNY KING
COMEDIAN/FRIEND

In addition to being able to sing an impressive array of styles, Elvis had an impressive vocal range.

Charlie Hodge: Elvis had one of the strongest voices; most people have an octave, maybe an octave and a half range and that's it; Elvis had almost a three-octave range; cause you take the first song and he'd go out there and hit maybe an A above middle C, and then the second song's "I Got a Woman" and he goes "Well, well, well, well…" that's an E almost two octaves below middle C; so that was almost three octaves right there that he was using in the first two songs.

CHARLIE HODGE
FRIEND/SINGER/GUITARIST/
MEMPHIS MAFIA

But even the King wasn't above learning some new tricks.

Ray Walker: We were doing "Surrender;" he took a break, which was unusual for him; he stepped over to me, he said, "You teach voice, don't you?" I said, "Well sometimes;" he said "I want to go up real high on the end of this song," and he said "I'm afraid to go for it cause I don't know how to say 'to-night.'" Well "oo" is the hardest vowel to say when you're getting up out of your register; it's one of the easiest ones down low; I said "Well sure, come on;" and I said "Now do what I do." I said "Bend over and put your hands on your knees," and he did, and I said, "Now can you throw up?" he said "What?" I said, "Can you throw up? Can you act like you're throwing up?" Hut! Hoot! And so he looked at me kind of funny; I said "Well do it," so he went "Hut," I said "No, go HOOT!" so he got that sound…I said "That's it, just try to throw up and go for it;" he went back and recorded one time and got "To-night!" you know, on that song?

RAY WALKER
SINGER - JORDANAIRES

Charlie Hodge: And Elvis, when you'd tell him something like that that he could use in his career, he was like a sponge; it became his; and by the time we started in Vegas, he had his tone placement, he had his projection, and not one time during touring did he ever have a sore throat from singing, because he sang correctly.

The eternal quest for just the right sound extended to the other musicians as well.

D.J. Fontana: You know for the JAILHOUSE ROCK movie, they said "Well guys, we need something that sounds like prisoners breaking rocks on a chain gang," so Scotty and I, we got in a corner, we was playing around with it and I played that lick, "Da-da," and he'd play the guitar lick in-between those and boy, them producers come running out saying, "What are you guys doing?" I says, "Well, we were trying to do something like prisoners breaking rocks;" they says "Great! Do it some more! That's exactly what we need; it was a sheer accident is what it was.

Robert Relyea: We were doing the pre-recordings on JAILHOUSE ROCK and we were in the fancy sound-recording stage and he liked to record at night; he could do, unlike any entertainer I've ever known, he could do 14 songs and six versions and they'd go gold and platinum and we'd do it in one night; it's just unheard of.

But while he was recording a song for BLUE HAWAII, Elvis hit a snag.

Bob Moore: He asked me on a playback, said "What about that right there? That's a tough line," I said "Sing it like Bing Crosby," just kidding, you know; he said, "What do you mean?" I sang "I could love you longer annnnd forever;" he said "Okay," so, I won't forget, we went back in the studio and I had the earphones on, I'm looking right in his face and hearing him as we put it down and he sang "I could love you longer annnnd forever" and looked at me and I said "Yeah!" I thought it was great.

Even though the movies may have varied in quality, they afforded Elvis the opportunity of working with new songs - and new songwriters.

Ben Weisman: They were doing a movie called LOVING YOU, we sat in the control room, so he's recording, recording, but he wasn't doing my song called "Got A Lot of Living To Do," which he was supposed to record. So I got scared, so what happened was in between the takes, I ran out. He was playing his guitar next to a piano and I sat down and I started playing the blues with him and he looked up and he says, "Who are you?" and I said "My name is Ben Weisman," and he says," Wait a minute, didn't you write a song called "Got A Lot of Living to do?" He says, "Hold it, Ben," and he got his musicians together and they recorded the song right on the spot.

Barry Gibb: LOVING YOU is amazing. The songs in LOVING YOU, what's that one? Got a lot of living to do, aweful lotta of loving to do. That was it.

Bob Moore: We'd listen to a lot of demos and the guy from Hill and Range, I think it was a publishing company, would bring a stack of demos this high. At that time demos were like seventy-eight records almost. And they'd play several and we'd stop on one song sometimes and run it for a while and decide. Everybody would decide, naw, we could do something better.

Mark James: Elvis had an ear, because a lot of times he didn't really try to change the demo or something; if the record sounded like a hit or a smash, he didn't try to change it too much, he kind of stayed with the melody and stayed with it.

D.J. Fontana: He didn't like to overdub tunes at all. He said "Once you lose the feel of the record, you've lost the record, let's don't waste time; we'll do the things as good as we can… He always done a good job on whatever he was tryin' to do. But he just didn't like to waste a lot of time because he just said "You lose it, you lose it after an hour or so, it goes downhill, everything just falls apart;" and he was right.

Ben Weisman: Elvis had different moods; he'd kid around sometimes or sometimes very serious; many times he would cut, like, as much as 32 takes just to get the right feel for it.

Patti Page: Even when I was at the recording sessions at Paramount, when he recorded the songs for the movies, he was always moving.

Ben Weisman: Each scene called for a certain type of song, and I would try to fit the song to fit the scene; that's why Elvis did fifty-seven of my tunes.

Also trying to come up with just the right tune to fit the scene was a young singer-songwriter named Mac Davis.

Mac Davis: All Elvis movies in those days was situation, you know; the situation led to the song and that's all the movies were written for was the music, really.

One of my real goals was to hear someone whistling a song I'd written, someone that didn't know me, just walking around whistling. And the first time that happened I was at the Palomino Club…I was back in the men's room and I heard a guy whistling the B side of "Memories," which was a theme song I wrote for one of his movies called CHARRO; and I recognized the melody and I went "Hey, what are you whistling?" He says, "Chair-o or something like that."

I heard someone say once that, "Mac has written songs for some of Elvis's lesser movies, which boils it down to some 40 or 50 movies."

MAC DAVIS
SINGER/SONGWRITER

Unfortunately, the composers' tireless efforts to come up with appropriate songs sometimes resulted in tunes that just didn't work outside the context of a motion picture.

Charlie Hodge: Some songs are good for the picture, but they're not good played on the radio. Like there was a song called "The Walls Have Ears," but you had to see the movie to see the walls bouncing back and forth and things coming off of there and everything. You can't see that on a record and that was the only bad thing about having some of the recordings that was done on a recording session for pictures. "Stay Away Joe" was so funny to me. We were cutting that session, and Elvis had a song in there where he had to sing to a bull. "Moo, moo, move your little foot, do!" Well, when they played the demo, Scotty Moore looked over at Elvis and said, "Elvis, has it come to this?"

CHARLIE HODGE
FRIEND/SINGER/GUITARIST/
MEMPHIS MAFIA

D.J. Fontana: Of course now we know some of those tunes out of the movies weren't that good and he knew that, he was no idiot at all. He knew the songs but he'd always tell us, says, "Guys, now we've got to do these songs whether we like them or not. It's for a picture. It's for a reason that they've written this into the movie. There's a reason for it. So let's all go in and work as hard as we do on our single records," and that's what he did.

D.J. FONTANA
ELVIS'S DRUMMER

Elvis's last real movie allowed him to indulge one of his first real loves – gospel music.

Ben Weisman: He was going to do a movie called CHANGE OF HABIT, and it was about three nuns and he was a doctor in this movie, so I wanted to make sure I got the right songs for him; so there's a church in Westwood called St. Paul's Church and I went there with my wife and I listened to the songs and to how they would pray, and they would say, one of the ministers would say "Let us pray." "Let Us Pray" was one of my favorite gospel songs I wrote for Elvis.

But even though gospel was one of Elvis's childhood influences, he didn't get around to recording a gospel album until the 1960s.

Gordon Stoker: We sat around many, many nights at Graceland singing gospel music. I just couldn't even begin to tell you how many nights we would sing gospel songs. Probably all night long. He'd get on one song and sing it two hours; he'd take a break, go back and sing it again for another fifteen or twenty, thirty minutes and he'd sing every part and every part good.

Patti Page: I could feel that he was very partial to gospel music, but then he kind of fused them all together: the rock, the gospel, the country, and that made him set apart.

Mac Davis, who would also have a career fusing rock, gospel, and country, and who had come through for Elvis with some movie tunes, provided Presley with some of his best-loved latter-day hits.

Mac Davis: I grew up with a little boy who lived in the ghetto, and I'd always wanted to write a song about it. Just one day I started thinking about the ghetto as a title for the song and the same day a friend of mine named Freddie Willard showed me a lick on the guitar that he was playing and I thought it sounded good and I took it home that night and I wrote this song.

Bobby Wood: Mac Davis came in and played "In the Ghetto" in person…We were in the control room; there was a couch in front of the board and Mac was playing his guitar and singing his song and sitting on the back of that couch and Elvis and Chips was behind the control board and Elvis just shook his head when Mac got through with that song; Mac was shaking like a leaf; he was scared to death!

BOBBY WOOD
ELVIS'S PIANIST

Tony Orlando: I like the "In the Ghetto" Elvis. I mean there was a soulfulness in that, that opening line "In the Ghetto." I mean the way he just dug in on that.

TONY ORLANDO
SINGER

Mac Davis: "Don't Cry Daddy;" He had told me. Elvis had told me, the first time I went over to his house that he was going to record that; I played it to him over there; I'll never forget him; it got real quiet, you know "Don't Cry Daddy" is a pretty sad song; we got to the end of it and it was just real quiet and Elvis says, "I'm going to cut that someday for my daddy;" and I went "Okay," and by golly, he did; he lived up to his word.

MAC DAVIS
SINGER/SONGWRITER

Another young singer-songwriter in the Mac Davis mold was Mark James, who penned what would turn out to be Elvis's first number-one song in nearly a decade.

Mark James: "Suspicious Minds" came from a song that I had written for myself; I was on Scepter Records and actually, I recorded it in 1968; it wasn't until years later when Elvis booked the studio for two weeks. Chips played it to Elvis and he said "Let's hear that again;" they must've recorded 40 or more songs, and I had heard that they were actually leaving the studio and George said, "Hey E! You forgot to cut 'Suspicious Minds,'" and they went back and they recorded it.

MARK JAMES
SONGWRITER, SUSPICIOUS MINDS

And it was the #1 record in 27 countries, I mean it was a great feeling and I was glad to be part of that, you know.

Music legend Jimmie Rodgers also shared one of his songs with Elvis. It was called "It's Over."

Jimmie Rodgers: After I wrote it, I recorded it and then Eddy Arnold recorded "It's Over" and it went to #1 Country. And then I get a call from the Colonel's management company and asked me if I would mind if Elvis recorded my song "It's Over." And I said, "Are you kidding? Of course I wouldn't mind." He sang it "out." You know, how he would get to the big finish and just keep going and keep going with that voice. And he did it his own way, of course, and I thought it was great. I still think it's great.

Another crowd-pleaser from Elvis's Vegas years was actually a medley of three traditional songs. It was called "American Trilogy."

Joe Guercio: The first night we did "Trilogy" in Atlanta, Georgia, James started with the intro and Elvis said "Oh I wish I was in the land of cotton…"and they started with those calls and people stood and screaming and every hair I mean, just, just unbelievable, I mean, we stood 30 seconds, which can be like a year, until they stopped and slowed down and we continued on with the song.

Joe Esposito: Elvis loved dynamic songs, powerful songs, big endings, big singing, hard, big buildups, and that song had the big buildup, let's face it; it starts off so slow; I mean that was Elvis's song; he loved to do those kinds of songs.

Jimmie Rodgers: He had that wonderful way of laying back for a while and doing things very quietly, and then all of a sudden boom! He would take it like an opera singer almost over the top.

Tony Brown: They were arena shows but in a sense you were in his living room, you were right there with him; he didn't go out there, he didn't – he entertained you, but I think he felt like you were just, you know, sitting in his living room.

People from every corner of show business were impressed with the power and emotion of Elvis's performances.

Sonny King: I mean Frank Sinatra made "My Way" a very famous song, you know that, but when Elvis sang it, it was tear jerking.

SONNY KING
COMEDIAN/FRIEND

Bobby Wood: The thing I guess that sticks in my mind about Elvis, you couldn't fool him about "feel;" I mean this guy knew soul and he knew feel.

BOBBY WOOD
ELVIS'S PIANIST

Anita Mann: One of the things that he would say to me is "Is it natural? Does it feel right?" and I'd always remember him saying, "That doesn't feel right, it's got to be natural."

ANITA MANN
CHOREOGRAPHER

> **Elvis Presley:** I like to mix them up; I like to do a song like "Bridge Over Troubled Water," or "American Trilogy," or something and then mix it up and do some rock 'n' roll, some of the hard rock stuff.

But finding that "hard rock stuff" was becoming increasingly difficult.

Jerry Scheff: It was hard for him to find the good rock songs to record, because rock songs were getting to become parodies of themselves. They loved the old stuff you did, and they want you to do that kind of stuff, but you become a parody of yourself when you start doing it too much; and I personally believe that Elvis knew that and really didn't want to do that kind of rock 'n' roll anymore.

JERRY SCHEFF
BASS GUITAR

Ronnie Tutt: I think it was really hard for him to get the songs that were best-suited for him, and I think there were always a lot of people pitching songs at him, from the inner circle people to; all the influences around him made it real difficult to get what was best for him.

Elvis Presley: It's hard to find good material nowadays; You know for everybody; it's very difficult to find any good hard rock songs; if I could find them I would do them.

Others felt it wasn't Elvis's inability to find good rock songs so much as his lack of interest in singing them.

Jerry Scheff: I don't think he wanted to do that rock 'n' roll anymore; he was, you know; he was middle-aged...he wanted to do songs, I think, that he could use his voice on more. See that's why he loved doing "Impossible Dream" and all that Vegas kind of stuff; cause he was a great singer.

But regardless of his choice of songs and styles, Elvis continued to impress audiences, critics, and colleagues for the remainder of his life.

Kenny Rogers: He loved music and I think he loved getting out and performing in front of people and he became a much better singer in the later part, before the very end of his life; there was a point in there where he was really singing well; he had great chops and he was doing good music and I think he was very proud of himself at that point, too.

Jerry Scheff: When he sang a song, he wasn't sitting there going "Oh boy, how do my nails look tonight?" or anything like that; that song was computing and he was putting it out there, and that was part of his love for the audience.

Tony Orlando: Elvis always understood the power of an entrance and the power of an exit. Not just the power of an opening song or the power of a closing song, but the power of making that first entrance.

Anita Mann: There's hardly a song that he performed or sang or made famous or covered or did that is not a part of your growing-up memories, I mean, he means the same thing to me that I think he means to you or he means to everybody that still pays tribute to his music, to his style, to his soul.

Patti Page: He just had a charisma that very few people have; I think it's something that just came from inside.

Even a quarter of a century after his passing, Elvis's musical magic continues to inspire new generations of fans and performers alike.

Dick Clark: Over the years, I must've talked to thousands of musicians and I always say, "Who influenced you?" You'd be amazed, even to this day, people will tell me, "Oh, Elvis, of course," and then so-and-so; he's on everybody's list.

Sheila E: He just had a charisma about him as an entertainer onstage and I think people really loved that about him, so his music and his soul lives on.

Jackie DeShannon: He was the king of rock 'n' roll and will always be; he's what's made it possible for everyone to be performers and to do the things they do now; we all owe that to Elvis.

Barry Gibb: With Elvis, he was completely and utterly natural and I think that the world recognized that. The world of music recognized it. This was a very unique human being and I don't think we'll ever see that again.

Tony Orlando: He copied nobody. There's only one. Everything you saw about him reflected only him. There was nobody in Elvis that appeared other than Elvis.

Joe Guercio: He was the original cast of Elvis Presley; I mean that was it; there was nothing off-Broadway about Elvis; he was what it was; You know, he was real.

Trent Carlini: His music was God's gift to mankind, his integration of Soul, Gospel, Country and Blues in his music was pure magic. As a performer I am always amazed at how much I learn from him, every time I play his songs.

Kenny Rogers: I think because he was so unique in his approach, that, in itself, will last him forever; he was one of a kind, and for that, the music business will always be indebted and those of us who are out there now can only hope to come close to what he did.

EXCERPT OF JAYCEE'S AWARD CEREMONY

Elvis Presley: Every dream that I ever dreamed has come true a hundred times; I learned very early in life that without a song, the day would never end, without a song, a man ain't got a friend, without a song, the road would never bend, without a song... so I keep singing the song.

SWEET SWEET SPIRIT

"AS LONG AS I LIVE ON THIS EARTH, I SOLEMNLY SWEAR WITH GOD'S HELP TO TRY TO BRING JOY AND HAPPINESS THROUGH SINGING."

— ELVIS PRESLEY

Elvis Presley. It is a name that conjures up many images. The greasy haired young rocker, who left girls in an ecstatic frenzy. The black leather clad king of rock 'n' roll, pouring his heart into his music.

Cars, women, Graceland, planes, and all manner of excess are associated with his name. But what many people don't realize is that there was a quieter side to the 20th century's most potent cultural icon. A side that reflected on what it meant to actually be Elvis Presley, the man, the husband, the father and son. To be Elvis Presley, the legend.

Elvis Presley: Well the image is one thing, and a human being is another, you know. It's, it's, it's very hard to live up to an image, put it that way.

CHRISTINA FERRA
FRIEND

Christina Ferra: Everybody talks about Elvis and rock 'n' roll or Elvis and sex or Elvis and drugs. But there was a side to Elvis that is the side that I know, which was the loving, nurturing, very strong, wonderful side of Elvis, and a very spiritual side.

Although Elvis would forever be linked with the rock 'n' roll music he made so successful in the 1950s, his musical roots stretched back much farther than the rhythm and blues that were the foundation of his rockabilly sound.

STEVE BINDER
PRODUCER COMEBACK
SPECIAL

Steve Binder: I was blown away with the fact that here's a man to this day he's never won a, a Grammy for rock 'n' roll.

The only Grammies he picked up were in the gospel area.

WILLIAM CAMPBELL
CO-STAR - LOVE ME TENDER

William Campbell: He was extremely religious. Not religious in a – in a mass – you know, not, not overbearing where he was trying to beat you into believing what he believed. But he loved spiritual music, and he said to me on a couple of occasions he said, this is what got me started.

DEBORAH WALLEY

Deborah Walley: Elvis loved gospel, more than any other kind of music. And it was part of his childhood, as it was also part of my childhood.

But Elvis's love for gospel music and its soulful sound went much deeper than just his musical tastes.

Chris Beard: Elvis had a supernatural something to him. He was very spiritual. He, he was connected to the spirit. And, a lot of people don't know this and Colonel didn't want that to be out there 'cause it would've made him appear to be a little bit sort of like wiggy. All of us that believe in spirit understand each other and, Elvis was right there. He wanted to have that knowledge. He wanted to go to other places.

Joe Esposito: There was always a mystery to Elvis. And it always bothered him tremendously. Why he was picked to be this major, major star of the world and idolized by millions and, have all this talent and, he was always searching. Trying to figure out why. I mean, he thought he was reincarnated, because he felt he lived in the past, in the Roman days. That was one of his things he was always searchin' all the time. Why me Lord? Why me God? Why? Why was I picked to be this person?

Sandy Ferra-Martindale: Oh, he knew the Bible from cover to cover. He could quote scripture. He was a very spiritual man. He loved God.

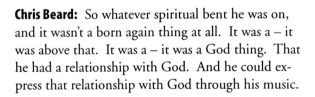

Shirley Dieu: He had a lot of Bibles that he read, and he was always searching and searching. But I thought it was just really interesting to see somebody literally wear the pages out on a Bible.

Chris Beard: So whatever spiritual bent he was on, and it wasn't a born again thing at all. It was a – it was above that. It was a – it was a God thing. That he had a relationship with God. And he could express that relationship with God through his music.

Early on in Elvis's career, it was evident that this was no ordinary celebrity. His values dictated his responses to everything from rock 'n' roll to the controversy his performances generated. When a writer named Herb Rowe referred to Presley's fans as idiots in his column, Elvis responded not to the criticism of himself, but to the attack on his audience.

EXCERPT FROM PRESS CONFERENCE

Elvis Presley: Herb Rowe, or whatever his name is. I mean, I'm not – I'm not running Mr. Rowe down but I, I just don't see that he should call those people idiots. Because they're somebody's kids. They're somebody's decent kids probably that was raised in a decent home. And he's, he, he, he hadn't got any right to call those kids idiots. If they want to –If they want to pay their money and come out and jump around and scream and yell, that's their business. They'll grow up someday and grow out of that. but while they're young let 'em have their fun. Don't let some old man that's so old he can't get around, sit around and call 'em a bunch of idiots because they're just human bein's like he is.

When Rowe's column became a little more graphic in its critique, once again Elvis responded in a way that would be out of character with almost any other rock 'n' roll idol.

EXCERPT FROM PRESS CONFERENCE

Reporter: Back to the quotation. We're no prude but we might suggest a gift, in genuflecting to Elvis Presley, a solid slap across the mouth. Rowe means a slap across the mouth to these girls. Have you any comment to that?

Elvis Presley: Yeah, but I don't think I should say it, you know, because I'm a singer, I'm not a fighter.

Sam Phillips: The beat of his heart, was just like the rhythm that was in his soul, for people. Elvis loved people. But Elvis knew exactly how far he could take himself with someone, and not impose on that person. Or he would find their personality out and then have more darn fun with them. You were with one of the most honest, sweetest, decent, funniest, generous human bein's that had been through a lot as a child. That could've caused him to go exactly the opposite. It didn't. Elvis, to me, is a champion in every way that a human bein' can be a champion.

Malcolm Leo: It's a tough, tough thing. It's tough to be – to maintain a real sane life. Forget the entertainment side. But when you're elevated on a pedestal and, you know, it's hard. It's amazing that he held out for so long. You know, he wasn't an educated man. But he certainly was street smart, and had a very decent heart. Very decent heart. Condemned to be honest I think.

MALCOLM LEO
DIRECTOR, WRITER
PRODUCER, THIS IS ELVIS

John O'Hara: This is part of the appeal in a way, too. There's a lot of sadness in Elvis's story. I mean, there's a lot about the human condition. You know, everybody has great triumphs and great failures and, and Elvis had his share of, of both. And that's part of his appeal.

JOHN O'HARA
AUTHOR

Glen Campbell: Charisma is, is God shining through man, you know. And I like that, Elvis sayin' that. That's a good one, boy. You don't know what your, you know, your future is going to be. You're either blessed or you're cursed. There's no fortunate. There's no luck involved. There's no nothing. It's you're either blessed or you're cursed.

GLEN CAMPBELL
SINGER/FRIEND

The first glimpse that the public would have into this side of Elvis Presley, came on The Ed Sullivan Show when he insisted on singing a number that most people would not associate with a rock 'n' roll rebel.

Gordon Stoker: On the first show, as I remember, he wanted to do "Peace in the Valley" and the CBS officials said no. No! No way are we going to do a religious number. He said I have promised my mother, that I would do "Peace in the Valley," and I'm going to sing it. And we did.

GORDON STOKER
SINGER - JORDAINAIRES

His relationship with his beloved mother would influence more than just his choice of music. Her values were a road map to his life.

RED ROBINSON
HALL-OF-FAME DJ/FAN

Red Robinson: Elvis made me nervous before I met him because, I mean, you know, you're buying the aura. You're buying all of the appearances on Milton Berle and Steve Allen and, and the Tommy and Jimmy Dorsey Show, and Ed Sullivan. But he turned out to be a, a, you know, completely opposite to what I had expected. He wasn't wrapped up in himself. He was a down to earth gentleman. A guy that called me Sir when I'm two years younger. And, he said well that's how my mamma brought me up, you know.

GEORGE BARRIS
CUSTOM CAR DESIGNER

George Barris: He was very humble and nice. And I think that's what come from his mother's part because, he was just like her and, the fact that he was so considerate and he was such a giving young man and, so polite.

A.C. LYLES
PARAMOUNT PRODUCER

A.C. Lyles: When I met Elvis, and was around him a lot and got to know him, had I a son, I would loved for him to have been like Elvis. Not necessarily the music and the adulation and the tremendous wealth that he brought in, but as a person. I just thought Elvis was the – he was so well mannered and, so polite. I never heard him calling anybody other than Mr., Miss, and Mrs. Norman Taurog, the director, did five or six pictures with him. He still called him Mr. Taurog.

Due to his success as an entertainer, Elvis was able to indulge yet another side of his nature. One that would become almost as legendary as the man behind it.

JOE ESPOSITO
ROAD MANAGER & FRIEND

Joe Esposito: You know, Elvis's religious beliefs and generosity could've connected together in some way or another. He loved to help people. And I think he felt that religion helps people, too. And, he loved to make people happy. And since he could afford to do that, that's what he liked to do. He liked to see peoples' reactions, when he gave them something that they could never afford themselves.

Mike Freeman: And he was very generous with the material wealth that he had. He gave away a lot of it. Not necessarily in the form of cash, but if someone needed something he gave it to 'em.

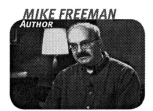

MIKE FREEMAN
AUTHOR

Marian Cocke: I know one night I went in and he said, do you have a microwave? I said why do you want to know if I have a microwave for? And he said well Miss Cocke, you work all day, and you come out here and you take care of me at night and I know you have to cook for your family. And I thought maybe you might need a a microwave. He said some nurse had told him that she needed a microwave, because it would make her – make her life easier with cookin' supper at night and things like that. And I said no, I don't need a microwave. I said, I got one and I don't use it.

MARIAN COCKE
ELVIS'S NURSE

Myrna Smith: To a fault, Elvis was generous to a fault I think. He, well he gave away most of his fortune, you know, when he was alive. He rewarded you because it made him feel good.

MYRNA SMITH
SINGER/BACK-UP GROUP,
SWEET INSPIRATIONS

A.C. Lyles: Don't admire anything and don't say you'd like that because the next day, it would show up to – in your office, or wherever it was.

A.C. LYLES
PARAMOUNT PRODUCER

Christina Ferra: If my mother said gee Elvis, that's a nice lamp. He'd say, you want it take it. I don't need your lamp. Well, do you want the car take it. It – he always was very generous and when he was in Vegas, everything was on the house, you know. From our room to our food. I could go into the gift shop and sign things. It was amazing.

CHRISTINA FERRA
FRIEND

Anita Wood: I would just maybe get a few things. If I liked 'em he'd get 'em, get 'em. Get some more. Get more. Little that's not enough Little, you know. Yeah, he was very generous, to a fault, I think.

But it wasn't just material goods that Elvis shared. He felt his wealth could be used to do some good for the people in his life.

Marian Cocke: And I remember very well, an instance where there was a child at one of the hospitals, that was in a service ward. And they didn't allow the parents to stay at night. They could visit during the day but not at night because it was a ward. And the child was real, real sick. And he had that child moved to a private room, which he paid for. So that mother could stay. And he made sure that mother had money to eat on. And the, the necessities that she needed for herself.

June Sayers: He said but if you ever need a friend? He said I'm here. I want you to know I'm here.

Pauline Sayers: And I'm not here just for you to look at.

June Sayers: No.

Pauline Sayers: He said – he said you're my friend, and I want to be your friend.

June Sayers: Your friends.

Pauline Sayers: When, when my mother passed away, the – we didn't know what to do because we had no money.

June Sayers: It was a – it was the – a Labor Day weekend. It was September the 5th.

Pauline Sayers: Labor Day weekend. No way of getting it.

June Sayers: In 1965. This was in 1965. We didn't know what to do. My father was devastated. And it was Elvis. We went up to Elvis and I think we got there at about 3:00 in the morning. He said honey he said, go on the phone and tell your daddy, not to worry about nothing. That we'll be down, you know, don't – don't worry about anything. Pauline went down and called, called my dad. And meanwhile Elvis says just holding, you know, hugging us and, telling us not to worry. And, and, and it was so devastating.

Pauline Sayers: They started makin' arrangements. And, they, they couldn't get us on a plane, that could take my mother's body from London Heathrow to Manchester, which is where we would have to go. And, and my dad called Elvis and Elvis said, if you can't get a plane, you charter one.

June Sayers: Charter one.

Pauline Sayers: But anyway Elvis took us out to the car. And, of course, he had his arms around us and we got in the car. And that man, lay at our feet inside the car. And he said honeys, he said, I'd come with you he said, but it'd be a circus.

June Sayers: Yeah.

Pauline Sayers: It'd be a circus. He said, you don't want me to come with you.

JUNE & PAULINE SAYERS
FANS & FRIENDS

Christina Ferra: I believe that that's – part of the strength of Elvis, is his faith and his belief spiritually. That's what attracts a lot of people to him. People can talk about, you know, the swiveling hips or his wonderful voice. And then this sexual attraction he had. But the biggest attraction of Elvis in my estimation, was his spiritual strength and his faith. And his being plugged into the power source so to speak. Plugged into God. And people are always attracted to that tremendous energy.

Chris Beard: Anything to do with a spiritual experience is difficult to explain, and Elvis definitely I think you could say was a spiritual experience to everybody who ever saw him or touched him or came in contact with him, because of that. Because he was a much deeper feeling person than even the people closely around him even had any idea.

Elvis's quest for spiritual growth would lead him down many paths. One that would be with him throughout his life was his devotion to the eastern discipline of karate.

PRESS CONFERENCE

Reporter: What do you do for relaxation?

Elvis Presley: Karate, If you can relax doin' this I don't know.

Mindi Miller: The guys started doing some karate moves and got me interested in that. So immediately I started taking classes in karate and he said well you need to go to Ed Parker and you need to go to this one and you need to take Kempo. And he started talking about all of these forms of, of karate. It was Shotokan, Kempo, Jujitsu, and how, you know, very into it he was. And he loved to, you know, he loved to share with people what his personal interests were.

Christina Ferra: I remember he scared the heck out of my mother once, because she saw him try to break a board in half with his head. But he succeeded. And he was a tough guy. His hands were all cut up from the karate when he experienced it and, and kept on trying to break boards. But he didn't care because he just had a mission. He was a man with on a mission. But he also was extremely well read. Very much into philosophy and spiritual books.

Sam Thompson: Elvis read books on eastern religions. Elvis questioned everything. I think of Elvis as this guy that was looking for answers. And, you know, when I think like that, most the people that I know are looking for answers. You know, we're just sort of trying to make it from A to B and do – and tryin' to get there without hurting anybody. And trying to be the best person we can and maybe leave the world a little bit better place than where we found it.

Ray Walker: A lot of people don't know he's a well read man. He – if he didn't know something he'd read about it. He'd look it up. He'd find out. Internet today would be an unbelievable thing for him. He'd just find out anything he wants to know. But he started studying world religions.

Lester Hoffman: I noticed that, one time he wore a necklace, a neck piece. And one of it had the cross, and the other was the Star of David. But I understand that when he was a young man, and his folks had to go to work, they would leave him, with people that were, were Jewish and he – I think he wore the Star of David for them.

George Nichopoulos *Elvis's Private Physician*

George Nichopoulos: Yeah, I think that was a very strong side of Elvis, the spiritual side. And the house that, that, that we built we – I had a chapel in that house. And, Elvis had bought me a cross to put in that chapel. And, he was always amazed that someone's got a little chapel in their home. But he was a very spiritual guy and talked about religion a lot. He had all kinds of thoughts about religion, I mean, pro and con. And, I guess some of the impact of that is, in the little thing he used to wear around his neck. He, he had a cross and he had a Star of David and he had, you know, he kind of covered the bases with everything. He didn't want to be – he didn't want to be left out of heaven on a technicality of any kind.

Patty Parry *Memphis Mafia*

Patty Parry: He loved all religions. He loved the Jewish religion. He used to wear a Jewish star and a cross 'cause he didn't want to get shut out of heaven on a technicality. He liked – he, he used to read the Bible. He'd make up his own things. He would say, God's name is hallowed because it says here, hallowed be thy name .

In the mid 1960s, Elvis had an experience that would change his outlook on life, and his place in it.

Sandy Ferra-Martindale *Girlfriend*

Sandy Ferra-Martindale: It was like in the desert. And there was a cloud formation. I mean, he saw Jesus. And he said that God spoke to him. And he just knew that he was gonna do something really big in life. And, and like bigger than life, but he didn't know what it was. Little did he know that, you know, it was gonna be after death, and not even in life, that he was gonna become this like phenomenon.

Gail Ganley Steele: He spoke about God and Jesus Christ in his life and I thought, wow. Here is this wonderful sensuous performer who gave everything he had in his entertaining, and he's able to sit and talk about God. He said, "Well I – a lot of people have come to think of me kind of like as a god," he said, "But I'm not a god." He says, "There's only one God," and he said, "People worship me. And it's really hard to keep up this image all the time, to be this person that they expect me to be, always perfect." He says, "I'm very imperfect." And he says, "I'm fighting demons all the time."

GAIL GANLEY STEELE
ACTRESS

Joe Esposito: Elvis always told us, "I'm an entertainer. I don't think I should influence other people, my fans, with the religion or politics. That is something they had to decide on their own. Just because I'm a Christian doesn't mean all my fans should be Christians." Same thing as democrat or republican. Elvis never said where he stood politically because, he didn't want to influence them. And he felt that's not his job in this world. He's an entertainer; he's there to perform, to sing, make people happy, but not get involved in their personal lives.

JOE ESPOSITO
ROAD MANAGER & FRIEND

In 1966, Elvis made the decision to record some of his favorite gospel numbers. The result was the legendary album, "How Great Thou Art."

Pat Broeske: What's interesting is, Elvis cut, you know, his greatest gospel album, you know, at the height of 60s radicalism. Which was really, when you think about it, a really daring move for Elvis Presley to do that. And, and that music has endured. That album, you know, is considered one of the great gospel albums today.

PAT BROESKE
AUTHOR

ANN ELLINGTON WAGNER
TENNESSEE GOVERNOR'S DAUGHTER

Ann Ellington Wagner: I think that's really where his, his love for music obviously began. But I think it's also where he felt comfortable, was with the gospel music.

Joe Esposito: Elvis's favorite music was gospel music. It's music from the heart, 'cause he was such a religious person and he felt so good when he sang it. And it was so strong and emotional that, that was probably his favorite music. And I think he carried that over into all his music. To sing with feeling.

Elvis never sang a song twice the same way. 'Cause he always, dependin' on how he felt that day and, how he put his heart into it. And, that's I think what made Elvis such a great singer because he put his heart and soul into every song he ever sang.

He probably sang gospel more than any music there was. He'd sit at the piano by himself, down in his music room at Graceland.

EXCERPT FROM INTERVIEW

Elvis Presley: Well we grew up with it, you know, from the time I was – I can remember, like two years old. When I got old enough I started to sing in church. And I started –

Reporter: That's how you got into singing?

Elvis Presley: Well that's one of the ways.

Reporter: One of the ways.

Elvis Presley: But this thing here, the gospel thing is, is just, is really all I grew up with, you know, more than anything else.

"How Great Thou Art" would go onto win Elvis his first Grammy.

Sam Thompson: We got artists now that are, are nominated for Grammies, that get up on stage and insult people and, and incite riots and offend people racially, ethnically, religiously on every level. And, and that was not what Elvis was about. His, you know, people felt good when they went to his concerts. They felt better when they left and, he wasn't about inflaming the passions of people and, and causing that type of situation to, to exist.

SAM THOMPSON
MEMPHIS MAFIA

Though most of those around him were very supportive of his spiritual side, there was at least one person who wasn't happy with Elvis's quest for enlightenment.

Shirley Dieu: If someone spent a lot of time with Elvis, like Larry spent all that time going over all the books and everything, the guys would get jealous. They would get, you know, and like one of 'em, in particular, well when's he comin' back down, you know, he's been up there for how long? You know, just really getting all upset because he was spending so much time with Larry Geller. But that's what he wanted to do, and thank God, that somebody was there to do something he enjoyed. To keep him going.

SHIRLEY DIEU
JOE ESPOSITO'S FORMER
GIRLFRIEND

Hal Kanter: Col. Parker wanted me to write somethin', for Elvis, so that Elvis could do something spiritual. And I said you've got the wrong fella. I said I, I, can't write spiritual. And he wanted some kind of a spiritual lyric. I said I don't write lyrics. That's somebody else. He says well no I don't want it to be lyrics I just want it to be lyrical, but not lyrics. It's something, he can say it in the middle of his act. And, I said I'll think about it. He never mentioned that to me after that.

HAL KANTER
DIRECTOR/ LOVING YOU, BLUE
HAWAII

What many fans do not know is that Elvis's sense of spiritual purpose extended even to the management of his personal finances. During his lifetime, Presley was the US's single largest private taxpayer, due to the fact that he never took a single deduction, and paid the full tax every year. He stated on more than one occasion that he felt that deducting his charitable contributions would negate their value. It wasn't a contribution, if you got something back for it.

RED ROBINSON
HALL-OF-FAME DJ/FAN

Red Robinson: I happen to know, not through any of Elvis's close friends because what he did, in many cases, charitable donations in the true sense of charity. The Christian sense of charity that he believed in, was that you give something away you don't expect anything in return. This is unique.

BILL MORRIS
SHERIFF/MAYOR MEMPHIS

Bill Morris: In any lifestyle, you know, this person – he wasn't the richest person in the world, but what he had, was a great deal by comparison to what most other people had, and he shared it. He shared it to charity. He gave to the top 50 charities in our city, in Memphis. He gave to individuals that he knew. He supported law enforcement. He supported church organizations. He supported his family, and he supported his friends in ways that they couldn't do things for themselves.

But it wasn't just money Elvis would donate to his favorite charities. In 1964, he purchased Franklin Roosevelt's presidential yacht, the Potomac, which at that time was in danger of being scrapped. After fixing up the yacht, he then donated it to Danny Thomas's St. Jude's Hospital for Children, to be used in a fundraising event for that cause.

After serving its purpose, the Potomac went onto become a national historic landmark, and is now a floating museum. But the Potomac wasn't the only part of our national history that Elvis's good nature was responsible for preserving. If one goes to Pearl Harbor in Hawaii, there's a big reminder of Presley's charitable works, anchored on what used to be Battleship Road.

Tom Moffat: At the time there was no official memorial in Pearl Harbor, to honor those who went down in – with the Arizona. Colonel Parker read about this in Los Angeles that the commission that was trying to complete the project didn't have enough money. And they needed a big fundraiser to finish it off. A lot of people had donated, but they didn't have enough money.

The answer to the problem was simple in Elvis's mind. He would do a benefit show to build the memorial.

Tom Moffat: And we got a wire back from Elvis, saying that he would come to Hawaii and do his first performance here, after he was released from the army. That's how the Pearl Harbor Arizona Memorial benefit concert came to be.

Ray Walker: By 1961 when we did the Arizona Hawaii show, I'd never seen a crowd like that, of 30,000, 40,000, 50,000 people.

Bob Moore: And the navy had the welcoming committees for us and all and, we were just treated great. And then they put us in the Hawaiian Village Hotel which was the most beautiful place I guess in the world.

Unfortunately the United States Government has seen fit to take a move in recent years that has angered many of those close to Presley during his lifetime.

Bob Moore: I'll tell you this, since then I've been to Hawaii several times. And, last time I went we went to go out to the Arizona memorial, and Elvis's name was not there anymore. And so I asked about it and, I noticed a lot of senators' and politicians' names were up there and I said well where's Elvis? And they said well, they have decided that Elvis had a drug problem and so they've taken his name down.

But Elvis was kind of responsible, I'd say along with Colonel Tom, for settin' this whole thing up. They drew a lot of money for the families of the sailors that went down on the USS Arizona.

One of the problems that Elvis faced in his spiritual quest, was that by the mid 1960s, many people saw him as an aging rocker who had sold out his roots to do Roustabout. The rest of the world had undergone a transformation which included the study of yoga and other esoteric practices. At the forefront of this moment were the Beatles with their newfound devotion to the Maharishi Mahesh Yogi and his version of Transcendental Meditation. To many people, Elvis seemed more and more out of touch with the reality of the times in which he was living. They couldn't have been more wrong.

DEBORAH WALLEY

Deborah Walley: The self realization center was started by an Indian named, Yoganonda. And he was the first I believe, to bring Hindu philosophy and yoga techniques, to the west. The lake shrine, is where we would go. It's a very peaceful, beautiful place. And, Elvis took me there one day when we got off early. And we spent the afternoon there. Went back again several times. But, he introduced me to the teachings of Yoganonda, there, and bought me all of Yoganonda's books. And then on, you know, as we got closer, our relationship turned very spiritual. And Elvis began to share with me, things he had learned. Books he had read. And so our discussions became very deep and esoteric. We explored, you know, the nature of God. You know, different religions. And I spent a, a great deal of time. It changed my life.

DR. LESTER HOFFMAN
ELVIS'S DENTIST

Dr. Lester Hoffman: We were doing a little dental surgery on Elvis. I was taking out a, an old broken root tip. And, of course, I reached for the syringe to get him numb and he says what's that? I said well I'm gonna get you numb he says no, just give me a moment. He went into sort, sort of like a trance and at the end of the minute he said okay, I'm ready. And I reached for the syringe again. And he said no he said, that won't be necessary. He had gone into some deep meditation. I says come on Elvis, I said, this – he says you go ahead. If it bothers me I'll, I'll stop you. I went ahead and did the surgery. Got the root tip out, sewed him up. He never blinked, he never moved. And when he finished it I said hey Elvis I'm through. He says I never felt a thing. He could put himself into this meditative trance. He was a student of meditation, and he used it.

Jerry Schilling: Elvis being the thinker that he was, and the reader that he was, and the human that he was, you know, he wasn't obsessed his whole life about it but yeah, he did question it. He did search. And he did read and he did think of past lives, if you will, and he was a very bright man.

JERRY SCHILLING
MEMPHIS MAFIA/FRIEND

In the end, faith was not enough to save Elvis from the pressures of being the best known man in the world. But his thoughts and actions towards others offer a redemption that he could not find in life.

Kanani Seanoa: He said that we don't pay attention, most of us. That we float through life. And I really notice this as time has passed on that most people float, and it's just whatever you call getting by. And he says we have a, a responsibility, for everybody. Not just family members but we really need to think about that. We have a responsibility for everybody.

KANAI SEANOA
SPIRITUAL FRIEND

Sandy Basset: I mean, there's this whole huge universe. Why us here on this earth? And he always had us looking up in the stars and we could – I mean, you could see and you could relate and it really – I even do that now, you know. How could it possibly be? How special are we to be here? Well he was a very spiritual person and very in tune with God, and Jesus. It was very, very close to him. He lived it.

SANDY BASSET

CHRISTINA FERRA
FRIEND

SUSAN HENNING
GIRLFRIEND/DANCER

Christina Ferra: And the reason why, as a fan, somebody is attracted to him or people are attracted to him, so many people, and why he still lives on is because of who he was spiritually. There are a lot of good looking guys and gals out there in show business. And there are a lot of talented people out there. But there was only one Elvis.

Susan Henning: I think he knew there was something more. But I think when you're in the business, you're never quite satisfied with what it gives. And that's adoration. It's a very physical. There was times when I would cry that, nobody loved me for anything but my body. It was what I presented. I think he had a restlessness of an inner peace. And he had so much to give and I think, he was looking for maybe a peace that God might've give him. And I do think he had the Lord in him, but I think it was difficult to find in the circumstances he was in.

CHRISTINA FERRA
FRIEND

Christina Ferra: Unfortunately I think he died because that was a time when he started to get shaken, and lose the faith. And he was searching desperately in his spiritual books, trying to find it again. He was still reading them trying to get that faith reignited but a lot of people let him down.

In his brief lifetime, Elvis touched millions with his music. But to those who knew him, his greatest legacy is not that of the superstar king of rock 'n' roll, but of the Elvis Presley who was simply a human being.

MARIAN COCKE
ELVIS'S NURSE

Marian Cocke: After Elvis passed away, my husband and I were going to church one Sunday and I – it was about six weeks, after he had died. I was just thinking about all the things we had done and the fun we'd had and things like that. And so on the way home from church I told Bob I said pull in at Walgreen's. I want to pick up a, a notebook. And, so we did and I got me a notebook and he said what are you gonna do with that? And I said well, you know, honey I think I want to put down all I can remember about Elvis. I said because someday I'm gonna be too old to remember. And I want to be able to go back, and remember him.

D.J. Fontana: You still think about Elvis. I do. And, I thought he was one of the nicest guys that I'd ever met in my life.

Jerry Schilling: There's not really, I mean, this – no disrespect but there's not really a, another person worldwide, probably outside of Jesus, that had this affect on the world. I mean, I was in India several years ago. And it's amazing. I mean, the Indian Times did an article on me just because I was a friend of Elvis Presley, you know, which is amazing. And I'm very proud to be a friend of Elvis Presley.

Bill Morris: I hope that somewhere along the line as we go down through history, that the things that will not be missed about Elvis. He was more than a musician. He was more than a singer. He was a – more than entertainer. He was also a man of a great spirituality. Great character. Great capacity to love. Great capacity to share. And a great capacity to contribute. All of those make – And that's why when the time came an opportunity for me to do so, I named – as the mayor, I named the hospital, Elvis Presley Trauma Center. The, the place where people go with the greatest amount of hurt. And I thought, what better example could we have than to name it after Elvis, because there the hurt can be dealt with.

Dr. Lester Hoffman: Elvis brought a touch of magic into our lives. That's the way we put it. And when he passed away and I, I told my wife I said, you know, I said, the magic will now be gone. But here it is, years later, and it, it's still there.

THE IMPOSSIBLE DREAM

AUGUST 16, 1977

He was young. He was strong. And he knew how to stay healthy.

Joe Esposito: We didn't have alcohol in the house in the early 60s. Uh, he didn't care for any – no beer cans or booze.

Sandy Ferra-Martindale: He wasn't into, you know, like recreational drugs for any reason.

In those early Hollywood days, when Elvis Presley said, no booze and no drugs, he meant just that. But somewhere along the line, he started drawing an important distinction.

Joe Esposito: Elvis just had it in mind that it was prescription medicine. Got it from a doctor, so it's okay to take it.

Christina Ferra: And he said well they're prescription drugs. And the thing that I would like to share with other people is that Elvis had this innocent country boy kind of attitude. A doctor was someone he looked up to. If a doctor prescribed some sort of sedative, to him that was okay.

Sandy Ferra-Martindale: Originally when he'd come out to do a movie he would take diet pills because he was worried about his weight and wanted to be thin for the movies, because he'd eat a lot of hamburgers and stuff when he was back in, uh, Memphis.

Charlie Hodge: Did he have a drug problem? Yes, but it was necessary. Elvis had a twisted colon, which I understand is a very, very painful. And he had to take a heavy narcotic for that. He had glaucoma, which they had under control but he had to take narcotics for that. I mean, it, it would – he had to take it or he'd gone blind. But they had it under control.

George Klein: If you walked a mile in his shoes, you may understand what he was going through. Traveling, uh, you know, uh, doing shows, one nighters. Couldn't get to sleep. You're all wound up coming off stage. So you'd ta– go take sleeping pills. Then you got to get up the next day to travel a thousand miles and, and so you take some uppers.

GEORGE KLEIN
MEMPHIS MAFIA/FRIEND

In public, questions about Elvis's energy level were easily deflected.

PRESS CONFERENCE EXCERPT

Elvis Presley: I take vitamin E. I was only kidding. I don't know. It just – I embarrassed myself man. I, I don't know dear I just – I enjoy the business. I like what I'm doing.

Mary Ann Mobley: But I don't think that Elvis ever was involved in anything that was against the law. Any drugs such as heroine or, crack, or any, uh, cocaine. Uh, uh, maybe he was but I, I, I would have difficulty, uh, believing that. I do know that, uh, he had trouble with his weight. Um, I do know that, he had trouble sometimes sleeping. And, uh, I think that he did get hooked on amphetamines and, and then, sleeping pills.

MARY ANN MOBLEY
CO-STAR, HARUM SCARUM,
GIRL HAPPY

Sandy Martindale: So it would be like one diet pill and one sleeping pill and then his immunity, built up to that. And so then it would be two diet pills and two sleeping pills. And it was just like a vicious cycle. And, uh, at one point I, I flushed all those things down the toilet and he laughed because, of course, he could, you know, get plenty more.

SANDY FERRA-
MARTINDALE
GIRLFRIEND

Pat Broeske: The MGM years had an impact on Elvis Presley. I mean, this is the studio that was famous for shoving diet pills at a teenage Judy Garland, you know? There's, there's no question about it. The studio at the time had a legacy for sending stars to Dr. Feelgoods.

PAT BROESKE
AUTHOR

No one can say for sure when Elvis started abusing the drugs that would eventually lead to his death. But most friends and associates point to March 1972, when Priscilla announced to Elvis that she was leaving him. Whatever pills he may have taken before, he started taking more of them. And they in turn took more of a toll on him.

Joe Esposito: Elvis's personality changed. You know, he was not the happy go lucky, nice individual. Sometimes his moods would swing. Uh, he could be crabby in one minute and then, fine the next.

The amazing thing about Elvis was that, you know, then he would just clean his act up. He would just stop taking anything for long periods of time.

And he was great. In a good mood, had a great time. And then, maybe something bothered his mind and, instead of drinking, he'd take a pill.

Sometimes even Elvis's fans were witness to his anger. At concerts when talking to them between songs.

CONCERT EXTRACT

Elvis Presley: I don't pay any attention to rumors. I don't pay any attention to Movie magazines. I don't read 'em, because they're all junk. When I got sick here in the hotel, I got sick here that one night. I had a 102 temperature. They wouldn't let me perform. From three different sources I heard, I was strung out on heroine. Well by god I'll tell you somethin' friend, I have never been strung out, in my life, except on music. But all across this town, I was strung out. So I told 'em earlier and don't you get offended, ladies and gentlemen, I'm talkin' to somebody else. If I find or hear the individual that has said that about me, I'm gonna break your goddam neck you son of a bitch. That is dangerous. That is damaging to myself, to my little daughter, to my father, to my friends, my doctor, to everybody. My relationship with you. My relationship with you up on the stage. I will pull your goddam tongue out by the roots!

Wink Martindale: And I remember when we left and said goodbye. We walked out of the dressing room, closed the door behind us, and I looked at Sandy and she looked at me and I said, "You know what? That'll be the last time we're gonna see Elvis alive." And she said, "What do you mean?" And I didn't say anything else and we walked back to our hotel. We got a cab. We went back to our hotel. And we had no sooner gotten into our dressing room, and both of us just broke down and cried. Because we felt and it was so sad what we had just witnessed. And then, six months later he was dead.

Christina Ferra: I remember when I was 18 or 19, my mother and I were in West LA and my mother said I had a terrible dream. I dreamt that Elvis's mother came to me, and said save my son, save my son. And I think Elvis is in major trouble. And, we flew to Vegas, and we tried to get in. And it's the first time, ever, that Elvis didn't have us backstage. And, they said he's really sick. He can't see anybody right now. And I know that that's when, you know, things were getting really bad and I only wish that my mom could've been around him more. I wish that he could've had more loving female influences. You know, a lot of people cared about him but, a lot of people were afraid to help him.

Sheila Ryan: Drug use is insidious. You start out with a little bit. a little bit works so why not more works better? And, so by the time I met him he was always at the more works better stage. And, so that's what I had to deal with, you know. Just him taking a lot of medications and I, you know, would have to sometimes give him the medications or injections or whatever. He, he told me it was vitamin B12 and I, I don't think it was. Just between you and I. Don't tell anybody.

The people closest to Elvis were fiercely protective of his reputation. Initially, Joe Esposito denied Elvis's drug use.

Joe Esposito: I was just protecting my friend. I knew there was a problem there. I mean, you can't take all that medication. All that medication can't be good for you.

And Linda Thompson, Elvis's girlfriend from 1972 to 1976, never mentioned drugs to her brother, Sam, even when he went to work for Elvis as a bodyguard.

Linda Thompson: Sam, my brother Sam, he came to me after a few months of having been on the road with Elvis. And I'd been with Elvis about two years at the time I think, two and a half years. And he said, Baby Sister, I said yeah? He says, how come you never mentioned any of this? You never – we're close, right? I said yeah. He said, but you, you've never shared this with anybody. You've never told me anything about what's goin' on here. And, that, you know, Elvis is doin' these prescription drugs. And this is – this is a real distorted way of life. And I – and I was so protective of Elvis, that I didn't even share that with my only sibling, whom I was really, really close to and, and still very close to. And he was really taken aback by that, that I had never even shared with him, the kind of drug abuse that Elvis had succumbed to.

Sheila Ryan: I would be in charge of, of the medicine box. And it had all of this medicine in it. And, you know, sometimes we would try to fill some of the capsules with sugar and make him think he was getting a sleeping med when in fact it was a placebo. And, so, you know, it was all a game. Let's pretend Elvis isn't dying, you know. We didn't really talk about how serious it was. But it was.

As rumors of his drug use became more widespread, Elvis didn't help his own cause with rambling interviews like this one from 1973.

EXCERPT FROM PRESS CONFERENCE

Reporter: How do you pace yourself?

Elvis Presley: Sir?

Reporter: How do you pace yourself?

Elvis Presley: You mean physically, vocally, whatever?

Reporter: So you are up when you need to be up?

Elvis Presley: I just, I exercise every day. I vocalize every day. I practice. If I'm working or, or not. So I just try to stay in shape all the time. Vocally and mentally and —

RAY MANZAREK
KEYBOARDIST, THE DOORS

Ray Manzarek: You know what I think it might be? No one ever says no to them. You know? You say no to me you'll say no to you. Everybody gets said no to. No, no, no, no, no. Not to Jim Morrison. You didn't say no to Jim Morrison. He's the lead singer. He's the star, you know. He wants to do this he wants to do that. You kinda go along with 'em, you know. He wants to drink, how do you stop him from drinking? I think the same thing happened to Elvis. No one said, get that bottle out of your hand. Knocked it right out of his hand. No pills bamm! As a matter of fact, boom. Now go to sleep and sit down. You couldn't do that to Elvis Presley. You'd do that to anybody else, you know. You'd do that to the drummer in the band or the guitar player. But you don't do that to the lead singer. Elvis was the lead singer. And the biggest thing, until the Beatles. So how do you stop it?

Joe Esposito: We've all talked to him at one time or another. His dad, Priscilla, the guys, all the guys around him. We sat around and talked and said we got to do somethin' about this. And there were times Red and Sonny would be in the bedroom talkin' to Elvis and they would talk to him about his problem, Red would say somethin' about, Elvis you got to start cleanin' up your act. He said, yeah, I'll do it. When I'm ready to do it I'll do it. Then he'd get mad at ya and just tell you to get out of the room. He was very hard headed.

In 1977, bodyguards Red West, Sonny West, and Dave Hebler made what they maintain was a final attempt to help Elvis see what drugs were doing to him. They wrote the tell all book, "Elvis What Happened?"

When word of the book in progress leaked out, Elvis was devastated.

Joe Esposito: That pretty well haunted him the last year of his life. He got obsessed with it. Every night we'd sit and talk about it, after the shows. You know he was so concerned about what they're sayin' about him. What they're gonna write about me. What are the people gonna think about me? What are my fans gonna say? Or how about Lisa Marie when she reads this, when she gets older? It bugged him. But instead of doing something about it, it just sent him into a fatal emotional dive, it destroyed him.

The book was published on August 1, 1977. Two weeks later, Elvis had flowers delivered to his mother's grave, as he did every August 14th, the anniversary of her death. On the 15th, Elvis was getting ready to go on tour.

Joe Esposito: I came in that evening and, Larry Geller came in town, too, from LA. And I was stayin' at the Howard Johnson's Hotel down the street. And I came to the house that evening. And hung around, visited some of the people. Sam Thompson was there and the other guys just talking and, gettin' ready for tomorrow. And, Elvis went to the dentist.

JOE ESPOSITO
ROAD MANAGER & FRIEND

Dr. Lester Hoffman: It was just a routine visit to check him over. He was preparing to tour. And, he, he had Ginger Alden with him. And his comments to me were Dr. Hoffman, after you check me over if you can, please check Ginger over because I'm, would like to get her teeth fixed and straightened. And, it was a just a very, very enjoyable visit.

DR. LESTER
HOFFMAN
ELVIS'S DENTIST

Sam Thompson: And I was there when he got back. And, just before he went down to play racquetball, he called me upstairs and we were just talkin' about some of the songs of the upcoming tour. And I had actually been supposed to take Lisa Marie back, for several days, to, to Priscilla. And as always happened when Lisa came to visit Elvis would just want to add a few more days, a few more days cause he really loved his daughter and, was looking for an opportunity to stay with her. So my, my role the next day was to come back over, pick Lisa up, and fly commercially back to Los Angeles.

SAM THOMPSON
MEMPHIS MAFIA

I said good night to him. And left in the wee hours of the morning. And I went home and went to bed. And, as I recall we, we embraced which we often – we'd shake hands and then we'd give each other a little hug, you know. And I told him to get some rest or something like that. And, that – and then I went home and went to sleep.

JOE ESPOSITO
ROAD MANAGER & FRIEND

Joe Esposito: I called upstairs and I said Elvis, I'm here. Is there anything you need? Anything we should get ready for tomorrow? He said no, everything's fine. You know, make sure you wake me up tomorrow at 4:00 pm and, if I need anything I'll let you know. Basically that was it. So, I hung around a little bit. Went back to the hotel and went to sleep.

Early in the afternoon of August 16, 1977, Ginger Alden awoke to find that three hours after Elvis went into the bathroom to read, he still hadn't returned. She went back to sleep.

About 12:00 noon, I came back to Graceland, and Al Strada was there packin' the wardrobe cases. And, about 2:00, 2:10, the phone rang, the intercom. It was Ginger calling down, and one of the maids answered. And she asked if one of the boys was there and she said Al's here. So she gave the phone to Al. She asked Al to come upstairs. He went upstairs, went into the bathroom. And, Ginger apparently thought Elvis fainted. And as soon as Al got up there he called me real quick, on the intercom. And he said Joe, I need your help. Elvis has collapsed. So I ran upstairs. I went up to the bedroom and into the bathroom. Elvis had fallen off the toilet. He was readin' a book. And, he fell face down onto the carpeting. And I immediately turned him over. And the minute I touched him, I knew that he had been dead for awhile.

So I turned him over and I pulled up his pajamas. I could not give him mouth to mouth because his mouth was shut, closed. There was no way I could open it. And, I tried to do the heart thing, which I saw in movies. I'm not a CPR expert. I picked the phone up, called the operator and said I need an ambulance here at 3765 Elvis Presley Boulevard. Somebody has collapsed. We need somebody here quick.

Sam Thompson: My dad came over and took me to Graceland. He was gonna drop me off. 'Cause we were gonna have a, a car take us to the airport. And, as I was goin' into Graceland, a car came speeding down and it turned out it was David Stanley.

And I was just saying hi to David or something and, he said something like have you heard the news? Elvis just died or Elvis is dead or something like that. And I mean, my dad and I were just startled and, I thought well yeah, I must've heard that wrong.

Joe Esposito: I think Al or somebody called Vernon. He was down in the office, Elvis's father. He come upstairs. I was concerned about Vernon because Vernon had a bad heart and he's had some heart problems the last couple years. And, he came in and he got on his knees and he was sayin' Elvis please don't leave us. He was saying Elvis, my boy. And, and – it was a tough scene. All kinds of things were happening. Ginger was by the doorway and then Lisa Marie was in town. She was gettin' ready to go back to LA that day. She came by the door and looked into the bathroom and saw her father laying there. That was tough. I said let's get her out of here. And, it seemed forever, before the ambulance got there. And I come to find out later it was about 20 minutes it took 'em to get there, and we have no idea why.

Charlie Hodge: I had come in and I was, standing in the kitchen with my back to – you know, where, where there, there's this little part where it's flat there where the cabinets are. I'm standin' there lookin' through the paper. And, Patsy Gamble and Vernon came behind me. I thought they were laughing. You know, because laughter and s– sorrow are a lot alike sometimes. And, I turned around to look to see what was so funny. And I saw that, that they were both crying. And I went straight upstairs and, and Joe was already up there. And I began to, to do what I could.

Jerry Weintraub: And he was supposed to start a tour for me the next day in Maine. And my telephone rang. And it was Joe Esposito on one line. I don't even know if he remembers this but it, it was Joe. And, he said Jerry I got to talk to ya. And my other line rang. I said hold on one second, Joe. And, I hit the other line. And it was Roone Arledge from ABC News.

And he said to me, Jerry, Elvis is dead. I said what? What? He said he just di– I said hold on. I – and I – and I got back on with Joe I said Joe, what's the matter? Joe said I'm in the bathroom with Elvis. He just died. He hadn't go– they hadn't taken him away yet. Said I just want you to know 'cause your phone's gonna start ringin'. I, I said it's already rung. You know, Roone is on the phone. He was in the – Joe was a disaster. You know, he was a complete wreck. He'd lost his best friend and his – and he, he, he couldn't believe it. I mean, he was totally bummed out.

Joe Esposito: And we all went downstairs. Charlie Hodge was with me. Took him downstairs to the ambulance. Got him in the back and as I jumped in the back of the ambulance, Charlie Hodge jumped in the back with me. And just as we were getting' ready to pull out, Dr. Nick pulled up in front of the house, jumped out of his car, and jumped in the back of the ambulance with us. And we took off.

Charlie Hodge: I was telling him to breathe. Breathe for us 'cause, Elvis used to say that the last thing to go was your hearing. So with that in mind I was – I was, you know, but, in reality, rigor mortis had already set in. He'd been dead for some time but, you know, you don't want to give up. And like I said with, with your last thing – with him sayin' that the last thing to go is your hearing, I was saying breathe. Elvis breathe. And everything and then, the medics said later, that they believe that the time Elvis fell, if they'd have been there with the right equipment, it was too late. He was gone.

CHARLIE HODGE
FRIEND/SINGER/GUITARIST/
MEMPHIS MAFIA

Sam Thompson: And so I got up to the top of the hill there and I could see a, a fire department ambulance sitting at the front door. Well my first thought it was Vernon. 'Cause Vernon had had a bad heart and he'd had some problems. So I really thought, at that moment, that it was Vernon that, that, that, that, that David was talking about. And I went in and, and Vernon was sitting in a big high back chair in the jungle room, crying. And I just stood in the dark for a moment and stepped out. And then he – he saw me and he said somethin' like, is that you Sam? You know, well, you're here to get Lisa? Well there's no need to go. My, my boy's dead or something. And he just burst out and started crying. And the cops was, was there and it was quite a scene. It was pandemonium. And they'd already taken Elvis's body by that time.

SAM THOMPSON
MEMPHIS MAFIA

Joe Esposito: We went to the hospital. We got him to the emergency room. They ushered Charlie and me off into another room. And, they took him into the emergency room. And, Billy Smith showed up to the emergency room, and I forgot who else. I don't remember. It was starting to get very hectic.

JOE ESPOSITO
ROAD MANAGER & FRIEND

Marian Cocke: So I went to the emergency room, and they were working on him. And, when I went in, it was very evident that Elvis had been gone a long time. And I just asked 'em to stop. I said please, do not do this him. And, Dr. Nick – I said Dr. Nick, please don't do anything else. And so they worked him for a few more minutes and I said Dr. Nick, please don't do anything else. And so they stopped.

George Nichopoulos: I, I think probably the most amazing part of that was that, that, there were a few moments during this time period that we, we're trying to resuscitate him. There were – there a few moments where, we got some heart beat back. Which when you put things in perspective, how long he'd been dead, and how you got a heart beat back. I mean, it – when you look back on it it was just an amazing feat. You know, even though it wasn't sustained. Th– there was still some EKG evidence of the heart beating.

Marian Cocke: Elvis would not have wanted to be anything other than vibrant and able to sing and to live a normal life. And had they been able to resuscitate him, as long as he had been gone, it would've been bad. And God works for God. And so, I was glad he had the upper hand.

Joe Esposito: Then Dr. Nick came in there, and told us that he was gone.

George Nichopoulos: We felt like that Elvis died of some cardiac arhythmia problem where his heart just starts beating erratically and real fast.

Joe Esposito: That's when I, you know, I called Colonel Parker, in Portland, Maine, and told him what happened. And, there was a lot of silence on the other side of the phone. And he just says, we'll be there tonight. And then I called Priscilla, and told her. And, naturally she was in shock. She didn't know what to do and she asked naturally how's Lisa? I said Lisa's fine. You know, don't worry about her.

Linda Thompson: I was living in Los Angeles, and I think it was about 12:00 or 1:00. The phone rang and it was Lisa Marie. Linda, Linda my dad's dead. My, my daddy died, my daddy died. He's dead. I said, what? He's dead, he's dead. And I threw the phone in the air. It was like, it, it was such a, a nightmarish quality. I just couldn't even accept it so I threw the phone. And, and I'm standing there sayin' oh my god, oh my god. And I hear this little voice across the room on the receiver and, and, you know, I collected myself enough to realize, this little nine year old child has had the presence of mind to pick up the phone, dial my number long distance, to let me know that the person that she knew I loved, has passed on. So I somehow reached for the phone again and I said Lisa honey, are you sure? And she said I'm sure, I'm sure and she was hysterical. You know, she was crying. And then I just started trying to say things like, you know, you know how much your daddy loves you and how much your daddy's always loved you. And you're his little girl. And I was trying to say things to her to comfort her, on some level. I um while I was so distraught myself. And I was by myself in my apartment. And my brother took the phone from Lisa and he said Linda, I said Sam is it true? Is it just – she's – she's wrong, isn't she? He's just sick that he had a problem. They took him to the hospital? He said no, you better come home. And, I said well give me to Lisa again so he put Lisa back on and I said honey, I'm gonna come in. Just, just feel your daddy's love 'cause that's always with you. And, you know, we hung up and then I caught a flight, late in the evening and, and flew to Memphis right away.

LINDA THOMPSON
ELVIS'S GIRLFRIEND

Patty Parry: I got a call from Memphis in the morning of the, the day he passed away and to let me know before it was on television. Just so it wouldn't be a shock to me. I Freaked out. And I ran – I went over to Linda Thompson's house. And, she was getting ready to fly back, to Memphis.

Shirley Dieu: I get this phone call, from Joe. And, he said Shirley, Elvis is dead. And I said what? He said I'm tellin' you Elvis is dead. And I said Joe, don't joke around. And he started to cry and Joe is a strong man, that's when I knew it was real my god it killed me we both cried.

Mindi Miller: And I got a phone call. And I think, I think it was from Shirley, who at the time was Joe Esposito's girlfriend. I just was – I was shocked but I wasn't shocked. And I don't know how that can be but, you know, sometimes you have premonitions about things. And I hadn't seen him or spoken to him for about six months. But I had kept tabs on how he was and where he was because Shirley had become a very good girlfriend of mine and she was going with Joe at the time.

Shirley Dieu: I can remember running my nails across the, the wall. And the last I remember I was behind our apartment in the alley just crying. And then, after that, it was just getting everything together. And Joe remained pretty calm and, just kinda handled everything the best he could.

Joe Esposito: And I was getting calls from friends, Nancy Sinatra, Ann-Margret, different friends, different celebrity friends who wanted to come. And, you know, I said, you know, it was – it was tough, you know, just – I couldn't help em. It was a mad house there. And I suggested Nancy, you know, just don't come. It's gonna be crazy here. And Ann-Margret I said the same thing – the same thing to her. She says no, I'm coming.

Another celebrity who had been trying to call was singer Tony Orlando, who, like Elvis, and like Tony's good friend the late Freddy Prinze, also had a drug problem. Oddly though, Tony started calling the house several hours before Elvis died.

Tony Orlando: After what happened to Freddy, after what was going on with me, I became very frightened about Elvis. And the night before he died I started to call the house. And I called about – I started calling about 10:30. I was very concerned, and I kept calling well after midnight and I got no answer. On the morning of the 16th, I decided to walk down the street to St. Patrick's Cathedral. Now I know – I know Priscilla. I know Li– I knew Lisa as a child. And they used to come see me at the hotel, the shows, the front row. They'd sit in the front row, you know. And I decided to go to St. Patrick's Cathedral and light a candle for Elvis, and Lisa, and Priscilla. I kneeled down, I – lit three candles. I said my prayers. And I hoped them for the best. I walked back I kept to the hotel. Elaine opens the door. She says you'd better sit down. They found Elvis today, and he died today. And I don't know quite what it was that was making me pursue this feeling or this sense that he was in danger. But I'll never forget that. I'll never forget that I was trying to call him the night before. Didn't get through. Went to church, prayed for him. And that very morning, he was no longer.

TONY ORLANDO
SINGER

Myrna Smith: Well I just I lost it. And, they had to sedate me. Oh. But I had enough sense as soon as the plane landed back in Burbank, and I got home, I immediately got on the phone and made a plane reservation. And it's lucky that I did because, an hour later, I couldn't have gotten one.

MYRNA SMITH
SINGER/BACK-UP GROUP,
SWEET INSPIRATIONS

Kenny Rogers: I was in Dallas, Texas. And I – I couldn't believe it. I mean, I just – I, I – it reminds me so much of the John F. Kennedy thing. I mean, when I heard about John F. Kennedy for some reason it touched me in, in s– in a place I haven't been touched before except for those two deaths, and I don't know why.

KENNY ROGERS
SINGER/SONGWRITER

DICK CLARK
TELEVISION HOST/PRODUCER

JACKIE DeSHANNON
SINGER/FRIEND

PATTI PAGE
SINGER/FRIEND

JOE ESPOSITO
ROAD MANAGER & FRIEND

Dick Clark: I was in Las Vegas. I was on my way to a television station. Walking in the door, to do an interview to promote a show I was doing. And they said well, what do you think about Elvis? I said well what do you mean what if? I think he's the greatest. I went on and on and they went no, no he, he just died. And I said he what? Moments later I was on television. It was tough.

Jackie DeShannon: When I heard the news that Elvis passed away I believe that I was, here – I was in California in Los Angeles. And, I just remember, you know, breaking into tears and, feeling so empty.

Patti Page: I was appearing in Wildwood, New Jersey at, in the summer time, in August. I had my two children there, with me. And, we were I think just coming in from taking them out like on a – to the beach or something and we were coming inside to the hotel and I was to, you know, start getting ready for the show, and they had to get their dinner and so forth. And that's when I heard the news. And, naturally they were young. They didn't know really what had happened. But, it was quite a thing.

Joe Esposito: It really didn't sink in to me personally, 'cause I didn't even cry that much that whole time.

Joe Esposito was still shell shocked when the ever intrusive press peppered him with questions, even as Elvis's body lay in state inside Graceland.

Joe Esposito: I did a couple of interviews I think. I don't even remember to tell the truth. I know I was in front of a camera, answering questions for a few reporters. And I – a lot of it's a big blur.

EXCERPT FROM NEWS FOOTAGE

Reporter: Mr. Esposito, can you tell us anything about the family, how they are bearing up in this, this time?

Joe Esposito: Right now they're all in a state of shock. I don't think nobody real – can't realize it yet. I don't even realize it.

Reporter: What about Mr. Presley's former wife? How is she?

Joe Esposito: She's pretty upset.

Reporter: What's gonna be the procedure for the – for the funeral tomorrow?

Joe Esposito: I couldn't tell you till I sit down and we're gonna go over that in a little while.

But Joe couldn't afford the luxury of sitting down. He had a funeral to arrange.

Joe Esposito: It's just like putting on a show. We all had to do the, the right job. Like I say, Sam and Dick Grob. Sam Thompson and Dick Grob they handled the security situation. They had all the meetings with the police department and the highway patrol 'cause they knew it was gonna become pretty hectic

Sam Thompson: And then I guess for about the next four days I probably had 30 minutes worth of sleep. Because we had the whole funeral to put on and the security. And, and I stayed at the house and was in charge of guarding his body when they brought it back from the funeral home.

PATTY PARRY
MEMPHIS MAFIA

Patty Parry: I didn't get to go to the funeral. I wa– you know, I was married. And my – my husband didn't want me to go because of all the hoopla.

SHEILA RYAN

Sheila Ryan: I wouldn't even go to his funeral. I don't think I could've been at th– any help to anybody there. Joe would've just felt pressure to put, put me up. I didn't want to deal with Priscilla and Linda, and every other girl that thought she was the only one. You know, I just – I didn't want to be a part of the drama, you know. I didn't. I just didn't.

LINDA THOMPSON
ELVIS'S GIRLFRIEND

Linda Thompson: I was just so stunned and so grief stricken, and so at loss that I, I really didn't know what to expect of, of my own reactions, the fans' reaction, how many people would be there. family reactions. Would there be a celebrity contingent. You know, what, what – I, I – it didn't – nothing occurred to me. I was just kinda catatonic getting back to Memphis.

LOANNE PARKER
COLONEL PARKER'S

Loanne Parker: Tom Hulett I believe said Colonel, I need to get a, a suit. I, I don't have a suit with me. We can't go to the funeral in, in the clothes we wear on tour. And Colonel said Tom, these clothes were good enough for us to work for Elvis. They're good enough for us to wear at his funeral. He would understand. And if he saw me in a suit he wouldn't recognize me. So we went to the funeral in very basic work – work clothes, in our work clothes. I had slacks.

Appearance was also paramount to those making the arrangements for the King's final curtain.

JOE ESPOSITO
ROAD MANAGER & FRIEND

Joe Esposito: Vernon told him what kind of casket he wanted for Elvis and he wanted all limousines. White, all white. And there was not even that many limousines in Memphis and they had to get the limousines from Arkansas and Mississippi. They got 'em all to come in.

Linda Thompson: I still have this vision in my mind of all the big white limousines, that we rode in. And it was so appropriate that they were white, because he had such a purity of heart. And, celebrated life on such a level that it was so nice to not have just all black limousines and a black hearse. The white meant a lot to me.

Joe Esposito: George Hamilton, good friend of Colonel Parker and a friend of Elvis's. He came and – it – it was heck tryin' to, you know, coordinate who was gonna go in what limousine and, all that. And I, I know some people got their feelings hurt, some family members, because they weren't up in the front – in the front ones. But, you know, we, we did it, and it all worked out. And, I'm sure, Elvis is very proud of everybody, that put this together for him because it was hell.

Loanne Parker: They asked Colonel to ride in one of the limousines, in one of the front limousines with family. And Colonel said no. I have always been behind the scenes with Elvis. That's the way I want to maintain it. And he, he rode in a limousine but, but not, not with the – with the family group.

Joe Esposito: Every flower in the city was delivered to Graceland. They would come from all different parts of the state because all the florists ran out of flowers.

Linda Thompson: The body lay in state at the base of the stairs at Graceland and the fans could come through and view his body for the last time. Which I think was comforting to them. Just to be able to have that kind of closure, as they say. Just to be able to say one last goodbye. To see him. Maybe they'd never seen him while he lived but they saw him in his death.

Unfortunately those devoted fans had to make great sacrifices in order to say that one last goodbye to their hero.

Joe Esposito: The bad thing about August in Memphis is it's horrible. It's humid, hot. And then we had – there was no wind blowin' at all and, and people were outside the gate shoving and pushing. Wanted to get in. We opened the gates up for the people to come up around and come and say – give their goodbyes to Elvis. People collapsing, fainting from the heat, heat exhaustion. Ambulance was there, police department was there. And, and it was like, like a – like a battle zone almost. It really was. It was really horrible. I felt bad for the people but, nothing we could do about it.

Charlie Hodge: There was one la– lady that left her husband, and three children, and threw herself under a train, on the day that Elvis died. And they had a whole list of people who actually, killed themselves on the day Elvis died. What an effect that man had.

But even under such tragic circumstances, there was still humor to be found.

Linda Thompson: And I sat on the landing of the stairs, and watched all these people come through, and pay their last respects to Elvis. And, we alternately laughed hysterically and cried hysterically. And each of us would look at each other and know what Elvis would've said, as someone came through. A funny little remark he might've made about what they were wearing. Or, you know, some guy came in a neck brace, and we looked at each other and we said, he would've said the guy's in worse shape than he is, you know. What's he doin' here? He's in worse shape than I am.

Jerry Weintraub: It was pretty tough. It was – it was, it was pretty tough to see him laid out dead in the living room. And, and then when I got there I had a meeting with his father and the Colonel. And, a whole bunch of people were there. And, you know, it was the day of the funeral. Anyway, I'm gonna cry 'cause I miss him.

But not everyone who passed by Elvis's casket showed the same level of respect.

Joe Esposito: The picture of Elvis on the cover of the National Enquirer was the biggest selling issue they ever had in history. And a relative takes the picture, got paid $75,000 to sneak a camera, into his room, his own relative. Then sell them the picture.

Elvis's unusual appearance led to one of many urban myths that arose in the months and years following his death. The Elvis sightings.

George Nichopoulos: When we saw Elvis, at the time of the funeral, I mean, he just looked so different than, than he did. Because of, he'd lost all that bloatness. He'd lost all of his abdomen, because all those things were removed. And, and, which means some people didn't think it was Elvis, because he didn't look like, the obese Elvis that we, we thought of before.

Joe Esposito: Some fans are very gullible and they'll believe that Elvis is still alive. You got these people – there's people today saying they still talk to him. Elvis died man. Elvis died August 16, 1977. And, it just makes me mad. It really does. You know, then I feel sorry for the fans 'cause a lot of people are gullible and they believe it.

Once Elvis was laid to rest, it was time for those closest to him to go on with their lives. Or at least try.

Linda Thompson: The thing that struck me most was that life went on. I think when you're grieving and you're at such a personal loss and you feel such personal loss, the television news would allude to Elvis passed away today. Elvis died yesterday. The funeral was held today, and then onto something else. And I, I wanted to say no wait, you can't go on. There, there is nothing else. That's all that matters right now. And I – that's what struck me personally, that the world could go on and that life could go on without him.

Joe Esposito: It was about three months later, one evening at my home, I just said, I'm not gonna see him again. I'm n– you know, he's gone. And, and I became very depressed and my girlfriend Shirley and thank God she was there. She helped me out tremendously. I just realized that he is not coming back. We're not going on tour anymore. We're not making movies. Not singin' anymore. And that depressed the heck out of me for a long time. Luckily I had some friends like Jerry Weintraub and Tom Hulett around and Jerry asked me, he told me ac– actually at the funeral. He says, you know, when you want to go to work, just let me know. And I went to work for Jerry Weintraub about after 10 months after Elvis passed away. And, it was tough.

Patty Parry: I know he's gone but to me he's still here. I mean, he's, he's all over the media. I mean, I think about him every day. I think all of us, as I say I miss him terribly. But, he's with me all the time, you know.

Sandy Basset: And I think Elvis was never meant to live very long. Who would want to see him old? You know? Can you imagine him old? I can't.

Ray Manzarek: Elvis lived a long time compared to Jim Morrison, Janice Joplin, Jimmy Hendrix, Brian Jones, and Kurt Cobain, who all died at 27. We had Elvis for a long time, you know. We were lucky to have him that long. There's something about genius that carries – that level of genius that carries the seeds of its own destruction.

Marian Cocke: Elvis had his faults, you know. However he did tell me one time, Miss Cocke, I don't know but two people in this world that are perfect. One's you and the other one's me. And he's gone and I have this awesome responsibility to myself now. But, he was a very kind and warm and loving man.

Christina Ferra: His fire that burned within him came from his spiritual strength and his faith. And the passion that he let out in his singing, in the gospel like singing that he did, was passion coming straight from the strong soul that he, he is today, wherever he is.

Kenny Rogers: He didn't have a life. He was a professional Elvis Presley, you know. And there – there's a sadness to that. At the same time, I mean, he was what he was.

Bill Medley: A lot of guys have come and gone and this and that. But, he's Elvis Presley. And, the people that were raised in that era, couldn't let go of it even if, if they wanted to, you know. I mean, he's an, an enormous part of their life. He's a part of my life so that's never gonna go. And then, and then different generations on down, hear about him and, you know, he was a phenomenon. He was – he– pretty much started rock 'n' roll.

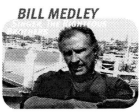

Patti Page: He was unique. And I think the charisma that he had, with his fans, was, was something else. It's too bad he didn't realize how much he was loved.

Connie Stevens: I for one am sorry, that I didn't reach out more. Because I think at the end of where his life ended, was when we should've been there more. And I've often regretted that but, as what happens with a very big star, you have a tendency to think that, they're okay. They're surrounded. Which he was, most of the time. But, you know, instinctively we all feel we should've been there, a little bit more for him.

UNDYING LOVE

ELVIS HAS LEFT THE BUILDING, BUT THE LIGHTS ARE STILL ON, BRIGHTENING THE WORLD WITH THE GIFT OF HIS SONG.

— QUOTE BY MARION LINDSAY

Jacquelyn Kilgore, Garden City, MI — *Elvis you will always be my Teddy Bear...miss you but you are alive in my heart and soul.*

Pauline Cuss, Hampshire, UK — *You were the most beautiful talented man ever.*

Jennie Nightingale, Kent, England — *A very unique and talented man. Luv you Elvis. X*

Anthony Willis, Billingham, Cleveland, UK — *Only eight when Elvis died but been alive and part of my life ever since.*

Nancy Bazajou, Normangee, Texas — *Elvis, you will forever be in my heart.*

Ruby Clinard, Lexington, Texas — *It's amazing but Elvis' talent touched an entire generation of people. It's even more amazing when that same influence affects several generations. Elvis made an impression on the world of music unequaled by any other single performer.*

Jacquie Ulmo, Sao Paulo, BRAZIL — *Elvis, you are and will always be the sunshine of my life...no matter what!*

Sandra Cooley, England — *Elvis was and is the most incredibly gifted musician of all time, he is the epitome of cool!!!!!!!!!!*

Liz Gutsell, Kent, United Kingdom — *Elvis you are a treasure that will live on forever.*

Sergio Salazar, Los Angeles, CA — *Every time I listen to Elvis records, I'm amazed by the huge talent and his wonderful voice.*

Ruth Shephard, Silver Spring, MD — *Elvis, you were so Near but always so Far...could almost be touched but then, you couldn't be. You surround me every day at work, my office is every inch Elvis, walls, all sides of desk, every file cabinet, every table...everyone knows the Elvis Lady...just look for the red Corvette convertible with the L VIS Maryland Tags!!! Elvis, you were one of a kind and we love you!!*

Gloria Basham, Mount Washington, Kentucky — *I became an Elvis fan at 6 yrs old. A love that continues to this day (I'm 44 now). His music and movies got me through some really tough times in my life. I will always love him.*

Betty Ridgley, Frederick, MD, United States — *A fan always and forever. His gospel music was wonderful.*

Bud Jones, Chino, CA, United States — *Thank you, Elvis, for living in our life-time and sharing that life with us. The world will never be the same-thanks to you. We will always remember you!*

Peter Spierings, Australia — *Remembering the one and only true King of Rock 'n' Roll.*

Bruce Marks, Simi Valley, CA, USA — *I met Elvis a few times during the movie years, when I was starting my music career, and found him to be real and funny. I miss you friend.*

Sheryl Smith, Houston, TX — *Elvis has had a place in my heart for 51 years and always will.*

Mark Scrivens, London, England — *Elvis the greatest artist. The voice of the 20th century. Loved and respected by millons all over the world.*

Danielle Genest, Charlesbourg, Quebec, Canada — *Elvis is always stay alive in my heart.*

Steve Gungel, Arlington Heights, IL, USA — *Thank You, Elvis for the music and the inspiration you have brought to my life. Heartfelt gratitude to you, Joe for all you have done to preserve the greatness of your best friend! God Bless! WE WILL NEVER FORGET YOU EP!!*

Casey DeFalco, Millville, NJ, USA — *Elvis you will always be an inspiration for many generations to come. My love & respect for you as a human being continues to grow.*

Helen Wilkins, Sacramento, CA, USA – *The greatest fan ever, my mom at 85 yrs. Still rockin. Skip Wilkins.*

Donna Herring, Ypsilanti, Michigan, USA – *Elvis was a big part of my teenage life. His music the enjoyment of his movies helped me through a tough time. I have made some forever friends through Elvis. I usually know most of the songs by heart at church if it is one Elvis sang. He touched my life and still does.*

Jeff Fetterman, Bradford, PA, USA – *As a musician myself, I know what made up Elvis' heart@soul, MUSIC, it's born in you and can't be taken away no matter what, it's the blood that runs through your veins. Only a few are lucky enough to become celebrities, but only 1 was ever handpicked by God 2 become a leader besides his only son, that would be Elvis, a leader, an inspiration, and the ONLY human on this earth to be remembered for eternity.*

Heidi May, Springfield, Illinois, USA – *You have angels on earth helping us to remember you and keeping your spirit alive.*

Jason Redfern, Pontefract, England – *Elvis is great Elvis is smart we love Elvis with all our hearts. Long live the King.*

John Corrie, Whitehaven, Cumbria, England – *Every aspect of my life was influenced by ELVIS. Strong, generous, talented, warm, handsome & modest; it's what I always aspired to be. What a star! What a man.*

Lori Fidler, New York City, USA – *Iconoclast, saddened past, you left too soon after you came, and charmed my darkest hours, it's close again, and things are not the same. I remember you...did you know you are the ghost who dries my tears? I was conceived to you...and I have the scarf you gave me at 2. You are more beautiful than all the sunrises and sunsets put together.*

Elaine, Buffalo, New York, USA – *Elvis, thank YOU very much for all the joy you have given millions of people. You raise me up when I am sad. I teach many children about your kindness, generosity, love and talent. I love and miss you.*

Charlene Frydberg, Staten Island, New York, USA – *I will always love Elvis*

Adela 'AJ' Caputo, Salinas, CA, USA – *My first memory of Elvis was seeing him on Ed Sullivan singing 'Hound Dog' which led me to sing to Sister Mary Roseanne for a first grade interview when I was 6 years old (and not too badly at that); to being allowed to see my very first movie VIVA LAS VEGAS. And oh, how I envied Ann-Margret. Ah, May 1st, the day Elvis and Priscilla got married, always meant a lot to me...it was so grand that he picked my birthday of all days to get married on. I always felt so special because of that. As I believe in one God, I also believe that there will only be one Elvis. To Elvis...forever TCB wherever he may be...and I thank him for the wonderful legacy he left us.*

Brad Money, London, KY, USA – *Can't wait to get a copy of this book, Thanks Joe :D*

Gina Wilson, South Bend, Washington, USA – *You have always been a huge part of my life and you always will*

Tony Gentili, East Brookfield, MA, USA – *This is for the greatest entertainer that ever lived. We miss you Elvis and will always remember you.*

Katherine Baysdon, Lumberton, NC, USA – *No one will ever take your place.*

Katherine Howe, Sheffield, England – *Elvis will always be number one and I'll always love him forever.*

John Campolo, Kenosha, WI, USA – *ELVIS YOU WILL BE IN MY HEART AND MIND FOR-EVER.*

Randall & Kelly Bart, Bartlett, IL, USA – *Elvis, you will forever live in our hearts.*

Frode Klement Kjellevold Klementsen, Bergen, Norway – *Elvis! You took care of business, we'll take care of your legacy... and never let the world forget how great thou art!!!*

Susie Smith, Greenleaf, KS, USA – *TCB all the time!*

Bobbie Jones, New York, NY, USA – *My boy, my boy*

Bev McKinlay, Brisbane, QLD, Australia – *Elvis & his music reached in and touched a corner of my heart. The fingerprints will stay there forever.*

Eric Murray, Toms River, NJ, USA – *Words can not express what Elvis means to me, I listen to his music almost 24hrs a day.... Coming up from nothing & becoming what he is today & remaining a down to earth person & not some stuck up kind of guy, That's why I will always love ELVIS !!!!!!!!!*

Becky Hyatt, Blountsville, AL, USA – *You are Always on my Mind*

Julie Brown, St. Louis, MO, USA – *Elvis will forever reach generations through his music and persona. Young people will not forget him!*

Todd Boothroyd, Victoria, British Columbia, Canada – *Elvis was not just the ultimate entertainer, he was also a good man. That is rare. He will always be a part of me.*

Denise Migliorati (Lallier), Wethersfield, CT, USA – *I will always LOVE you, Elvis. Please listen to Elvis sing, 'How the Web Was Woven' because, I want the world to FEEL my love for Elvis instead of reading it, So close your eyes, as you hear Elvis sing the depth of my love for him.*

Martha Atha, Frankfort, KY, USA – *Reading about Elvis always makes me happy. I love all the good memories of him.*

Margaret Petrovich, Allentown, PA, USA – *Nobody Noticed.*

Paul W Collins, Bruce, Mississippi, USA – *I sure wish Elvis could walk out on the stage again...*

Andrea Stoeckle, San Mateo, CA, USA – *November, 1970, Cow Palace, SF, CA is a night I will never forget. You came into my heart and soul and never left.*

Simona Khan, Bucharest, Romania – *Today, Tomorrow and Forever. An incredible voice, a unique soul, a carrying and loving heart from the first to the last bit, an irresistible charm, a breathtaking appearance, a strong well defined sense of value and a such intense aura which is just impossible to put into words & mixed all together & could have just one result called simply Elvis Presley. There will never be another Elvis Presley and we will all keep his legacy alive.*

Bill Bryan, Orland Park, IL – *It would be an under-statement to say that Elvis' popularity has taken any dive in modern society. Take it from me, Bill Bryan, who is an Elvis fan that is only 15 years old! Ever since I was 10 I have enjoyed Elvis' music. Of course, to be a true fan, it is one thing to love the music, but another to admire the legacy of Elvis Presley. Nobody deserved the title of 'artist of the century' more than Elvis did, and still does.*

Katrina Parrish, Orlando, FL, USA – *Elvis....Always on my mind and forever in my heart!*

Gaylon Spencer, Huntsville AL, USA – *When I lose my way, I look toward the Northern Star when I want to return to the past I look toward The Southern Star! The music of ELVIS PRESLEY.*

Audrey Wurtz, Linn, KS, USA – *Elvis will always be with us. Now and forever.*

Maggie Smith, Palmer, KS, USA – *E's biggest fan.*

Gary, Palmer, Wales, UK – *Congratulations Elvis on your home becoming a national Historic Landmark.*

Phyllis Davis, Long Beach, CA, USA – *Elvis was the most powerful and influential performer in history of music. Not a day goes by that I do not listen to his music or play his movie videos. He will always be number one. What a voice.*

Corinne Loomis, Yorba Linda, CA, USA – *Elvis, your music has been a constant source of joy and comfort to me for 40 years. I know you are singing with the angels and I will see you again.*

Shelley Apa, Keswick, Ontario, Canada – *Elvis asked. 'What is my purpose here?' The answer. You lived it in the gifts you gave the world. Your music, charm, generosity, and love for family, friends, fans and life. We well receive that gift til the end of time. Elvis really did 'Take Care of Business.' Thank you from a grateful fan Shelley Apa.*

Michael Otto, Sandusky, OH, – *There is only one King of Rock 'n' Roll, so we will always keeping singing your song Elvis.*

Deni Davis, Houston, TX, USA – *Your positive impact on my life is indescribable and unforgettable. The way you interpret songs is profound and unmatched. You have my unconditional love and gratitude... forever!*

Mary McCoy, Gulfport, FL, USA – *Elvis will be a very special part of our lives forever...Loved you then and still do.*

Ivette Naranjo, Santiago, Chile – *Elvis is very important in my life...Always on my mind.*

Maria Elefante, Oceanside, NY, USA – *I will always be grateful for my 'Memories of Elvis.'*

Vicky Hohenschutz, Terrytown, Louisiana – *Your 'purpose in life' is now eternal. Thanks for all the help you've given me.*

Juanita Thompson, Montrose, Michigan, USA – *Elvis to this day you still are in the hearts of many, and always will be from generation to generation. The love of your fans will remain eternity.*

Michelle R. Sheehan, Bethlehem, PA, USA – *The profound impact of Elvis' music, both to people on a personal level and to the world on a historical level, will never be seen again.*

David Maye, Pointe Claire, Quebec, Canada – *Elvis, you are missed. You were simply the best!*

Dianna Weisner, Rockville, MD, USA – *My love for Elvis will never die.*

Norah West, Isle of Man – *He was the greatest singer the world has ever known and no one will ever match him.*

Audrey, Devon, United Kingdom – *Your music is a huge legacy which will continue for generations to come.*

Alicia Gregory, Dallas, Georgia, USA – *I have loved Elvis since I can remember. I saw him in concert at the Omni in Atlanta May 2, 1975. This was my 15th birthday present.*

Karen Evans, Dallas, Texas, USA – *I love Elvis.*

Rhonda McKinney, Lynchburg, TN, USA – *I will always remember and love you, Elvis.*

Christie Massey, Swansea, Illinois, USA – *Elvis will always be my king.*

Paul Teahan, England – *A fantastic performer a fantastic person long live the king.*

Forrest W. Erickson, USA – *Elvis, you gave the world love with your voice and music.*

Michele Kissil, Tucson, AZ, USA – *Always & Forever.*

Tangerine Erin Martinz, Stockholm, Sweden – *I adored you and will keep doing so till the end of time. Not a day passes by without me seeing you on my precious dvds. My prayers are always for you!*

Mario Miranda, Brasil – *Elvis was and always will be amazing!*

Natasha Burnett, Springdale, AR, USA – *Elvis, you are and always will be THE KING! No one will ever replace you, you are forever in my heart. Love, Natasha*

Regina Lorenzen, Waco, Texas, USA – *Your memory has not left the building..and never will!!*

Ray Covey, LaPorte, Texas, USA – *All my life, ever since I could remember, Elvis is all I listened to. He could sing any song great. I don't know any other entertainer that can do that.*

Donna Ruff, Arlington, Texas, USA – *I will always love you & admire you, Elvis.*

Reggy Gagne, Montreal, Qc, Canada – *My life was always based from Elvis Great Style & Music.*

Adam Schaffer, New York City – *We will always remember him for everything he was, everything he is and everything he will always be.*

Janet Bates, Westbank, B.C. Canada – *I met my husband because of my love for Elvis, so we went to Vegas and had an Elvis wedding. He will always hold a special place in my heart.*

Gary M. Balaban Jr., Potsdam, NY – *First heard him at the age of 8, and have been hooked ever since. Just a fantastic person in so many ways, TCB!*

Erich Leutgeb, Wr. Neustadt, Austria – *I'm a fan since 2002 and he changed my life by the same way what he changed the life in the world thanks ELVIS.*

Donnie Brown, Hartselle, AL, USA – *Elvis' spirit will always be with us.*

Karen Fanara, Maui, Hawaii, USA – *Elvis, It seems I've followed you all my life, and I've loved you even longer than that. Aloha and Love, Karen.*

Rita Orr, Las Vegas, Nevada, USA – *Elvis was and will be king of the world from 1935 until eternity.*

Joe & Sue Carlozo, Fallston, MD, USA – *Elvis is, and will always be, the King and we will never forget him.*

Linda Roberts, Tamworth, Staffordshire, England – *Elvis was someone very special, He was one in a million, He brought so much joy to millions of fans, that he's memory will always live on. He'll always have a special place in my heart. God bless you Elvis. From a very devoted fan. TCB*

Shirley Mott, Vancouver, BC Canada – *My memories of Elvis started when I was just a little girl at the age of about six. I loved his music then and always will. Listening to his songs has given me the understanding of love, caring, and the belief in god. My future thoughts of Elvis is what keeps me going on in life and believing that he is still with us in heart and soul. He has given the world more than anyone ever thought was possible. I will always love him for what he has given to each and everyone of us around the world. Priscilla made that possible and very real that he loved everyone.*

Michele Altamirano, Chicago, IL, USA – *Our King will always be remembered!*

Marian Ferrier, Brechin, Scotland, UK – *Always on my mind, always in my heart.*

Brian Flynn, Gold Coast, Australia – *Elvis changed my life forever, I will be Forever Grateful.*

Patrick Thompson, Portageville, MO, USA – *Elvis your are the greatest.*

David Castagna, Carmel, CA, USA – *Thanks for all the shakin', rattlin' ...So we can keep rollin'*

Christie Massey, Swansea, IL, USA — *Elvis will always be my king.*

Marawan Kamel, Cairo, Egypt — *Elvis, you will always be the king of music no matter what! There could never be another Elvis Presley again!!*

Kathy B. Fischer, St Louis, Missouri, USA — *Elvis, I'm so glad I finally discovered you. Back in the day, I was a Ricky Nelson fan, but I'm thrilled I've finally caught up with you. My life is certainly richer for having learned about you. Elvis - You Rock!!*

Renee D. Dorsey, San Jose, CA — *There will never be another like Elvis. He will always be in our hearts and so very loved.*

Michael Brandenburg, Sparta, TN, USA — *Elvis formed my life.*

Harry Young, Elk Grove, CA — *Before Elvis there was nothing...After Elvis there was musical history.*

Gilbert Laurent, France — *Merci pour tout monsieur Elvis Presley.*

Stephanie Williams, Fort Worth, Texas, USA — *I was only 9 months old when Elvis died. I knew about Elvis but not a lot of details until I met Sandi Pichon in 2004!! She gave me a wonderful enlightenment into what Elvis was really like behind closed doors away from the media. Elvis was a caring soul! He was truly a GIFT FROM GOD! He is truly missed! Heaven is lucky to have such a heavenly again such as Elvis!! We will always Miss and Love You!!!!*

Steve Gungel, Arlington Heights, IL, USA — *Thank You, Elvis for the music and the inspiration you have brought to my life. Heartfelt gratitude to you, Joe for all you have done to preserve the greatness of your best friend! God Bless! WE WILL NEVER FORGET YOU EP!!*

Danielle Genest, Charlesbourg, Quebec, Canada — *Elvis is always stay alive in my hearth.*

Casey DeFalco, Millville, NJ, USA — *Elvis you will always be an inspiration for many generations to come. My love & respect for you as a human being continues to grow.*

Vickie Csurny, Clinton, TN, USA — *Elvis has owned my heart since I found out who he was when I was 8 years old...that 46 years ago! He will own it until the day I die...and even then I hope I can take his love with me.*

C. Sahin, Germany — *I will always remember you.*

Dorothy Dutton, Selkirk, NY, USA — *Elvis, you will forever live in our hearts. You live on through generations of people who never had the chance to know what the world was like with you in it.*

Kim de Koning, Souris, MB, Canada — *You rocked my world with your awesome voice.*

Charles L Taylor, Carnation, WA, Canada — *Seeing Aloha for the first time when I was 7 years old was, what I imagine, very similar to kids seeing the Ed Sullivan show. In short, AMAZING! I was glued to the TV set the entire time!*

Dawn Stedman, Atlanta, Georgia, USA — *Elvis passed away before I got to see him in concert, I still have the tickets. In all my life I have had one wish, I wish I could have seen him. He is a huge part of my life, and will always be. I love him very much. In short, AMAZING! I was glued to the TV set the entire time!*

Vera White Phipps, Abbotsford, British Columbia, Canada — *I have had but one true unconditional love in my life, ever steady and for always, Elvis lives in my heart and mind. Never to be forgotten as long as I can breath. I wear an 'Elvis record' around my neck and TCB tattooed on my ankle. Part of my life forever, always with me.*

Marina and Monica Pizano, Chicago, Illinois – *I asked Marina what she thought of Elvis during the Vegas years. Her response was "I love the way his hair would fall into his face and then KABAM! There is his voice!" This is the impression a nine year old has of our King. His voice exceeded his presence and we all know his presence was quite powerful!*

Chuck Barron, Fayetteville AR, USA – *Greatest entertainer of the 20th century. We will never see his likeness again!!*

Kevin Cline, Nederland, Texas, USA – *Elvis has inspired me to be a better person.*

Jeanette, Devon, England – *I admired Elvis from a early age when my dad used to play his records over and over. One particular song I loved as a child was wooden heart. And that's why I grew up to love Elvis like my dad did.*

Charlotte Hendry, Carmel, CA, USA – *Even though I was only 12 years old when Elvis left this world, he was and always will be the biggest influence for many reasons in my life! There will never be another Elvis Presley. I will always love Elvis for who he was and what he stood for and what he gave to all of us. I miss you Terribly!*

Anna White, Lexington, KY, USA – *Elvis you will always hold an eternal flame in my heart. Thank you for the music and so much more.*

Margo Wade, Las Vegas, Nevada, USA – *Thru his music he is still with us. Thank you for writing this book.*

Jim McCrann, London, UK – *The legacy of Elvis lives on now and forever.*

Jacqueline Simms, Hampshire, England – *Thanks to our love of Elvis I met a very dear friend for 20 yrs until she died. For that and all the other things I've been able to do and people I have met because of you, I thank you. Most of all Thank god for you.*

Maria Hesterberg, Bonn, Germany – *You will waste your life without loving ELVIS!*

Lori Reed, Thomasville, Georgia, USA – *I will always love you and your music. Your voice was a beautiful gift from God.*

Sebastiano Cecere, Torino, Italy, Europe – *Elvis overcame any geographical and cultural barriers to become a timeless cornerstone of modern music.*

Julie Myers, Vancouver, WA, USA – *I saw you in Las Vegas when I was 9 years old. I'll never forget it. God Bless you Elvis.*

Janet Roberts, Wales, United Kingdom – *Joe, thank you for sharing your life with Elvis. We all love Elvis and appreciate you giving us the chance to read the facts and not the rubbish that has been written in the past.*

Candice Pike, Ohatchee, AL – *Elvis, you will always remain number one. And I will always love you.*

Teresa Bush, Seymour, IN, USA – *I will never forget the day the music died. I was seven years old that day on a very humid dreary August day and the world seemed to change at that instant. I will never forget you Elvis. I love you and all you gave to me. My dream was to one day meet you and marry you, but at seven that seems to be a dream that was taken from me like a thief in the night. That was my first lesson on death, I will never forget you and I will continue being your fan until I am but a memory as you are.*

Ann Edmonson, Petal, MS, USA – *ELVIS IS THE GREATEST ENTERTAINER THAT EVERY LIVED. HE WAS VERY GOOD LOOKING & WONDERFUL SENSE OF HUMOR!!!!*

Desiree Anderson, London, Ontario Canada – *Elvis was the one that got my into doing karate. Also, I remember the soul and passion that he put into every song he did, the amazing jumpsuits he had, and the way that he interacted with the audience, you could see that he loved his fans.*

Larry Dillon, New Jersey – *What Elvis means to me, Being born in 1965 I will always remember Elvis as the "Best of the Best" while I was growing up! My parents and family loved him and thought he was the coolest. From his Cadillacs, personal charm and way he lived, he had it all! I can remember when in the early seventy's Elvis was playing Madison Square Garden and I was about 8 years old. The buzz was big in the area that he was coming to town and all of my uncle's and aunt's were going to the show. I wanted to go but there was no way, this was their night out and I missed a chance of a life time! And to this day I bring that moment in time up at family gatherings, how I was left behind. But the one event I did not miss was the ALOHA from Hawaii concert live on TV. I didn't even know it was on that night but luck was on side and instead of doing my home work I WAS WATCHING THE KING OF ROCK 'N' ROLL!!! My mother was on her way out the door when the show started but she never made it to her destination, she sat next to me and watched the whole show. To this day when the concert is replayed on TV, we remember when in our younger days we caught that historic moment Live on TV. I will say that Elvis left a great impression on me from the way he handled himself and from the goodness in his heart. We all heard of the stories of giving cars and money away to people in need and to the average working guy. That was something he did not have to do but his heart was in the right place. On the day that man passed away, the world lost a good hearted person. I wish I could have meet him and shook his hand and said THANKS!*

To view the rest of this list please visit us at www.tcbjoe.com under TCB Fan Corner.

My warmest thanks and appreciation goes out to the following people that have given so generously of their time, energy, and effort, and for granting the incredible interviews that made this project into an unforgettable experience.

Valerie Allen
Eddy Arnold
Rona Barrett
George Barris
Billy Barty
Sandy Basset
Chris Beard
Bill Belew
Steve Binder
Kathy Blondell
Susan Brodsky
Pat Broeske
Stan Brosette
Earl Brown
Tony Brown
Dr. Joyce Brothers
James Burton
Glen Campbell
William Campbell
Trent Carlini
Jeanne Carmen
Matt Cimber
Dick Clark
Marian Cocke
Norman Crosby
James Darren
Christine Dashner
Mac Davis
Richard Davis
Joe Delaney
Jackie DeShannon
Shirley Dieu

Donovan
Sheila E
Barbara Eden
Janice Fadal
Art Fein
Christina Ferra
Mary Lou Ferra
Bob Finkel
D.J. Fontana
Buzzy Forbes
Mike Freeman
Teri Garr
Barry Gibb
Sandy Giles
Glen Glenn
Paul Gongaware
Laurel Goodwin
Reeca Gossan
Billy Graham
Shecky Greene
Joe Guercio
Glen Hardin
Susan Henning
Charlie Hodge
Dr. Lester Hoffman
Tab Hunter
Jim Hydlach
Mark James
Jackie Joseph
Jackie Kahane
Hal Kanter
Buddy Killen

Gene Kilroy
Sonny King
George Klein
Bernard Lansky
Lance Legault
Dixie Locke-Emmons
A.C. Lyles
Bernard Lansky
Barbara Leigh
Malcolm Leo
L.H. Leslie
Gary Lockwood
Anita Mann
Ray Manzarek
Ann-Margret
Sandy Ferra-Martindale
Wink Martindale
Marlyn Mason
Diane McBain
Marion Kesker-McGuiness
Phyllis McGuire
Bill McKenzie
Ed McMahon
Barbara McNair
Bill Medley
Emilio Micelli
Mindi Miller
Mary Ann Mobley
Tom Moffat
Bob Moore
Michael Moore
Bill Morris
Mike Morris
Bob Morrison

Jim Mydlach
George Nichopoulos
Chris Noel
Mike Norman
Sheree North
Hugh O'Brian
Michael Ochs
John O'Hara
Roy Orbison
Tony Orlando
Patti Page
Gloria Pall
Loanne Parker
Julie Parrish
Patty Parry
Gloria Paul
Cynthia Pepper
Carl Perkins
Cassandra "Elvira" Peterson
Dewey Phillips
Sam Phillips
Vernon Presley
Juliet Prowse
Robert Relyea
Bill Reynolds
Red Robinson
Jimmie Rodgers
Kenny Rogers
Rita Rogers
Alex Romero
Robin Rosaaen
Steve Rossi
Sheila Ryan
June Sayers

Pauline Sayers
Jerry Scheff
Jerry Schilling
Kanai Seanoa
Mary Jo Sheeley
Sharon Sheeley
Jan Shepard
Sammy Shore
Myrna Smith
Ben Speer
Gail Ganley Steele
Connie Stevens
Stella Stevens
Steve Stevens
Gordon Stoker
Danny Striepeke
Linda Thompson
Johnny Tillotson
Vicky Tiu
Ronnie Tutt
Ann Ellington Wagner
Ray Walker
Deborah Walley
Jerry Weintraub
Ben Weisman
June Wilkinson
Anita Wood
Bobby Wood
Ken Wynn
Steve Wynn
Celeste Yarnall
Henry Young
Reggie Young

I would also like to thank the many fans from all over the world that have participated and contributed to this project.

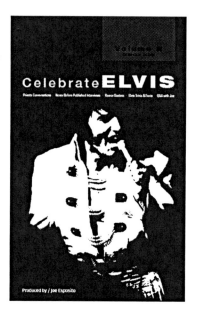

Printed in the United States
89813LV00003BA/2/A